Expert MVS/XA JCL

Expert MVS/XA JCL

Mani Carathanassis

Intertext Publications
McGraw-Hill Book Company

New York St. Louis San Francisco Auckland Bogotá
Hamburg London Madrid Mexico Milan Montreal
New Delhi Panama Paris São Paolo
Singapore Sidney Tokyo Toronto

Library of Congress Catalog Card Number 89-83764

10 9 8 7 6 5 4 3 2 1

ISBN 0-07-009816-6

Intertext Publications/Multiscience Press, Inc.
One Lincoln Plaza
New York, NY 10023

McGraw-Hill Book Company
1221 Avenue of the Americas
New York, NY 10020

Composed in Ventura Publisher by Context, Inc.

To my lovely wife
Rosemarie

Contents

Preface   **xiii**

Chapter 1   Introduction   **1**

1.1 Historical Perspective   1
1.2 Reasons for JCL Complexity   3
1.3 Multiprogramming And Virtual Storage   4
1.4 Data Set Organizations   8
      1.4.1 Non-VSAM Data Set Organizations   8
      1.4.2 VSAM Data Set Organizations   9
1.5 Record Formats   10
1.6 VTOC, PDS, and the Catalog   12
1.7 Jobs, Steps, and Initiators   15
1.8 Types of JCL Statements   20
1.9 The Syntax of JCL   22

**Chapter 2   Discussion of JOB and EXEC Statement
Parameters**   **31**

2.1 The Job Statement — General   31
      2.1.1 Accounting Information   33
      2.1.2 Programmer's Name   35
      2.1.3 The MSGLEVEL Parameter   36
      2.1.4 The ADDRSPC Parameter   37
      2.1.5 The Region Parameter   38
      2.1.6 The COND Parameter   40
      2.1.7 The Class Parameter   41
      2.1.8 The PRTY Parameter   42
      2.1.9 The Time Parameter   43
      2.1.10 The Notify Parameter   44
      2.1.11 The PERFORM Parameter   45
      2.1.12 The MSGCLASS Parameter   46
      2.1.13 The RESTART Parameter   46
      2.1.14 The TYPRUN Parameter   48

2.2 The EXEC Statement — General   50
   2.2.1 The PGM Parameter   50
   2.2.2 The PARM Parameter   52
   2.2.3 The ADDRSPC Parameter   54
   2.2.4 The Region Parameter   54
   2.2.5 The COND Parameter   56
   2.2.6 The TIME Parameter   58
   2.2.7 The PERFORM Parameter   59
   2.2.8 The ACCT Parameter   60

Chapter 3   **Failures Under MVS/XA**   **63**

3.1 General   63
3.2 JCL Errors   63
   3.2.1 Syntactical JCL Errors   64
   3.2.2 Allocation JCL Errors   65
3.3 ABEND Failures   67
3.4 Bypassing Execution Because of a Return Code   70

Chapter 4   **Controlling Execution**   **73**

4.1 General   73
4.2 A Return (or Condition) Code   73
4.3 The COND Parameter   76
   4.3.1 The COND Parameter in the JOB
       Statement   76
   4.3.2 The COND Parameter in the EXEC
       Statement   80
4.4 Practical Examples   86
   4.4.1 Ordinary Examples   86
   4.4.2 Conditional Execution in Job Recovery   87
   4.4.3 The Warning Last Step   89
   4.4.4 Innovative Ways of Controlling Execution   92

Chapter 5   **Discussion of DD Statement Parameters**   **95**

5.1 The DD Statement — General   95
5.2 The DSN Parameter   96
   5.2.1 How a Program Finds a Data Set   100
5.3 The DISP Parameter   101
5.4 The UNIT Parameter   109
5.5 The VOL (VOLUME) Parameter   115
5.6 The SPACE Parameter   122
5.7 The LABEL Parameter   129
5.8 The DCB Parameter   133
5.9 The FREE Parameter   138

Chapter 6   Using the Catalog   141

6.1 Definitions   141
6.2 The Contents of a Catalog Entry   143
6.3 When and How the Catalog Is Used   144
6.4 Adding a New Entry in the Catalog   150
6.5 When an Attempt to Catalog Fails   151
6.6 Cataloging an Existing Data Set   155
6.7 Uncataloging a Tape Data Set   160

Chapter 7   Retrieving Data Sets   165

7.1 Definition   165
    7.1.1 Required and Optional Parameters for
        Retrieval   166
7.2 Retrieval With and Without the Catalog   167
7.3 The Logic of Allocation, Program Execution, and
    Step Termination for Retrieval   171
    7.3.1 Disk Data Set Retrieval   171
    7.3.2 Tape Data Set Retrieval   174
    7.3.3 Tape Data Set Retrieval with Deferred
        Mounting   175
    7.3.4 Retrieving and Deleting Data Sets   176
7.4 Retrieving Partitioned Data Sets   180
7.5 DISP=OLD vs DISP=SHR   182
7.6 Retrieving with NL, BLP, AND LTM   183
7.7 Retrieving Multivolume Data Sets   185
7.8 Retrieving Using MOD   186
7.9 Altering Secondary Allocation and Releasing
    Unused Space   189
7.10 Dcb Considerations for Retrieval   191
7.11 Using Unit Affinity and FREE=CLOSE   193
7.12 Retrieving Concatenated Data Sets   195
7.13 Retrieving VSAM Data Sets   197

Chapter 8   Creating Data Sets   199

8.1 Definition   199
    8.1.1 Required and Optional Parameters for
        Creating   199
8.2 The Logic of Allocation for Creating Disk Data Sets   201
    8.2.1 Creating Nontemporary Sequential Disk
        Data Sets   201
    8.2.2 Creating Temporary Sequential Disk
        Data Sets   203
    8.2.3 Creating Partitioned Data Sets   205

	8.2.4 Creating Direct Data Sets	206
	8.2.5 SPACE Parameter Considerations	207
	8.2.6 Creating Multivolume Disk Data Sets	218
	8.2.7 Public/Private Considerations	221
	8.3 The Logic of Allocation, Open, and Close for Creating Tape Data Sets	224
	8.3.1 Creating Tape Data Sets with Deferred Mounting	227
	8.3.2 Creating Nonlabeled Tape Data Sets	228
	8.3.3 Creating Multivolume Tape Data Sets	229
	8.3.4 Creating Multifile Tape Volumes	230
	8.3.5 Using Unit Affinity and FREE=CLOSE	235
	8.4 DCB Considerations for Creating Data Sets	236
	8.5 Selecting a Proper Blocksize	240
	8.6 Creating Using MOD	246
Chapter 9	**Passing and Receiving Data Sets**	**249**
	9.1 Definitions	249
	9.2 Passing and Receiving	250
	9.3 Passing WIthout Receiving	252
	9.4 Other Problems With Passing	257
	9.5 Passing Temporary Data Sets	260
	9.6 When to Use Pass	265
	9.7 Pass and Restart Recovery	267
Chapter 10	**Special DD Statements and Parameters**	**271**
	10.1 DD * and DD DATA — Supplying SYSIN Data	271
	10.2 The SYSOUT Parameter	274
	10.2.1 Parameters Used with SYSOUT	276
	10.3 The OUTPUT Statement	287
	10.3.1 Parameters Common to Both SYSOUT DD and OUTPUT Statements but with Different Syntax	288
	10.3.2 Selected Parameters Available only in the OUTPUT Statement	290
	10.3.3 Examples of the OUTPUT Parameter and the OUTPUT Statement	294
	10.4 The DUMMY Parameter	296
	10.5 The DDNAME Parameter	298
	10.6 The JOBLIB and STEPLIB DD Statements	300
	10.6.1 The JOBLIB DD Statement	301
	10.6.2 The STEPLIB DD Statement	302
	10.7 The JOBCAT and STEPCAT DD Statements	304

10.8 The SYSUDUMP, SYSMDUMP, and SYSABEND
      DD Statements   305
      10.8.1 The SYSUDUMP DD Statement   305
      10.8.2 The SYSMDUMP DD Statement   305
      10.8.3 The SYSABEND DD Statement   306
10.9 Virtual I/O (VIO)   307
10.10 Concatenation   309

Chapter 11   Generation Data Groups   315

11.1 How GDGS Work   315
11.2 Preparing for a GDG   318
11.3 Changing the Characteristics of a GDG   320
11.4 Using a GDG Model   321
11.5 Peculiarities of GDGS   323
11.6 Concatenating Generations of a GDG   326
11.7 Generation 9999   327
11.8 Using Different Versions of a GDG Generation   327
11.9 Recovering from a Bad Generation   328
11.10 Using BLP With GDGS   330

Chapter 12   Using Procedures   333

12.1 General   333
12.2 The Use of Procedure Libraries   334
12.3 Invoking a Procedure   335
12.4 Restrictions   336
12.5 Overriding Procedures   336
12.6 The Output of a Procedure   349
12.7 Overcoming Some Restrictions   352
12.8 COMPILE-LINKEDIT-GO Procedures   353
12.9 Referring to a Procedure from Outside   356
12.10 Special Overrides   358
12.11 Executing a Procedure more than Once   365
12.12 Symbolic Parameters and Symbolic Overrides   369
12.13 The PROC Statement   373
12.14 Rules for Symbolic Overriding   374
12.15 Choosing Symbolic Parameters   378
12.16 In-stream Procedures   380
12.17 Rules for In-stream Procedures   381
12.18 Using In-stream Procedures   383

Chapter 13   Utilities and IDCAMS   387

13.1 JCL for Utilities   388
13.2 Utility Control Statement Syntax   389

13.3 The IEBGENER Utility   390
13.4 The IEHPROGM Utility   393
13.5 The IEBCOPY Utility   398
13.6 The IEBPTPCH Utility   402
13.7 The IEHLIST Utility   405
13.8 IDCAMS   407
   13.8.1 Required JCL for IDCAMS   407
   13.8.2 IDCAMS Command Syntax   408
   13.8.3 Examples of IDCAMS Used with VSAM
          Objects   409
   13.8.4 Examples of IDCAMS Used with
          Non-VSAM Data Sets   418

Chapter 14   MVS/ESA JCL Considerations   429

14.1 JCL Changes for MVS/ESA   430
14.2 New JCL Parameters   431
   14.2.1 The AVGREC Parameter   431
   14.2.2 The DATACLAS Parameter   433
   14.2.3 The KEYOFF Parameter   434
   14.2.4 The LIKE Parameter   435
   14.2.5 The MGMTCLAS Parameter   436
   14.2.6 The RECORG Parameter   437
   14.2.7 The REFDD Parameter   438
   14.2.8 The STORCLAS Parameter   439
14.3 Modified JCL Parameters   441
14.4 Alternative Parameters   442
14.5 Miscellaneous Changes   442
14.6 Effect of ESA on Existing JCL   444

Appendix A   Disk Characteristics   447

Appendix B   3380 Disk Capacity Table   449

Appendix C   3375 Capacity Table   451

Appendix D   3350 Capacity Table   453

Appendix E   3330 (MOD 1 or MOD 11) Capacity Table   457

Bibliography   461

Glossary   463

Preface

WHY ANOTHER BOOK ON JCL?

I came in contact with OS JCL for the first time in 1965 while working for IBM in Poughkeepsie, New York. It was my first assignment to code JCL for someone else's program. And it was a struggle. From the very beginning JCL struck me as a language full of peculiarities, ambiguities, grey areas, contradictions, inconsistencies, pitfalls, and events that seem to defy reasonable explanation. Yet, the available IBM literature at the time on the subject explained virtually none of the above and was generally confusing.

Nearly 25 years later, JCL remains a language with basically the same handicaps. Documentation provided by IBM has improved considerably over the years but is still difficult to read. Many books by other authors have been written, often easier to understand. Still, many of the areas that make JCL difficult are often misdocumented, poorly documented, or completely omitted. I have even read some books that claim JCL is easy (it is not!!). Explanations are often theoretical in approach, ignoring the practical aspects and neglecting to mention the potential pitfalls. Many of the examples provided are divorced from the "real world" and would either not work at all in a real environment or create serious problems. And sometimes certain parameters or subparameters are recommended when they are in essence useless or counterproductive. Here are some interesting examples taken from various pieces of documentation (though not verbatim):

• "DISP=OLD defaults to (OLD,KEEP)."

   Comment: It often does, but not always! Under certain conditions, (OLD,DELETE) becomes the default. That will cause a nasty surprise to a user who accepted the above statement as gospel (see Section 9.4 in Chapter 9)!

- "//DD1 DD DSN=ABC,...."
  Comment: You may work with JCL for years and never use an unqualified (simple) name like ABC in the DSN parameter (see Section 5.2 in Chapter 5). It has little to do with the real world.

- "...DISP=(NEW,CATLG),DCB=(LRECL=80,RECFM=FB,BLKSIZE=80)"
  Comment: 80 is a *terrible* blocksize that will result in serious inefficiencies (see Section 8.5 Chapter 8).

- "If a step is bypassed, it issues a return code of zero."
  Comment: This is strictly untrue (see Section 4.3.2 in Chapter 4)!

- "...deferred mounting is recommended"
  (with no explanation why).
  Comment: Deferred mounting is usually not recommended and, if it is, an explanation should be provided (see Section 5.4., 7.3.3 and 8.3.1 in Chapters 5, 7 and 8 respectively).

- ". . . use IEHPROGM to delete the data set."
  Comment: IEHPROGM is hardly ever a good choice for deleting a data set. Much better ways exist (see Section 7.3.4 in Chapter 7 and Section 13.4 in Chapter 13).

- ". . . code VOL=(PRIVATE, . . ."
  Comment: For the life of me, I can find absolutely no usefulness for the PRIVATE subparameter when nonremovable disk volumes are used. And these are the only kind of volumes we use in today's disk environment (see Section 5.5 in Chapter 5).

It is the objective of this book to fill the gaps in the existing documentation and provide answers to the many unanswered JCL questions. This will be accomplished by:

- Explaining how the MVS/XA system reacts to various JCL statements.
- Using "real-world" examples.
- Focusing on common and safe practices.
- Addressing the myriad of problems that can be encountered in a normal day-to-day use of JCL.
- Identifying the precise failure (by code) when a problem occurs.
- Emphasizing what to do as well as what *not* to do in JCL.

You may find some information in this book that other documents do not contain. Much of it comes from my experience working for IBM in the development and implementation of JCL. This experience gave me the rare opportunity to view JCL from an "inside the system looking out" perspective. Later, as a user and teacher, I viewed JCL from an "outside the system looking in" perspective. The two can be very different. In this book JCL is treated from the viewpoint of an *average user*. The logic used by the operating system in handling the user's JCL will be carefully examined.

WHO IS THIS BOOK INTENDED FOR?

By its title alone, this book is clearly not intended for the beginner. It is intended for the JCL user (systems programmer, applications programmer, technical manager, technical support specialist, and operator) with experience. Although basic and elementary topics are covered for reference purposes, the book focuses by and large on the difficult, the ambiguous, and the unexpected. Even individuals with many years of intensive JCL experience are very likely to find useful information, providing answers to some mysteries and dispelling some popular myths.

CAN A BEGINNER IN JCL READ THIS BOOK?

The answer is a qualified yes. The book covers basic topics (without emphasizing them) so that even a beginner can derive a substantial benefit from reading it. Some of the advanced topics, however, may be difficult for the uninitiated in JCL to digest. Ideally, reading a more basic document on JCL first and/or getting hands-on exposure would put an individual in a position to derive maximum benefit from this book.

IS THIS A REFERENCE BOOK OR A USER'S GUIDE?

Actually, it is both. It can be read from cover to cover as a guide or selectively as a reference manual. As a result, the reader may find occasional repetition on certain topics. This is unavoidable if the book is to be an effective reference document.

DOES THIS BOOK COVER EVERY DETAIL ON JCL?

The answer to this question is "no" — with an explanation. There are many topics in JCL that are completely obsolete, and this book will not discuss them. For example, ISAM was replaced by VSAM in the mid-1970s, and it is very seldom used today. The 3850 Mass Storage device is obsolete with barely any active users. Seven-track tape is long gone from the average MVS/XA installation. None of these topics is covered in this book.

Certain parameters or subparameters in JCL are seldom or never used for various reasons. They will be either briefly mentioned or completely omitted. The book concentrates on what is used in a real environment *today* and avoids burdening the reader's brain with useless or near-useless information.

OPERATING SYSTEM ENVIRONMENT

The main operating system covered is MVS/XA (MVS/SP Version 2). However, users of MVS/SP (MVS/SP Version 1) will find that JCL for both of these systems is virtually identical. The reader can assume that MVS/XA and MVS/SP work identically from a JCL standpoint unless otherwise noted. Differences between the two will be identified when they exist. They will rarely be found.

All that applies to MVS/XA JCL also applies to MVS/ESA (MVS/SP Version 3). Additional features and differences for MVS/ESA JCL will be covered separately in Chapter 14.

Software packages (with the exception of TMS and TLMS) that may be installed in an MVS/XA system are not taken into consideration. Some of them may have an impact on the way JCL is handled. Security restrictions based on a security package (such as RACF ACF2 or Top Secret) also cannot be taken into consideration. Each user must be aware of her or his security profile and the restrictions it entails.

TO WHAT EXTENT IS VSAM COVERED?

MVS/XA JCL was intended for non-VSAM data sets and has severe restrictions when it comes to VSAM. With the exception of retrieving, JCL can do little with a VSAM data set. For example, a VSAM data set can neither be created nor deleted via JCL. For such functions, IDCAMS must be used. Although some examples of IDCAMS are given in Chapter 13, this book does not claim to cover VSAM to any degree of completeness.

As will be seen in Chapter 14, JCL acquires many more capabilities in relation to VSAM under MVS/ESA.

CAN YOUR INSTALLATION BENEFIT FROM THIS BOOK?

Absolutely! JCL can be written in many different ways to accomplish a particular goal. Some of the ways may result in:

• Inefficiency of execution
• Poor resource utilization
• Excessive operator intervention
• Frequent (and unnecessary) JCL changes
• Frequent failures
• Intermittent failures
• Difficulty in fixing problems
• Difficulty in implementing change management

This book focuses on ways to avoid such problems and provides information helpful in establishing good practices. It can also serve as a guide in setting up JCL standards.

ACKNOWLEDGMENTS

It is a pleasure to say thanks to those who helped in some way with the writing and publishing of this book.

I wish to express my appreciation to Jay Ranade, Senior Editor of McGraw-Hill, for his guidance and for all his useful suggestions and recommendations, without which this book would have been much more difficult to write.

My thanks also go to my many friends, associates, and students, too numerous to mention by name, who gave me support and help. A special thanks to Judy Kelly of Met Life for her valuable assistance in providing a comprehensive technical review for the material in the book.

Last but not least, I must thank my wife, Rosemarie, and my two daughters, Stacy and Christina, for their moral support and encouragement and for putting up with me when I was not available to them for long periods of time while working on the book. I hope I can justify their faith in me.

About the Author

Mani Carathanassis began his data processing career with IBM in March 1965 in Poughkeepsie, N.Y. He was a member of the systems programming team which implemented and debugged the initial versions of the Operating System, PCP, MFT and MVT. His specific area of responsibility was Job Management, which put him in daily contact with JCL and where he began developing his expertise on the subject.

After his departure form IBM in March 1968, he worked as Director of Systems Software for CBS, Inc., responsible for systems programming, technical support, standards, technical training, online systems, etc., until February 1972.

Between February 1972 and February 1980 he worked for SIAC as Director of Technical Services, holding a variety of software related responsibilities. For a period of two years, he was also responsible for hardware evaluation, planning and installation.

For about a year after SIAC, he was with Coopers and Lybrand, as a Consultant Manager completing several technical engagements.

Between February 1981 and November 1984 he held the position of Vice President with Citibank, responsible for a variety of software-related areas, including contingency backup.

In February 1981, he founded Technical Computer Seminars, located in Englewood, New Jersey, a company mainly dedicated to conducting in-house and public classes in MVS-related subjects. In late 1984 he resigned his position at Citibank to assume full-time responsibility as the head of Technical Computer Seminars, a position he still holds.

In February 1970, be began teaching in the School of Continuing Education of New York University where he taught a variety of classes; the main one was OS/VS JCL. He still teaches at the school's Institute of Information Technologies and holds the title of Adjunct Associate Professor of Management.

1

Introduction

1.1 HISTORICAL PERSPECTIVE

MVS/XA is an evolutionary system. It is part of OS (or OS/VS for virtual systems), which has been in existence for a long time. After many years of development, IBM released the first version of OS in 1965. It was called PCP (Primary Control Program) and was the first of several versions intended for the System/360 mainframe, which was the marvel of its day.

PCP was meant to be a primer system and had limited capabilities. It offered no multiprogramming (one of the main features of System/360), no priority scheduling, and no input or output spooling to speak of. In addition, it was an unreliable system which "crashed" with regular and predictable frequency. Interestingly, the Job Control Language (JCL) used by PCP was very similar to the one used today. PCP became obsolete in 1969.

In 1966, a more advanced version, MFT (Multiprogramming with a Fixed number of Tasks) was released. It offered limited multiprogramming and was a small improvement over PCP.

MVT (Multiprogramming with a Variable number of Tasks) was released in 1967. It was the first relatively reliable system with a comprehensive set of features the other versions lacked. MVT was the predecessor to MVS.

In 1968 a much improved version of MFT, MFT II, was released. Eventually, the original version of MFT became obsolete and MFT II was renamed to just MFT.

MVT and MFT were the systems of the late 1960s and early 1970s. Both had one serious deficiency: They provided very limited and inefficient input/output spooling capabilities. A team of IBM employees, without official IBM sanction, developed a supplementary software package which could be superimposed on MFT or MVT and provide good spooling capabilities. The package was called HASP (Houston Automatic Spooling Priority). It was free to MFT/MVT users, and it became instantly popular. Eventually IBM made it an official product and assumed support for it. At the same time IBM developed another supplementary package, intended for MVT only, which would allow several mainframes to work together under one operating system in a master/slave relationship. This system, which also provided spooling capabilities comparable to those of HASP, was called ASP (Attached Support Processor). Relatively few users took advantage of ASP.

In 1973 IBM announced a new series of mainframes, System/370, which was a continuation of the System/360 series but with virtual storage capabilities. New OS systems, now referred to as OS/VS, were made available to support the new hardware: VS1 (Virtual Storage 1) and VS2 (Virtual Storage 2). VS1 was basically an MFT system in a virtual environment. VS2 consisted of two versions, SVS (Single Virtual Storage) and MVS (Multiple Virtual Storage). From an internal standpoint, SVS was a "virtual" MVT, but MVS was almost an entirely rewritten system. From an external standpoint, both worked very much like MVT. In the mid- to late 1970s, all versions except VS1 and MVS became obsolete. VS1 became obsolete in 1987, leaving MVS as the only remaining version of OS. It is interesting to note that today several terms have become synonymous: OS, OS/VS, VS2, and MVS. All of these terms are likely to appear in documents, especially older ones.

HASP and ASP migrated to MVS (but not VS1) under the names of JES2 (Job Entry Subsystem 2) and JES3 (Job Entry Subsystem 3), respectively. This explains why all operator console messages emanating from JES2 contain the word HASP. They also became integral parts of MVS as opposed to optional packages. An MVS installation must choose from the beginning to use JES2 or JES3. One or the other must be used. The great majority of MVS sites (perhaps over 90%) use JES2.

MVS provides far greater reliability, integrity, and performance than all the previous versions. It had, however, from its beginning a serious handicap. It had a virtual storage limit of 16 megabytes (approximately 16 million bytes). This was often inadequate for large systems such as CICS, database systems, etc. In the early 1980s,

IBM released a much heralded version of MVS which increased storage availability to 2 gigabytes (approximately 2 billion bytes) and also increased the maximum number of channels and devices. This version is known as MVS/Extended Architecture or MVS/XA. The original version of MVS is referred to as MVS/SP. Actually, the official names are MVS/SP Version 1 (normally referred to as MVS/SP), MVS/SP Version 2 (normally referred to as MVS/XA), and MVS/SP Version 3 (normally referred to as MVS/ESA).

MVS/ESA is a system announced by IBM in February of 1988. As of the writing of this book, MVS/ESA was scheduled for release in early 1989. MVS/ESA increases the virtual storage availability of each user to an incredible 16 terabytes (approximately 16 trillion bytes). To demonstrate how large this amount is, consider a large installation with 500 triple density 3380 devices. Its total disk capacity would be 500 x 1.890 = 945 megabytes or 0.945 terabytes, only a fraction of the virtual storage every user in an MVS/ESA is theoretically entitled to.

JCL has been an upward compatible language since its inception. Several new features have been added over the years, but JCL that worked in 1965 under PCP would work today with minor or no changes. Several new and modified parameters have been introduced under MVS/ESA. They will be discussed in Chapter 14.

For the remainder of this book, MVS/XA (or whichever version of MVS is being discussed) will be referred to as "the system."

1.2 REASONS FOR JCL COMPLEXITY

Syntax is one of the least complex areas in JCL. As a language, however, JCL can be very complex. There are many reasons why this is so.

JCL was designed in the early 1960s. The designers had no previous language on which to base their design. There were no operating systems in existence then. While the designers did an admirable job viewed from today's vantage point and level of sophistication, JCL leaves a lot to be desired.

One of the reasons for its complexity is the tremendous amount of freedom JCL gives to the user. As the ancient Greeks said, excessive freedom amounts to anarchy. Many techniques and practices that can achieve results ranging from the undesirable to the disastrous are readily available to the JCL user. Unless the installation restricts their use or the user understands the potential dangers, JCL becomes a problem waiting to happen. Installations can protect against some of these practices but not all of them. The average user is unlikely to understand all the dangers involved because many of them are of subtle nature, poorly documented and difficult to understand.

Another reason for complexity is the frequent reluctance of the system to keep the user informed. In most cases when JCL parameters or subparameters are being ignored or altered by the system, no messages are issued spelling out the facts to the user. Wrong assumptions and the problems that follow them become a natural consequence.

The reasons stated above offer no distinct advantage to the user. There is, however, some justifiable complexity which provides the user with some important advantages and benefits. Consider a program where some changes are needed:

• Instead of writing at the beginning of a data set, writing is to begin at the end, allowing the data set to be extended.
• Instead of processing a nonlabeled tape data set, a standard labeled data set is to be processed.
• Instead of reading in one data set, several data sets of comparable characteristics are to be read in.

In many other systems, the program must be modified to implement the above-stated changes. In MVS/XA this is accomplished by changing JCL, not the program. These are only a few examples of how JCL can act as a supplementary language to the programming language.

One of the main functions of JCL is to shield the program and insulate it from the external environment. As a result, environmental changes seldom require programming changes. An installation can go through numerous configuration changes with its programs remaining unaltered. JCL may change, but this is much easier than changing programs. This feature of JCL constitutes a considerable advantage to the user and the entire installation. It also accounts for some of the complexity in the language.

1.3 MULTIPROGRAMMING AND VIRTUAL STORAGE

System/360 was the first IBM mainframe to offer multiprogramming capabilities. Previous systems could only execute one program at a time, resulting in a very poor utilization of the Central Processing Unit (CPU). The reason for this was the fact that input/output operations, which usually constitute the most time-consuming part of a program's execution, use the CPU very little or not at all.

Multiprogramming allows two or more programs to execute concurrently using the same CPU. Figure 1.1 explains the basic mechanism of multiprogramming.

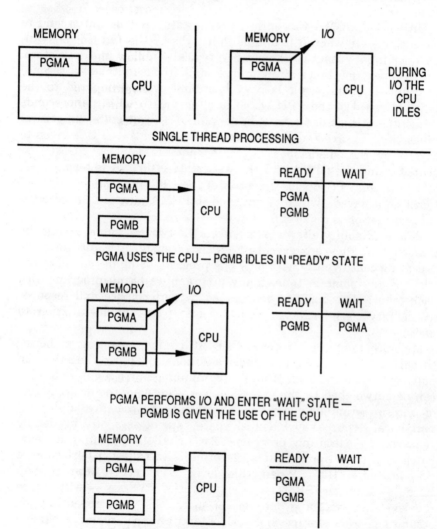

Figure 1.1 Multiprogramming.

Two programs, PGMA (high priority) and PGMB (lower priority), reside in storage. PGMA is using the CPU, and PGMB is in a "ready state." A program is said to be in this state when it is ready to use the CPU but cannot because another program is using it. One must keep in mind that a CPU can never have more than one user at a time.

Ultimately, PGMA will enter a "wait state." A program is said to be in this state when it is unable to use the CPU, even if it is available. An input/output (I/O) operation typically results in a wait state. An I/O operation takes a few milliseconds (thousandths of a second) to complete. This is a relatively long time when compared to the internal speed of the CPU which is often measured in nanoseconds (billionths of a second). As PGMA enters the wait state, its critical information is saved automatically and control of the CPU is given to PGMB by the "dispatcher," a component of MVS/XA. PGMB executes, using the CPU, until the wait state of PGMA is terminated, at which point PGMB loses control of the CPU (its critical information also is saved), which is returned to PGMA (after its saved critical information is restored).

CPU availability alternates between the two programs, giving the illusion that they are executing simultaneously. Actually they are executing concurrently with only one program being in control of the CPU at any point in time. Many programs can multiprogram with each other. How many is determined by performance and resource availability considerations, and it varies from one installation to another.

Multiprogramming improves CPU utilization, resulting in better throughput, but it also introduces additional overhead (i.e., the dispatcher). When the level of multiprogramming is too high, its benefit can be outweighed by the excessive overhead. Also, the desired level of multiprogramming can be dependent on the availability of peripheral resources such as disk space, tape devices, etc., needed by concurrently executing programs. An installation defines its own batch target multiprogramming level in its Installation Performance Specifications (IPS). When this level is exceeded, the System Resource Manager (SRM) — a component of MVS/XA — will reduce the level by "swapping out" one or more jobs. A swapped out job occupies no real storage and resides entirely on disk (or expanded storage) until it is swapped back in by SRM to resume execution, when the condition that caused the swap has been eliminated.

Many IBM mainframes contain several CPUs (as many as six) and all of them can work together as a unit under one operating system. This is known as multiprocessing.

Virtual storage is a technique that avails the user of much more usable storage than real storage can provide. Virtual storage is basically a combination of real storage and EPS (External Page Storage — usually disk). Figure 1.2 shows in a non-detailed way how a program executes in real and virtual storage. In a real storage environment (which is no longer in use), a program was loaded from disk into a "region" or "partition" of real storage and executed holding on to the entire amount of storage even though it may have needed only a fraction of it.

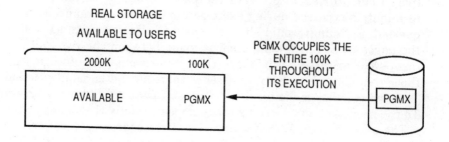

A PROGRAM EXECUTING IN A REAL (NONVIRTUAL) SYSTEM

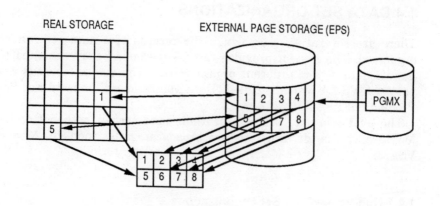

VIRTUAL STORAGE OF PGMX

A PROGRAM EXECUTING IN A VIRTUAL SYSTEM
(RELATIONSHIP OF REAL STORAGE, EPS, AND VIRTUAL STORAGE)

Figure 1.2 Real and virtual storage.

In a virtual storage environment, the program to be executed is first placed on EPS and divided into equal parts, or pages, of 4K each. EPS is usually disk, but it can also be cash storage on some 3880 control units and, in some advanced 3090 models, Expanded Storage (real storage dedicated to EPS activity). Then the first logical page of the program (#1 page in Figure 1.2) is loaded into real storage and execution begins. When another page is needed, say #5, this page is loaded in real storage and execution continues. Page #1 can be overlaid by a page of another concurrently executing program. If this happens, the page's contents, if altered, will be written out (paged out) to EPS to preserve the page's integrity. If an abnormal termination occurred during execution and a storage dump were requested, the dump would show the pages in real storage as well as the pages in EPS. No distinction is made between the two and it is impossible to distinguish pages that came from real storage from those that came from EPS. In essence there should be no distinction. The two together make up the virtual storage used by this program. To the user, real and virtual storage appear exactly the same.

The concept of an MVS/XA virtual address space is covered in Section 2.1.5 of Chapter 2 as part of the discussion of the REGION parameter.

1.4 DATA SET ORGANIZATIONS

There are several ways in which the records of a data set can be organized: The system provides "access methods," each designed to handle data sets of different organizations. The access methods are part of MVS/XA which is called "Data Management" or Data Facility Product (DFP).

The available data set organizations (and access methods) under MVS/XA can be divided into two broad categories: non-VSAM and VSAM.

1.4.1 Non-VSAM Data Set Organizations

Four data set organizations were made available to the user from the very beginning of OS:

• Sequential Organization. This is divided into two categories: QSAM (Queued Sequential Access Method). This access method allows the user to read and write sequentially, at the logical record level. The program deals with logical records and the system reads and writes blocks on behalf of the program. It can be used for either disk or tape. This is the most frequently used access method in a batch environment. BSAM (Basic Sequential Access Method). This access method allows the user to read and write sequentially, at the block level. It can be used for either disk or tape. This is not a frequently used access method.

- Direct (Random) Organization or BDAM (Basic Direct Access Method). This access method allows the user to read and write directly (without processing previous records) at the block level. It is used for disk only. This is not a frequently used access method.
- Partitioned Organization or BPAM (Basic Partitioned Access Method). This access method divides the data set into many sequentially organized members. It is used for disk only. This is not a frequently used access method. Paradoxically, partitioned data sets are very common. This apparent discrepancy is due to the fact that members of partitioned data sets are most often processed individually using QSAM or BSAM.
- Indexed Sequential Organization or ISAM (Indexed Sequential Access Method). This access method is obsolete. It was meant to be phased out and replaced by VSAM a long time ago. ISAM data sets can still be found in some installations, but ISAM would never be used in designing a new application. It will not be discussed in this book.

1.4.2 VSAM Data Set Organizations

VSAM (Virtual Storage Access Method) is an organization that became available with virtual operating systems (VS1 and VS2) and can be used only for disk.

Three organizations are available under VSAM:

- Sequential Organization. This is referred to as ESDS (Entry Sequenced Data Set). It supplements QSAM and BSAM rather than replacing them.
- Direct Organization. This is referred to as RRDS (Relative Record Data Set). It supplements BDAM rather than replacing it.
- Indexed Organization. This is referred to as KSDS (Key Sequenced Data Set). It replaced ISAM.

JCL was originally designed for non-VSAM data sets. Most JCL facilities are either invalid or ignored for VSAM data sets (except under MVS/ESA). IDCAMS is an IBM-supplied product which provides many facilities for VSAM data sets that are unavailable via JCL. The bottom line is that JCL provides few services to VSAM data sets. In the following chapters of this book, many statements will be made in reference to disk data sets, disk volumes, and a disk environment in general. Unless VSAM is specifically mentioned, the statements will refer only to non-VSAM. This is necessary to avoid possible confusion, in view of the fact that VSAM and non-VSAM data sets are considerably different from each other.

1.5 RECORD FORMATS

There are three record formats available in a non-VSAM environment:

1. Fixed format. This is by far the most frequently used record format. All logical records are the same size. All blocks (physical records) are also the same size except for the last block of the data set which could be smaller. In the majority of cases there are several logical records in a block, and the record format is called fixed blocked — RECFM=FB (Figure 1.3). The maximum size of a block as well as a logical record is 32760.
2. Variable format. Logical records can be different sizes and each one is preceded by a 4-byte field describing its length. Blocks can also be different sizes and each one is preceded by a 4-byte field describing its length. In the majority of cases there are several logical records in a block and the record format is called variable blocked or VB (see Figure 1.3). The maximum size of the block and logical record are 32760 and 32756, respectively. When a record format is defined as variable blocked spanned (VBS), the logical record can exceed the size of the block. VBS is a rarely used record format.
3. Undefined format — RECFM=U. Logical records do not exist and the program can only deal with blocks. The blocks can be any size up to the maximum of 32760. This is a seldom used record format, except in load (executable program) libraries which are always of undefined record format.

Regardless of record format used, a physical separation always exists between any two blocks. This separation is known as an Interblock Gap (IBG) or Interrecord Gap (IRG). Logical records do not have separations. The last byte of one logical record is immediately next to the first byte of the next logical record.

Formats under MVS/XA

1) Fixed Blocked Format (FB)

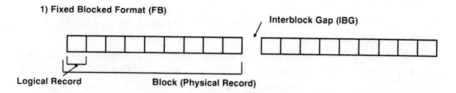

Note: All logical records are the same size
      Limit 32,760 bytes

      All blocks are the same size (except the last one)
      Limit 32,760

2) Variable Blocked Format (VB)

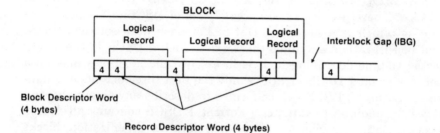

Note: Logical records in a block can have different sizes.
      The first 4 bytes define the size of each record.

      Blocks can have different sizes.
      The first 4 bytes of each block define its size.

3) Undefined Format (U)

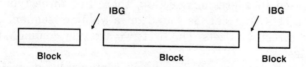

Note: Blocks can be of any size up to the limit of 32,760.
      Logical records do not exist.

Figure 1.3 Record formats.

1.6 VTOC, PDS, AND THE CATALOG

Every disk volume must have a Volume Table of Contents, most often referred to by the acronym VTOC (see Figure 1.4).

A disk device comes from the factory with a nonremovable volume already mounted on it and a VTOC already on the volume. (Disk devices with dismountable volumes, such as 3330, became obsolete a long time ago, and they are unlikely to be found in a real environment. This book will basically ignore them.)

The VTOC may be changed in size and repositioned by the personnel responsible for initializing the volume. The VTOC can be placed anywhere on a volume. For certain types of volumes (scratch or work volumes), positioning the VTOC in the middle may offer a performance advantage.

The VTOC contains entries known as DSCBs (Data Set Control Blocks). There are several different types of DSCBs, the most common of which is a Format 1 DSCB. For each data set (non-VSAM and non-ISAM) on a volume there exists such a DSCB in the VTOC of the volume describing it. It is in essence the label of a disk data set. A Format 1 DSCB identifies only the first three extents of a data set. A Format 3 DSCB will be formed to describe any extents beyond three. In addition to extents, a Format 1 DSCB contains all details about a data set's characteristics (i.e., data set organization, blocks size, logical record length, record format, creation date, expiration date, etc.).

When a data set is deleted, using any means at all, its DSCB is logically removed from the VTOC and the space it occupied becomes immediately available for reuse. However, the data inside the data set is not erased. It remains on the volume until another data set allocates the same space and writes over it. Although the data of a deleted data set is at best difficult to use, its presence on the volume can be considered a possible security exposure.

As discussed in a previous section, there are three types of non-VSAM data sets that can be found on a volume: sequential, partitioned, and direct data sets. The first two are very common, the third one much less so.

A partitioned data set (PDS) requires some explanation. It is basically a data set which contains suballocated sequential data sets, except that the suballocated data sets are called members (see Figure 1.4, data sets TST.LIBA and TST.LIBB). At the beginning of a PDS there exists a directory which contains entries for the members inside the PDS. Each PDS directory entry provides information about

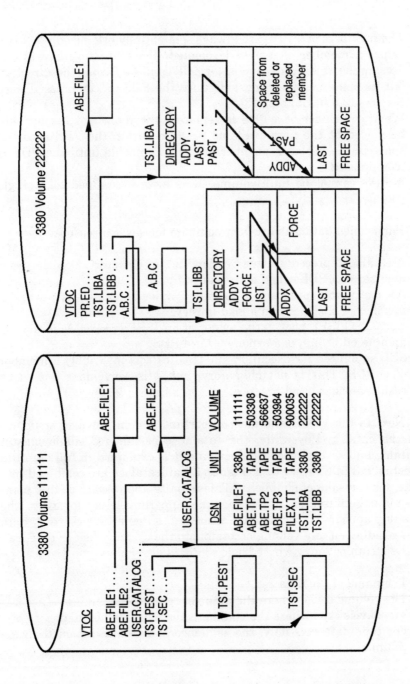

Figure 1.4 Symbolic representation of VTOC, PDS, and catalog (NON-VSAM)

a member, including its exact location. Entries in the directory are alphabetically organized and reusable. A PDS, which is also called a *library*, is subject to certain restrictions and peculiarities:

• The members of a PDS are always sequentially organized.
• When a member of a PDS is deleted (there are several ways to accomplish this), its entry is logically removed from the directory but its space becomes unusable until the PDS is "compressed" (see Section 13.5 in Chapter 13).
• When a member of a PDS is replaced, the replacing member will be placed at the first available position within the PDS, and the space of the replaced member becomes unusable until the PDS is "compressed."
• A PDS cannot be multivolume. It is always confined to a single volume.

Partitioned data sets are very common for several reasons:

• A cataloged procedure (see Section 12.1 in Chapter 12) is always a member of a PDS called a procedure library.
• An executable program, also called a load module, is always a member of a PDS called a load library.
• Each TSO/ISPF user is the owner of an ISPF library. A library, as mentioned before, is a synonym for a PDS.
• JCL submitted for execution via TSO/ISPF is invariably a member of a PDS. This is not obligatory, but it is convenient and, as a result, a widespread practice.

Next to the VTOC, the most important system-provided structure is the catalog. Physically, the catalog consists of a single master catalog and several user catalogs, and it is explained in full detail in Section 6.3 in Chapter 6. In Figure 1.4 all catalogs are combined into one, for the sake of simplicity. This is quite appropriate at this point in time because, as it will become apparent later, logically, the catalog appears to the average user as a singular structure. A data set residing on any volume accessible to the system, disk or tape, can have a catalog entry whose basic contents are:

• The name of the data set.
• The volume serial where the data set resides.
• The device type where the volume is (or is to be) mounted.
• For tape data sets only, the sequence of the data set on the tape volume.

Although cataloging a data set (not including GDGs) is optional, it is so important that it becomes almost mandatory from a practical standpoint. Several data sets, some cataloged and some not, are shown in Figure 1.4. Consider cataloged data set TST.LIBA. The user need know only the name of the data set to be able to retrieve it. The catalog can supply device and volume information needed by the system in order to find the appropriate VTOC. The data set's DSCB will yield detailed information about the data set's exact location on the volume and other characteristics.

Now consider noncataloged data set TST.PEST. It is now the user that must know and supply via JCL device and volume information. This is not just inconvenient, it is also risky. User-supplied information is far less reliable than that supplied by the catalog.

The vast majority of data sets in an ordinary environment (excluding nonlabeled tape data sets) will be cataloged. It is not easy to find a justifiable reason for not cataloging a data set when it is created. Here is an example: A tape data set which is to be sent to another site should not be cataloged when it is created. Cataloging such a data set would be useless, since its catalog entry would never be used. Few such valid reasons for not cataloging exist.

1.7 JOBS, STEPS, AND INITIATORS

There are three types of work that a user can perform under MVS/XA:

• Time-sharing (TSO)
• Online
• Batch

The first two appear very much alike to the user. Under both the user logs on, using a userid and a password, and begins to work interactively. A transaction is entered and a response received, normally in very few seconds. Technically, the two can be very different from each other, but they appear similar to the user. A unit of work for both is called a *session*.

Batch processing is not interactive. It is deferred execution. It can be executed as soon as it is submitted, or much later. Also, the execution of batch work can be time-consuming, as opposed to interactive, which is usually very quick.

JCL must be used in order to submit batch work. The unit of batch work is a "job." A job can be defined as one or more steps, up to 255.

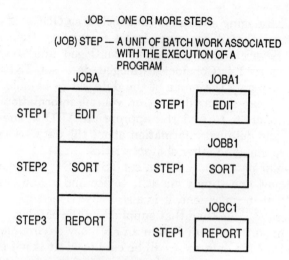

JOB — ONE OR MORE STEPS

(JOB) STEP — A UNIT OF BATCH WORK ASSOCIATED
WITH THE EXECUTION OF A
PROGRAM

HOW DO THE TWO METHODS DIFFER?

• STEPS WITHIN A JOB HAVE PREDEFINED SEQUENCE

• STEPS WITHIN A JOB CANNOT
  MULTIPROGRAM WITH ONE ANOTHER

• A STEP WITHIN A JOB CAN INTERROGATE THE STATUS OF
  PRECEDING STEP'S EXECUTION AND DETERMINE
  WHETHER TO EXECUTE OR NOT.

Figure 1.5 The concept of work under MVS/XA.

A step can be defined as a unit of batch work that executes a program. It is also referred to as a job step.

Consider Figure 1.5. On the left, a job is shown with three steps. STEP1 executes program EDIT, STEP2 executes program SORT, and STEP2 executes program REPORT. On the right, the same three steps appear but as parts of three different jobs. Both setups can achieve the same goal, but the two don't work the same way. The steps on the left must be executed in sequence, and the execution of steps STEPB and STEPC can be controlled based on what happened to preceding steps. The steps on the right are within different jobs and can be executed concurrently (although sequential execution can be forced), and there is no communication between jobs. If these steps require sequential execution and execution control, then the setup on the left is much better. If not, the one on the right is preferable.

Figure 1.6 shows in a general, nondetailed way how a job is submitted to the system.

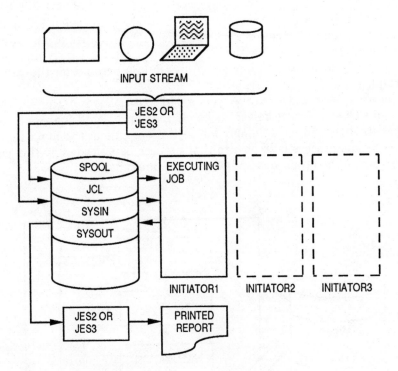

Figure 1.6 Processing of JCL.

Input stream is JCL and, optionally, data which comes together with JCL (80-byte records), known as sysin data or input stream data.

Cards and tape are rarely used for submitting work to the system (especially cards). Disk is sometimes used, and a time-sharing terminal is by far the most common device used in submitting jobs.

JES2 or JES3 reads the JCL in the input stream and places it on the spool pack. JCL goes though more than one level of syntax checking (not shown here). Sysin data, if any, is also read in and placed on the spool pack by JES2 or JES3. If the JCL is syntactically correct, it is queued for execution in what is known as the Job Queue.

An "initiator" must be available to execute this job. An initiator is a group of routines whose sole function is to select a job from the Job Queue and execute it under its control. During the job's execution sysin data, if any, will be read in and print-lines, if any, will be placed on the Spool pack for later printing. They can be printed by the printer routines of JES2 or JES3 normally after the job terminates. There are several initiators available, and each one performs the same service for a different job. The number of initiators available varies according the the hardware configuration and the amount of concurrent time-sharing and online activity on the same system.

Figure 1.7 shows the workings of an initiator. The initiator goes to the Job Queue and asks for a job. If an appropriate job exists, it takes its JCL and goes though Job Initiation. One of the main functions of this process is to ensure that no data sets needed by this job are reserved by other jobs and, therefore, unavailable.

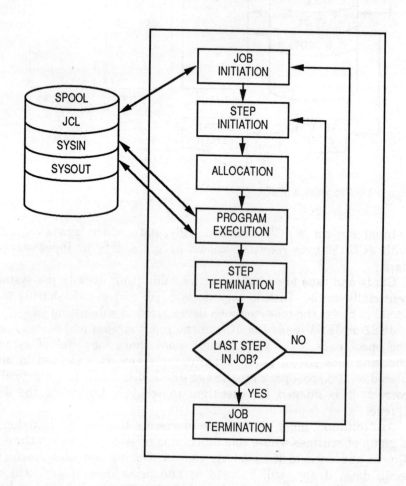

Figure 1.7 The execution of a job by an initiator.

If some data sets are reserved, it places itself in a wait state and informs the operator. If not, the initiator takes the first step of the job and goes to the next process, Step Initiation. This process will check the COND parameter of the EXEC as well as the JOB statement. For the first step the COND parameter either does not exist or is ignored (except COND=ONLY).

Next comes the Allocation process (or Allocation routines), which performs the following functions:

- Allocates the required devices for all DD statements in the step. Disk devices may already be allocated and, if so, the "use count" of the device is incremented. For JES3 tape devices may be preallocated in which case the Allocation routines take no action. JES3 normally preallocates a high water mark of tape devices needed in a job, before the job begins execution. JES2 does not.
- For old data sets on disk, it makes certain that any needed (non-dismountable) volumes are available.
- For new data sets on disk it makes certain that the requested volumes are available or assigns volumes when none are requested specifically. Then it creates the data set with the space requested in the primary quantity, if possible. If not possible, the result is a JCL error.
- For tape data sets (NEW or OLD) not preallocated by JES3 and not using deferred mounting, a mount message is routed to the operator console, requesting that a volume be mounted on the allocated device. The Allocation routines do not wait for the operator to satisfy the mount request. When all required allocations for a step are complete, the next phase (Program Execution) will be entered even though the requested mount may not yet be satisfied.

If the Allocation routines are successful, Program Execution begins. The program to be executed is frequently written by the user (it can also be written by a vendor) and it is normally the most time-consuming part of a step's entire process. Sysin records, saved during reading process, will be read in by the program. Sysout (print-line) records, if any, will be saved on the Spool pack for later printing or viewing.

The Step Termination process is entered when the program execution terminates normally or abnormally (ABEND). This process:

- Deallocates all devices allocated in the Allocation process. Devices containing "passed" data sets or "retained" volumes will also not be deallocated. For JES3 some tape devices will not be deallocated if they will be needed later in the job.

• Performs disposition processing. It attempts to satisfy what is requested in the normal or abnormal field of the DISP parameter (keep, delete, catalog, uncatalog, or pass the data set).
• Verifies that all data sets opened were closed during the program's execution and closes those that were not.

If there is another step in the job, the entire Step Initiation/Allocation/Program Execution/Step Termination sequence is repeated. It will be repeated as many times as there are steps in the job, except for steps that are not executed (i.e., because of the COND parameter which is checked during Step Initiation).

When the last step in the job has been executed, the Job Termination process is given control. This process is responsible for tying up loose ends. For example, when a data set is passed and not received, Job Termination will determine the ultimate status of the passed data set.

Then control is passed to the Job Initiation routines, which query the Job Queue for another job to execute.

In Figure 3.2 the output of an executed job is shown with the Allocation and Step Termination messages for each step identified.

1.8 TYPES OF JCL STATEMENTS

The types of available JCL statements are:

1. **The JOB Statement.**

A JOB statement must be at the beginning of each job. It identifies the name of the job and its characteristics. All records preceding the JOB statement will be ignored by the system.

A JOB statement signals the beginning of a job during the reading process. All statements following a JOB statement belong to the job until a delimiter is encountered. Another JOB statement is a possible delimiter. A null statement is also a delimiter (see #6) as is an end-of-file condition on the reading device.

2. **The EXEC Statement.**

An EXEC statement must be at the beginning of each step. It identifies the name of the step, if any, and its characteristics.

An EXEC statement signals the beginning of a step during the reading process. All statements following an EXEC statement belong to the STEP until a delimiter is encountered.

Another EXEC statement is such a delimiter. JOB statement delimiters will also act as EXEC statement delimiters.

A job can have a maximum of 255 EXEC statements.

3. **The DD (Data Definition) Statement.**

DD statements normally follow EXEC statements. The basic function of a DD statement is to describe a data set which the executing program intends to open and read from or write to.

With the exception of dynamic allocation and operator console-routed messages, if a program must read from or write to a data set, a DD statement must be included in the step to describe the data set. Additional DD statements describing data sets which the program has no intention of using will have no effect on the execution of the program. They can, however, have a detrimental effect on resource utilization.

There are also certain special DD statements that serve different functions. DD statements such as JOBLIB, STEPLIB, STEPCAT, SYSUDUMP, etc. provide the system with certain needed information rather than describing data sets to be used by the executing program.

The sequence of DD statements in a step is not important, except where referbacks are used.

A maximum of 3273 DD statements are allowed per step (1635 if Data Facility Product before Version 2.3 is in use).

4. **The Default Delimiter Statement (/*).**

This statement begins with /* in the first two positions and blanks in the remainder of the statement up to position 71. It serves to delimit sysin (input stream) data. This data consists of 80-byte records and is submitted together with JCL.

5. **The Comment Statement.**

This statement begins with //* in the first three positions and anything at all for the rest of the statement up to position 71. Its contents are ignored by the system but are displayed for the user to see. It is coded for strictly visual purposes.

It can be placed anywhere in the input stream after the JOB statement, except inside sysin data.

6. **The Null Statement.**

This statement begins with // in the first two positions and blanks in the remainder of the statement up to position 71. It serves to delimit a job during the reading process. Any record found in the input stream after this statement will be ignored unless it is a JOB statement.

7. **The Command Statement.**

A number of operator commands which are normally issued at the operator console can also be issued through a command statement. This statement, if used improperly by someone not familiar with operations, can cause serious problems to the entire system, and it is usually unavailable to all but some very technical authorized personnel. It will not be discussed further in this book.

8. **The PROC Statement.**

The PROC statement is used for two reasons:

- To supply symbolic override defaults in a cataloged or instream procedure. It is optional for cataloged procedures but practically always used when symbolic parameters are used. When coded, it must be the first statement in the procedure.
- To signal the beginning of an in-stream procedure during the reading of a job. It is a required statement for an in-stream procedure.

9. **The PEND Statement.**

The PEND statement is used to signal the end of an instream procedure during the reading of a job. It must be the last statement of an in-stream procedure.

10. **The Output Statement.**

The output statement is intended to contain attributes normally assigned to an output (sysout) data set which can be scheduled for local or remote printing. By itself, an output statement has no effect on a step's execution. A sysout DD statement, however, can acquire some or all the attributes of an output statement by making an explicit or implicit reference to it.

1.9 THE SYNTAX OF JCL

Syntactically, JCL is a fairly simple language. Although there are some syntactical peculiarities, most rules are easy to learn and follow.

All JCL statements begin with two slashes, //, in the first two positions (except /*). All positions of a line, from 1 to 71 (included), can be used for coding a JCL statement. Position 72 is used (rarely) for imbedded comment continuation, and positions 73 through 80 are used for numbering purposes.

With the exception of the null (//), delimiter (/*), comment (//*), and command statements, all other statements follow the same general format:

```
//[name]   operation  parameter field   [comments]
```

Expressions in brackets, [ ], are optional.

name — Every JCL statement can or must have a name. A name must consist of a minimum of 1 and a maximum of 8 alphabetic, numeric, or national ($, #, and @) characters, but the first character cannot be numeric. A hyphen is also permitted. One or more blanks must follow the name. If no name is coded, at least one blank must follow the two slashes (//).

operation — JOB, EXEC, DD, PROC, PEND, or OUTPUT. One or more blanks must follow the operation.

The parameter field consists of one or more parameters (under rare conditions none), separated by commas. No imbedded blanks between parameters are permitted.

```
//[name]    operation   [parameter][,parameter][,parameter]...
```

In general, there are two types of parameters: *positional* and *keyword*. A positional parameter, when coded, must be placed at the beginning of the parameter field. Exception: The programmer's name parameter is positional but must be coded second in the JOB statement. A keyword parameter can be coded in any sequence in relation to other keyword parameters. The great majority of parameters are keyword.

Parameters can have several different syntactical formats. Some of the values in a parameter must have "predefined spelling." While describing the syntax, "predefined spelling" will indicate that a particular spelling or one of a limited selection of spellings must be used. "No predefined spelling" will indicate that the user has a wide choice of spellings or values within certain syntactical constraints. For example, DSN=USER1.F99. DSN will be described as having predefined spelling; only DSN or DSNAME can be used. However, USER1.F99 has no predefined spelling, as the user can select any name desired as long as it does not violate certain syntactical rules.

• A parameter can appear as an expression with no predefined spelling:

  Example:

```
//USER1A JOB AZ31,...
```

AZ31 is the account number parameter in the JOB statement. It has no predefined spelling (the installation determines account numbers).

A parameter can also appear as several expressions with no predefined spelling separated by commas and enclosed in parentheses. The fields, or subparameters, inside the parentheses must appear in a particular sequence.

Example:

```
//USER1A JOB (AZ31,243),...
```

(AZ31,243) is the accounting information parameter in the JOB statement containing an account number and a room number. Neither has predefined spelling, and they must be coded in the sequence shown.

• A parameter can appear as a keyword with predefined spelling followed by an equal sign and a value or a name. This name or value may or may not have predefined spelling.

Example:

```
//DD1 DD DSN=USER1.FILE3,UNIT=TAPE,...
```

DSN and UNIT are keywords with predefined spelling. USER1.FILE3 in the DSN parameter has no predefined spelling (although it must adhere to syntactical rules). TAPE in the UNIT parameter has predefined spelling.

• A parameter can appear as a keyword with predefined spelling followed by an equal sign and one or more subparameters separated by commas and enclosed in parentheses. The subparameters are often (but not always) in a given sequence, some with and some without predefined spelling.

```
keyword=(subparameter1,subparameter2,...)
```

Example:

```
//DD1 DD DISP=(OLD,KEEP),LABEL=(2,BLP),...
```

DISP and LABEL are keywords with predefined spelling. OLD and KEEP are subparameters that must appear in the sequence shown, and both have predefined spelling. 2 and BLP are subparameters that must appear in the sequence shown, but only BLP has predefined spelling.

A subparameter can be a set of subsubparameters (some with and some without predefined spelling, but always in a given sequence) separated by commas and enclosed in parentheses.

```
keyword=(subparameter1,(subsubparameter1,subsubparameter2),..)
```

Example:

```
//S2 EXEC ...,COND=(EVEN,(0,LT,S1))
```

COND is a keyword with predefined spelling. EVEN is a subparameter with predefined spelling. 0, LT, and S1 are three subsubparameters that must appear in the sequence shown, and of the three only the second (LT) has predefined spelling. EVEN and (0,LT,S1) can be coded in any sequence.

A subparameter can also be a keyword with predefined spelling followed by an equal sign and one subsubparameter, or several subsubparameters separated by commas and enclosed in parentheses. A keyword that exists within another keyword is called a minor keyword. The other is called a major keyword. The subsubparameter(s) of a minor keyword have no positional significance and no predefined spelling.

```
keyword=(subparam1,minor-keyword=(subsuparam1,subsubparam2))
```

Example:

```
//DD2 DD VOL=(,RETAIN,SER=(111111,222222)),
//       UNIT=AFF=DD1,
//       LABEL=(2,BLP,EXPDT=98000),
//       DCB=(BLKSIZE=8000,BUFNO=10),...
```

In this example, SER, AFF, EXPDT, BLKSIZE, and BUFNO are minor keywords. VOL, UNIT, LABEL, and DCB are major keywords.

Comments can be coded at the end of a line provided there is at least one blank after the last valid character of the line. Comments are ignored by the system but appear in the output listing. These are known as imbedded comments to differentiate them from a comment statement where the entire line is a comment.

Comments can be continued by coding a nonblank character in position 72 and continuing the comments beginning in any position of the next line. The entire continued line will be treated as a comment. Example:

```
//DD1 DD DSN=USER1.F4,DISP=SHR THIS STATEMENT WAS   X   pos. 72
//                              ADDED ON 4/18/90
```

Syntactical notes and peculiarities:

• When it is permissible to omit a subparameter of positional significance, a comma can be coded in its place to indicate its absence. Normally, a default value is assumed.

Example: DISP=(,CATLG,DELETE) in the DD statement. In this case the first subparameter defaults to NEW.

When this comma is followed by at least one subparameter, as in the example above, it is called a *leading* comma. Leading commas are often used in JCL. When it is followed by no subparameters, it is called a *trailing* comma.

Example: DISP=(,CATLG,,) in the DD statement.

Trailing commas are never necessary. The above parameter should be coded as DISP=(,CATLG). The presence of the right parenthesis indicates that no more subparameters exist. In most cases trailing commas are benign, but sometimes they create syntactical problems. They should never be used, with only one exception: SYSOUT=(,). This a very special case, which will be explained in Section 10.2. of Chapter 10.

• When no commas exist within an expression enclosed in parentheses, the parentheses become optional. Example:

```
//DD1 DD UNIT=SYSDA,SPACE=(CYL,50)
//DD1 DD UNIT=(SYSDA),SPACE=(CYL,(50))
```

are both acceptable.

• When subparameters of positional significance that precede a minor keyword are omitted, more than one comma is never needed, even if several subparameters have been omitted. If none are coded, no commas at all are needed. Example:

```
//DD1 DD VOL=(,RETAIN,SER=000394),
//        LABEL=RETPD=5,...
```

```
//DD1 DD VOL=(,RETAIN,,,SER=000394),
//        LABEL=(,,,,RETPD=5),...
```

are both acceptable.
- A few parameters may contain special characters other than commas and parentheses. Expressions containing special characters must be enclosed in single apostrophes (quotes). Keep in mind that a blank is treated as a special character. Example:

```
//S1 EXEC .....,PARM='X+Y=Z'
```

When an apostrophe is coded in a parameter where it is permitted, the JCL syntax checker will bypass syntax check for all that follows until the delimiting apostrophe is found. Then normal syntax checking resumes. Having served their purpose, the apostrophes are stripped away and not used again. They do not contribute to the length of the expression they enclose. Apostrophes that are intended to be part of the information must be coded as two apostrophes. They count as only one character in the length of the field. Example:

```
//S2 EXEC ....,PARM='THREE O''CLOCK AM'
```

Rules of Continuation   If necessary or desired, a JCL statement can be continued in a simple way. The statement must be interrupted at a comma. This means that the last valid character of the line must be a comma followed by at least one blank. Then the statement can be continued into the next line by coding two slashes at the beginning of the line and continuing the parameter field starting anywhere between positions 4 and 16 (4 and 16 included). Note that the comma which indicates continuation, is not an extraneous character but part of the statement.

Any comma in a JCL statement can be used for continuation, including a comma in a subparameter field. There is, however, an exception: A comma enclosed in apostrophes cannot be used for continuation.

Examples of valid continuation:

```
//OUTPT DD DSN=USER1.TRANS,DISP=(,CATLG),
//        SPACE=(TRK,(100,,5)),...

//OUTPT DD DSN=USER1.TRANS,DISP=(,CATLG),SPACE=(TRK,(100,
//        ,5)),...
```

Example of invalid continuation:

```
//STEP2 EXEC PGM=RET2,PARM=('A,BC,OPT=19,FAF=Q22,
//           FORM=DUP')
```

The comma used for continuation is enclosed in apostrophes, which makes it an invalid continuation.

The erroneous statement above can be corrected as follows:

```
//STEP2 EXEC PGM=RET2,PARM=('A,BC,OPT=19,FAF=Q22',
//            'FORM=DUP')
```

Since the comma used for continuation is no longer within apostrophes, the continuation is valid.

The problem can also be corrected by placing the entire PARM parameter in the continuing line:

```
//STEP2 EXEC PGM=RET2,
//           PARM=('A,BC,OPT=19,FAF=Q22,FORM=DUP')
```

When continuing a JCL statement, one must be careful to begin the continuation line within the 4 to 16 position range. If the rule is violated on the low side, the result will always be a JCL error. Assume the continuation begins with position 3.

```
//OUTPT DD DSN=USER1.TRANS,DISP=(,CATLG),
//SPACE=(TRK,(100,,5)),...
```

The word SPACE in the second line will be mistaken for a name (only a name can be coded immediately after the two slashes) indicating a new statement. The previous line indicates continuation and the contradiction results in a JCL error.

If the rule is violated on the high side, the result may or may not be a JCL error. Assume the first continuation begins with position 17. The System places //* in the beginning of the line and makes it into a comment statement.

```
//OUTPT DD DSN=USER1.TRANS,
//                UNIT=SYSDA,
//           VOL=SER=PACK02,
//           DISP=(,CATLG),
//           SPACE=(TRK,(100,50))
```

The continuation line containing the UNIT parameter will become a comment statement.

```
//*              UNIT=SYSDA,
```

The absence of the UNIT parameter causes, luckily, a JCL error.

But now consider the same statement with the second continuation violating the continuation rule:

```
//OUTPT DD  DSN=USER1.TRANS,
//          UNIT=SYSDA,
//              VOL=SER=PACK02,
//          DISP=(,CATLG),
//          SPACE=(TRK,(100,50))
```

The continuation line containing the VOL parameter will become a comment statement, and the second line continues into the fourth line, as comment statements are ignored by the system.

```
//*              VOL=SER=PACK02,
```

Unfortunately, the absence of the VOL parameter causes no JCL error. The system simply allocates the data set to a volume of its own choice, rather than volume PACK02, a detail that can easily go by unnoticed. No error message of any sort is given by the system. This data set, because its volume is system assigned, is likely to be deleted overnight while the intent of the DD statement was to create a permanent data set.

2

Discussion of JOB and EXEC
Statement Parameters

In this chapter a brief description of the JOB and EXEC statements and their associated parameters will be given.[1] Parameters and subparameters that are rarely or never used will be deemphasized or omitted. Also, clues about how most installations treat certain parameters will be mentioned.

2.1 THE JOB STATEMENT — GENERAL

A JOB statement must be at the beginning of every job submitted to the system for execution. Until a JOB statement is found in the input stream, the system will not accept any JCL statement other than a command statement. When a JOB statement is found, the system accepts all JCL statements that follow as belonging to the job, until a delimiter is found. There are three possible delimiters for a job during the reading process:

Another JOB statement is the input stream. It signals the end of (reading) one job and the beginning of (reading) another:

---

1. Much of the information covered in this chapter is basic and is intended mostly for review or reference purposes. The experienced reader may wish to bypass or read this chapter selectively.

- A null statement. This is a statement with two slashes in the first two positions followed by blanks. Following a null statement all JCL statements, except a JOB statement, will be ignored.
- End-of-file on the reading device, meaning there are no more statements to read in.

A JOB statement must have a name. The absence of a jobname will result in a JCL error.

```
//[jobname]  JOB  parameters
```

There are many names in JCL, jobname, stepname, membername, ddname, etc. All names (except a qualified name) have the same syntax: A name consists of 1 to 8 alphabetic, numeric, and national characters (there are three national characters: $, #, and @). The first character cannot be numeric.

Following the operation (sometimes referred to as the verb) is the parameter field. In discussing parameters, a syntactical notation found in many IBM manuals will be used. The symbols of this notation will be explained:

Braces: {A|B|C} indicate that A or B or C must be coded. No more than one can be coded.

Brackets: [A|B|C|] indicate that A or B or C or none may be coded. No more than one can be coded. When none is coded, a default will be assumed. If the default is fixed (always the same), then one of the options will be underlined as being the default — [A|B|C|].

[n] indicates n is optional.

Upper and lower case characters: Expressions shown in upper case (caps) indicate that the expression must be coded as it appears. When in lower case, expressions indicate that a value or a name must be coded in their place. Example:

```
DSN=name
```

DSN must be coded as shown. A data set name must be coded in the place of "name."

Periods: ... indicate the preceding item can be coded more times. Example:

```
VOL=SER=(volser1,volser2,...)
```

These syntactical notations will be used throughout the book.

2.1.1 Accounting Information

Accounting information is a positional parameter. If present (it normally is), it must be the first in the parameter field. It can have a maximum of 142 characters (including parentheses and commas but not apostrophes) and can consist of many subparameters enclosed in parentheses. If any portion of the field contains a special character other than a "," (comma) or a "-"(hyphen), the portion must be enclosed in apostrophes.

```
//jobname JOB
([account-number][,additional-accounting-information])
```

The account number is an alphanumeric field from 1 to 4 characters long (many installations permit the use of more than 4 characters). It is normally used to account for resource utilization based on SMF (System Management Facility) records. An installation has the option of making the account number mandatory and most installations do. If so, its absence will cause a JCL error.

Additional accounting information is installation dependent except when JES2 is in use. In JES2 the fields have particular meaning, determined by their position. Many of the fields are not very important and are not often used. Also, except for the account number, all other subparameters can be supplied through the /*JOBPARM JES2 control statement (JES2 control statements are not covered in this book).

The general syntax of the JES2 account number parameter is:

```
                     x1000
([acctno][,room][,time][,lines][,cards][,forms][,copies][log]
[,lincnt])
```

room — Specifies room or any other identification, 1 to 4 alphanumeric characters long.

time — Specifies the estimated elapsed time of the JOB in minutes (1–4 decimal digits). If this field is omitted, an installation-defined default is used. In either case when the time is exceeded, a message appears on the operator console. This message repeats for every multiple of the estimated (or default) time. Note that no failure occurs.

This field should be supplied only for a very long-running job, many times longer than the default. For such a job, if the field were not coded, the operator would see a message repeating several times. Such repeated messages may lead the operator to assume that the

job is in a loop and cancel the job. Coding a high number for time
will stop the messages.

```
//USER1A  JOB  (FT62,236,180)
```

lines x 1000 — Specifies the estimated number of print lines for
the entire JOB x 1000 (1–4 decimal digits) — 5 indicates 5000 lines.
If this field is omitted, an installation-defined default is used. In
either case, when the number of lines is exceeded, a message appears on the operator console. This message repeats for every multiple of the estimated (or default) number of lines. Note that no failure
occurs.

This field should be supplied only when a job produces a very large
print output, many times greater than the default. For such a job, if
the field were not coded, the operator would see a message repeating
several times.

Such repeated messages may lead the operator to assume that the
job is in a write loop and cancel the job. Coding a high number for
lines will stop the messages. Some installations may limit the number of print lines for nonproduction jobs.

```
//USER1A  JOB  (FT62,236,180,200)
```

cards — Specifies the estimated number of punch cards for the
entire JOB. This field works basically the same as the lines field (not
x 1000). In view of the almost complete absence of cards in today's
environment, this field should always be omitted. Syntactically, this
is done by coding a comma in place of the subparameter, unless the
omitted subparameter is the last one in the parameter.

forms — Specifies the forms to be used for printing all the sysout
data sets of the job (1–4 characters). If this field is omitted, the installation default forms will be used. Forms can better be controlled
at the individual report level, using SYSOUT DD and OUTPUT
statements (see Section 10.2 in Chapter 10).

```
//USER1A  JOB  (FT62,236,180,200,,3PLY)
```

copies — Specifies the number of times the entire job's output is to
be printed (max 255). If this field is omitted, the default is 1.

Copies can also be requested at the individual report level, using
SYSOUT DD and OUTPUT statements (see Section 10.2 in Chapter
10).

2 — All JCL will be shown, but not procedure statements.

messages — 0 or 1

0 — No messages will be shown.

1 — All messages will be shown. The most important of these are allocation and termination messages (see Figure 1.7).

If the entire parameter or either of the two fields is omitted, an installation-defined default is assumed.

```
MSGLEVEL=1   ----> MSGLEVEL=(1,default)
MSGLEVEL=(,1)  ----> MSGLEVEL=(default,1)
parameter omitted  ----> MSGLEVEL=(default,default)
```

In view of the fact that having the JCL and its associated messages available is very important (essential when debugging), the default of practically all installations is (1,1). As a result, the MSGLEVEL parameter is often absent from the JOB statement. If an installation's default is different, then MSGLEVEL should be coded.

```
//USER1A  JOB  FT62,JONES,MSGLEVEL=(1,1)
```

If the job encounters an ABEND failure, the second field always defaults to 1 even if coded as 0.

2.1.4 The ADDRSPC Parameter

The ADDRSPC parameter specifies if the job will use real or virtual storage.

General Syntax

```
ADDRSPC {VIRT|REAL}                    keyword parameter
```

VIRT — The REGION will be virtual storage (default).

REAL — The REGION will be real storage.

If the ADDRSPC parameter is coded in both the JOB and an EXEC statement (within the job), the value in the JOB statement will be used.

This is a rarely used parameter. ADDRSPC=REAL is a parameter that is disallowed in practically all installations. It can cause serious performance problems and it is never required. The ADDRSPC parameter should be omitted, allowing the default (VIRT) to be used.

2.1.5 The Region Parameter

The REGION parameter specifies the limit of available storage for each of the steps in the job within the job's address space. Or, in other words, it specifies the amount of storage needed by the step (within the job) with the highest storage requirements.

General Syntax

```
REGION=value{K|M}                        keyword parameter
```

value — 1 to 2096128 if K (1024 bytes) is used. It should be an even number. If an odd number is used, it will be rounded to the next higher even number.

value — 1 to 2047 if M (1024 K or 1048576 bytes) is used. M is not available to MVS/SP, only to MVS/XA. REGION=1000K can also be coded as REGION=1M.

When a job is selected by an initiator for execution, it is given an address space. This address space is 2 gigabytes (minus what MVS/XA uses) (see Figure 2.1) and, conceivably, all of it is available to the job's steps. However, a step normally requires only a small fraction of this huge storage, below the 16M line (an ordinary COBOL — or any other language — program seldom needs more than 1000K). This is normally what the value in the REGION parameter represents. Few jobs have the need to expand to storage above the 16M line. Large software packages, like CICS, IMS, DB2, VTAM, etc., often require storage beyond the 16M line. An ordinary batch job seldom has such requirements and, as a result, will normally be confined to storage below the 16M line. Storage availability below this line varies in different installations, but it is generally around 9M (storage between COMMON AREAS and EXTENDED COMMON AREAS is not available to the user). Storage above the

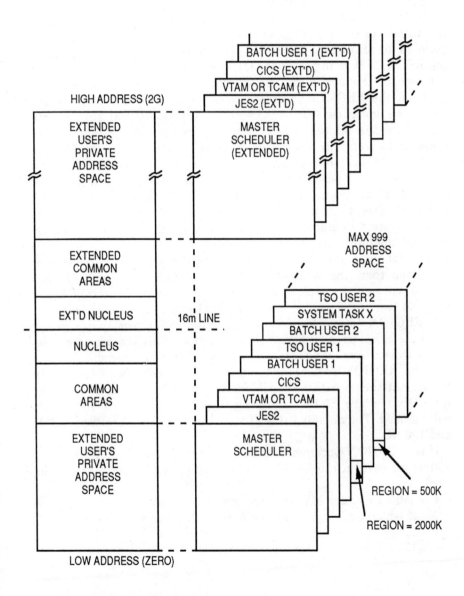

Figure 2.1 MVS/XA address space.

16M line can be acquired by coding a value higher than 16M. However, it may be restricted by the installation to only those jobs that need it.

Assume REGION=1100K was coded in the job statement. All the steps in the job are limited to this value. If more storage is needed, the usual result is a S878 or S80A or S804 ABEND failure. It is possible for an installation to supply more storage than requested in the REGION by using the IEALIMIT or IEFUSI routines.

If one of the above failures occurs, the user must increase the value in the REGION parameter. The amount by which the value should be increased can be generous. Any additional storage will come from the address space belonging to the job and will not be taken away from any other user. Also, an ordinary program does not make use of any unnecessary additional storage and, therefore, will have no effect on performance. There are, however, a number of vendor-written programs, like DFSORT, SYNCSORT, and CASORT, which, if asked to, will make use of all available storage. Then some overall system degradation is possible, depending on the REGION size and the hardware of the installation.

When the amount of storage requested in the REGION parameter is higher than the address space can provide, an S822 ABEND failure will be the result. If, for example, the available storage below the 16M line is 9M, coding REGION=10M will cause this failure.

If REGION=0K (or 0M) is coded, the entire address space (except for those areas used by MVS/XA) is available. This provides for maximum storage availability, but the exact size is unpredictable.

If the REGION parameter is omitted, the REGION parameter in EXEC statements within the job will be used. If it is coded in neither the JOB nor the EXEC statement, an installation-defined default will be used. The default value of most installations is between 500K and 1000K.

If the REGION parameter is coded in both the JOB and an EXEC statement (within the job), the value in the JOB statement will be used.

For job run under MVS/SP, the entire address space is limited to 16M, of which usually less than 8M is available to the user.

```
//USER1A   JOB   FT62,JONES,REGION=800K
```

2.1.6 The COND Parameter

The COND parameter can perform a test (or multiple tests) at the beginning of each step against the return (condition) codes issued by previous steps. If a test is satisfied, none of the steps from that point on will be executed.

General Syntax

```
COND=(test[,test][,test]...)              keyword parameter
```

test — (code,operator)

code — a number between 0 and 4095

operator —   LT (less than)
              LE (less than or equal to)
              NE (not equal to)
              EQ (equal to)
              GT (greater than)
              GE (greater than or equal to)

```
COND=((12,LT),(8,EQ))
```

If only one test is coded, the outside parentheses are not required.

```
COND=(4,LT)
```

If the COND parameter is coded in both the JOB and an EXEC statement (within the job), both will be in effect for that step. However, the COND parameter in the JOB statement will be tested first. (The COND parameter is fully discussed in Chapter 4.)

```
//USER1A   JOB   FT62,JONES,REGION=800K,COND=(0,LT)
```

2.1.7 The Class Parameter

The function of the CLASS parameter in to assign a class to a job.

General Syntax

```
CLASS=jobclass              keyword parameter
```

jobclass — A letter from A to Z or a number from 0 to 9.

A job is selected and executed by an initiator. Each initiator is assigned from 1 to 36 classes by either the JES2 or JES3 initialization process or by an operator command. Only those initiators whose classes include the one assigned to the job can execute the job. Consider an installation with four initiators as follows:

I1 — classes A, B & F
I2 — classes K, L & T
I3 — classes J, K & A
I3 — class T

and the JOB statement below:

```
//USER1A   JOB   FT62,JONES,REGION=800K,COND=(0,LT),
//                CLASS=T
```

Job USER1A can be executed by initiators I2 and I4 — they are the only ones assigned class T.

Frequently, installations develop a testing class structure that favors short-running jobs with minimal resource requirements and penalizes long-running jobs with heavy resource demands. This is done by assigning the class used by trivial jobs to many initiators and the class used by heavy jobs to few. To keep people honest (one can gain an unfair advantage by coding the wrong class), the CLASS parameter in a testing environment is often tied to several other parameters (such as TIME, PRTY, PERFORM, etc.) For example, a job coding CLASS=A can be given TIME=(,5), PRTY=2, and PERFORM=9. The values assigned to these parameter may not show in the output. If any of these parameters were coded in the JOB statement, they would be ignored.

If the CLASS parameter is omitted, an installation-defined default will be assumed.

2.1.8 The PRTY Parameter

The PRTY parameter determines the scheduling priority of a job in relation to other jobs in the Job Queue of the same class.

General Syntax

```
PRTY=priority                              keyword parameter
```

priority — A number from 0 to 15 for JES2 or 0 to 14 for JES3. The higher the number, the better the priority.

Comparing the PRTY parameter of two jobs belonging to different classes is meaningless. Looking at the initiators I1 through I4 discussed in the preceding section, a job of class L and priority 13 would execute after a job of class K and priority 1. This is due to the fact that I2 will execute all jobs of class K before any of class L. K appears before L in the definition of the initiator I2, and that is how initiators work.

This parameter is seldom of use in a testing environment. Since high priority would be used by practically all users, negating the very purpose of the parameter, in most installations the PRTY, whether coded or not, will default to an installation-defined value or will be supplied by the CLASS parameter.

2.1.9 The Time Parameter

The TIME parameter specifies the total amount of CPU time that all steps in a job can use collectively.

General Syntax

```
TIME=(minutes,seconds|1440)                keyword parameter
```

minutes — A number from 1 to 1439.

seconds — A number from 1 to 59.

TIME=(5,30). All the steps in the job are allowed collectively 5 minutes and 30 seconds of CPU time. If this amount is exceeded, the result will be a S322 ABEND failure.

TIME=1440. The job will not be timed for CPU. It will also not "time out" (S522 ABEND) when a single wait state exceeds the installation-defined limit (often 10 to 20 minutes). TIME=1440 is rarely used, and most installations disallow its use in a testing environment. It is seldom needed in view of the fact that with

TIME=(1439,59) — a second less than 24 hours — a job could be literally running for over a month. CPU time is only a very small fraction of the elapsed time. TIME=1440 should be used by an on-line system which stays up 7 days a week, 24 hours a day.

If the TIME parameter is coded using only minutes, seconds default to zero. For example, TIME=5 is the same as TIME=(5,0).
If the TIME parameter is coded using only seconds, minutes default to zero. For example, TIME=(,5) is the same as TIME=(0,5).
The TIME parameter is intended almost exclusively for a testing environment and should be coded when:

• Installation guidelines require it.
• A CPU loop may occur in testing a program.

The TIME parameter can also be supplied by the CLASS parameter, as mentioned before.
When the TIME parameter is omitted and the CLASS parameter does not supply it, the job will not be timed for CPU time. However, each step will be individually timed (EXEC TIME parameter, or its installation-defined default), unless it contains TIME=1440.
If the TIME parameter is coded in both the JOB and an EXEC statement (within the job), both will be in effect, and either can cause a S322 ABEND failure.
It is possible for a job to get more CPU time than that is specified in the TIME parameter by a maximum 10.5 seconds. This is due to the fact the system checks for violations every 10.5 seconds.

```
//USER1A  JOB  FT62,JONES,REGION=800K,COND=(0,LT),
//             CLASS=T,PRTY=6,TIME=(1,50)
```

2.1.10 The Notify Parameter

The NOTIFY parameter informs a TSO user when her or his job terminates.

General Syntax

```
NOTIFY=userid                 keyword parameter
```

userid — A name from 1 to 7 characters, identifying a valid TSO user.

This a very simple parameter. If coded, a message will appear on the user's TSO terminal when the user's job terminates. The message indicates if the job ABENDed or got a JCL error. If the job terminates while the user was logged off, the message will appear when the user logs on.

If the NOTIFY parameter is omitted, no message will appear when the job terminates.

```
//USER1A   JOB  FT62,JONES,REGION=800K,COND=(0,LT),
//         CLASS=T,PRTY=6,TIME=(1,50),NOTIFY=USER1
```

2.1.11 The PERFORM Parameter

The PERFORM parameter determines the availability of three major resources during the job's execution: CPU, real storage pages, and I/O operations. It is basically an in-execution priority parameter.

General Syntax

```
PERFORM=n                            keyword parameter
```

n — A number from 1 to 999. It identifies the performance group that the job will belong to. Only a few numbers within the range will be valid in a given installation, usually under 15.

Each installation has its own Installation Performance Specifications (IPS), and the numbers assigned to performance groups are arbitrary within the acceptable range. There is no implication (as with the PRTY parameter) that a higher number will give better resource availability.

A job belonging to a performance group will be limited to a certain number of service units (SUs) per second, which varies according to the workload of the system. CPU, I/O, and real storage use is always translated to service units.

This parameter is seldom permitted in a testing environment. It is, however, used for certain production jobs (i.e., CICS) where high resource availability is essential.

If the PERFORM parameter is not coded, or coded using a number which is not a valid performance group for the installation:

- An installation-defined default will be used.
- If no installation-defined default exists (that's possible), a system default will be used: 1.

• The CLASS parameter will determine the performance group.

If the PERFORM parameter is coded in both the JOB and an EXEC statement (within the job), the value in the JOB statement will be used.

```
//USER1A  JOB  FT62,JONES,REGION=800K,COND=(0,LT),
//            CLASS=T,PRTY=6,TIME=(1,50),NOTIFY=USER1,
//            PERFORM=12
```

2.1.12 The MSGCLASS Parameter

The MSGCLASS parameter assigns a sysout class to the job log. The job log consists of what is known as system or JES data sets:

• JES2 or JES3 log — appears after the separator page.
• JCL and its associated messages.
• Allocation and Termination messages (see Figure 1.7).

General Syntax

```
MSGCLASS=class                    keyword parameter
```

class — A character from A to Z or a number from 0 to 9

All data sets to be printed must have a class. This is normally called the output class, sysout class or message class. Sysout data sets created by executing programs are assigned a class by the SYSOUT DD statement (see Section 10.2 in Chapter 10). After the job terminates (and earlier, if FREE=CLOSE is coded in a DD statement), the sysout data sets, which are saved on the spool pack, will be selected and printed by a JES2 or JES3 component called a printer. There are several printers available, and each one is assigned one or more sysout classes (from 1 to 36). The sysout class assigned to the MSGCLASS parameter (and SYSOUT DD statement) schedules a sysout data set to a printer in a similar way as a job class schedules a job to an initiator. The sysout class, therefore, can be thought of as a print-scheduling class.

If the MSGCLASS parameter is omitted, an installation-defined default will be used.

```
//USER1A   JOB   FT62,JONES,REGION=800K,COND=(0,LT),
//                CLASS=T,PRTY=6,TIME=(1,50),NOTIFY=USER1,
//                PERFORM=12,MSGCLASS=C
```

2.1.13 The RESTART Parameter

The RESTART parameter requests that a job begin its execution with a step other than the first one.

General Syntax

```
RESTART={stepname|procexec.stepname|*}       keyword parameter
```

stepname — The name of the step where execution is to begin.

procexec.stepname — The name of the EXEC statement invoking a procedure and the name of the step within the procedure where execution is to begin.

* — Indicates that execution of the job is to begin with the first step. This represents the default and need not be coded. It will be used only when Checkpoint/Restart is in effect and execution is to begin at a checkpoint within the first step. Checkpoint/Restart is a rarely used feature, and its JCL-related parameters are not discussed in this book.

The RESTART parameter does nothing to make restart, a difficult operation at best, possible. It simply obeys blindly the user's request to begin execution with a particular step. If the conditions for restarting are not proper, a variety of problems are possible.

The following is a list of what to avoid and be mindful of:

Things to avoid:

- Duplicate names for EXEC statements invoking procedures. If RESTART=procexec.stepname is used, the first procexec found will be used.
- Duplicate stepnames within a procedure. If RESTART=procexec.stepname is used, the first stepname found within the procedure will be used.
- Duplicate stepnames. If RESTART=stepname is used, the first stepname found will be used.
- EXEC statements (invoking procedures) without names. RESTART=procexec.stepname cannot be used to restart within a proce-

dure, RESTART=stepname must be used and then the first step-name found, inside or outside a procedure, will be used.

- Steps with no stepnames inside or outside procedures. No restart is possible at such a step.
- Creating and passing temporary data sets. Such data sets are always deleted by the time the job terminates and, therefore, unavailable for restarting.
- Creating and passing nontemporary data sets. If such a data set is not received and assigned a permanent disposition, Job Termination will delete it, making restart impossible.
- Using VOL=REF referring to a previous step. If the previous step is not executed in a restart situation, VOL=REF generates a JCL error. VOL=REF referring to the same step is acceptable.
- Using DISP=MOD, intended to add more records to a data set. If an ABEND failure occurs while writing, the data set becomes useless. This is a problem independent of restarting.
- Deleting a data set, not created in the job, before the job successfully completes. This data set will be unavailable for restarting.
- Removing or commenting out JCL prior to the step to be restarted. This has nothing to do with the RESTART parameter, but it can be thought of as an alternative to the RESTART parameter. It is not. It can cause JCL errors because all references to the eliminated steps become invalid.

Things to be watched carefully:

- DSN=gdgindex(+1),DISP=OLD. If the step that contains the same data set name with a NEW disposition is not being executed in a restart, the (+1) must be changed to (0).
- DSN=gdgindex(0),DISP=OLD. If the (+1) generation was created in a preceding step that will not be executed during the restart, the (0) must be changed to (-1).
- DISP=(,CATLG). If the step ABENDs, the data set will be cataloged. To be able to restart at that step or before, the data set must be uncataloged and (if on disk) deleted. DISP=(,CATLG,DELETE) will alleviate this problem to a degree. If an ABEND occurs, the data set will be deleted and not cataloged. However, there are other failures beside ABENDs, and then the data set will be cataloged, requiring intervention to delete and uncatalog it before restarting.

```
//USER1A   JOB   FT62,JONES,REGION=800K,COND=(0,LT),
//                CLASS=T,PRTY=6,TIME=(1,50),NOTIFY=USER1,
//                PERFORM=12,MSGCLASS=C,RESTART=S4
```

2.1.14 The TYPRUN Parameter

The TYPRUN parameter requests special processing for the job allowing:

• Execution of the job to be withheld temporarily.
• Syntactical check to be performed without execution.
• To print JCL with no syntax check and no execution (JES2 only).

General Syntax

```
TYPRUN={HOLD|JCLHOLD|SCAN|COPY}      keyword parameter
```

HOLD — Job will be held (and not executed) until the operator uses a command to release it. A job will be held only if syntacticly correct.

JCLHOLD (JES2 only) — Job will be held (and not executed) until the operator uses a command to release it. The job has not gone through all its processing and syntax checking. Held job can still have syntactical errors after it is released. Rarely used.

SCAN — Job will be scanned for all syntactical JCL errors but will not executed.

COPY (JES2 only) — Job will be printed. No execution and no syntax checking takes place. Rarely used.

TYPRUN=HOLD is often used in a production environment. Jobs that will be executed late at night are submitted with TYPRUN=HOLD in the early afternoon. Then the operator releases each job when the time comes.

TYPRUN=SCAN is a useful parameter but should not be treated as a catch-all-JCL-error facility. It only detects syntactical errors. There are other types of JCL errors that TYPRUN=SCAN will not detect (see Section 3.2.2 in Chapter 3).

```
//USER1A   JOB   FT62,JONES,REGION=800K,COND=(0,LT),
//                CLASS=T,PRTY=6,TIME=(1,50),NOTIFY=USER1,
//                PERFORM=12,MSGCLASS=C,RESTART=S4,
//                TYPRUN=HOLD
```

Note: The JOB statement shown above is the result of coding most of the parameters discussed. Clearly it is not a typical JOB statement. Far too many parameters are coded. A typical JOB statement may look like this:

```
//USER1A   JOB   FT62,JONES,CLASS=T,NOTIFY=USER1,
//                MSGCLASS=C
```

2.2 THE EXEC STATEMENT — GENERAL

An EXEC statement identifies a step during the reading process when a job is submitted to the system. When an EXEC statement is found, the system accepts all JCL statements that follow as belonging to the step, until a delimiter is found. There are four possible delimiters for a step during the reading process:

• Another EXEC statement in the input stream. It signals the end of (reading) one step and the beginning of (reading) another.
• A JOB statement.
• A null statement. This is a statement with two slashes in the first two positions followed by blanks. Following a null statement, all JCL statements will be ignored except a JOB statement.
• End-of-file on the reading device, meaning there are no more statements to read in.

The last three of the above are also job delimiters.

An EXEC statement need not have a name. The absence of a stepname is acceptable but undesirable. When the stepname is omitted, no reference can be made to that step. Referring to a step is sometimes necessary, and, therefore, it is recommended that a stepname always be supplied.

```
//[stepname]   EXEC   parameters
```

A job can contain a maximum of 255 EXEC statements.

2.2.1 The PGM Parameter

The PGM parameter identifies the program to be executed in a step.

General Syntax

```
PGM={pgmname|referback}        positional parameter
```

pgmname — Name of the program to be fetched and executed

referback — This can have two formats:

- *.stepname.ddname — Refers to a program defined in DD statement "ddname" in a previous step "stepname." This program is to be executed. Found almost exclusively in Compile-Linkedit-Go procedures. Rarely used elsewhere.
- *.procexec.stepname.ddname — Refers to a program defined in DD statement "ddname" in a previous step "stepname," found within a procedure "procexec" (name of EXEC statement invoking the procedure). This program is to be executed. Rarely used.

The PGM parameter is positional. It must be coded first.

```
//S1      EXEC PGM=PERSONL
```

The program specified in this parameter is always a member of a library (PDS). This is commonly known as an executable program library or a load library. The EXEC statement can identify only the member. It has no parameter available to identify the library. If necessary, this must be done by using a JOBLIB or a STEPLIB DD statement (see Section 10.6 in Chapter 10).

```
//USER1A  JOB  FT62,JONES,CLASS=T
//JOBLIB  DD   DSN=TEST.LOADLIB,DISP=SHR
//S1      EXEC PGM=PERSONL
```

or

```
//USER1A  JOB  FT62,JONES,CLASS=T
//S1      EXEC PGM=PERSONL
//STEPLIB DD   DSN=TEST.LOADLIB,DISP=SHR
```

If neither JOBLIB nor STEPLIB is coded, the system searches certain predefined libraries. They are the system default libraries. If the specified member is found, it is executed. If not found, the result is a S806 ABEND failure.

When the referback is used,

```
PGM=*.LKED.SYSLMOD
```

neither JOBLIB nor STEPLIB is needed. The system finds DD statement SYSLMOD in step LKED and extracts a member for execution. The SYSLMOD DD statement can appear in two formats:

```
//SYSLMOD   DD   DSN=&&LOADSET(RUN),DISP=(,PASS),UNIT=SYSDA,
//               SPACE=(TRK,(10,5))
```

or

```
//SYSLMOD   DD   DSN=&&LOADSET,DISP=(,PASS),UNIT=SYSDA,
//               SPACE=(TRK,(10,5))
```

In the first format, program (member) RUN will be executed. In the second format, the first program found in the temporary library will be executed.

2.2.2 The PARM Parameter

The PARM parameter provides a way to supply data of limited size to the executing program. There are normally two ways for a program to receive data: by reading records from a data set or by requesting some information from the operator (this is strongly discouraged). The PARM parameter provides a third way.

General Syntax

```
PARM=string
```

string — A string of characters up to 100. If commas are part of the string, the entire field must be enclosed in parentheses (apostrophes can also be used). If any portion of the string contains special characters (other than a hyphen), that portion or the entire string must be enclosed in apostrophes. Any parentheses used count toward the maximum. Apostrophes do not.

All information after the "=" in the PARM parameter, excluding apostrophes, will be saved by the system within the step's own region. When the program begins execution by using the appropriate instructions, it can find the saved information in storage. What the program does with this information is the program's own business.

In Assembly Language, Register 1 contains an address which contains the address of the PARM information, preceded by 2 bytes indicating the length of the information.

```
L    2, 0(1)
```

Register 2 now points to an area in storage which contains the PARM information preceded by the length.

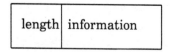

2 bytes   variable — max 100 bytes

In COBOL the following must be coded:

```
LINKAGE SECTION
        01    PARM
               05   PLENGTH   PIC  S9(4) COMP
               05   PCONTNT   PIC   X(100)
```

The length of the PARM field will be found in PLENGTH and its contents in PCONTNT. Any valid names can be used in place of PARM, PLENGTH, and PCONTNT.

In PL1 the following must be coded:

```
name: PROC(PARM) OPTIONS(MAIN);
       DCL PARM CHAR (100) VAR;
```

The string is stored in PARM and the PARM length is set to the length of the string. Any valid data name may be used in place of PARM.

Examples:

```
PARM=VERIFY3
PARM='12/20/1992'          apostrophes are required
PARM=(A,B,C,D)
```

This can also be coded as

```
PARM='A,B,C,D'
```

The two, however, are not the same. When parentheses are used, the information found by the program is (A,B,C,D). If apostrophes are used, the information found by the program is A,B,C,D.

When the PARM information is lengthy, continuation problems can arise.

```
//S1 EXEC PGM=P1,PARM=('MAP,DO,EXPLAIN,LIMIT=1000,BUF=4,SELL=10,BUY=20')
```

This PARM field contains special characters and is enclosed in apostrophes. Its length, however, can create a continuation problem, since an expression in quotes cannot be continued. The problem can be resolved by rewriting the parameter as follows:

```
//S1 EXEC PGM=P1,PARM=(MAP,DO,EXPLAIN,'LIMIT=1000','BUF=4',
//          'SELL=10','BUY=20')
```

2.2.3 The ADDRSPC Parameter[2]

The ADDRSPC parameter specifies if the step will use real or virtual storage.

General Syntax

```
ADDRSPC {VIRT|REAL}              keyword parameter
```

VIRT — The REGION will be virtual storage (default).

REAL — The REGION will be real storage.

---

2. Most of the discussion below is a repetition of Section 2.1.4, which discussed the same parameter for the JOB statement.

If the ADDRSPC parameter is also coded in the JOB statement, the value in the JOB statement will be used.

This is a rarely used parameter. ADDRSPC=REAL is a parameter disallowed in practically all installations. It can cause serious performance problems and is never required. The ADDRSPC parameter should be omitted, allowing the default (VIRT) to be used.

2.2.4 The Region Parameter[3]

The REGION parameter specifies the limit of available storage for the step within the job's address space.

General Syntax

```
REGION=value{K|M}                    keyword parameter
```

value — 1 to 2096128 if K (1024 bytes) is used. It should be an even number. If an odd number is used, it will be rounded to the next higher even number.

value — 1 to 2047 if M (1024 K or 1048576 bytes) is used. M is not available to MVS/SP, only to MVS/XA. REGION=1000K can also be coded as REGION=1M.

When a job is selected by an initiator for execution, it is given an address space. This address space is 2 gigabytes (minus what MVS/XA uses (see Figure 2.1), and, conceivably, all of it is available to the job's steps. However, a step normally requires only a small fraction of this huge storage, below the 16M line (an ordinary COBOL — or any other language — program seldom needs more than 1000K). This is normally what the value in the REGION parameter represents. Few jobs have the need to expand to storage above the 16M line. Large software packages, like CICS, IMS, DB2, VTAM, etc., often require storage beyond the 16M line. An ordinary batch job seldom has such requirements and, as a result, it will normally be confined to storage below the 16M line. Storage availability below this line varies in different installations, but it is generally around 9M (storage between COMMON AREAS and EXTENDED

---

3. Most of the discussion below is a repetition of Section 2.1.5., which discussed the same parameter for the JOB statement.

COMMON AREAS is not available to the user). Storage above the 16M line can be acquired by coding a value higher than 16M. However, it may be restricted by the installation to only those jobs that need it.

Assume REGION=1100K was coded in the job statement.

All the steps in the job are limited to this value. If more storage is needed, the usual result is a S878 or S80A or S804 ABEND failure. It is possible for an installation to supply more storage than requested in the REGION by using the IEALIMIT or IEFUSI routines.

If one of the above failures occur, the user must increase the value in the REGION parameter. The amount by which the value should be increased can be generous. Any additional storage will come from the address space belonging to the job and will not be taken away from any other user. Also, an ordinary program does not make use of any unnecessary additional storage and, therefore, it will have no effect on performance. There are, however, a number of vendor-written programs, like DFSORT, SYNCSORT, and CASORT, which, if asked to, will make use of all available storage. Then some overall system degradation is possible, depending on the REGION size and the hardware of the installation.

When the amount of storage requested in the REGION parameter is higher than the address space can provide, an S822 ABEND failure will be the result. If, for example, the available storage below the 16M line is 9M, coding REGION=10M will cause this failure.

If REGION=0K (or 0M) is coded, the entire address space (except for those areas used by MVS/XA) is available. This provides for maximum storage availability, but the exact size is unpredictable.

If the REGION parameter is omitted, and no REGION parameter is coded in the JOB statement, an installation-defined default will be used. The default value of most installations is between 500K and 1000K.

If the REGION parameter is coded in both the JOB and an EXEC statement (within the job), the value in the JOB statement will be used.

For jobs run under MVS/SP, the entire address space is limited to 16M, of which usually less than 8M is available to the user.

```
//S3        EXEC PGM=PERSONL,PARM=(X,Y),REGION=1200K
```

The REGION parameter in the JOB statement is used much more often than the one in the EXEC statement. This is justifiable since there is no great advantage to coding different values for different steps. Coding the same value for all steps would have the same effect as the REGION parameter in the JOB statement.

2.2.5 The COND Parameter

The COND parameter can perform a test (or multiple tests) before a step begins execution against the return (condition) codes issued by previous steps. If a test is satisfied, the step will not be executed.

General Syntax

```
COND=(test[,test][,test]....,[EVEN|ONLY])   keyword parameter
```

test — (code,operator,[stepname]) or (code,operator,[procexec.stepname]).

code — a number between 0 and 4095.

operator —   LT (less than)
LE (less than or equal to)
NE (not equal to)
EQ (equal to)
GT (greater than)
GE (greater than or equal to)

stepname — The name of the step whose return code will be tested.

procexec.stepname — the name of the EXEC statement invoking a procedure and the name of the step within the procedure whose return code will be tested.

EVEN — Requests that execution be allowed even if a previous (any previous) step ABENDed.

ONLY — requests that execution be permitted only if a previous (any previous) step ABENDed.

Example:

```
COND=((8,LT,S1),(6,EQ),EVEN)
```

EVEN and ONLY are mutually exclusive.

A maximum of eight tests is allowed. If EVEN or ONLY is coded, it counts as a test.

If only one test is coded, the outside parentheses are not required.

```
COND=(4,LT,S2)
COND=EVEN
```

If the COND parameter is also coded in the JOB statement, both will be in effect for that step. However, the COND parameter in the JOB statement will be tested first.

The COND parameter if fully discussed in Chapter 4.

```
//S3      EXEC PGM=PERSONL,PARM=(X,Y),REGION=1200K,
//              COND=((4,LT,S1),(8,LE,S2))
```

2.2.6 The TIME Parameter[4]

The TIME parameter specifies the amount of CPU time that the step is allowed to use.

General Syntax

```
TIME=(minutes,seconds|1440)          keyword parameter
```

minutes — A number from 1 to 1439.

seconds — A number from 1 to 59.

TIME=(5,30). The step is allowed 5 minutes and 30 seconds of CPU time. If this amount is exceeded, the result will be a S322 ABEND failure.

TIME=1440. The step will not be timed for CPU. It will also not "time out" (S522 ABEND) when a single wait state exceeds the installation defined limit (often 10 to 20 minutes). TIME=1440 is rarely used, and most installations disallow its use in a testing environment. It is seldom needed in view of the fact that with

---

4. Most of this discussion below is a repetition of Section 2.1.9, which discussed the same parameter for the JOB statement.

TIME=(1439,59) — a second less than 24 hours — a step could be literally running for over a month. CPU time is only a very small fraction of the elapsed time.

If the TIME parameter is coded using only minutes, seconds default to zero. For example, TIME=5 is the same as TIME=(5,0).

If the TIME parameter is coded using only seconds, minutes default to zero. For example, TIME=(,5) is the same as TIME=(0,5).

The TIME parameter is intended almost exclusively for a testing environment and should be used when:

• Installation guidelines require it.
• A CPU loop may occur in testing a program.

When the TIME parameter is omitted, an installation-defined default will be used. This default is usually very high and unlikely to cause an S322 ABEND.

If the TIME parameter is also coded in the JOB statement, both will be in effect and either can cause a S322 ABEND failure. It is not advisable to use them both.

It is possible for a step to get more CPU time than that specified in the TIME parameter or the default by a maximum 10.5 seconds. This is due to the fact the system checks for time violations every 10.5 seconds.

```
//S3      EXEC  PGM=PERSONL,PARM=(X,Y),REGION=1200K,
//              COND=((4,LT,S1),(8,LE,S2)),
//              TIME=(2,20)
```

2.2.7 The PERFORM Parameter[5]

The PERFORM parameter determines the availability of three major resources during the step's execution: CPU, real storage pages, and I/O operations. It is basically an in-execution priority parameter.

General Syntax

```
PERFORM=n                        keyword parameter
```

---

5. Most of the discussion below is a repetition of Section 2.1.11, which discussed the same parameter for the JOB statement.

n — A number from 1 to 999. It identifies the performance group that the job will belong to. Only a few numbers within the range will be valid in a given installation, usually under 15.

Each installation has its own Installation Performance Specifications (IPS), and the numbers assigned to performance groups are arbitrary within the acceptable range. There is no implication that a higher number will give better resource availability.

A step assigned to a performance group will be limited to a certain number of service units (SUs) per second, which varies according to the workload of the system. CPU, I/O, and real storage use is always translated to service units.

This parameter is seldom permitted in a testing environment.

If the PERFORM parameter is not coded, or coded using a number which is not a valid performance group for the installation, and no PERFORM parameter is coded in the JOB statement, an installation-defined default will be used, or if no installation-defined default exists (that's possible), a system default will be used: 1.

If the PERFORM parameter is also coded in the JOB statement the value in the JOB statement will be used.

```
//S3       EXEC PGM=PERSONL,PARM=(X,Y),REGION=1200K,
//             COND=((4,LT,S1),(8,LE,S2)),
//             TIME=(2,20),PERFORM=21
```

2.2.8 The ACCT Parameter

The ACCT parameter specifies accounting information to be used for the step as opposed to the accounting information in the JOB statement.

General Syntax

```
ACCT=(acctno,[additional acct info])       keyword parameter
```

acctno — The account number to be used for the step.

additional acct info — Same as in the JOB statement but without any JES2 meaning.

The ACCT parameter is seldom used, and when it is, only the account number normally appears. It permits the relatively unusual

| PARAMETER | IF A PARAMETER APPEARS IN THE JOB STATEMENT AND IN ONE OF ITS STEPS EXEC STATEMENT, FOR THIS STEP: | | |
	JOB STATEMENT PARAMETER PREVAILS	EXEC STATEMENT PARAMETER PREVAILS	BOTH STATEMENT PARAMETERS ARE IN EFFECT
REGION	X		
ADDRSPC	X		
COND			X
TIME			X
PERFORM	X		
ACCT*		X	

* THE SYNTAX IS NOT THE SAME IN JOB AND EXEC

Figure 2.2 Common JOB and EXEC statement parameters.

practice of charging resource utilization for a step to a different account number than the one coded in the JOB statement.

If an account number is also coded in the JOB statement, the account number in the EXEC statement will be used.

```
//S3        EXEC PGM=PERSONL,PARM=(X,Y),REGION=1200K,
//               COND=((4,LT,S1),(8,LE,S2)),
//               TIME=(2,20),PERFORM=21,ACCT=FJ12
```

Note: The EXEC statement shown above is the result of coding most of the parameters discussed. Clearly, it is not a typical EXEC statement. Too many parameters are coded. A typical EXEC statement may look like this:

```
//S3       EXEC PGM=PERSONL,PARM=(X,Y),COND=(4,LT)
```

There are several common parameters that can be coded in both the JOB and EXEC statements. As discussed, the results can be different for different parameters. Figure 2.2 represents a summation of these results. The ACCT parameter is treated as a common parameter even though its syntax is not the same in the JOB and EXEC statement.

3

Failures Under MVS/XA

This chapter will discuss the types of failures a JCL user can encounter in an MVS/XA environment. The use of proper terminology and the effect of each type of failure will also be discussed.

3.1 GENERAL

There are three types of failures that a job can encounter under MVS/XA. This chapter will discuss the nature of each type, its causes, and its implications.

Terminology is often a problem when a failure is communicated from one person to another. Expressions such as "the job bombed" or "the job failed" or "the job went down" are ambiguous, using nontechnical terms, and they simply convey the fact that something went wrong without being specific. This chapter will emphasize the use of proper terminology for failing conditions.

The three general causes of failures are:

- JCL errors
- ABEND failures
- Bad return (or condition) codes

3.2 JCL ERRORS

There are two types of JCL errors:

- A syntactical error
- An allocation error

3.2.1 Syntactical JCL Errors

A syntactical JCL error is detected when a job is submitted and read into the system. It will occur when a JCL statement or parameter violates the syntax rules of JCL.

None of the steps of a job that contains a syntactical JCL error can be executed, regardless of which step the error was detected in. Since the entire JCL of a job is read in before execution can begin, a JCL error in the first step has the same effect as a JCL error in the last: None of the steps of the job will be executed.

A message always appears in the output of the job that describes the error. In most cases, such messages are self-explanatory.

Example 1:

```
//D1   DD   DSN=USER1.FILEA,DISP=(OLD,DLETE)
```

Message "IEF630I UNIDENTIFIED KEYWORD IN THE DISP FIELD" will appear in the output. It is easy to detect that instead of DELETE, DLETE was coded. An example of the same type of syntactical error, representing an actual job submission, is shown in Figure 3.1.

Example 2:

```
//S3   EXEC   PGM=ERRT,COND=((0,NE,S1),ONLY))
```

Message "IEF622I UNBALANCED PARENTHESIS IN COND FIELD" will appear. It is easy to detect that there are two left and three right parentheses.

If the message supplied by the System is not clear, IBM Manuals #GC28-1367 and #GC28-1377 (MVS/Extended Architecture Message Library: System Messages — Volume 1 and Volume 2) can be consulted. (Note: The reader should be aware that the explanations provided in these manuals are not always easy to understand.)

Under certain conditions, it is possible for a message to appear indicating that a particular parameter is at fault and yet the parameter appears to be perfectly correct. The preceding (and even the following) parameter should then be checked. It may be the one responsible.

```
1     //OPRSMAN2 JOB 96150PRS,MC,CLASS=1,MSGCLASS=3,TIME=1,
      // NOTIFY=OPRSMAN

2     //S1  EXEC PMG=IEFBR14
3     //DD1 DD  DSN=STU.FILEA,DISP=(NEW,CATLG),UNIT=SYSDA,
      //          VOL=SER=TECH03,SPACE=(TRK,1)
4     //S2  EXEC PMG=IEFBR14
5     //DD3 DD  DSN=STU.FILEA,DISP=(NEW,CATLG),UNIT=SYSDA,
      //          VOL=SER=TECH02,SPACE=(TRK,1)
6     //S2  EXEC PMG=IEFBR14
7     //DD3 DD  DSN=STU.FILEA,DISP=(NEW,CATLG),UNIT=SYSDA,
      //          VOL=SER=TECH03,SPACE=(TRK,1)
```

STMT NO.   MESSAGE

2   IEF630I UNIDENTIFIED KEYWORD ON THE EXEC STATEMENT

Figure 3.1 Example of syntactical JCL error.

3.2.2 Allocation JCL Errors

An allocation JCL error is detected when a step goes through the Allocation routines (see Figure 1.7). A problem is detected while attempting to allocate or locate a resource (such as a data set, a volume, a device, etc.) needed by a DD statement in the step.

The step where the error was encountered and all the following steps will not be executed. However, since every step has its own allocation process, previous steps may well have executed.

The allocation type of JCL error can be far more painful that its syntactical counterpart because when it occurs in the late steps of a job, it can result in loss of time and restart problems.

Example 1:

```
//OUT DD  DSN=USER1.FILEX,DISP=(,CATLG,DELETE),UNIT=SYSDA,
//         SPACE=(CYL,(60,10)),VOL=SER=PROD47
```

Message "IEF257I USER1C STEP9 OUT SPACE REQUESTED NOT AVAILABLE" will appear in the output (USER1C is the jobname and STEP9 is the stepname).

The allocation routines are unable to find 60 free cylinders on SYSDA volume PROD47.

Example 2:

```
//IN  DD  DSN=USER1.FILEY,DISP=SHR
```

Message "IEF212I USER1E STEP4 IN DATA SET NOT FOUND" will appear in the output (USER1E is the jobname and STEP4 is the stepname).

Data set USER1.FILEY is neither passed nor cataloged and, as a result, the allocation routines cannot find it. An example of the same type of allocation JCL error representing an actual job execution is shown in Figure 3.2.

TYPRUN=SCAN cannot detect allocation JCL errors.

The effect of allocation JCL errors may differ in certain instances between JES2 and JES3. JES3 performs certain preallocation functions that will cause some (but not all) allocation type of JCL errors to be detected before the job begins execution. When this happens, these errors have the same effect as syntactical errors: None of the steps in the job execute. The above-mentioned error, "DATA SET NOT FOUND," is typically one of them. When possible, JES3 will detect the error before the job begins execution, causing the entire job not to execute.

```
 1     //OPRSMAN2 JOB 96150PRS,MC,CLASS=1,MSGCLASS=3,TIME=1,
        // NOTIFY=OPRSMAN                                          00010269

 2     //S1  EXEC PMG=IEFBR14                                      00010892
 3     //DD1 DD  DSN=STU.FILEA,DISP=(NEW,CATLG),UNIT=SYSDA,        00010992
        //        VOL=SER=TECH03,SPACE=(TRK,1)                     00011092
 4     //S2  EXEC PMG=IEFBR14                                      00011192
 5     //DD3 DD  DSN=STU.FILEA,DISP=(NEW,CATLG),UNIT=SYSDA,        00011292
        //        VOL=SER=TECH02,SPACE=(TRK,1)                     00011392
 6     //S2  EXEC PMG=IEFBR14                                      00011492
 7     //DD3 DD  DSN=STU.FILEA,DISP=(NEW,CATLG),UNIT=SYSDA,        00011592
        //        VOL=SER=TECH03,SPACE=(TRK,1)                     00011692
```

```
IEF236I   ALLOC. FOR OPRSMAN2 S1          ⎫
IEF237I   151 ALLOCATED TO DD1            ⎬  ALLOCATION MESSAGES FOR STEP S1
IEF237I   17F ALLOCATED TO SYS00584       ⎭
IEF142I   OPRSMAN2 S1 - STEP WAS EXECUTED - COND CODE 0000
IEF285I   STU.FILEA                       CATALOGED    ⎫  STEP TERMINATION MESSAGE
IEF285I   VOL SER NOS= TECH03.                         ⎬  FOR STEP S1
IEF285I   TECH.NABG.CATALOG               KEPT         ⎭
IEF285I   VOL SER NOS=TECH01.
+ --------------------------------------------------------------------------------

IEF236I   ALLOC. FOR OPRSMAN2 S1          ⎫
IEF237I   151 ALLOCATED TO DD1            ⎬  ALLOCATION MESSAGES FOR STEP S2
IEF237I   17F ALLOCATED TO SYS00584       ⎭
IEF142I   OPRSMAN2 S1 - STEP WAS EXECUTED - COND CODE 0000
IEF285I   STU.FILEA                       NOT CATLGD 2 ⎫  STEP TERMINATION MESSAGE
IEF285I   VOL SER NOS= TECH03.                         ⎬  FOR STEP S2
IEF285I   TECH.NABG.CATALOG               KEPT         ⎭
IEF285I   VOL SER NOS=TECH01.
+ --------------------------------------------------------------------------------

IEF253I   OPRSMAN2 S3 DD3 – DUPLICATE NAME ON DIRECT ACCESS VOLUME
IEF272I   OPRSMAN2 S3 – STEP WAS NOT EXECUTED.          JCL ERROR IN STEP S3
+ --------------------------------------------------------------------------------
```

Figure 3.2 Example of allocation JCL error.

3.3 ABEND FAILURES

The abbreviation ABEND is a combination of the words "Abnormal" and "End." "Abnormal Termination" is sometimes used as an alternative expression (but the abbreviation ABTERM is not used).

An ABEND failure occurs under the following conditions: A program, while executing, attempts to perform (knowingly or unknowingly) an instruction or operation which the system recognizes as being impossible or unacceptable (for whatever reason). The program loses control and is instantly removed from execution. The last action taken by the program in an ABEND situation is the offending instruction. The system associates the failure with a code known as a "completion code" or an "ABEND code." The purpose of this code is for the user to look it up in the appropriate manual (IBM Manual #GC28-1157, MVS/Extended Architecture Message Library: System Codes), where an explanation can be found. The explanation frequently makes reference to messages discussed in the aforementioned manuals #GC28-1367 and #GC28-1377.

The last two digits of many completion codes have a meaning. With the exception of S0Cx ABEND failures (where x is 1 to F and which are known as program checks or program exceptions), the last two digits of code represent the SVC (Supervisor Call) where the failure occurred. During the execution of a program, many nontrivial functions are performed not by the code of the program but by SVC routines invoked by the program. These are highly complex, sophisticated and privileged routines that constitute an integral part of MVS/XA and reside in system library, SYS1.SVCLIB. Functions such as open, close, read, write, and many others are performed by SVCs. A S013 ABEND indicates that the failure happened while opening a data set — SVC 13 is open. A SB37 ABEND indicates that the failure occurred during End of Volume (EOV) processing — SVC 37 is EOV. Remembering that there is a relationship between a completion code and an SVC can be useful because there are similarities between ABENDs whose last two digits are the same. It is also helpful in understanding that, as an example, without an open there can be no Sx13 type of ABEND failure.

Frequently, but not always, a two-digit "reason code" follows the completion code (i.e., S013-18) identifying one of the several different meanings assigned of the same completion code. The reason code is also occasionally referred to as a return code. This is unfortunate. A return code in this case is unrelated to the one that will be discussed at length in Chapter 4, which can be interrogated by the COND parameter.

In the vast majority of cases, an ABEND failure occurs during the execution of a program (see Figure 1.7). There are, however, some exceptions: If a program (coded in the PGM parameter of the EXEC statement) cannot be found, the result is an S806 ABEND failure. It can hardly be claimed that the program ABENDed during its execution, since it could not be found. If the REGION parameter specifies (or defaults to) a value that is inadequate, an S80A (or S804 or S878) ABEND failure will occur. If the REGION parameter specifies a value too large, an S822 ABEND failure will occur. In both of the last two cases, the ABEND failure occurred before the program began execution. These are the exceptions.

Some programming languages have the ability to intercept ABENDs (for example, by using STAE or SPIE macros in Assembly Language). By requesting that, if an ABEND failure occurs, control not be lost but rather be returned to a specified routine within the program's code. In such cases, the step will not be considered as having ABENDed.

When a step ABENDs (as well as when it completes without ABENDing), the step termination routines (see Figure 1.7) get control.

In general, an ABEND failure can be caused by:

1. Program Error. A logic error in the program. For example, a program may attempt to add two numbers, both of which are expected to have packed decimal format. One (or both) of the numbers has a different format. The result will be a S0C7 ABEND failure. Although some will argue that a S0C7 ABEND failure is often caused by bad data, it is also easy to argue that the program failed to detect the invalid nature of the data, which led to the ABEND failure. Proper editing might have prevented it.

2. JCL Error. The expression "JCL error" can be a little confusing. JCL error was discussed before as a different category. These were syntactical or allocation errors. Mistakes, however, can be made in JCL which do not fall under either of those categories, and can result in ABEND failures. Many examples can be shown. Here are some:
   The program name is misspelled in the PGM parameter.

```
//S3  EXEC  PGM=PI
```

The program name is P1 but was instead coded as PI. This is an error in JCL which is not syntactical — PI is a perfectly valid program name, but it is the wrong one. This error also

has nothing to do with allocation. The result will be an S806
ABEND failure. This is not to suggest that when an S806
ABEND failure occurs it is always a JCL error that caused it.
It may be that the program name was coded correctly, but the
program has been deleted from the library.
Here is another example:

```
//JOB2   JOB   EJ74,MC,REGION=200K
```

The intent was to code REGION=2000K, but somehow a zero
was dropped. Again, the value of a parameter was coded incorrectly. In the absence of a better name such an error must be
called a JCL error. The result will be an S878 (or S80A or
S804) ABEND failure.

3. Resource Unavailability. A needed resource has been
    eliminated, or is simply unavailable. Depending on the
    resource, an ABEND failure can occur. An S806 ABEND again
    can be used to demonstrate this type of failure:

```
//S3   EXEC   PGM=PI
```

PI is the correct name but the program has been deleted from
its library. Result: S806 ABEND.

4. Exceeding Limits. A system-defined, installation-defined, or
    user-defined limit is exceeded. When it is a user-defined limit
    controllable through JCL, exceeding a limit can also be con-
    sidered the fault of JCL and as a result a JCL error (category
    2). Consider a job which exhausts its CPU availability as
    specified in the TIME parameter of the JOB or EXEC state-
    ment. The system will cause an S322 ABEND failure. A dif-
    ferent TIME parameter could have prevented the failure.
    There are, however, some limits that JCL has no control over.
    Here is an example: A wait state caused by a mount message,
    requesting that the operator mount a volume on a tape device,
    takes longer than the installation-defined limit, say 15
    minutes. The result is an S522 ABEND failure. JCL could not
    have determined the allowable duration of the wait state.
    Another example: A DD statement creating a disk data set con-
    tains SPACE=(CYL,(50,10)). Suppose that, after having gotten
    several secondary allocations of 10 cylinders, the next one
    needed would cause the total number of extents for the data
    set (on a single volume) to exceed 16. The result will be an
    SB37-04 ABEND failure. The limit of allowable extents is
    defined by the system, and neither JCL nor the installation

has control over it. One can argue, with good cause, that this is really an error in JCL causing the ABEND failure (category 2). Clearly, the values for the primary and/or secondary allocations were not large enough. This ABEND can actually be assigned to either category.

5.   Hardware Malfunction. Such a malfunction would typically be a hard I/O error. When the system is unable to read or write a block (after having retried several times) and the volume cannot be swapped to another device, the result will be an S001-1 ABEND failure. Given the relative reliability of today's peripherals, this failure is infrequently encountered.

6.   User ABEND. A program has the ability to request an ABEND failure and supply its own a completion code. This is known as a user ABEND and the code will be preceded by the letter "U" followed by a 4-digit hex number (i.e., U1101). For programs in production, such ABENDs must be carefully documented. User ABENDs are also often issued by software packages and certain languages. In those cases the package or language documentation will provide the explanation.

7.   Operator Intervention. An operator cancellation. The operator has the ability to cancel a job via an operator command. This is an S122 (if a memory dump is requested) or S222 (if no dump is requested) ABEND.

8.   Operating System Failure. If a job is executing while the entire MVS/XA system fails, when the system is re-IPLed the job will appear to have failed with an S2F3 ABEND code. This is likely to occur very seldom.

From all the ABEND causes mentioned above, #2 and #3 cover the majority of cases.

A note should be made here. Following an operator cancellation (S122 or S222 ABEND) or a S322 ABEND caused by the TIME parameter of the JOB (not EXEC) statement, no steps can ever be executed regardless of the presence of EVEN or ONLY in the COND parameter.

3.4 BYPASSING EXECUTION BECAUSE OF A RETURN CODE

A program has the ability to issue a return code (also called a condition code) to indicate whether its execution has been successful or not. A subsequent step can interrogate this return code via the

COND parameter and, if the return code is bad, bypass execution. Chapter 4 fully explains the COND parameter.

This last type of failure, however, should be treated with a grain of salt. Bypassing a step's execution frequently indicates that a previous step did not execute well. Frequently, but not always. Consider a job where the last step will be executed (and issue a warning message to the operator) only if one of the preceding steps issues a bad return code. In this case the last step not being executed indicates that all is well in the job. This is the opposite of what normally happens and constitutes an uncommon occurrence.

4

Controlling Execution

This chapter will discuss how a user can control the execution of steps within a job, with the emphasis on the COND parameter.

4.1 GENERAL

A step within a job may be executed or it may be bypassed without execution. Bypassing the execution of a step can be caused by:

- A syntactical JCL error.
- An allocation-type JCL error (see Section 3.2.2 in Chapter 3) in a step or those that follow.
- The COND parameter in the JOB statement.
- The COND parameter in the EXEC statement of the step.
- An ABEND failure.

4.2 A RETURN (OR CONDITION) CODE

The main tool for controlling the execution of steps within a job is the COND parameter. Before the COND parameter can be discussed, it is important to understand what a *return code* is. First of all, the terms *"return code"* and *"condition code"* are synonymous. This book will use "return code," but the reader should be aware that both terms are commonly used.

A return code is a number, between 0 and 4095, issued by an executing program just before its execution is finished. It is intended to identify an important event found (or not found) during the execution. For example, a program may issue a return code of 12 to indicate that a problematic event (such as a record with an invalid field) was detected during the execution or a return code of 0 to indicate that the execution was trouble-free. The return code issued by a program is saved by the system for the duration of the job. Any subsequent step of the same job can interrogate this return code by using the COND parameter either in the JOB or EXEC statement. The result of this interrogation is to permit or bypass the execution of the step. Note that providing control is the joint responsibility of programming and JCL. The program is responsible for issuing the return code, JCL for interrogating it. A return code is never available to a job other than the one that issued it. The step that interrogates the return code must be in the same job as, and subsequent to, the step that issued it.

All languages provide a means by which the return code can be issued. In Assembly Language, for example, a return code of 12 can be issued as follows:

```
LA   15,12    PLACE 12 IN REGISTER 15 - 12 IS THE RETURN CODE
BR   14       EXIT...PROGRAM EXECUTION HAS ENDED
```

The return code is simply the contents of Register 15 when the program completes its execution (without an ABEND failure). In COBOL, the same can be done by coding:

```
MOVE 12 TO RETURN-CODE
```

In PL/1 the following will issue a return code of 12:

```
CALL PLIRET(12);
```

The instruction that issues the return code is optional. It is recommended that all programs be written to contain such an instruction, but the fact remains that it can be omitted. If so, a default return code will be supplied:

- For high-level languages, such as COBOL, the default is 0.
- For Assembly Language, the default is unpredictable (whatever the contents of Register 15 happen to be).

A program can issue any return code between 0 and 4095. Arbitrary selection of return codes by the writer of a program must be discouraged. If a job contains several steps and the return codes issued by each step are different than those of the other steps, the COND parameter becomes very difficult, if not impossible, to code. It is highly recommended that all programs issue meaningful return codes which follow IBM-established conventions:

- Return code of 0 indicates complete success.
- Return code of 4 indicates a warning. The warning is benign, so that a return code of 4 will normally be treated as acceptable.
- Return code of 8 indicates questionable results.
- Return code of 12 indicates bad results.
- Return code of 16 indicates a terminal condition.

This convention is followed by the majority of IBM-written programs, such as language processors, the Linkage Editor, Utilities, IDCAMS, and others. Other programs, however, use an abbreviated version of this convention. The DFSORT program, for example, issues a 0 to indicate a successful sort and a 16 to indicate an unsuccessful one. Return codes of 4, 8, and 12 are not used. Programs written by other software vendors adhere to similar conventions. Applications or systems programmers should do the same.

When executing a vendor-written program that utilizes all of the above return codes, in many cases a return code of 8 or 12 or 16 should be treated identically. Take as an example the IEBGENER utility (see Section 13.3 in Chapter 13). This utility always performs a single function during a single execution (i.e., copy a sequential data set). A questionable result (return code of 8), a bad result (return code of 12), or a terminal result (return code of 16) basically have the same meaning: The utility has not performed well and subsequent steps that rely on its successful execution should be bypassed. There are, however, programs that permit many functions to be performed in a single execution. IDCAMS is an example. When such a program executes, there is a difference between 8, 12, and 16. A return code of 8 issued during a given function means that the results are questionable, but execution continues with subsequent functions. A return code of 12 issued during a given function means that the results are bad, but execution continues with subsequent functions. A return code of 16 issued during a given function means that the results are bad and execution terminates. Subsequent functions will not be executed.

The discussion thus far brings into focus an unfortunate fact: A return code of zero can have more than one meaning. To elaborate, consider this scenario: A job in production executes and all its steps issue a return code of 0. The average observer may assume that all is well with this job, as 0 being a return code indicative of success is a well-known fact. This may or may not be true. Unless the programs being executed are vendor-written or are known to issue meaningful return codes adhering to conventions, a return code of 0 has an ambiguous meaning. A program, for example, may not have issued a return code. In this case, a return code of 0 will be issued by default, and it is meaningless. There is no way to distinguish between a return code issued by a program and one issued by default. In both cases a message will appear in the output:

```
IEF142I USER1A  STEP3  STEP WAS EXECUTED - COND CODE 0000
```

(USER1A is the jobname and STEP3 is the stepname)

The only saving grace is the fact that vendor-written programs always issue return codes that adhere to convention. Unfortunately, the same cannot be said about user-written programs.

4.3 THE COND PARAMETER

The COND parameter can be coded in the JOB as well as the EXEC statement. It is mostly used in the EXEC statement.

4.3.1 The COND Parameter in the JOB Statement

The general format of the COND parameter of the JOB statement is:

```
COND=((code,operator)[,(code,operator)]......)
```

"code" is a number between 0 and 4095.

"operator" provides a comparison between a return code and the "code." There are six operators:

- LT — Less than
- LE — Less than or equal to
- NE — Not equal to
- EQ — Equal to
- GT — Greater than
- GE — Greater than or equal to

"(code,operator)" is called a test. There can be a maximum of eight tests in the COND parameter. If a test is satisfied, meaning it is true as it is read from left to right, the job stops execution at that point.

An example can best illustrate the mechanism of the COND parameter. Consider a job with five steps. Assume that none will ABEND.

```
//USER1A   JOB   SE44,TEST,COND=((12,LT),(8,EQ))
```

STEP1 issues a return code of 0
STEP2, if executed, issues a return code of 4
STEP3, if executed, issues a return code of 8
STEP4, if executed, issues a return code of 0
STEP5, if executed, issues a return code of 4
(Warning: This example does not adhere to conventions.)

STEP1 is executed. No previous return codes exist and the COND parameter in the JOB statement will be ignored for the first step.

Before STEP2 begins execution, the system interrogates the existing return code (0), using the tests in the COND parameter and reading the test from left to right.

- Is 12 less than 0? The answer is "no." The first test of the COND parameter was not satisfied. The second test is tested.
- Is 8 equal to 0? The answer is "no." Neither of the two tests was satisfied, and, therefore, STEP2 is executed.

Before STEP3 begins execution, the system interrogates the existing return codes (0 and 4), using the tests in the same COND parameter. Since the result for return code 0 is already known, only 4 will be tested:

- Is 12 less than 4? The answer is "no." The first test of the COND parameter was not satisfied. The second test is tested.
- Is 8 equal to 4? The answer is "no." Neither of the two tests was satisfied, and, therefore, STEP3 is executed.

Before STEP4 begins execution, the system interrogates the existing return codes (0, 4 and 16), using the tests in the same COND parameter. Since the results for return codes 0 and 4 are already known, only 16 will be tested:

• Is 12 less than 16? The answer is "yes." The first test of the COND parameter was satisfied. There is no need for the second test. Execution of the job stops. STEP4 and all remaining steps will not be executed.

A message will appear in the output:

```
IEF201I  USER1A  STEP4 — JOB TERMINATED BECAUSE OF CONDITION CODES
```

The COND parameter is probably the most confusing parameter in JCL. Its design makes its use difficult. One of the reasons is the fact when the answer to a test is "yes" (something positive), the result is no execution (something negative). And conversely, when the answer is "no," all is well. Some poetic soul came up with a little poem that may lend assistance to the user in remembering that "yes" means "no" and "no" means "yes." It goes like this:

If it's true,
You're through

Not great poetry, to be sure, but any help in understanding this parameter should be welcome.

How the system handles the COND parameter must be understood before it can be coded correctly. Unless one has had significant exposure to the COND parameter, coding it can be an unnerving experience. Considering its negative logic, it is difficult to code it and be able to foresee that it will achieve the desired result. The user may have to code a COND parameter that seems correct and then, by selecting various possible return codes, desk-check it to ensure that it works, and if it does not, change it and check it again. A rather strange way to write a JCL parameter.

To wit, assume that the COND is needed in a JOB statement where all the steps issue return codes closely adhering to conventions: A return code from 0 to 4 will be considered successful, from 5 on, unsuccessful. The user writes COND=(4,GT) — that is what most users unfamiliar with the COND parameter are likely to write. It appears reasonable. Now the parameter must be tested. Several hypothetical return codes must be tested: 0 (it is the most common one); 4 and 5 (they are important because they are threshold values — 4 is the last good return code, 5 the first bad one); 6 (one more test within the failing range).

Start with 0. If STEP1 issues a return code of 0, STEP2 should be executed. Examine the test (4,GT). Is 4 greater than 0? The answer is "yes," which means that STEP2, which should be executed, will not be. Nor will any following steps. No need to continue testing. Back to the drawing board to rewrite the COND parameter. The user writes COND=(4,LE) on the second attempt and again proceeds to test.

Start with 0. If STEP1 issues a return code of 0, STEP2 should be executed. Examine the test (4,LE). Is 4 less than or equal to 0? The answer is "no," which means that STEP2 will be executed, as it should. Now try 4 (a good return code). Is 4 less than or equal to 4? The answer is "yes," inappropriately stopping the execution of the job. On the third try the user writes COND=(4,LT) and tests again.

0 tests the same as with COND=(4,LE); 4 now will work well. Is 4 less than 4? The answer is "no," allowing STEP2 to be executed, as it should. Try 5. Is 4 less than 5? The answer is "yes," stopping the execution of the job. Since 5 is a bad return code, this is appropriate. 6 will give the same result as 5.

COND=(4,LT) is the proper COND parameter.

The above process may be described as horrendous, and, thankfully, it can be avoided in most situations. If return code conventions are followed, a useful observation regarding the frequency of use of each operator can minimize some of the complexity.

Operator	Frequency of Use
LT	High
LE	High
NE	Occasional
EQ	Low
GT	Low
GE	Low

Even a formula can be devised and used to code the COND parameter, if return code conventions are strictly adhered to (the importance of sticking to conventions cannot be overemphasized).

COND=(last-good-return-code,LT)

or

COND=(first-bad-return-code,LE)

Apply the formula to the example given earlier, where 0-4 is a good return code:

4 is the last good return code...COND=(4,LT)

or

5 is the first bad return code...COND=(5,LE)

The two COND parameters are logically equivalent to each other, and it makes no difference which one is used.

Try another example, where 0 is the only good return code:

0 is the last good return code...COND=(0,LT)

or

1 is the first bad return code...COND=(1,LE)

In this case, COND=(0,NE) can also be used to achieve the same result. This is because 0 is the one and only good return code.

If the COND parameter is not coded in the JOB statement (and also not coded in any of the EXEC statements within the job), all steps will be executed regardless of previous return codes, except for steps that follow an ABEND failure. Such steps are never executed.

The COND parameter in the JOB statement is relatively inflexible. For this reason, the COND parameter is usually coded in the EXEC statement where more flexibility is available.

4.3.2 The COND Parameter in the EXEC Statement

The COND parameter in the EXEC statement uses the same basic mechanism as the one in the JOB statement. If a test is satisfied (reading from left to right), the step (which contains the COND parameter) will not be executed. Following steps may or may not be executed, each guided by its own COND parameter. This is noticeably different from what happens when a test is satisfied in the COND parameter of the JOB statement (none of the following steps execute).

There are several differences between the two, and a summary of them is presented below:

- The tests that appear in the COND of the JOB statement repeat for each step (except the first one). For every new step, of course, there is a new return code to be tested.

  The COND in the EXEC statement allows each step to have its own tests.
- Each test in the COND of the JOB statement is tested against all previously issued return codes.

  The COND in the EXEC statement allows the same, but also allows to selectively test against the return code of a particular (previous) step.
- When a test is satisfied in the COND of the JOB statement (a "yes" answer), no steps can execute from that point on. It is impossible to bypass one step and execute a subsequent one.

  When a test is satisfied in the COND of the EXEC statement (a "yes" answer), only the step that contains the COND parameter will not be executed. Following steps may or may not be executed based on their own COND parameter.
- The COND of the JOB statement does not provide a way to allow execution of steps subsequent to an ABEND failure.

  The COND of the EXEC statement does.
- The COND in the JOB statement is ignored for the first step of the job. As a result, the first step will always be executed.

  The COND in the first EXEC statement may:
- — be ignored
- — cause a JCL error
- — cause the step to be bypassed without execution

The general format of the COND parameter of the EXEC statement is:

```
COND=((code,operator[,stepname])[,(code,operator[,stepname])]...
     [,EVEN],[,ONLY])
```

"code" — A number between 0 and 4095.

"operator" — Provides a comparison between a return code and the "code." There are six operators, as in the COND parameter of the JOB statement.

- LT — Less than
- LE — Less than or equal to
- NE — Not equal to
- EQ — Equal to
- GT — Greater than
- GE — Greater than or equal to

"stepname" — Identifies the name of a preceding step whose return code will be interrogated. It can also appear as two names: procexec.stepname where "procexec" identifies the name of the EXEC statement invoking a procedure and "stepname" the stepname within the procedure.

"(code,operator[,stepname])" is called a test. There can be a maximum of eight tests in the COND parameter. However, if EVEN or ONLY is coded, a maximum of seven can be used.

If a test is satisfied, meaning it is true, the step that contains the COND parameter will be bypassed. Following steps can be executed.

A test can assume one of two formats:

• (code,operator,stepname) — The "code" will be tested against the return code of a designated (by stepname) step.
• (code,operator) — The "code" will be tested against the return codes of all previous steps.

EVEN requests that execution be permitted even though a previous (any previous) step has ABENDed.

ONLY requests that execution be permitted only if a previous (any previous) step has ABENDed.

EVEN and ONLY cannot make reference to a particular step. They refer to any previous step that has ABENDed.

Neither EVEN nor ONLY guarantees execution following an ABEND failure, unless each appears alone in the COND parameter (i.e., COND=EVEN or COND=ONLY). If other tests are included in the COND parameter, they will be tested and that can cause the step not to be executed.

Following an ABEND failure, a step cannot be executed unless it contains EVEN or ONLY in the COND parameter of its EXEC statement.

EVEN and ONLY are mutually exclusive and cannot be coded together in the same COND parameter.

EVEN and ONLY have no positional significance. Each can be coded anywhere in the COND parameter in relation to other tests.

The EVEN and ONLY subparameters will have no effect under the following conditions:

• If a job is cancelled by the operator (ABEND code S222 or S122), no steps after the cancellation can be executed.
• If a job exhausts available CPU time (ABEND code S322) supplied by the TIME parameter in the JOB statement, no steps after this ABEND can be executed (no CPU time is available). If the same

ABEND, however, is caused by the TIME parameter in the EXEC statement, following steps can be executed.

If the COND parameter is not coded in an EXEC statement (and it is also not coded in the JOB statement), the step will be executed regardless of previous return codes. However, it will not be executed if a previous step has ABENDed.

If the COND parameter is coded in both the JOB statement as well as an EXEC statement within the job, both will be tested. The COND parameter of the JOB statement is tested first. If none of its tests are satisfied, then the COND parameter of the EXEC statement is tested. If a test is satisfied, the COND parameter in the EXEC statement will not be tested. Such a test would be meaningless since no further execution is possible. Considering the complexity of the parameter, it is recommended that the two never be coded together.

The COND parameter in the EXEC statement has the same mechanism as the one in the JOB statement regarding how tests are performed. Specifically, "If it's true/You're through" still holds.

Consider the JCL below. This is an example unlikely to be used in a real environment. Its purpose is to provide a demonstration of what has been discussed and raise some facts not mentioned yet:

```
//USER1B   JOB   MC21,MCAR,CLASS=T,NOTIFY=USER1
//S1       EXEC  PGM=P1
//S2       EXEC  PGM=P2,COND=((0,LT,S1),EVEN)
//S3       EXEC  PGM=P3,COND=(8,LT,S2)
//S4       EXEC  PGM=P4,COND=(4,LT)
//S5       EXEC  PGM=P5,COND=((4,LT,S1),(0,LT,S3))
//S6       EXEC  PGM=P6,COND=(EVEN,(0,LE,S5))
//S7       EXEC  PGM=P7,COND=((0,LT,S1),(12,LT,S3))
//S8       EXEC  PGM=P8,COND=((16,EQ,S6),ONLY)
//S9       EXEC  PGM=P9,COND=EVEN
//S10      EXEC  PGM=P10,COND=ONLY
```

(Warning: This example does not adhere to conventions.)

The anticipated return codes are shown below. Which steps will and which will not be executed?

S1, if executed, issues return code of 4
S2, if executed, issues return code of 12
S3, if executed, issues return code of 0

S4, if executed, issues return code of 8
S5, if execution begins, ABENDs
S6, if executed, issues return code of 16
S7, if executed, issues return code of 0
S8, if executed, issues return code of 0
S9, if executed, issues return code of 4
S10, if executed, issues return code of 0

- S1 will be executed. Assuming the RESTART parameter is not coded in the JOB statement, the first step will always be executed, unless COND=ONLY appears in the EXEC statement. COND=ONLY would cause the first step to be bypassed, since no previous ABEND failures could have occurred. Any other COND parameter in the first EXEC statement will either be ignored (i.e., COND=(5,LE) or COND=EVEN) or will result in a JCL error (i.e., COND=(5,LE,stepname) — stepname is an invalid reference, since there are no previous steps).
- S2 contains COND=((0,LT,S1),EVEN). The EVEN has no effect — no previous ABEND failure exists. The return code of S1 is 4. Is 0 less than 4? The answer is "yes." The test was satisfied so S2 will not be executed.
- S3 contains COND=(8,LT,S2). Had S2 been executed, the return code would have been 12 and the message below would have appeared in the output:

```
IEF142I USER1B  S2 STEP WAS EXECUTED - COND CODE 0012
```

But the step was not executed and the program responsible for issuing the return code was not even loaded into storage. As a result, *no return code can exist* and the message above will not appear. Any test of the COND parameter that attempts to interrogate this nonexistent return code ((8,LT,S2) is such a test) will be ignored. It will, however, be syntactically checked. In essence, step S3 does not have a COND parameter and it will be executed.
- S4 contains COND=(4,LT). Since no stepname is coded, all available return codes must be tested. Is 4 less than 4 (the return code of S1)? The answer is "no." S2 has no return code, so no test is performed. Is 4 less than 0 (the return code of S3)? The answer is "no." No tests were satisfied, so S4 will be executed.
- S5 contains COND=((4,LT,S1),(0,LT,S3)). Is 4 less than 4 (the return code of S1)? The answer is "no." Is 0 less than 0 (the return code of S3)? The answer is "no." No tests were satisfied, so S4 will begin execution and, as indicated, it will ABEND.

- S6 contains COND=(EVEN,(0,LE,S5)). The EVEN permits execution despite the ABEND failure of Step S5. (0,LE,S5) is a test which, if a return code existed, would always give a "yes" answer and, as a result, step S6 would not execute. But what can be said about the return code of an ABENDing step? A program always issues a return code (intentionally or by default) if it reaches the end of its execution and intentionally returns control to the system. When an ABEND occurs, the program loses control instantly and is "evicted" from execution by the system. As a result, *when a step ABENDs, no return code exists* (a completion code does).

   Since an ABENDing step issues no return code, the (0,LE,S5) test is ignored (it will be syntactically checked) and S6 will be executed.
- S7 contains COND=((0,LT,S1),(12,LT,S3)). A step that follows an ABEND failure can never be executed unless it contains either EVEN or ONLY in its COND parameter. S7 does not and will not be executed. There is no need to interrogate the tests in its COND parameter.
- S8 contains COND=((16,EQ,S6),ONLY). The ONLY requests execution only in the event of a previous ABEND failure and such a failure has occurred (S5). Is 16 equal to 16 (the return code of S6)? The answer is "yes" and S8 will not be executed proving that ONLY does not guarantee execution following an ABEND failure, unless coded alone in the COND parameter.
- S9 contains COND=EVEN. The EVEN permits execution despite the previous ABEND failure, and since no tests are included in the COND parameter, S9 will be executed.
- S10 contains COND=ONLY. The ONLY requests execution only in the event of a previous ABEND failure and such a failure has occurred (S5). Since no tests are included in the COND parameter, S10 will be executed.

There are two important facts that came out of the analysis of the example above that were not discussed before:

Fact 1: A step that is not executed issues no return code. An attempt to interrogate the return code of such a step in the COND parameter of a subsequent step will be ignored.

Fact 2: A step that ABENDs issues no return code. An attempt to interrogate the return code of such a step in the COND parameter of a subsequent step will be ignored.

There is, however, an exception. Certain programs, usually vendor-written, have the ability to intercept ABEND failures and allow the program to continue executing (STAE and SPIE macros in Assembly Language can accomplish this). If that happens, then the program can issue a bad return code without advertising the fact that an ABEND failure occurred. The user is none the wiser seeing only the return code. This is perfectly OK because the intercepted ABEND has no impact on the user. But, again, an exception exists. IDCAMS, which is an often used program, intercepts most ABEND failures during its execution, issues the appropriate return code, but sometimes still displays a message identifying the ABEND. This is likely to be confusing. The user must keep in mind that if a message

```
IEF142I jobname stepname  STEP WAS EXECUTED — COND CODE nnnn
```

appears in the output of a step, even if a message describing an ABEND failure also appears, the step will not be treated as an ABENDing step by the system.

4.4 PRACTICAL EXAMPLES

This section will discuss situations that may arise in a real environment and ways to handle then. Some of the situations will be ordinary, others unusual.

4.4.1 Ordinary Examples

In an ideal situation, all the steps in a job will issue return codes that adhere to IBM conventions. Typically, return codes of 0 through 4 can be considered successful and all others unsuccessful.

Control can be established in two ways:

Using the COND in the EXEC statement:

```
//PROD55   JOB   JJ19,'DAILY JOB #3'
//S1       EXEC  PGM=K1
//S2       EXEC  PGM=K2,COND=(4,LT)
//S3       EXEC  PGM=K3,COND=(4,LT)
//S4       EXEC  PGM=K4,COND=(4,LT)
```

and so on...

Using the COND in the JOB statement

```
//PROD55   JOB   JJ19,'DAILY JOB #3',COND=(4,LT)
//S1       EXEC  PGM=K1
//S2       EXEC  PGM=K2
//S3       EXEC  PGM=K3
//S4       EXEC  PGM=K4
```

and so on . . .

In essence, the two ways boil down to the same thing. In both cases, if a return code greater than 4 is issued by any step, all subsequent steps will not be executed.

If 0 were deemed to be the only good return code, then the same two examples can be used, but with (0,LT) instead of (4,LT). As mentioned before, (5,LE) can be used in place of (4,LT). Also, (1,LE) or (0,NE) can be used in place of (0,LT)

4.4.2 Conditional Execution in Job Recovery

It is frequently desired, especially in a production environment, that the first step of a job save a file (or files) to be updated. This ensures that the file can always be restored to its original status in case something goes wrong later in the job. The second step of the job contains JCL to restore the file.

Under normal conditions, the first step will be executed, the second bypassed, and all the rest executed as the job requires.

In a recovery situation, the first step will not be executed, the second will be, restoring the file, and then the job will proceed normally.

The following JCL can accomplish this goal:

```
//PROD55A  JOB   JJ19,'DAILY JOB #43'
//CONTR    EXEC  PGM=IEFBR14
//SAVE     EXEC  PGM=SAV1,COND=(0,NE,CONTR)
//REST     EXEC  PGM=RES1,COND=(0,LE,SAVE)
//S1       EXEC  PGM=P1,COND=(4,LT)
//S2       EXEC  PGM=P2,COND=(4,LT)
//S3       EXEC  PGM=P3,COND=(4,LT)
```

In a normal execution, step CONTR will be executed and issue a return code of 0 (IEFBR14 always issues a return code of 0).

Step SAVE will be executed (the answer to the question: Is 0 not equal to 0? is "no"). This step saves the file.

Step REST will not be executed because no matter what the return code of step SAVE is, the question: Is 0 less than or equal to any number? is always "yes."

The rest of the steps will be executed normally.

In a recovery situation, it is desired that step SAVE be bypassed and step REST executed. To accomplish this, the COND of step SAVE must be changed to COND=(1,NE,CONTR).

Step CONTR will be executed and issue a return code of 0.

Step SAVE will not be executed (the answer to the question: Is 0 not equal to 1? is "yes").

Step REST will be executed because step SAVE was not executed, it issued no return code, and, as a result, the test (0,LE,SAVE) will be ignored.

The rest of the steps will be executed normally.

This is best done by creating a procedure containing the JCL, coding COND=(&C,NE,CONTR), and also coding C=0 in the PROC statement.

```
PROCEDURE UPFIL
-----------------------------------------------
//UP        PROC  C=0
//CONTR     EXEC  PGM=IEFBR14
//SAVE      EXEC  PGM=SAV1,COND=(&C,NE,CONTR)
//REST      EXEC  PGM=RES1,COND=(0,LE,SAVE)
//S1        EXEC  PGM=P1,COND=(4,LT)
//S2        EXEC  PGM=P2,COND=(4,LT)
//S3        EXEC  PGM=P3,COND=(4,LT)
-----------------------------------------------
```

In a normal execution,

```
//NR  EXEC  UPFIL
```

0 will be substituted for &C, and the substitution JCL will be COND=(0,NE,CONTR).

In a recovery execution,

```
//RR  EXEC  UPFIL,C=1
```

1 will be substituted for &C, and the substitution JCL will be COND=(1,NE,CONTR).

The same can be accomplished with a variation of the previous JCL:

```
PROCEDURE UPFILX
----------------------------------------------
//UPX      PROC C=0
//CONTR    EXEC PGM=IEFBR14
//SAVE     EXEC PGM=SAV1,COND=(&C,NE,CONTR)
//REST     EXEC PGM=RES1,COND=(&C,EQ,CONTR)
//S1       EXEC PGM=P1,COND=(4,LT)
//S2       EXEC PGM=P2,COND=(4,LT)
//S3       EXEC PGM=P3,COND=(4,LT)
----------------------------------------------
```

In this example, the procedure would contain two parameters with the same symbolic parameter &C, COND=(&C,NE,CONTR) and COND=(&C,EQ,CONTR).

The rest is very similar to the preceding example: In a normal execution,

```
//NR  EXEC  UPFILX
```

C=0 (the default), step SAVE will be executed and step REST will not.

In a recovery execution,

```
//RR  EXEC  UPFILX,C=1
```

C=1, step SAVE will not be executed and step REST will. The rest of the steps will execute normally in both situations.

4.4.3 The Warning Last Step

There are three types of failures that can occur during a job's execution: A JCL error, an ABEND failure, or a bad return code (see Section 3.1 in Chapter 3).

For a job in production, it is often a good idea to make certain that the operator knows, as soon as possible, when a failure occurs.

JCL errors and ABEND failures generate messages that appear on the operator's console. Bad return codes, however, generate no such messages, and one may not be aware of the problem until the output is scrutinized. This can produce an unacceptable delay.

A last step can be added to the job, whose function will be to inform the operator that a bad return code has been encountered somewhere in the job by routing to the console a message such as:

```
*** ATTENTION - A STEP WITHIN JOB PROD53 HAS ISSUED A BAD RETURN
    CODE...INFORM TECH SUPPORT. REPLY 'A' TO ACKNOWLEDGE.
```

Note that the message will not roll off the screen until the operator replies. This guarantees that the message will be seen.

Assuming a normal return code situation — 0 through 4 is good — the JCL below will accomplish the desired goal.

```
//PROD53    JOB  JJ19,'DAILY JOB #53'
//S1        EXEC PGM=P1
//S2        EXEC PGM=P2,COND=(4,LT)
//S3        EXEC PGM=P3,COND=(4,LT)
   |           |    |      |
   |           |    |      |
   |           |    |      |
   |           |    |      |
//S12       EXEC PGM=P12,COND=(4,LT)
//OPSTEP    EXEC PGM=WTOR,COND=(4,GE,S12)
```

Note that the COND parameter of the last step refers to the immediately preceding step.

Consider a normal situation where all steps, including S12, issue a return code of 4 or less. Assume the return code of step S12 is 4. Step OPSTEP will not be executed because the answer to the question: Is 4 greater or equal to 4? is "yes." The same would happen if the return code of OPSTEP were less than 4. This is appropriate. The last step that writes the warning message should not be executed when all is well.

Now consider a failing situation where any step between S1 and S11 has issued a bad return code. To be specific, pick step S3 to have issued a return code of 8.

- Steps S4 through S12 will not be executed because all contain COND=(4,LT).
- Step OPSTEP will be executed because step S12 was not executed, issued no return code and, therefore, test (4,GE,S12) will be ignored.

If step S12 were the one issuing the bad return code, step OPSTEP will again be executed because the answer to the question: Is 4 greater than or equal to 8? is "no."

It is easy to modify the above example to work when the only good return code is 0 (rather than 0 through 4):

```
//PROD53    JOB  JJ19,'DAILY JOB #53'
//S1        EXEC PGM=P1
//S2        EXEC PGM=P2,COND=(0,LT)
//S3        EXEC PGM=P3,COND=(0,LT)
    |          |     |     |
    |          |     |     |
    |          |     |     |
    |          |     |     |
//S12       EXEC PGM=P12,COND=(0,LT)
//OPSTEP    EXEC PGM=WTOR,COND=(0,EQ,S12)
```

The technique just discussed can be enhanced to include an ABEND failure anywhere in the job. The message to be issued by the last step will now be:

```
*** ATTENTION - A STEP WITHIN JOB PROD53 HAS ISSUED A BAD RETURN
    CODE OR ABENDED...INFORM TECH SUPPORT. REPLY 'A' TO
    ACKNOWLEDGE.
```

The JCL to accomplish this is identical to the previous example except for the COND parameter of the last step (0 through 4 being a good return code is assumed).

```
//PROD53    JOB  JJ19,'DAILY JOB #53'
//S1        EXEC PGM=P1
//S2        EXEC PGM=P2,COND=(4,LT)
//S3        EXEC PGM=P3,COND=(4,LT)
    |          |     |     |
    |          |     |     |
    |          |     |     |
    |          |     |     |
//S12       EXEC PGM=P12,COND=(4,LT)
//OPSTEP    EXEC PGM=WTOR,COND=(EVEN,(4,GE,S12))
```

For a normal execution (good return codes and no ABEND failures) this JCL will work exactly the same as in the previous example. The only difference between the two is the presence of EVEN in the COND parameter of the last step. When no ABEND occurs, EVEN is ignored.

For an execution when a bad return code is issued, again the two examples work identically. EVEN has no effect on return codes.

What remains to be shown is that if an ABEND failure occurs anywhere between steps S1 and S12, step OPSTEP will be executed.

To be specific, pick step S3 to have ABENDed.

- Steps S4 through S12 contain neither EVEN nor ONLY in their COND parameters, and they cannot be executed.
- Step OPSTEP will be executed. EVEN permits execution and since step S12 was not executed, it issued no return code, and therefore, COND=(4,GE,S12) will be ignored.

If S12 were the ABENDing step, step OPSTEP will again be executed. EVEN permits execution and, since step S12 ABENDed, it issued no return code, and therefore test (4,GE,S12) will be ignored.

This method works very well and has been used repeatedly in a real production environment. There are, however, two instances for which the last step will not be executed.

- If the operator cancels the job (ABEND code S222 or S122), no steps following the cancellation are ever permitted to execute (EVEN and ONLY notwithstanding).
- If CPU time is exhausted based on the TIME parameter of the JOB statement (ABEND code S322) no step can execute following this failure because there is no CPU time available.

Those two exceptions are mostly benign and are unlikely to reduce the effectiveness of this method. If the operator cancels a job in production, she or he knows the job has been canceled and there is no need for a warning message. A S322 ABEND failure is extremely unlikely to happen in a production job. Production jobs are seldom given CPU time limitations.

4.4.4 Innovative Ways of Controlling Execution

Under certain conditions it becomes impossible to code a COND parameter that will provide a desired control. Here is an example. A program issues return code 0 or 40 to indicate successful completion. All other return codes are bad. A COND parameter that will handle this situation cannot be coded. One may ask why a program would be coded in this fashion. It should not, of course, but let's assume it exists.

Let us explain why no effective COND parameter can be coded. To cover the "0 as a good return code," (0,LT) (or (1,LE) or (0,NE)) must be included in the COND parameter. Unfortunately, this makes 40 a bad return code. To cover the "40 is a good return code," (40,NE) must be included in the COND parameter. Unfortunately, this makes 0 a bad return code.

An observation can be made here. While a COND parameter cannot be coded that will allow execution if the return code is either 0 or 40, the exact opposite is easy. A parameter can be coded to bypass execution if the return code is either 0 or 40: COND= ((0,EQ),(40,EQ)).

Based on that, the JCL below will establish a semblance of control by using an auxiliary step AUX executing IEFBR14.

```
//S1    EXEC   PGM=P040
//AUX   EXEC   PGM=IEFBR14,COND=((0,EQ),(40,EQ))
//S2    EXEC   PGM=PABC,COND=(0,EQ,AUX)
```

Assume that S1 issues a (good) return code of 0. Step AUX will not be executed because the answer to the question: Is 0 equal to 0? is "yes." The fact that step AUX is not executed allows S2 to be executed, since the test (0,EQ,AUX) will be ignored (AUX has no return code). The same will happen if S1 issues a (good) return code of 40.

If a bad return code is issued by step S1, say 20, step AUX will be executed (is 0 equal to 20? "no." Is 40 equal to 20? "no.") and issue a return code of 0. That, of course, will cause step S2 to not be executed.

Some control is established, but it is limited, cumbersome, confusing and probably not worth using. Altering the offending program to issue conventional return codes is a much better idea.

Now let's consider another area of concern. What if the steps of a job issue condition codes not adhering to conventions, with each step being different than the others. Since only eight tests are permitted in the COND parameter, the job can have no more than nine steps if the COND is used in every step. This is actually true if only the first two steps do not issue the same return codes. Here is an example.

The first step of a job uses 0 as the only good return code. All remaining steps use 0 through 4 as the only good return codes. Using the convenient COND=(4,LT) or COND=(0,LT) in all the steps of the job is not possible. Each step in the job must be referenced explicitly in the COND parameter of all following steps, limiting the maximum number of steps to nine.

```
//S1  EXEC  PGM=R1
//S2  EXEC  PGM=R2,COND=(0,LT,S1)
//S3  EXEC  PGM=R3,COND=((0,LT,S1),(4,LT,S2))
//S4  EXEC  PGM=R4,COND=((0,LT,S1),(4,LT,S2),(4,LT,S3))
//S5  EXEC  PGM=R5,COND=((0,LT,S1),(4,LT,S2),(4,LT,S3),(4,LT,S4))
//S6  EXEC  PGM=R6,COND=((0,LT,S1),(4,LT,S2),(4,LT,S3),(4,LT,S4),
//          (4,LT,S5))
//S7  EXEC  PGM=R7,COND=((0,LT,S1),(4,LT,S2),(4,LT,S3),(4,LT,S4),
//          (4,LT,S5),(4,LT,S6))
//S8  EXEC  PGM=R8,COND=((0,LT,S1),(4,LT,S2),(4,LT,S3),(4,LT,S4),
//          (4,LT,S5),(4,LT,S6),(4,LT,S7))
//S9  EXEC  PGM=R9,COND=((0,LT,S1),(4,LT,S2),(4,LT,S3),(4,LT,S4),
//          (4,LT,S5),(4,LT,S6),(4,LT,S7),(4,LT,S8))
```

The tenth step would have required a COND parameter with nine tests, one over the limit of eight. Not only is the job limited to nine steps, but the COND parameter gets progressively messier with every following step.

For such jobs a method exists to provide control, a method that resembles the first example in this section. As in that example, an auxiliary step will be utilized. This step will execute a program which causes an immediate ABEND failure — one can easily be coded to provide a user ABEND.

```
//S1    EXEC  PGM=R1
//AUX1  EXEC  PGM=ABEND,COND=(0,EQ,S1)
//S2    EXEC  PGM=R2
//AUX2  EXEC  PGM=ABEND,COND=(4,GE,S2)
//S3    EXEC  PGM=R3
//AUX3  EXEC  PGM=ABEND,COND=(4,GE,S3)
//S4    EXEC  PGM=R4
//AUX4  EXEC  PGM=ABEND,COND=(4,GE,S4)
```

Whenever a bad return code is issued by any step, the following auxiliary step will be executed, resulting in an ABEND failure and causing all subsequent steps not to be executed. Whenever a good return code is issued by any step, the corresponding auxiliary step will be bypassed and the execution of the job will continue. This method creates an inflexible environment where a step can never be executed after a bad return code has been issued by any of the preceding steps and where EVEN and ONLY can serve no useful purpose. Come to think of it, it resembles the limitations of the COND parameter in the JOB statement.

5

Discussion of DD Statement Parameters

This chapter will provide a description of DD statement parameters.[1] Emphasis will be placed when discussing parameters and sub-parameters prominently used in a day-to-day environment, whereas those that are rarely or never used will be deemphasized or omitted. When appropriate, how most installations use some of these parameters will also be mentioned.

Parameters that are used only with special DD statement parameters (such as SYSOUT, DUMMY, etc.) will be discussed in Chapter 10.

5.1 THE DD STATEMENT — GENERAL

A DD (Data Definition) statement must appear in a step when the executing program expects to read from or write to a data set. The DD statement is responsible for describing the data set. There are two exceptions to this rule:

---

1. Some of the information covered in this chapter is basic and is intended mostly for review or reference purposes. The experienced reader may wish to read this chapter selectively.

- When a program writes to the operator console, a practice that is not encouraged, no DD statement is needed (actually, none can be supplied). The console is a special device and it is always available to all executing programs.
- A program has the ability to perform the same function as a DD statement through its own code. This is called dynamic allocation. However, only a few languages (e.g., Assembly Language) have this facility, and it is very rarely used.

In all other cases, if a program intends to perform I/O operations to a data set, a DD statement must be supplied.

Some DD statements describe data sets which the executing program neither reads from nor writes to (such as JOBLIB, STEPLIB, SYSUDUMP, etc.). These will be discussed in Chapter 10.

The maximum number of DD statements in a step is 3273 (1635 prior to Data Facility Product Version 2.3).

A DD statement, with the exception of DUMMY, either *creates* or *retrieves* a data set.

5.2 THE DSN PARAMETER

The DSN (or DSNAME) parameter identifies the name of the data set to be created or retrieved.

General Syntax

```
DSN=name|NULLFILE            keyword parameter
```

name — several formats are possible:

- A simple or unqualified name. This name consists of from one to eight alphabetic, numeric, or national characters (a hyphen is also permitted). The first character must be alphabetic or national.

```
DSN=FAILSAFE
```

This type of name is seldom, if ever, used. It is virtually impossible to catalog a data set with a simple name (see Section 6.3 Chapter 6). Given the significance of the catalog, simple names should be completely avoided. No examples will be presented in this book using simple names.

- A qualified name. This name consists of two or more simple names separated by periods for a maximum of 44 characters (periods included). Each level (preceding or following a period) is called a qualifier, a qualification level, or an index. Qualifier is the most common, and that is what will be used in this book.

Qualified names are practically always used in the DSN parameter for technical (being able to catalog) as well as practical reasons. It allows the user to supply a name that is unique and meaningful at the same time. The name can, for example, contain information about the user, the user's department, the application the user is working with and many other pieces of information. This could not be achieved with a simple name.

```
DSN=USER1.DEPT19.PAYROL.MASTER
```

In most installations, the user's id must be the high qualifier of all the user's data set names.
- library(member) — This notation identifies a library (PDS) and a particular member in it.

```
DSN=USER1.CTLLIB(SE24)
```

In the example above, member SE24 within PDS USER1.CTLLIB is requested. Only member SE24 is available to the executing program. This DD statement will be treated as if it were describing a sequential data set (members of a PDS are always sequentially organized), and a program using an ordinary sequential access method, such as QSAM, can handle it. The only difference between a DD statement describing a member of a PDS and one describing a sequential data set is that MOD cannot be used in the DISP parameter to extend the data of a member (see Section 7.4 Chapter 7).
Without the member the DSN parameter means something quite different.

```
DSN=USER1.CTLLIB
```

Now the entire PDS with all its members is available to the program, but BPAM (Basic Partitioned Access Method) must be used to access the data set. This is a rarely used access method and is unavailable to many high-level programming languages.
- &&name — A simple name preceded by two ampersands. This identifies a temporary data set name. A single ampersand can also

be used. A double ampersand, however, is preferable, because &name, when found inside a procedure, is a symbolic parameter and becomes a temporary name only when no substitution for it occurs. This can result in undesirable substitutions and confusion. &&name is always a temporary name, never a symbolic parameter.

```
DSN=&&TEMP
```

The system generates a name with the following format:

```
SYS90122.T051645.RV001.USER1A.TEMP
```

— First level, SYS90122: The word SYS followed by the Julian date.
— Second level, T051645: The letter T followed by the time in hours, minutes, and seconds. This is not the current time. It is the time when JES2 or JES3 was initialized and will remain the same until the next initialization.
— Third level, RV001: System provided information in reference to the reader used.
— Fourth level, USER1A: The jobname as it appears in the JOB statement.
— Last level, TEMP: Whatever is coded after &&, or &.

This name is unique (another job cannot generate such a name), and it is also temporary. Temporary means that it cannot be retained beyond job termination.

Note that if DSN=&&TEMP is used again by the same job or another job with the same jobname, the resulting data set name will be the same. However, the danger of duplication is remote because DD statements creating temporary data sets are normally nonspecific (contain no VOL=SER or VOL=REF). If the system finds a duplicate name while trying to create the data set on a PUBLIC or STORAGE disk volume, it will go to a different volume, when possible.

• referback — This can have three formats:
— *.stepname.ddname — Requests that the data set name be copied from DD statement "ddname" found in a previous step "stepname."

```
DSN=*.STEP2.OUT
```

— *.ddname — Requests that the data set name be copied from a previous DD statement "ddname" found in the same step. This reference is seldom used.

```
DSN=*.DD1
```

— *.procexec.stepname.ddname — Requests that the data set name be copied from DD statement "ddname" found in a previous step "stepname" found within a procedure "procexec" (name of EXEC statement invoking the procedure).

```
DSN=*.PS4.STEP6.DD3
```

• 'name'— A name containing unacceptable special characters. Apostrophes must never be used around the data set name when creating a data set. It may become necessary when attempting to retrieve a tape data set whose label was created by a system other than MVS/XA, when it is an acceptable label, but the dsname contains special characters, or is otherwise unacceptable. Very rarely used.

```
DSN='OTHJ.%STEPSIDE'
```

• gdgbase(number) or gdgbase — Both of these pertain to Generation Data Groups, which are discussed in Chapter 11.

If the DSN parameter is omitted from a DD statement (DD *, SYSOUT and DUMMY not included), the system generates a name with the following format:

```
SYS90122.T051645.RV001.USER1A.R00000002
```

This is the same format as generated when DSN=&&name was coded, except the last level contains the character R followed by seven numeric digits, which change for every new data set name being generated in a job. This name is completely unique. No other data set can have the same name in the same or another job. It is also temporary and it cannot be retained beyond job termination.

When a step requires a work data set (a data set created at the beginning of the step's execution and deleted at the end), omitting the DSN parameter achieves two goals. It guarantees the uniqueness of the data set name (avoiding possible duplication) and the temporary status of the data set (avoiding possible future intervention to delete the data set).

NULLFILE — Indicates that no I/O operations will be performed for the DD statement. No other parameters except DCB are required. If any are coded, they will be syntactically checked and ignored.

The DSN=NULLFILE parameter works identically as the DUMMY parameter, except that it is not positional as DUMMY is (see Section 10.4 in Chapter 10).

5.2.1 How a Program Finds a Data Set

Figure 5.1 shows how a data set is located when it is opened by the program. A data set must be opened before it can be read from or written to. The open instruction in the program points to a DCB (Data Control Block).

If a program intends to read from or write to a (non-VSAM) data set, a DCB must exist within the code of the program. The instructions of the program may never refer to the acronym DCB. The compiler collects information from various parts of the program and constructs a DCB. It contains such information as the logical record length, the blocksize, the record format, the data set organization, the expiration date, the creation date, the *ddname*, and much more.

Note that when an ordinary access method is used, it is not the data set name but the ddname that resides in the program (and specifically inside the DCB). In COBOL, the SELECT ASSIGN clause supplies the ddname. In Assembly Language, the DCB macro includes a DDNAME=ddname parameter.

The ddname is in essence the connecting link between the program during the execution (and specifically during the open) and the corresponding DD statement. The ddname in the program's DCB and the ddname in the DD statement *must* be spelled the same way.

The DD statement contains the data set name. Either directly, when VOL and UNIT information are coded in the DD statement, or preferably through the catalog, the volume that contains the data set has already been found.

The VTOC of the volume contains a DSCB for the data set with its exact location on the volume. The open has now physically found the data set where I/O will be performed. With all the pointers in place, the system knows the exact location of the data set the program will be reading from or writing to.

An interesting point can be made here. Preceding any I/O activity, it is necessary for the program to open the data set. It is not, however, necessary to close the data set. It is certainly advisable that a program contain code to close a data set, but it is not mandatory. Even if the close were coded, it may not be executed if an ABEND failure prematurely terminates the step. The step termination routines (see Figure 1.7) will close all data sets that the program failed to close.

5.3 THE DISP PARAMETER

The DISP parameter specifies:

- if the data set is to be created or retrieved
- how to dispose of the data set when the step terminates
  General Syntax

```
         ┌─────┐  ┌──────────┐  ┌──────────┐
         │ NEW │  │ ,DELETE  │  │ ,DELETE  │
         │ OLD │  │ ,KEEP    │  │ ,KEEP    │
  DISP=  │ SHR │  │ ,CATLG   │  │ ,CATLG   │       keyword parameter
         │ MOD │  │ ,UNCATLG │  │ ,UNCATLG │
         │     │  │ ,PASS    │  │          │
         └─────┘  └──────────┘  └──────────┘
```

The three fields of the DISP parameter are: The status field; the normal disposition field; the abnormal (or conditional) disposition field.

The status field: This field tells the system whether that data set is to be created or retrieved.

NEW — Indicates that the data set will be created in this step.

OLD — Indicates that an existing data set will be retrieved. It also indicates that this data set may not be shared with any other users.

SHR — Indicates that an existing data set will be retrieved. It also indicates that this data set, if on disk, can be shared with one or more other users.

SHR will be changed to OLD if DISP=(SHR,DELETE) is used (no message will appear to that effect).

MOD — This subparameter has two possible meanings:

- Indicates that an existing data set will be retrieved. This will be true if:
  — The data set is either cataloged or passed.

  or

  — The DD statement contains either VOL=SER or VOL=REF (a VOL=REF referring to a DD statement, which is a nonspecific request for a new data set, is not included).
- Indicates that the data set will be created. This will be true if:
  — The DD statement contains neither VOL=SER nor VOL=REF and it describes a data set which is neither cataloged nor passed.

  or

  — The DD statement contains VOL=REF referring to a DD statement, which is a nonspecific request for a new data set.

When MOD is used, the system assumes the data set to be existing. If the volume on which the data set resides can be found and it was not supplied by a VOL=REF parameter referring to a DD statement which itself contained neither VOL=SER nor VOL=REF (*new* nonspecific request), then the assumption is taken to be correct. When the data set is opened for output, the system will position the read/write mechanism of the device after the last record of the data set. As the program writes records, the data set will be extended (if the program opens for input, MOD will default to OLD).If the volume cannot be found through any means, MOD defaults to NEW (no message appears explaining what MOD defaults to).

Consider the DD statement below where the data set is cataloged:

```
//EXT  DD  DSN=USER1.MODAT,DISP=(MOD,CATLG),UNIT=TAPE
```

The system assumes USER1.MODAT to be an existing data set. Since the DD statement contains neither VOL=SER nor VOL=REF, the system searches the Catalog and gets volume information from the catalog entry. The volume having been found, USER1.MODAT will be treated as an existing data set.

Had the data set been neither cataloged nor passed, the system would have been unable to find volume information and MOD would default to NEW.

Misconceptions about how MOD works are common. The most popular is that if the data set exists, MOD will extend it, and if it does not, MOD defaults to NEW and will create it. This is not a correct description of how MOD works, although it is admittedly easier to understand. Consider the DD statement below where the data set does not exist.

```
//D22   DD   DSN=USER1.SELLE,DISP=(MOD,CATLG),UNIT=SYSDA,
//            VOL=SER=PACK25,SPACE=(TRK,(50,20))
```

The system has volume information supplied in the DD statement (VOL=SER). As a result, the fate of MOD is sealed. Whether or not it exists, it will be treated as OLD (with the appropriate positioning). In this case the result will be an S213-04 ABEND failure.

Using MOD can cause short blocks to exist in the middle of data. Consider a data set containing 150 80-byte records blocked at 100 (BLKSIZE=8000). The data set will have two blocks.

8000-byte block	IBG	4000-byte EOF block

A short block is very common at the end of data and it never creates any problems. RECFM=FB and RECFM=FBS both anticipate it and handle it.

If MOD is used to add more records to the data set, the short block will remain and new blocks of standard size will be added.

8000-byte block	IBG	4000-byte IBG block	IBG	8000-byte block	...

RECFM=FB anticipates short blocks in the middle of data and takes care of them. RECFM=FBS does not. When a short block is found, it acts as an end-of-file condition. Data beyond that point will not be read. It will appear as a normal EOF, and the user will not know that some of the data is missing. For this reason, RECFM=FBS, which has a minor speed advantage over RECFM=FB, is not recommended when reading. FBS should *never* be used when writing.

Sharability considerations: With the exception of SHR, all other status fields demand exclusive usage of a data set. This means the following:

If a job containing a DD statement (in any step) with OLD, NEW, or MOD begins execution, no other job which contains a DD statement (in any step) with the same data set name can begin execution, regardless of DISP used. It is placed in a wait state (no S522 ABEND can occur) and the operator is informed. When the last step that uses the data set with OLD, NEW, or MOD terminates, then the data set is freed and other jobs can begin execution. Note that if this step were the last one of the job, no other job can begin execution throughout the execution of the first job despite the fact that only the last step uses the data set.

If a job containing a DD statement (in any step) with a DISP of SHR begins execution, no other job which contains a DD statement (in any step) with the same data set name can begin execution, if the DISP is OLD, NEW, or MOD. It is placed in a wait state (no S522 ABEND can occur) and the operator is informed. When the last step that uses the data set terminates, then the other job can begin execution.

DISP=SHR should be used whenever retrieving and reading a disk data set.

DISP=OLD should be used whenever retrieving and updating a disk data set. Using DISP=SHR while updating creates an exposure. If two jobs use SHR for the same data set and both update it, with the right timing, the data set can be destroyed.

For tape data sets DISP=OLD is normally used, but DISP=SHR is also acceptable. Tape is a nonsharable device. DISP=SHR can be useful if two jobs contain a DD statement each describing a data set by the same name but on different volumes.

TSO/ISPF users are similarly affected when they attempt to access data sets being used by jobs.

The normal disposition field: This field is used to tell the system how to dispose of the data set when the step terminates normally (without an ABEND).

DELETE — Indicates that the data set is to be deleted when the step terminates. For an existing data set, OLD SHR or MOD (not defaulting to NEW), the data set will also be uncataloged if the catalog were used while retrieving the data set. It will only delete if the catalog were not used during retrieval.

When a disk data set is deleted, the system removes its DSCB from the VTOC and makes its space immediately available. The data of the deleted data set is not erased. It remains until it is written over.

When a tape data set is deleted, nothing happens. A tape data set cannot be deleted through the DISP parameter. It is effectively deleted when the data set is written over.

A VSAM cluster cannot be deleted via the DELETE of the DISP parameter. For VSAM DISP=(OLD,DELETE) defaults to DISP=(OLD,KEEP).

When a data set is deleted, disk or tape, a step termination message appears.

```
IEF285I data set name                              DELETED
IEF285I VOL SER NOS=volume ser
```

This message is meaningful only for a disk data set.
   If a disk data set cannot be deleted, the message will be.

```
IEF283I data set name                         NOT DELETED n
IEF283I VOL SER NOS=volume ser
```

(n indicates the reason for failing to delete)

KEEP — Indicates that the data set is to be kept when the step terminates. The system takes no action and issues a message indicating the data set was kept.

```
IEF285I data set name                              . KEPT
IEF285I VOL SER NOS=volume ser
```

This message always appears when KEEP is coded or implied regardless of whether or not the data set exists. The only time this message will not appear is when DISP=(NEW,KEEP) is coded for a nonspecific tape request and the data set is not opened.
   A "NOT KEPT" message does not exist.
   Note that KEEP does not imply CATLG. As a result, DISP=(NEW,KEEP) should be a rarely used parameter.
   For VSAM clusters, KEEP is always in effect no matter what the DISP parameter contains.

CATLG — Indicates that the data set is to be kept and an entry for it placed in the catalog when the step terminates. If cataloging is successful, a message is issued.

```
IEF285I  data set name                           CATALOGED
IEF285I  VOL SER NOS= volume ser
```

If cataloging fails, for a NEW data set, the message will be

```
IEF287I   data set name                         NOT CATLGD n
IEF287I   VOL SER NOS= volume ser
```

(n indicates the reason for failing to add the catalog entry)
   If the data set to be cataloged is OLD or MOD, which was opened but did not extend into additional volume(s), the message will be

```
IEF287I   data set name                         NOT RECTLGD n
IEF287I   VOL SER NOS= volume ser
```

(n indicates the reason for failing to update the catalog entry)
   If the data set to be cataloged is OLD or MOD and has extended into additional volume(s), the message will be

```
IEF285I   data set name                          RECATALOGED
IEF285I   VOL SER NOS= volume ser, volume ser,...
```

CATLG implies KEEP. Since all data sets, with rare exceptions, should be cataloged, DISP=(NEW,CATLG) is a very common parameter.
   Chapter 6 is entirely dedicated to discussing the catalog.

UNCATLG — Indicates that the data set is to be kept but its entry removed from the catalog when the step terminates. If uncataloging is successful, a message is issued.

```
IEF285I data set name                         UNCATALOGED
IEF285I VOL SER NOS=volume ser
```

If uncataloging fails, the message will be

```
IEF287I   data set name                        NOT UNCTLGD n
IEF287I   VOL SER NOS= volume ser
```

(n indicates the reason for failing to uncatalog)
UNCATLG implies KEEP.

PASS — Indicates that an entry for the data set (containing dsn, volume, and unit information) be placed on a table in storage (Passed Data Set Queue). This entry is to be used in a subsequent step to "receive" the passed data set. A message will appear.

```
IEF285I data set name                        PASSED
IEF285I VOL SER NOS=volume ser
```

This message always appears when PASS is coded or implied. The only time this message will not appear is when DISP=(NEW,PASS) is used for a nonspecific tape request and the data set is not opened.

A "NOT PASSED" message does not exist.

When passing a tape data set, its device remains allocated and its volume normally remains mounted between steps so that the data set can be received in a later step of the same job with no operator intervention to mount the tape volume again.

Passing does not always guarantee that this will happen. If there is a long time between the step that passes and the step that receives, the system can dismount the volume, allocate the device to a different job or a later step of the same job, and then go through a normal mount request when the step that receives the data set is executed. If, on the other hand, the step that receives the data set immediately follows the step that passes it, the system never gives up the device to another job.

When PASS is used, the tape volume will not rewind at the end of the step. When the data set is received, the open will do the rewinding.

Chapter 9 is entirely dedicated to discussing passing and receiving data sets.

The abnormal (or conditional) disposition field: This field is used to tell the system how to dispose of the data set when the step terminates abnormally (ABENDs). It is required only if this disposition is different from the normal disposition.

DELETE, KEEP, CATLG, and UNCATLG have the same meaning they do in the normal disposition field. Note that PASS is not permitted in the abnormal disposition field.

The best example of using the abnormal disposition field is DISP=(NEW,CATLG,DELETE). If there is no ABEND, the data set is to be cataloged. If there is an ABEND, the data set is to be deleted. This eliminates future manual intervention to delete and uncatalog the data set in order to restart.

Defaults: Some defaults in the DISP parameter are fixed and others are variable.

• If the DISP parameter is omitted, the default is always (NEW DELETE).

```
//SORTWK01  DD  UNIT=SYSDA,SPACE=(CYL,(20,5))
//*          (NEW,DELETE) IS THE DEFAULT
```

- If the status field is omitted, the default is always NEW.

```
DISP=(,CATLG) ---> DISP=(NEW,CATLG)
```

- If the normal disposition field is omitted,
  — If the status field is NEW, the default is DELETE.
  — If the status field is OLD or SHR and the data set name non-temporary
    — If the DD statement is not receiving a passed data set, the default is KEEP.

```
//D1   DD   DSN=USER1.PERT,DISP=SHR
```

  — If the DD statement is receiving a passed data set, which was created during the execution of the job and was never given a permanent disposition, the default is DELETE.

```
//S1    EXEC   PGM=PR
//DD1   DD     DISP=(,PASS),DSN=USER1.PDST,UNIT=SYSDA,
//             DCB=(BLKSIZE=23440,LRECL=80,RECFM=FB),
//             SPACE=(TRK,(50,10),RLSE)
//S2    EXEC   PGM=PC
//DD2   DD     DISP=OLD,DSN=USER1.PDST
```

In DD2 DISP=OLD defaults to DISP=(OLD,DELETE)

  — If the DD statement is receiving a passed data set, which was created during the execution of the job but was given a permanent disposition since being created, the default is KEEP.

```
//S1    EXEC   PGM=PR
//DD1   DD     DISP=(,PASS),DSN=USER1.PDST,UNIT=SYSDA,
//             DCB=(BLKSIZE=23440,LRECL=80,RECFM=FB),
//             SPACE=(TRK,(50,10),RLSE)
//S2    EXEC   PGM=PC,COND=(4,LT)
//DD2   DD     DISP=(OLD,CATLG),DSN=USER1.PDST
//S3    EXEC   PGM=PF,COND=(4,LT)
//DD3   DD     DISP=(OLD,PASS),DSN=USER1.PDST
//S4    EXEC   PGM=PK,COND=(4,LT)
//DD4   DD     DISP=OLD,DSN=USER1.PDST
```

In DD4 DISP=OLD defaults to DISP=(OLD,KEEP)

— If the DD statement is receiving a passed data set which existed before the job began execution, the default is KEEP.

```
//S1    EXEC   PGM=PR
//DD1   DD     DISP=(SHR,PASS),DSN=USER1.LONE
//S2    EXEC   PGM=PK,COND=(4,LT)
//DD2   DD     DISP=SHR,DSN=USER1.LONE
```

```
In DD2 DISP=SHR defaults to DISP=(SHR,KEEP)
```

Despite the several possible defaults for DISP=OLD or DISP=SHR, their use is extremely common. When not receiving a passed data set, they always safely default to DISP=(OLD,KEEP) and DISP=(SHR,KEEP), respectively.

— If the status field is OLD or SHR and the data set name temporary, the default is PASS.

```
//DD1   DD   DISP=OLD,DSN=&&TEMP
```

DISP=OLD defaults to DISP=(OLD,PASS) and the following message will appear in the output.

```
IEF648I   INVALID DISP FIELD - PASS SUBSTITUTED
```

— If the status field is MOD, which defaults to an existing data set, MOD works the same as OLD and SHR.
— If the status field is MOD, which defaults to NEW, the default of the second field is DELETE.

DISP=MOD can default to (MOD,KEEP), (MOD,DELETE), (MOD,PASS), and (NEW DELETE). In view of all these possibilities, it is recommended that defaults not be practiced with MOD.

— If the abnormal disposition field is omitted, the default is the normal disposition field.

5.4 THE UNIT PARAMETER

The UNIT parameter identifies:

- The device type or device address where the volume is mounted or, for tape, will be mounted. The volume is the one where the data set resides (or will reside, if DISP is NEW).
- The number of devices to be allocated to the data set.
- When the mount message is to be shown to the operator.

The UNIT parameter must be included in a DD statement when:

- Device information is not supplied by any other facility, specifically:

  — The catalog
  — The Passed Data Set Queue (see Section 9.2 in Chapter 9)
  — VOL=REF

- Multiple devices must be allocated (retrieving a multivolume disk data set and creating a multivolume disk data set by specific volume serials not included).
- Deferred mounting is desired
- Two tape data sets must be allocated to the same device.
- The data set to be retrieved is cataloged but the device specified in the catalog entry is too general, and a subset of this device must be specified.

General Syntax

The UNIT parameter can have two formats:

```
        ┌                      ┐ ┌              ┐ ┌         ┐
        │ device address       │ │              │ │         │
UNIT=(  │ generic device name  │ │ ,device count│ │ ,DEFER )│   keyword
        │ generated device name│ │ ,P           │ │         │   parameter
        └                      ┘ └              ┘ └         ┘
```

or

```
UNIT=AFF=ddname                    keyword parameter
```

device address — Identifies the exact device address. This notation is almost never used because:

- Users are seldom aware of device addresses.
- A particular device may not be available (may be offline).
- Device addresses may change when an installation reconfigures.

```
UNIT=724
```

generic device name — Identifies the device type using a universal system-supplied name.

```
UNIT=3380    UNIT=3400-5    UNIT=3480
```

generated device name — Identifies the device type using an installation-defined name. This is also known as a group name or an esoteric name.

```
UNIT=SYSDA    UNIT=DISK    UNIT=TAPE
```

Of the three, the generated name is by far the most commonly used. There are two reasons for this: First, they allow the UNIT parameter in JCL to remain the same when migrating from one model to another of the same device type. Rather than changing the UNIT parameter, the definition of the name is changed to correspond to the new device. If generic names were used, the UNIT parameter would have to be changed. Second, they permit a much more detailed description of devices than generic unit names, providing better control of device usage.

The generated names can be made to mean whatever an installation wishes them to mean. For example, UNIT=SYSDA can mean all 3380 devices of any density, or single density only, or a subset of double density devices, or a combination of all 3380 and 3350 devices. Actually, each generated name is associated with a number of device addresses decided by those responsible for generating the system.

SYSDA and TAPE are the most commonly used generated names, and they will be used throughout this book. Of course, for each installation their meaning can be different.

device count — Specifies the number of devices to be allocated for the data set. The limit is 59 devices. If omitted, the default is 1 except when DD statement describes a disk multivolume data set. In such case, device count default=number of volumes.

```
UNIT=(TAPE,2)    UNIT=(SYSDA,3)
```

UNIT=(,2) can also be used if the device is being supplied by the catalog

P — Requests the numbers of devices to be allocated be equal to the number of volumes explicitly requested (through VOL=SER or

VOL=REF) or gotten though the catalog (or Passed Data Set Queue). This is known as the parallel mount.

Parallel mount should never be used. It is automatic for disk and unreasonable (as well as dangerous) for tape. Allocating multiple devices for multivolume tape data sets is not always advisable, and when it is, it should never be more than two.

DEFER — Requests that the mount message to the operator (to mount a tape volume to a system-assigned device address) not be issued by the allocation routines (see Figure 1.7) but by the open routines when, and if, the data set is opened.

The common misconception about DEFER is that it postpones device allocation. It does not! It only postpones the mount message until the open occurs and eliminates it if there is no open. Device allocation is identical whether or not DEFER is used.

If UNIT=TAPE is coded, the mount message is issued by the Allocation routines. Even if the volume is never needed because the data set is not opened, the mount message still appears.

If UNIT=(TAPE,,DEFER) is coded, the mount message will appear only if the data set is opened. This is the basic usefulness of DEFER: to eliminate the unnecessary (and possibly confusing) mount message when there is no open.

Using DEFER for a data set that is opened is counterproductive. Since the operator will not see the message until open time, the volume cannot be mounted ahead of time and be ready at open.

DEFER should be used when the data set is not opened or opened conditionally (sometimes) (see Section 7.3.3 in Chapter 7 and Section 8.3.1 in Chapter 8).

DEFER must never be used with disk. Disk volumes are non-removable and not subject to mount messages.

For a JES3-managed device, DEFER is ignored when the device is premounted.

```
UNIT=(TAPE,,DEFER)
```

UNIT=(,,DEFER) can also be used if the device is being supplied by the catalog

AFF=ddanme — Requests that the device to be allocated must be the same as the one allocated in a previous DD statement, "ddname," of the same step.

This allows the user to allocate the same nonsharable device to two or more DD statements of the same step, thus saving one or more devices. Since two data sets could not possibly be active at the exact same time on the same (nonsharable) device, certain restrictions exist:

The DD statement that UNIT=AFF references must be closed before the DD statement that contains UNIT=AFF opens. (This restriction does not apply to concatenated DD statements; see Section 7.11 in Chapter 7 and Section 8.3.5 in Chapter 8.)

```
//D1        DD   DSN=USER1.TP1,DISP=OLD     tape data set
//D2        DD   DSN=USER1.TP2,DISP=(,CATLG),UNIT=AFF=D1
```

D1 and D2 will be allocated to the same device, but D1 must be closed before D2 opens. If not, the result will be S413-04 ABEND failure. When using a SORT product (DFSORT, SYNCSORT, or CASORT), DD statement SORTOUT can always use UNIT=AFF= SORTIN if both use tape. They are never open at the same time.

```
//SORTIN  DD   DSN=USER1.ITBS,DISP=OLD     tape data set
//SORTOUT DD   DSN=USER1.SOT,DISP=(,CATLG),UNIT=AFF=SORTIN
```

UNIT=AFF can be safely used for concatenated DD statements without being concerned about opening or closing.

```
//IN  DD   DSN=USER1.TP1,DISP=OLD
//    DD   DSN=USER1.TP2,DISP=OLD,UNIT=AFF=IN
//    DD   DSN=USER1.TP3,DISP=OLD,UNIT=AFF=IN
```

UNIT=AFF implies DEFER.

UNIT=AFF provides no practical benefit when used for disk, which is a sharable device. In today's nonremovable disk volume environment, requesting that two data sets be allocated the same physical device is tantamount to requesting that they reside on the same volume. To accomplish this, VOL=REF (or VOL=SER), not UNIT=AFF, should be used. Although it is often benign, UNIT=AFF can inhibit nonspecific allocation for new disk data sets and even cause a JCL error:

```
IEF702I jobname stepname ddname - UNABLE TO ALLOCATE
```

Generic names for tape and disk   Although generic names are seldom used in JCL, they may be needed for utilities or IDCAMS. In any case, it is a good idea to know them, because they can always be used if one is not familiar with the generated names. Generic names obsolete since long ago are omitted.

Tape:

Generic name	Requests
3400-3	A 3420 model tape device which contains 1600 BPI density.
3400-4	A 3420 model dual density tape device with 800 BPI and 1600 BPI density. This type of device is practically obsolete and rarely used.
3400-5	A 3420 model tape device which contains 6250 BPI density.
3400-6	A 3420 model dual density tape device with 1600 BPI and 6250 BPI density. This is the most common 3420-type device.
3480	A 3480 model tape device which uses cartridges (its density is 38000 BPI). Heavily used.

Disk:

Generic name	Requests
3330	A 3330 device, Model 1. This is an obsolete device.
3330-1	A 3330 device, Model 11. This is an obsolete device.
3350	A 3350 device. This is a near-obsolete device, but a few are still in use as of the writing of this book.
3375	A 3375 device. This is a near-obsolete device with few still in use as of the writing of this book.
3380	A 3380 device. This is the only device in heavy use. Single, double, or triple density.

Defaults:

There is no default for the device name. If it is not coded in the UNIT parameter and it is also not supplied by the catalog, the Passed Data Set Queue, or VOL=REF, the result will be a JCL error:

```
IEF210I jobname stepname ddname - UNIT FIELD SPECIFIES INCORRECT
                                  DEVICE NAME
```

This message may imply that a default exists and it is incorrect. Not true! The message actually means that the device name was needed but not coded.

In view of the fact that there is no default, it is always a good idea to code the UNIT parameter when DISP is NEW. It will always be needed, except when VOL=REF is also coded (not a very common occurrence), in which case the device type identified in the UNIT parameter will be ignored (unless it is a subset of what is supplied by VOL=REF). However, DEFER and device count, if coded, will not be ignored.

The device count, if omitted, defaults to one.

5.5 THE VOL PARAMETER

The main function of the VOL (or volume) parameter is to identify the volume(s) by serial number where an existing data set resides or where a new data set will reside.

The VOL parameter can also request:

- That a tape volume remain mounted between steps.
- For a multivolume data set, the sequence of the volume with which processing is to begin.
- The number of volumes that can be used for creating or extending a tape data set.
- The number of devices to allocate for a disk data set.

The VOL parameter must be coded:

- When retrieving a data set which is neither cataloged nor passed
- When retrieving a data set which is cataloged but the catalog must not be used.
- When creating a data set which must reside on a particular volume
- When a tape volume must remain mounted between steps and PASS cannot be coded
- When retrieving a multivolume data set and the volumes must be processed beginning with other than the first volume
- When creating a cataloged multivolume tape data set with more than five volumes.

General Syntax

```
{ VOL    }                                        [ ,SER=(vol1,vol2,...) ]
{ VOLUME } =([PRIVATE][,RETAIN][,volseq][,volcount] | ,REF=referback      | )
                                                  [ ,REF=dsname          ]
```

PRIVATE — This subparameter was intended for removable disk
volumes and allowed for a volume to be mounted and be given a
"PRIVATE" use attribute (see Section 8.2.7 in Chapter 8) for the
duration of the step.

For all practical purposes this is impossible with nonremovable
disk volumes and, therefore, PRIVATE should *never* be used. Disk
volumes assigned the "PRIVATE" use attribute are normally the
most common in an installation. However, a volume cannot be assigned this attribute by coding PRIVATE in the VOL parameter. The
attribute can only be assigned by the Initial Program Load (IPL)
process or by the MOUNT operator command.

Coding PRIVATE when creating a disk data set provides no benefit and can easily result in the cancellation of the job (by the operator). When retrieving a data set, coding PRIVATE is equally useless
but quite benign.

Coding PRIVATE for a tape data set is (and always was) unnecessary but benign. The volume of an old tape data set is always PRI-
VATE. The volume of a new tape data set is treated as PRIVATE if
the data set is opened and:

• Specific volume information is coded (VOL=SER or VOL=REF).

or

• Anything other than DELETE is coded in the DISP parameter.

RETAIN — Requests that a tape volume remain mounted between
steps so that it can be used in a later step of the same job with no
operator intervention to mount the tape volume again. The device
containing a RETAINed volume is not deallocated during step termination processing.

Under certain conditions, RETAIN may not have the intended effect. If a long time elapses between the step where RETAIN is coded
and the step where the volume is used again, the system can dis-

mount the volume, allocate the device to a different job or to a later step of the same job, and then go though a normal mount request when the step that needs the volume is executed. If, on the other hand, the step that uses the RETAINed volume immediately follows the step where RETAIN was coded, the system never gives up the device to another job.

When RETAIN is used, the volume will not rewind at the end of the step. If the same data set is opened in a subsequent step, the open will do the rewinding.

RETAIN is unnecessary if PASS is used in the DISP parameter.

```
VOL=(,RETAIN)
VOL=(,RETAIN,SER=000465)
```

Note that the commas normally found in place of omitted subparameters, volseq and volcount, are in this case omitted.

```
VOL=(,RETAIN,,,SER=000465)
```

This is due to the fact that SER is a minor keyword, as explained in Section 1.9 of Chapter 1. It is for the same reason that VOL=SER=111111 need not be coded as VOL=(,,,,SER=111111).

volseq — Determines the volume with which a multivolume data set will begin processing. Rarely used. The default is one.

```
VOL=(,2)
```

If the data set consists of two or more volumes, processing will begin with volume # 2. Volume # 1 will not be used.

volcount — Determines the number of volumes to be used. The meaning of the subparameter is different for tape and disk.

For Tape

Specifies the number of tape volumes that can be mounted when creating or retrieving a tape data set which is opened for output.

```
//OUT   DD   DSN=USER1.TPX,DISP(,CATLG,DELETE),UNIT=CART,
//             DCB=(BLKSIZE=32700,LRECL=100,RECFM=FB),VOL=(,,,40)
```

If volcount were not coded in the example above, the data set would be limited to five scratch volumes. A scratch tape volume is normally an expired volume whose contents are of no value to anyone. If more were needed, the result would be an SE37-04 or S837-08 ABEND failure. VOL=(,,,40) will allow up to 40 volumes to be mounted. Actually the true limit in effect is the nearest multiple of 15 plus 5 that is higher than the coded volcount and no higher than 255. The true limit in this case is 3 x 15 + 5 or 50. The same limit would be in effect if the coded volcount were any number between 36 and 50. Any attempt to exceed this limit causes the same ABEND failure mentioned before.

```
//OUT   DD  DSN=USER1.TPA,DISP(,CATLG,DELETE),UNIT=CART,
//          DCB=(BLKSIZE=32700,LRECL=100,RECFM=FB),
//          VOL=(,,,40,SER=(002034,000301))
```

The above example is basically the same as the previous one except that the first two volumes to be mounted will be those coded in SER. The remainder, up to the limit, will be scratch volumes.

```
//OUT   DD  DSN=USER1.TP2,DISP(MOD,CATLG),VOL=(,,,15)
//          UNIT=(,,DEFER)
```

In the above example, data set USER1.TP2 can extend into additional scratch volumes as long as the total of existing (as per catalog entry) and additional volumes does not exceed 15. The limit actually in effect will be 1 x 15 + 5, or 20. If more are needed, the result will be an SE37-04 or S837-08 ABEND failure.

If volcount were not coded in this example, the total of existing and additional (scratch) volumes cannot exceed 5.

```
//OUT   DD  DSN=USER1.TP3,DISP(MOD,CATLG),UNIT=(TAPE,,DEFER),
//          VOL=(,,,22,SER=(002372,001288,000287))
```

The above example is basically the same as the previous one except that the volume serials in this example are being supplied by SER rather than the catalog and the volcount is 22. The limit actually in effect will be 2 x 15 + 5, or 35.

DEFER was used in both of the preceding examples in order to prevent a mount message for the first volume from appearing on the operator console. If data set USER1.TP2 is assumed to be multi-volume, the first volume in either example will not be used. DEFER will cause the mount message to call directly for the last volume, which is the one needed.

The volcount subparameter will be ignored if it is less than or equal to the number of volumes identified in the catalog (for retrieving), or supplied by either VOL=SER or VOL=REF (for retrieving or creating).

If volcount is omitted or is coded with a value of less than 5, the default is 5.

The volcount for tape cannot exceed 255.

For Disk

Specifies the number of volumes to be allocated by a multivolume disk data set if:

- A DD statement creates a data set, contains VOL=SER or VOL=REF (specific request), and the coded volcount is greater than the number of volumes supplied by VOL=SER or VOL=REF.

Example:

```
//OUT   DD   DSN=USER1.DK2,DISP(,CATLG,DELETE),UNIT=SYSDA,
//           SPACE=(23440,(800,300),RLSE),DCB=BLKSIZE=23440
//           VOL=(,,,4,SER=(PACK23,PACK04))
```

In the example above, four volumes will be allocated, PACK23, PACK04 and two "STORAGE" volumes assigned by the system.

Coding UNIT=(SYSDA,4) and omitting the volcount would produce the same result.

- A DD statement retrieves a data set, and the coded volcount is greater than the number of volumes supplied by the catalog, VOL=SER or VOL=REF. Examples:

```
//OUT1 DD   DSN=USER1.DK3,DISP=(MOD,CATLG),VOL=(,,,2)
```

In the above example, if data set USER1.DSK3 resides on a single volume, two volumes will be allocated, the one identified in the catalog entry and the one "STORAGE" volume assigned by the system.

```
//OUT   DD   DSN=USER1.DK4,DISP(MOD,CATLG),UNIT=SYSDA,
//           VOL=(,,,2,SER=PACK01)
```

In the above example, two volumes will be allocated, PACK01, and one "STORAGE" volume assigned by the system.

Coding UNIT=(SYSDA,2) and omitting the volcount in either of the preceding two examples, would produce the same result.

The volcount subparameter will be ignored if it is coded in a DD statement:

- Which creates a data set and contains neither VOL=SER nor VOL=REF.
- When the coded volcount is less than or equal to the number of volumes identified in the catalog (for retrieving), or supplied by either VOL=SER or VOL=REF (for retrieving or creating).

If volcount is omitted, it will default:

- To n if UNIT=(SYSDA,n) is coded.
- To the number of volumes identified in the catalog (retrieving), or supplied by either VOL=SER or VOL=REF (retrieving or creating).
- To the greater of the two above, if both are present.
- To 1, if neither is present.

The volcount for disk cannot exceed 59.

SER=(vol1,vol2....) — Specifies the serial number(s) of the volume(s) to be used. The maximum number of volumes is 255.

A volume serial is a combination of alphabetic, numeric, and national characters ($ @ #) up to 6. A hyphen is also permitted. In a real environment, the number of characters is almost never less than 6. Volume serial PRIVAT and SCRTCH must not be coded. They are used by the system in operator messages.

REF=referback

referback — This can have three formats:

- *.stepname.ddname — Requests that the volume be the same as for DD statement "ddname" found in a previous step "stepname."

```
VOL=REF==*.STEP2.OUT
```

- *.ddname — Requests that the volume be the same as for a previous DD statement "ddname" found in the same step.

```
VOL=REF=*.DD1
```

- *.procexec.stepname.ddname — Requests that the volume be the same as for DD statement "ddname" found in a previous step "stepname" found within a procedure "procexec" (name of EXEC statement invoking the procedure).

```
VOL=REF=*.PR4.STEP6.DD3
```

Referbacks are not encouraged. They should be used only when they are necessary. A referback with a "stepname" will cause a JCL error if the referenced step does not execute. Such referbacks must be avoided for jobs where restart is required.

REF=dsname — Requests that the volume be the same as the one where data set "dsname" resides on. The data set must be cataloged (or passed). The data set does not even have to exist, as long as it is cataloged or passed. The name of the referenced data set need not appear anywhere else in the job.

```
VOL=REF=USER1.FILEA
```

When VOL=REF (referback or dsname) is used, the system supplies the volume as well as the unit information. Therefore, the UNIT parameter is usually unnecessary. If UNIT is coded with VOL=REF, the coded device name:

- Will be ignored if VOL=REF supplies a different device type, an identical device type, or a device type that is a subset of what is coded in the UNIT parameter.
- Will be used if it is a subset of the device type supplied by VOL=REF. This can result in a JCL error,

```
IEF702I jobname stepname ddname - UNABLE TO ALLOCATE
```

To avoid such an error, it is best to omit the UNIT parameter when VOL=REF is used, unless UNIT=AFF is needed when tape is used. UNIT=AFF is never ignored.

Even when the device name in the UNIT parameter is ignored, other subparameters in the UNIT parameter will not be ignored.

```
//OUT   DD   DSN=USER.NEWF,DISP=(,CATLG,DELETE),VOL=REF=USER1.TAP3
//            UNIT=(SYSDA,2,DEFER),SPACE=(TRK(500,100)),
//            DCB=(BLKSIZE=15000,LRECL=100,RECFM=FB)
```

In the example above, if the device supplied by VOL=REF is tape, SYSDA coded in the UNIT parameter will be ignored; however, 2 and DEFER, which appear in the UNIT parameter, will be used.

When VOL=REF (referback or dsname) references a multivolume data set, all volumes will be supplied if the data set is on disk, but only the last volume will be supplied if the data set is on tape.

If VOL=REF=USER1.F4 is coded and data set USER1.F4 is neither cataloged nor passed, the result will be a JCL error:

```
IEF212I jobname stepname ddname - DATA SET NOT FOUND
```

Defaults:

- There is no default for VOL=SER or VOL=REF. However, when both are omitted, no JCL error results. Instead, the meaning of the DD statement changes. For example, when retrieving and either VOL=SER or VOL=REF is coded, the catalog will not be used. If neither is coded, the catalog will be used.
- Volseq defaults to 1 and volcount defaults to 5 for tape and 1 for disk (assuming that one device requested and VOL=SER or VOL=REF does not supply multiple volumes).

5.6 THE SPACE PARAMETER

The SPACE parameter is used to:

- Request an initial amount of disk space to be allocated to a new data set.
- Request additional disk space for a new data set in the event that the initially allocated space is exhausted.
- Request additional disk space for an old data set when available space is exhausted.
- Release unused disk space for a new or old data set.
- Request space for PDS directory.

The SPACE parameter must be included in a DD statement when:

- A new disk data set is created.

- An old data set needs to alter its entitlement to additional space.
- An old disk data set must free up all unused space.

General Syntax

$$
\text{SPACE} = (\left\{\begin{array}{l} \text{TRK,} \\ \text{CYL,} \\ \text{blksize,} \end{array}\right\} (\text{prim-alloc[,sec-alloc][,directory]})
$$

$$
[\text{,RLSE}]\left[\begin{array}{l} \text{,CONTIG} \\ \text{,MXIG} \\ \text{,ALX} \end{array}\right] [\text{,ROUND}])
$$

TRK — Requests that space be allocated in tracks

CYL — Requests that space be allocated in cylinders

blksize — Specifies the average blocksize of the data set. The system will compute how many tracks (or cylinders if **ROUND** is coded) to allocate.

prim-alloc — Primary allocation or primary quantity. It identifies the number of tracks (if TRK is coded) or cylinders (if CYL is coded) or the number of blocks (if blksize is coded) that must be allocated during the allocation process for a new data set (see Figure 1.7) before the step begins execution. The system will allocate the requested space in one extent (one contiguous area of disk space). If this is not possible (and CONTIG is not coded), two extents will be used, then three and so on up to five extents. If as many as five extents still cannot satisfy the request, the result will be a JCL error:

```
IEF257I jobname stepname ddname - SPACE REQUESTED NOT
                                     AVAILABLE
```

If the request is nonspecific (no **VOL=SER** or **VOL=REF**), needing a storage volume, the JCL error message will be different:

```
IEF246I jobname stepname ddname - INSUFFICIENT SPACE ON
                                     STORAGE VOLUMES
```

The system will always allocate the primary quantity in the least number of extents possible on a single volume. The primary quantity cannot be split over multiple volumes.

The primary allocation cannot be omitted (coding 0 is allowed). It is ignored if the data set is old. Examples:

```
SPACE=(CYL,20)

SPACE=(TRK,100)

SPACE=(23440,200)
```

sec-alloc — Secondary allocation or secondary quantity. It identifies the number of tracks (if TRK is coded) or cylinders (if CYL is coded) or the number of blocks (if blksize is coded) that are to be allocated when all available space is exhausted while writing to the data set. The system will allocate the secondary quantity in the least number of extents possible, and just like the primary quantity, it can be given in as many as five extents, if necessary.

The system will always supply the specified secondary allocation when one is needed unless one of two events occurs:

• The allocated volume does not have enough space to satisfy the secondary allocation and no other volumes are allocated.
• The needed secondary allocation, if granted, will cause the data set to exceed 16 extents on the volume and no other volumes are allocated.

If either of these two conditions arises, the result will be a SB37-04 ABEND failure. For a PDS the ABEND can also be SE37-04. If another volume were allocated, the data set would keep on getting additional secondary allocations on this volume as long as space is available and the number of extents on the volume does not exceed 16. Please note that a PDS is confined to a single volume, while a sequential data set can extend into a maximum of 59 volumes (see Section 8.2.5 in Chapter 8).

The 16 extent-per-volume limit for a data set is system-supplied and cannot be altered.

The secondary allocation is optional. If omitted, it defaults to 0. When no secondary allocation is coded and the primary allocation is exhausted, the result is an SD37-04 ABEND failure.

The secondary allocation can be used for new as well as old data sets. The secondary allocation requested when the data set is created is recorded in the data set's DSCB (VTOC entry). If space is exhausted when the data set is retrieved as OLD and extended, the system attempts to provide the secondary allocation appearing in the DSCB. If, however, a SPACE parameter is included in the DD statement, the secondary allocation will be based on what is coded in this SPACE parameter rather than what appears in the data set's DSCB.

Note that the words "allocation" or "quantity" are not synonymous with the word "extent." Whenever possible an allocation (primary or secondary) will be one extent. However, an allocation can also be as many as five extents.

If a single extent secondary is allocated contiguous to a single extent primary (or another secondary), the two allocations will be treated as two extents rather than one despite the fact that the two extents together occupy contiguous space.

Consider a data set whose primary quantity of 50 tracks is in a single extent. A 20-track secondary quantity is allocated, also in a single extent, immediately adjacent to the primary. Even though the two allocations occupy 70 tracks of contiguous space, they will be treated as two extents, rather than one.

Secondary allocation should not be coded for direct (DSORG=DA) data sets.

Examples:

```
SPACE=(CYL,(20,5))
```

```
SPACE=(TRK,(100,30))
```

```
SPACE=(23440,(200,50))
```

directory — Specifies the number of directory blocks (256 bytes each) to be assigned to the directory of a partitioned data set.

On the average, six directory entries can fit into a directory block. Theoretically, this number can be used to estimate the size of the directory. In view of the fact that the directory does not expand dynamically and six is only an approximation, three or four (number of entries per block) are a better choice to use for estimating. When the directory is exhausted, the result is an S013-14 ABEND failure.

The directory quantity, if not coded, defaults to zero; therefore, the directory quantity must be specified for a new PDS. If it is not, S013-14 ABEND failure will occur if an attempt is made to add the first member to the PDS.

If the directory quantity is coded for a sequential data set, it will be ignored. When the program begins to write to the data set, it will start at the beginning of the data set, writing where the directory is supposed to be. No failure will occur and the resulting data set is sequential.

The directory quantity is taken away from the beginning of the primary allocation if TRK or CYL is coded in the SPACE parameter. When blksize is coded, the system adds the directory blocks to the data blocks and then computes the amount of primary space.

Examples:

SPACE=(CYL,(20,5,10)) or SPACE=(CYL,(20,,10)) if no secondary

SPACE=(TRK,(100,30,8)) or SPACE=(TRK,(100,,8)) if no secondary

SPACE=(23440,(200,50,9)) or SPACE=(23440,(200,,9)) if no secondary

RLSE — Requests that any unused space be freed when the data set is closed. This works for both new and old data sets, provided they were opened for output. Space will be released on the boundary used in the SPACE parameter. If tracks were allocated, unused tracks will be released. If cylinders were allocated, entirely unused cylinders will be released.

Using RLSE is highly recommended for data sets not intended for future expansion. Temporary data sets are ideal candidates. For data sets that expand in future runs, RLSE can result in a larger number of extents and, possibly, a premature SB37-04 ABEND failure.

RLSE will be ignored if:

• The data set is opened by another user.
• The data set is shared by another job.
• The step ABENDs

RLSE is optional. If not coded, unused space remains allocated. Examples:

```
SPACE=(CYL,(20,5),RLSE)

SPACE=(TRK,(100,30),RLSE)

SPACE=(23440,(200,50),RLSE)
```

CONTIG — Requests that the primary allocation be allocated in one extent (contiguous). If contiguous space is not available, the result will be a JCL error.

```
IEF257I jobname stepname ddname - SPACE REQUESTED NOT
                                   AVAILABLE
```

or

```
IEF246I jobname stepname ddname — INSUFFICIENT SPACE ON
                                   STORAGE VOLUMES
```

In view of the fact that the system will always allocate contiguous space, if possible, coding CONTIG is counterproductive in the vast majority of cases. It should be used only for direct data sets which are often used online, and, if they have intensive activity, multiple extents can have a degrading effect.

CONTIG applies only to the primary allocation. Secondary allocations are not bound by CONTIG. Examples:

```
SPACE=(CYL,20,,CONTIG)
```

```
SPACE=(TRK,100,,CONTIG)
```

```
SPACE=(23440,200,,CONTIG)
```

MXIG — Requests that the largest single extent equal to or larger than the primary quantity be allocated. It provides a way to allocate a large extent without risking a JCL error. The amount of space allocated, however, is unpredictable. Rarely used. Example:

```
SPACE=(CYL,2,,MXIG)
```

ALX — Requests that the largest five extents equal to or larger than the primary quantity be allocated. It provides a way to allocate a lot of space without risking a JCL error. The amount of space allocated, again, is unpredictable. Rarely used. Example:

```
SPACE=(CYL,2,,ALX)
```

Note that if MXIG or ALX is coded on a DD statement allocated to an empty volume, the entire volume's space will be allocated.

ROUND — Requests that cylinders rather than tracks be allocated when the blocksize type of SPACE parameter is used. ROUND is ignored if used with TRK or CYL.

When ROUND it omitted, the system will allocate in terms of tracks. Example:

```
SPACE=(23440,(200,50),,,ROUND)
```

There exists a way to request that the primary allocation begin at a particular track. This method is almost never used.

```
SPACE=(ABSTR,(500,99,10))
```

This example requests that 500 tracks be allocated beginning with track #99. 10 represents directory blocks. This parameter is unreasonable, inconvenient, and risky because:

- The exact location of a data set is seldom of interest to the user.
- The user is seldom familiar with the exact contents of a volume and cannot know if the requested tracks are available.
- The primary allocation can only consist of one extent.
- No secondary allocations are available.
- Space cannot be requested in terms of blocks.

This type of SPACE parameter will not be used or mentioned again in this book.

The blksize value in the SPACE parameter is never compared to the BLKSIZE subparameter of the DCB parameter (which may or may not be coded). During the allocation process (see Figure 1.7) the system has no way of knowing if it reflects the true blocksize of the data set and will use it to compute the primary allocation. For secondary allocations, however, the actual blocksize will be used.

Section 8.2.4 in Chapter 8 contains a section with an extensive discussion on space considerations.

Defaults:

Secondary allocation and directory space default to 0 when omitted. RLSE, CONTIG, MXIG, ALX and ROUND are optional subparameters. Primary allocation and type of allocation (TRK, CYL or blksize) have no default and must be coded.

For Virtual I/O (VIO) data sets (see Section 10.9 in Chapter 10), a default exists:

```
SPACE=(1000,(10,50))
```

A default also exists for Mass Storage (3850) data sets. However, 3850 is an obsolete device and is not discussed in this book.

5.7 THE LABEL PARAMETER

The LABEL parameter can specify:

• The sequence of a tape data set on a volume.
• The type of label of the data set.
• Expiration date for the data set.

Note: The LABEL parameter can also provide password protection, and for a BSAM data set which is opened for both input and output (INOUT or OUTIN), disallow either of the two. However, these functions are very rarely used (password protection is almost always supplied by one of the available security packages, RACF, Top Secret, or ACF2), and they will only be briefly mentioned later.

The LABEL parameter must be coded when:

• A tape data set is created and its sequence on the volume is greater than one.
• A noncataloged tape data set is retrieved and its sequence on the volume is greater than one.
• A data set other than standard labeled is created or retrieved.
• A data set with ASCII labels is created or retrieved.
• An expiration date must be supplied for a new data set.

General Syntax

```
                                  ┌,PASSWORD ┐ ┌,IN ┐ ┌,EXPDT=nnnn ┐
LABEL=([seq-no][,type] │,NOPWREAD │ │,OUT│ │,RETPD=yyddd│)
                                  └          ┘ └     ┘ └            ┘
```

seq-no — Identifies the sequence number of the data set on a tape volume. 1 to 4 digits. If omitted, it defaults to 1. If 0 is coded, it defaults to 1. Maximum: 9999.

The sequence number is ignored when:

• Retrieving or creating a disk data set. The sequence number is meaningless for a disk data set.
• Retrieving a tape data set through the catalog. The sequence number will be supplied by the catalog.

• Receiving a passed tape data set. The sequence number will be supplied by the Passed Data Set Queue.

Example:

```
LABEL=2
```

type — Identifies the type of label for the data set

There are many types of labels:

SL — Indicates IBM standard label. If the subparameter is omitted, SL is the default. All disk data sets are SL (the DSCB of a disk data set is its label) and so is the vast majority of tape data sets. Figure 5.2 shows how the labels are positioned on a tape volume.

NL — Indicates that no labels are used. NL is not commonly used. Normally, NL is used for a tape coming from or going to another installation which has no SL capabilities (i.e., a mini). Figure 5.2 shows the contents of a volume with NL data sets.

BLP — Bypass Label Processing. Indicates that labels will not be recognized and will be treated as ordinary files. BLP is used as a last resort when neither SL nor NL can accomplish what is required.

LTM — Leading Tape Mark. Indicates that no labels are used and the volume begins with a tape mark. DOS/VSE nonlabeled volumes begin with a tape mark, and LTM is specifically designed for them.

The first three of the four above are the most commonly used (LTM is likely to be used only in a VSE to MVS conversion or when a VSE NL tape must be processed in an MVS environment). Chapters 7 and 8 describe how they are used to retrieve and create data set.

Two others are rarely used, but are worth a brief mention:

SUL — Indicates IBM standard and user labels. Up to eight additional 80-byte records in addition to header 1 and header 2 can be used. The installation must develop its own software to write and process the additional labels.

AL — Indicates IBM standard label recoded in ASCII code, as opposed to the normally used EBCDIC code. The data is also recorded in ASCII.

Two remaining type of labels, NSL (Nonstandard Label) and AUL (ASCII Standard and User Label), are almost never used. Examples:

```
LABEL=(2,SL)
```

```
LABEL=(,NL)
```

```
LABEL=(2,BLP)
```

```
LABEL=(,LTM)
```

PASSWORD and NOPWREAD — Both refer to a password protection system which basically stopped being used when comprehensive security packages (such as RACF, ACF2, and Top Secret) were made available. No explanation will be provided here.

IN and OUT — IN indicates that a data set opened for INOUT using BSAM can only be read. OUT indicates that a data set opened for OUTIN using BSAM can only be written to. Very rarely used.

EXPDT=yyddd — Identifies the Julian date until which the data set will remain unexpired. yy identifies the last two digits of the year. ddd identifies the day, from 1 to 366. Unexpired data sets on disk (seldom used) cannot be deleted through JCL (IEHPROGM or IDCAMS must be used). Expiration dates on tape are almost exclusively used for the benefit of tape library software packages (such as TMS or TLMS, both non-IBM software), which use the expiration date to determine when a volume becomes "scratch." A scratch volume is an expired volume whose contents are not important.

If Data Facility Product (DFP) Version 2.3 (or later) is installed, the expiration date can also be coded as EXPDT=yyyy/ddd allowing for dates after December 31, 1999, up to year 2155. yyyy identifies the last two digits of the year. ddd identifies the day, from 1 to 366. With this version of DFP, EXPDT=99365, EXPDT=99366, EXPDT=1999/365, and EXPDT=1999/366 will be treated as "never-expire" dates. Data sets with these expiration dates will not expire even if the indicated dates are passed. Examples:

```
LABEL=EXPDT=93001 data set remains unexpired until 1/1/1993
```

```
LABEL=EXPDT=2005/365 data set remains unexpired until 12/31/2005
```

RETPD=nnnn — Specifies the number of days that the data set will remain unexpired. nnnn is a number from 1 to 9999. The system adds the number coded in EXPDT to today's date and makes that the expiration date.

With Data Facility Product (DFP) Version 2.3 (or later), if RETPD results in an expiration date of 1999/365, it will be treated as 2000/001. Example:

```
LABEL=RETPD=10
```

Note that both EXPDT and RETPD result in an expiration date. The first is more convenient when a far-off date must be given: LABEL=EXPDT=94365. The second is better suited for repetitive executions, like production jobs. EXPDT would have to be changed every day for a data set created daily which must remain unexpired for 5 days. LABEL=EXPDT=5 requires no changes at all.

Label verification: When retrieving an SL tape data set, both the volume serial and the data set name will be verified. When creating an SL tape data set with VOL=SER or VOL=REF, only the volume serial will be verified.

When retrieving an NL tape data set, neither the volume serial nor data set name can be verified. However, only an NL tape volume can be mounted. An SL volume will be rejected. When creating an NL tape data set, an SL scratch tape volume can be used, if the installation permits it. If so, the label will be overlaid and destroyed (see Section 8.3.2 in Chapter 8).

Defaults: If omitted, the LABEL parameter defaults to (1,SL). There are four ways to supply the same information:

• Omit the LABEL parameter
• Code LABEL=(1,SL)
• Code LABEL=(,SL) 1 is the default
• Code LABEL=1 SL is the default

If neither EXPDT nor RETPD is coded, the default expiration date is 00000. For installations using TMS or TLMS, a default retention period (installation defined) for tape data sets will exist. To avoid getting this default, LABEL=EXPDT=00000 must be coded.

5.8 THE DCB PARAMETER

The DCB parameter specifies values used to complete the Data Control Block (DCB) when a data set is opened. A DCB is constructed by the language processor (compiler or assembler), based on the appropriate instructions of the language being used, and resides inside the code of the program. In many languages, the acronym DCB does not appear in any of the instructions. The compiler, however, collects information and defaults from various parts of the program and constructs the DCB. A DCB will exist for every non-VSAM data set to be opened by the program (for input or output). Certain values must be "hard-coded" in the DCB by the program itself. Others can be left out, giving the user the option of supplying these values via the DCB parameter (as well as other means).

There are three suppliers of DCB information:

- Values supplied by the program, referred to as hard-coded. When a value is hard-coded, it cannot be changed unless the program is changed.
- Values coded in the DCB parameter of the DD statement. These values will be ignored if they are already hard-coded. Note that, regretfully, no messages will appear identifying the ignored values or the hard-coded ones in use.
- Values from the standard label of the data set. The values supplied by the label are limited to: BLKSIZE, LRECL, RECFM, DSORG, OPTCD, KEYLEN, and RKP. The last two are strictly ISAM sub-parameters, and OPTCD is mostly for ISAM data sets also (ISAM is obsolete and is not discussed in this book). Values from the label will not be used if they are hard-coded inside the program or coded in the DCB parameter.

The DCB parameter must be coded when:

- A data set is retrieved using NL, BLP, or LTM in the LABEL parameter and the DCB in the program is incomplete.

- An SL data set, disk or tape, is retrieved, the DCB in the program is incomplete and the values needed to fill it out cannot be supplied by the label.
- A data set is created and the DCB in the program is incomplete.
- A (+1) GDG generation is created and a cataloged model DSCB is used (see Section 11.4 in Chapter 11).

General Syntax

```
DCB=([referback]|[model][,subparameter][,subparameter],...)
```

referback — This can have three formats:

- *.stepname.ddname — Requests that the DCB parameter be copied from DD statement "ddname" found in a previous step "stepname."

```
DCB=*.STEP2.OUT
```

- *.ddname — Requests that the DCB parameter be copied from a previous DD statement "ddname" found in the same step.

```
DCB=*.DD1
```

- *.procexec.stepname.ddname — Requests that the DCB parameter be copied from DD statement "ddname" found in a previous step "stepname" found within a procedure "procexec" (name of EXEC statement invoking the procedure).

```
DCB=*.PS4.STEP6.DD3
```

Note that the DCB referback copies the DCB parameter as opposed to the DSN and VOL=REF referbacks which acquire the data set name and the volser, respectively, whether or not the DSN and VOL parameters are present in the referenced DD statement. If the DCB referback refers to a DD statement which contains no DCB parameter, nothing is copied and no message appears informing the user of that fact.

model — Specifies the name of a data set which:

- Must be cataloged. If it is not, the result will be a JCL error:

```
IEF212I jobname stepname ddname - DATA SET NOT FOUND
```

- Must be on disk (tape data sets cannot be used).
- Must reside on a volume that is accessible (online).

This data set is called a model DSCB. The DCB information from the label of the model is extracted and can be used (if not hard-coded in the program). In addition to DCB information, the expiration date is also provided. If the expiration date is undesirable, the LABEL parameter should be used to supply the desirable date.

subparameter — There is a vast number of subparameters, the great majority of which are seldom or never used. This book will discuss those that are likely to be used in an ordinary everyday environment.

- BLKSIZE — Specifies the size of the block (also known as the physical record). It can be as small as a few bytes (this varies for different devices) and as large as 32,760 bytes.

  For RECFM=FB, the blocksize must be a multiple of the logical record length, and it identifies the exact size of the block. For RECFM=VB, the blocksize can be any value up to the limit but at least 4 bytes larger than the logical record length. It identifies the maximum size block and it includes the 4 control bytes at the beginning of the block (see Figure 1.3).

  For RECFM=U, the blocksize can be any value up to the limit. It identifies the maximum size block.

  For tape data sets recorded in ASCII, the blocksize cannot exceed 2,048 bytes.

  There is no default for BLKSIZE.

```
DCB=BLKSIZE=23400
```

- LRECL — Specifies the size of the logical record. The maximum size is 32,760, and it cannot be larger than the blocksize, unless RECFM=VBS is used.

  For RECFM=FB, the logical record length can be any size up to and including the blocksize.

  For RECFM=VB, the logical record length can be any size up to 4 bytes less than the blocksize. It identifies the maximum size logical record, and it includes the 4 control bytes at the beginning of the logical record (see Figure 1.3).

  For RECFM=U, the logical record has no meaning. In the label, it will appear as LRECL=0.

  There is no default for LRECL.

```
DCB=(BLKSIZE=23400,LRECL=100)
```

- RECFM — Specifies the record format. There are several values (or combinations of values) that can be coded, the most common of which are:

  - F — All blocks and all logical records are fixed in size (see Figure 1.3).
  - V — Blocks as well as logical records are of variable size. The first 4 bytes of each block describe its size. The first 4 bytes of each logical record describe its size (see Figure 1.3).
  - B — One or more logical records reside in each block. B cannot be coded alone. It must follow F or V.
  - U — Blocks are of variable size. There are no logical records. This record format is rarely used except in load libraries which are always RECEM=U.
  - S — For fixed-size records, it indicates that no short blocks are permitted anywhere but the end of the data. For variable-size records, it indicates that a logical record can span more than one block. S cannot be coded alone. It must follow F, V, FB, or VB.
  - A — Indicates that the first character of each record is an ANSI control character to be used for printer carriage control. A cannot be coded alone. It must follow F, V, FB, VB, or U.
  - M — Indicates that that the first character of each record is a machine control character to be used for printer carriage control. Rarely used. ANSI code is much more common. M cannot be coded alone. It must follow F, V, FB, VB or U.
  - T — Requests the "track overflow" feature, and it is mentioned here only because coding it would be a waste of time. It specifies, in theory, that a block can begin in one track and continue into the next one, if necessary. However, this feature is not supported with currently available disk devices (3350, 3375, or 3380), and, if coded, it would be ignored.

```
DCB=(BLKSIZE=23400,LRECL=100,RECFM=FB)
```

If RECFM is not supplied through any means, U is the default. This is an unusual default considering that U is the least common record format.

- DEN — Identifies the density of a tape data set.

— DEN=2 indicates 800 BPI (bytes per inch) density. Near obsolete.

— DEN=3 indicates 1600 BPI density

— DEN=4 indicates 6250 BPI density

— DEN=0 and DEN=1 refer to 7-track tape, which is obsolete and not discussed in this book.

The DEN subparameter in needed only if the desired density for an output tape data set, using a 3420 model tape device, is other than 6250 BPI. It is never needed and, if coded, ignored, for input data sets. The DEN subparameter is meaningless for a 3480 tape data set, which can have only one density, 38000 BPI.

```
DCB=(BLKSIZE=32760,LRECL=100,RECFM=FB,DEN=3)
```

• BUFNO — Identifies the number of buffers to be constructed in virtual storage by the OPEN routines, which will contain the blocks to be read in or written out. If a small blocksize is used, a large number of buffers can improve I/O performance. If not coded, the default is 5. If an adequately large blocksize is used, the 5 default buffers are normally sufficient. The maximum is 255. Coding for BUFNO a number greater than 5 may require that the REGION parameter be increased.

• OPTCD — This subparameter can have several values. The most common is Q. When reading a tape data set coded in ASCII, OPTCD=Q will translate ASCII code to the native IBM EBCDIC. When writing, it will translate EBCDIC to ASCII. ASCII is used by several mainframe computers and practically all minicomputers.

```
DCB=(BLKSIZE=2000,LRECL=100,RECFM=FB,DEN=3,OPTCD=Q)
```

• EROPT — Specifies what action to take if an unrecoverable I/O error occurs while reading or writing a block.

ABE — Cause an ABEND failure (probably a S001 ABEND).

SKP — Skip the block containing the error.

ACC — Accept the block containing the error.

The default is ABE. The other two options are risky and they should not be used unless a way exists to correct a block with incorrect information (ACC) or provide missing data (SKP). Normally the default ABE is assumed.

```
DCB=(BLKSIZE=2000,LRECL=100,RECFM=FB,DEN=3,OPTCD=Q,EROPT=ACC)
```

DSORG — Identifies the organization of the data set.

> PS — Specifies physical sequential organization (mostly QSAM and sometimes BSAM. EXCP and TCAM are remote possibilities).

> PO — Specifies partitioned organization (BPAM and, rarely, EXCP). Programs written in many high-level languages (like COBOL) cannot use BPAM.

> DA — Specifies direct organization (BDAM and, rarely, EXCP).

This subparameter is practically never required in the DCB parameter. It is difficult to imagine a program that does not hardcode DSORG. If the data set is opened, the proper DSORG will be supplied whether or not it is coded in the DCB parameter. DSORG can be coded when creating a disk data set which will not be opened (until a later time) to identify the intended organization.

Section 7.10 in Chapter 7 and Section 8.4 in Chapter 8 discuss DCB considerations for retrieving and creating data sets.

5.9 THE FREE PARAMETER

The FREE parameter is used to:

- Deallocate a device during the close process as opposed to step termination.
- Release a data set from an exclusive usage status (caused by DISP of OLD, MOD, or NEW).
- To make a SYSOUT data set available for printing before the job terminates.

The FREE parameter is used only if one of the items mentioned above is necessary.

General Syntax

```
FREE={CLOSE|END}
```

CLOSE — Indicates that the device will be deallocated or the data set will be released from exclusive usage by the job when the data set is closed.

For a SYSOUT data set, it indicates that printing can begin when the data set is closed, rather than waiting for job termination.

END — Indicates that the device will be deallocated or the data set will be released from exclusive usage by the job when the step terminates. For a SYSOUT data set it indicates that printing is to begin after job termination.

Dangers:

- If the data set is opened more than once, since FREE=CLOSE deallocates the device when the data set is closed, there will be no device allocated during the second open (unless the program performs dynamic allocation). A message is issued:

```
IEC130I ddname - DD STATEMENT MISSING
```

  Although processing continues, an attempt to read or write will cause an unpredictable failure, most likely a program check (S0Cx ABEND failure).
- If FREE=CLOSE is used for a disk data set, the data set becomes sharable after closing, permitting another job, which updates the data set to begin execution. The data set, however, may be updated by later steps of the first job, resulting in possible concurrent updates, which can affect the data set's integrity.
- If FREE=CLOSE is used for many SYSOUT data sets in the same job, it becomes a logistical problem for the operator to collect all the printouts together as a job, without losing some.

FREE=CLOSE can be beneficial if a step uses a tape data set which is closed long before step termination.

In JES3, the FREE parameter should be avoided for JES3 managed devices.

Using FREE=CLOSE with a disk data set is pointless from a device utilization standpoint (disk is sharable) and still dangerous in the event of multiple opens. Example:

```
//OUT   DD   DSN=USER1.TPSETX,DISP=(,CATLG),UNIT=TAPE,
//           DCB=(BLKSIZE=32760,LRECL=100,RECFM=FB),
//           FREE=CLOSE
```

FREE=CLOSE will be ignored when:

• The DD statement is part of a concatenation.
• The step ABENDs before the data set is closed.
• The DD statement containing the FREE parameter is referenced by a DD statement in the same step using DSN=referback or VOL=REF=referback.
• The data set is passed or RETAIN is coded in the VOL parameter.

Defaults:

If the FREE parameter is omitted, FREE=END is the default.

6

Using the Catalog

Next to the VTOC, the most important structure for a non-VSAM data set is the catalog. Although use of the catalog is theoretically optional, it can be treated as virtually mandatory from a practical standpoint. For a nontemporary non-VSAM data set not to be cataloged, a good reason must exist. There are few such reasons.

This chapter will discuss the different catalog structures available, how the system uses the catalog, how the user can control the use of the catalog, and the dangers that exist when the catalog is used improperly.

6.1 DEFINITIONS

There are three different catalog structures and all or some of them could be in use in a given installation: CVOL catalogs, VSAM catalogs, and ICF catalogs. As of the writing of this book, the most commonly used catalog is ICF. Ultimately, all MVS/XA installations are expected to migrate to an ICF environment.

- A *CVOL catalog* (sometimes referred to as an OS catalog) is the original catalog used by all OS systems (such as PCP, MFT and MVT) before MVS. Under MVS, CVOL catalogs (which could not contain VSAM data set entries) were to be replaced by VSAM catalogs.
- A *VSAM catalog* became available with MVS and used VSAM as its organization. VSAM catalogs, which could be used for both

VSAM and non-VSAM data sets, were intended to replace CVOL catalogs. Instead, the two were used together: CVOL catalogs for non-VSAM and VSAM catalogs for VSAM data sets.
- An *ICF catalog* (Integrated Catalog Facility) was the replacement for the previous two catalogs and also uses VSAM as its organization. In 1983, MVS installations began converting from VSAM/CVOL to ICF catalogs. Since most MVS installations are in an ICF catalog environment, this book will focus on ICF catalogs, but the others will be mentioned when needed.

The difference between ICF and CVOL/VSAM catalogs may be transparent to the average user. ICF and VSAM catalogs basically work the same from an average user standpoint. CVOL catalogs work almost the same, with the following exceptions:

- CVOL catalogs, as mentioned above, can contain only non-VSAM data set entries.
- CVOL catalogs cannot be specified in a JOBCAT or STEPCAT DD statement.
- The IEHPROGM utility must be used to build a GDG base (index) in a CVOL (IDCAMS must be used for VSAM and ICF catalogs).
- Certain IDCAMS commands, such as DEFINE NONVSAM, will not work with CVOL catalogs.
- The name of a CVOL catalog has a particular format: SYSCTLG.Vvvvvvv (where vvvvvv is the volume on which the CVOL catalog resides). The names of ICF and VSAM catalogs have no particular format.
- A CVOL catalog entry does not contain creation/expiration date, owner information, or release number. VSAM and ICF catalog entries do.

There are two types of catalogs in use: master catalog and user catalog:

- The *master catalog* is a mandatory part of MVS/XA, and there is one master catalog per system. It must be an ICF (or VSAM) catalog. It contains entries for system data sets (those whose names normally begin with the qualifier SYS1), user catalogs, and alias names for user catalogs (the alias names will be explained in Section 6.3 in this chapter). It is write-protected and only a few individuals (such as systems programmers) have the authority to write in it. Consequently, entries for ordinary data sets will not normally be found in the master catalog. In a multisystem environment, the master catalog of one system is not available to (or sharable with) other systems.

• A *user catalog* contains entries for ordinary user data sets. Although it is theoretically optional, in practice every installation uses several of them. The number of user catalogs varies from one installation to another. Five to 15 user catalogs is a representative range, although many more are possible. Normally, user catalogs are sharable across all systems. A user is assigned a user catalog by the installation's technical staff.

A data set is said to be cataloged if it has an entry in a user catalog (or, rarely, the master catalog). In this book, "the catalog" is used to mean "the appropriate user catalog." "Master catalog" will be used infrequently to mean exactly what it says.

6.2 THE CONTENTS OF A CATALOG ENTRY

A catalog entry for a non-VSAM data set contains the following information:

• The data set name.
• The volume serial where the data set resides.
• The device type where the volume is meant to be mounted.
• The sequence of the data set on the (tape) volume (this number can be 1 to 9999; 0 means the same as 1). The number will always be 0 for disk data sets and is meaningless.
• Creation date and expiration date. This information is of relatively little importance (not available in a CVOL).
• Owner and release number. This information is of virtually no importance (not available in a CVOL).

The first three items above (the first four for tape) are the essential pieces of information for a non-VSAM catalog entry.

The contents of a non-VSAM catalog entry are shown in Figure 6.1 as produced by an IDCAM's command:

```
LISTCAT ENTRIES(USER1.FILEA) ALL
```

All information in this entry is self-explanatory, except the device type. The 8-digit hexadecimal number that appears under "DEVTYPE' is known as the UCB type, or the description of the device in the UCB (Unit Control Block), which resides in the nucleus

```
NONVSAM ------- USER1.FILEA
    IN-CAT --- ICFCAT.VPACK14
    HISTORY
        OWNER IDENT--------USER1     CREATION----------89.299
        RELEASE----------------2     EXPIRATION--------00.000
    VOLUMES
        VOLSER------------000331     DEVTYPE------X'78008080'

        FSEQN-----------------1
```

Figure 6.1 The contents of a catalog entry (ICF or VSAM).

of MVS/XA. For each device there exists a UCB. A list of the common UCB types, as well as which device they represent, is shown below:

UCB TYPE	DEVICE
X'3010200E	3380 disk (single, double or triple density)
X'3010200C'	3375 disk
X'3050200B'	3350 disk
X'78008080'	3480 tape (cartridge)
X'32008003'	3400-5 tape (3420)
X'32108003'	3400-6 tape (3420)
X'34008003'	3400-3 tape (3420)

6.3 WHEN AND HOW THE CATALOG IS USED

For non-VSAM data sets, the catalog will be used if the user explicitly or implicitly requests it.

An explicit request means the use of CATLG or UNCATLG. When these subparameters are coded in the DISP parameter, the step termination routines (see Figure 1.7) attempt to perform the requested cataloging or uncataloging operation (except when CATLG is requested for a nonspecific new tape data set that is not opened). Examples:

```
//OUT1  DD  DSN=USER1.FILEA,DISP=(,CATLG,DELETE),UNIT=SYSDA,
//          SPACE=(CYL,(25,5),RLSE),DCB=BLKSIZE=23440
```

In the example above a new entry will be added to the catalog.

```
//DDA    DD   DSN=USER1.TP1,UNIT=TAPE,DCB=BLKSIZE=32000,
//            DISP=(MOD,CATLG)
```

In the example above, if MOD defaults to an existing (cataloged) data set that extends into additional volumes, the existing catalog entry will be updated to contain the new volume serials.

```
//DD1  DD   DSN=USER1.FILEB,DISP=(SHR,CATLG),VOL=SER=PACK95,UNIT=SYSDA
```

In the example above a new entry will be added to the catalog for an existing data set. Note that the data set will be cataloged even if it does not exist.

```
//DD2   DD   DSN=USER1.FILEC,DISP=(OLD,UNCATLG)
```

In the example above an existing entry will be removed from the catalog.

The user can request the use of the catalog implicitly, as follows:

- By coding a DD statement with SHR, OLD, or MOD (not defaulting to NEW), and including no specific volume information (VOL=SER or VOL=REF). The absence of specific volume information causes the system to search the catalog. Example:

```
//DD3   DD   DSN=USER1.FILED,DISP=SHR
```

The catalog entry for this data set, when found, will provide volume, unit and (for a tape data set only) sequence number information. If VOL=SER or VOL=REF were coded in the example above, the catalog would not be used.

In JES2 the catalog will be searched by the allocation routines (see Figure 1.7). In JES3 the catalog may be searched before the job begins execution.

- By coding a DD statement that requests the deletion of an existing data set and uses the catalog when being retrieved. Example:

```
//DD4   DD   DSN=USER1.FILEE,DISP=(OLD,DELETE)
```

The DD statement above will use the catalog during its retrieval (no VOL=SER or VOL=REF is coded). The step termination routines will uncatalog the data set before deleting it. If VOL=SER or VOL=REF were coded in the example above, the catalog would not be used and the data set would only be deleted, even if it were cataloged.

- By coding a DD statement containing a VOL=REF=dsname parameter. Example:

```
//DD5   DD  DSN=USER1.FILEF,VOL=REF=USER1.MODLF,DISP=(,
//          CATLG,DELETE),DCB=BLKSIZE=9000
```

The catalog will be searched by the allocation routines for entry USER1.MODLF from which volume and unit information will be extracted and assigned to data set USER1.FILEF.

- By coding a DD statement containing a DCB=model parameter. Example:

```
//DD6   DD  DSN=USER1.FILEG,DISP=(,CATLG,DELETE),UNIT=SYSDA,
//          SPACE=(CYL,(25,5),RLSE),DCB=USER1.MODLDSCB
```

The catalog will be searched by the open routines for entry USER1.MODLDSCB from which volume and unit information will be extracted, used to locate the data set's DSCB which, in turn, will be used as a model of DCB information for data set USER1.FILEG.

- By coding a DD statement that retrieves or creates a GDG generation using a relative name in the DSN parameter (see Section 11.1 in Chapter 11). Examples:

```
//DD7   DD  DSN=USER1.GDGA(0),DISP=SHR
```

```
//OUT2  DD  DSN=USER1.GDGA(+1),DISP=(,CATLG,DELETE),
//          UNIT=SYSDA,SPACE=(CYL,(25,5),RLSE),
//          DCB=(TEST.GDGMODEL.BLKSIZE=23440)
```

The DD statements above will use the catalog to determine the respective absolute names (USER1.GDGA.GnnnnVmm).

For DD statement DD7, the catalog will also supply unit and volume information. Even if VOL=SER or VOL=REF were coded in this statement, the catalog would still be searched in order to determine the absolute name.

- By coding a DD statement that defines the concatenation of GDG generations and using the GDG base in the DSN parameter (see Section 11.6 in Chapter 11). Example:

```
//CONC DD DSN=USER1.GDGA,DISP=SHR
```

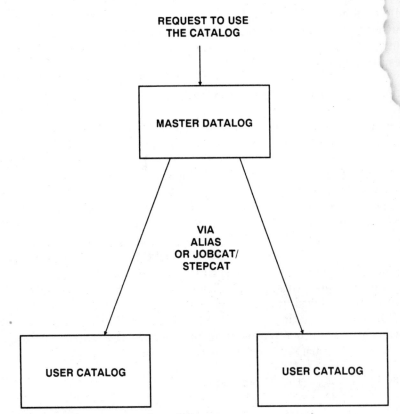

Figure 6.2 The MVS/XA catalog structure.

The DD statement above will use the catalog to determine all the generations that belong to GDG base USER1.GDGA, extract unit and volume information from their respective entries and concatenate them.

When a request is made to the system to use the catalog (either to create a new entry or to locate an existing one), the master catalog will always be used first. If neither JOBCAT nor STEPCAT is in use, the system takes the high qualifier of the data set name, in this case USER1, and determines if it is an alias name for a user catalog. If so, it is this user catalog that will be used to either locate an existing entry or create a new one (see Figure 6.2). Such an alias is more than likely to exist, because, as a matter of procedure, this alias name is placed in the master catalog (by someone with update authority) before the high qualifier is used. If this alias does not exist, then the activity is confined to the master catalog. An attempt to create a new entry will fail, since the average user has no update authority to the master catalog, and an attempt to locate an existing entry will most likely have the same fate for the very same reason, resulting in a JCL error:

```
IEF212I  jobname stepname ddname - DATA SET NOT FOUND
```

Note that the result will be the same if a data set name has no high qualifier; in other words it is a simple name (i.e., DSN=ABC).

The method of using the catalog, as discussed in the preceding paragraphs, is not the only one. However, for an average user, it may well be the only one.

The other method involves the use of JOBCAT and/or STEPCAT, and most installations do not allow their use. There is good reason for this restriction. First, if the high qualifier is an alias name for a user catalog, the use of JOBCAT/STEPCAT is seldom, if ever, needed. Second, JOBCAT/STEPCAT are probably the most dangerous statements in JCL. Their use will frequently cause new entries to be placed in the wrong catalog.

Still, an explanation of how JOBCAT and STEPCAT work will be given, if for no other reason than to persuade the reader not to use them unnecessarily. Consider the JCL below:

```
//USER1W    JOB    FF65,MC,NOTIFY=USER1
//S1        EXEC   PGM=R43
//IN        DD     DSN=USER1.F3,DISP=SHR
//OUT       DD     DSN=USER1.F4,UNIT=SYSDA,DISP=(,CATLG,DELETE),
//                 SPACE=(CYL,(10,5),RLSE),
//                 DCB=(BLKSIZE=23440,LRECL=80,RECFM=FB)
//STEPCAT   DD     DSN=ICFCAT.VPACK12,DISP=SHR
//          DD     DSN=ICFCAT.VPACK21,DISP=SHR
```

In this example, concatenated STEPCATs are used. No specific volume information is coded in DD statement IN, so the catalog must be used in retrieving the data set USER1.F3. The presence of STEPCAT dictates that the user catalog(s) defined in STEPCAT be used. The master catalog, which contains the entries for user catalogs, is accessed first. Having located the entries for the concatenated user catalogs, the system now searches ICFCAT.VPACK12 and then ICFCAT.VPACK21 (if necessary) for the entry of data set USER1.F3. If found in either, the entry will be used. If not found, the system returns to the master catalog, looks for the alias, etc.,taking the same action it did in the previous example when STEPCAT was not present.

Retrieval will be successful if the entry for data set USER1.F3 is located in any of the following catalogs.

- User catalog ICFCAT.VPACK12 (defined in STEPCAT)
- User catalog ICFCAT.VPACK21 (defined in STEPCAT)
- The user catalog of which USER1 is an alias name (if such an alias exists)
- The master catalog

By looking at the JCL above, one cannot tell in which catalog the entry was found. The process of locating a catalog entry is very flexible and forgiving.

There is nothing flexible, however, in the process that creates a new catalog entry for data set USER1.F4. The new entry will be added to the first concatenation of STEPCAT, ICFCAT.VPACK12. This user catalog may not be the one for which USER1 is an alias name. In such a case, the entry is added to the wrong user catalog. Note that data set USER1.F3 had no problem being retrieved even if STEPCAT defined the wrong user catalog. Unless one now remembers to include the appropriate STEPCAT (or JOBCAT), when data set USER1.F3 is retrieved later, a JCL error will be the result:

```
IEF212I  jobname stepname ddname - DATA SET NOT FOUND
```

JOBCAT works basically the same way as STEPCAT except it must be placed between the JOB and first EXEC statement (STEPCAT has no particular position — somewhere inside the step), and it is in effect throughout the job (as opposed to STEPCAT, which affects only the step where it is located). If both are present, STEPCAT negates JOBCAT (the relationship between JOBCAT and STEPCAT is the same as that between JOBLIB and STEPLIB). The results of the JCL below would be exactly the same as in the previous example where STEPCAT was used.

```
//USER1J   JOB    FF65,MC,NOTIFY=USER1
//JOBCAT   DD     DSN=ICFCAT.VPACK12,DISP=SHR
//         DD     DSN=ICFCAT.VPACK21,DISP=SHR
//S1       EXEC   PGM=R43
//IN       DD     DSN=USER1.F3,DISP=SHR
//OUT      DD     DSN=USER1.F4,UNIT=SYSDA,DISP=(,CATLG,DELETE),
//                SPACE=(CYL,(10,5),RLSE),
//                DCB=(BLKSIZE=23440,LRECL=80,RECFM=FB)
```

When adding a new catalog entry, STEPCAT (or JOBCAT) will always determine the user catalog where the entry will be placed, with one exception. Consider the JCL below:

```
//USER1G    JOB    FF65,MC,NOTIFY=USER1
//S1        EXEC   PGM=R43
//IN        DD     DSN=USER1.F3,DISP=SHR
//OUT       DD     DSN=USER1.DAY(+1),UNIT=SYSDA,DISP=(,CATLG,DELETE),
//                 SPACE=(CYL,(10,5),RLSE),
//                 DCB=(MODLDSCB,BLKSIZE=23440,LRECL=80,RECFM=FB)
//STEPCAT   DD     DSN=ICFCAT.VPACK12,DISP=SHR
//          DD     DSN=ICFCAT.VPACK21,DISP=SHR
```

While creating the data set in DD statement OUT, the system must search the catalog, locate the entry for the latest generation so that it can assign an absolute name to the relative name USER1.DAY(+1). Whichever user catalog this entry is found in, it is the same catalog the new entry will be added to, regardless of STEP-CAT or JOBCAT.

6.4 ADDING A NEW ENTRY IN THE CATALOG

When CATLG is coded in the normal or abnormal disposition field of the DISP parameter, it is the step termination routines (see Figure 1.7) that normally perform the cataloging operation.

If PASS is coded in the normal disposition and CATLG in the abnormal disposition field, job termination routines will perform the cataloging if an ABEND failure occurs (see Section 9.4 in Chapter 9).

Whether step termination or job termination routines, when the cataloging is successful, a message appears in the output:

```
IEF285I   data set name                          CATALOGED
IEF285I   VOL SER NOS= vol serial,vol serial,..
```

followed by a message identifying the user catalog where the entry was added.

```
IEF285I   user catalog name                      KEPT
IEF285I   VOL SER NOS= vol serial
```

Example:

```
//OUT1 DD   DSN=USER1.DSK1,DISP=(,CATLG,DELETE),UNIT=SYSDA,
//          SPACE=(CYL,(5,2),RLSE),VOL=SER=PACK05,
//          DCB=(BLKSIZE=23400,LRECL=100,RECFM=FB)
```

```
IEF285I   USER1.DSK1                              CATALOGED
IEF285I   VOL SER NOS= PACK05
IEF285I   ICFCAT.VTECH01                          KEPT
IEF285I   VOL SER NOS= TECH01
```

The same messages will appear when (OLD,CATLG) or
(SHR,CATLG) is used in the DD statement and there is no duplicate
entry in the catalog.
Example:

```
//DD1   DD   DSN=USER1.DSKA,DISP=(OLD,CATLG),
//            UNIT=SYSDA,VOL=SER=PACK09
```

```
IEF285I   USER1.DSKA                              CATALOGED
IEF285I   VOL SER NOS= PACK09
IEF285I   ICFCAT.VTECH01                          KEPT
IEF285I   VOL SER NOS= TECH01
```

6.5 WHEN AN ATTEMPT TO CATALOG FAILS

Under certain conditions, the attempt to catalog a new entry fails.
The step termination routines normally issue a message to inform
the user:

```
IEF287I   data set name                          NOT CATLGD n
IEF287I   VOL SER NOS= vol serial,vol serial,..
```

followed by a message identifying the user catalog where the attempt
to add the entry was made.

```
IEF285I   user catalog name                      KEPT
IEF285I   VOL SER NOS= vol serial
```

n identifies the reason for which the cataloging operation failed.
Often, n is 2. There are several reasons for failing to catalog a data
set. Most of them are seldom encountered. For instance, the failure
could be due to an I/O error or an out-of-space condition in the
catalog, both extremely rare. The examples that follow show some of
the more common reasons for failing to catalog a data set.
Example 1:

```
//OUT2 DD   DSN=USER1.DSK2,DISP=(,CATLG,DELETE),UNIT=SYSDA,
//            SPACE=(CYL,(5,2),RLSE),
//            DCB=(BLKSIZE=23400,LRECL=100,RECFM=FB)
```

If an entry for USER1.DSK2 already exists in the catalog, the step termination routines will not replace the existing entry with a new one. They will keep the data set and issue the following messages:

```
IEF287I   USER1.DSK2                          NOT CATLGD 2
IEF287I   VOL SER NOS= WORK03
IEF285I   ICFCAT.VTECH01                      KEPT
IEF285I   VOL SER NOS= TECH01
```

This is by far the most common reason for failing to catalog. The system will never replace an entry in the catalog. The existing entry must be removed before the one with the same name can be added.

One must pay close attention to a "NOT CATLGD" message. It must be treated as a danger signal.

It is interesting to note that an attempt to add a duplicate entry in the VTOC encounters a "DUPLICATE NAME ON DIRECT ACCESS VOLUME" JCL error. Yet an attempt to add a duplicate entry in the catalog results only in a warning message, which may easily be missed.

Using the above example, it is easy to see the potential for disaster if such a message is ignored. Assume that the existing catalog entry for data set USER1.DSK2 points to volume WORK05, which may or may not contain such a data set. As a result of DD statement OUT, the data set by the same name has been created and kept on volume WORK03 while the catalog entry remains unaltered.

Later, the user, who did not notice the "NOT CATLGD 2" message, submits a job containing a DD statement,

```
//IN   DD   DSN=USER1.DSK2,DISP=SHR
```

expecting to retrieve the data set that was created earlier in DD statement OUT.

If volume WORK05 does not contain a data set named USER1.DSK2, the result will be a S213-04 ABEND failure. If volume WORK05 contains a data set named USER1.DSK2, the result can be far worse. The (wrong) data set will be retrieved with no outward appearance of failure. The user may not ever realize that wrong data was read.

Had the user noticed the "NOT CATLGD 2" message, the problem could have been circumvented in two different ways:

• Remove the wrong entry from the catalog and add the right one. (how to catalog an existing data set will be discussed in Section 6.6

of this chapter) before submitting the job that retrieves the data set.

• Sidestep the use of the catalog altogether, by using DD statement

```
//IN  DD  DSN=USER1.DSK2,DISP=SHR,
//        UNIT=SYSDA,VOL=SER=WORK03
```

These circumventions are possible, of course, only if the data set is retrieved in a later job and the user gets the opportunity to see the output of the job that created and failed to catalog the data set. But what if the step that creates (but does not catalog) the data set and the step that retrieves it are in the same job? Then there would be no way to avoid the problem. Not only should the user be on the lookout for the "NOT CATLGD 2" message, he should take steps to prevent it from happening.

Figure 3.2 shows a "NOT CATLGD 2" message in an actual execution. Notice that data set STU.FILEA cannot be cataloged in step S2 because it was already cataloged in step S1. Also notice that the execution of step S2 was not adversely affected.

When dealing with a "NOT CATLGD 2" situation, other scenarios are possible:

• Consider the same DD statement OUT, resulting in the same "NOT CATLGD 2" message but with the following difference: data set USER1.DSK2 does not exist on any volume and the new data set is allocated to the same volume (WORK05) that the catalog entry points to. The user has "lucked out." Since the data set resides on the same volume as indicated by the catalog entry, the data set will be retrieved successfully.

• Consider the following JCL:

```
//S1    EXEC  PGM=IEFBR14
//DD1   DD    DSN=PROD.FILE1,DISP=(OLD,DELETE),UNIT=SYSDA,
//            VOL=SER=PACK25
//S2    EXEC  PGM=CR
//OUT2  DD    DSN=PROD.FILE1,DISP=(,CATLG,DELETE),UNIT=SYSDA,
//            SPACE=(CYL,(50,20),RLSE),VOL=SER=PACK25,
//            DCB=(BLKSIZE=23440,LRECL=80,RECFM=FB)
//S3    EXEC  PGM=RET
//OUT2  DD    DSN=PROD.FILE1,DISP=SHR
```

Assume that data set PROD.FILE1 is cataloged and exists. Let's follow the sequence of events:

— Step S1 deletes but does not uncatalog data set PROD.FILE1.
— Step S2 creates data set PROD.FILE1 on the same volume from where it was deleted, but fails to catalog it, resulting in a "NOT CATLGD 2" message.
— Step S3 retrieves the data set via the catalog. No problem will occur here because the old catalog entry correctly reflects the volume where the new data set resides.

Although the user got away scot- free, this example demonstrates what must be considered poor JCL, which should *not* be practiced.

The "NOT CATLGD 2" message can have another meaning, although this is rarely likely to surface. If an attempt was made to catalog a data set called USER1.DSK2.ABC when an entry for data set USER1.DSK2 already existed in the catalog, no cataloging will take place and the same message will appear. If the name of one data set is the same as the high qualifier of another, their entries cannot coexist in the catalog.

Example 2:

```
//OUTA   DD   DSN=USER1.TP1,DISP=(,CATLG,DELETE),UNIT=CTAPE,
//             VOL=SER=000327,DCB=(BLKSIZE=32004,
//             LRECL=32000,RECFM=VB)
```

If TAPE describes a 3420 type device, a dual density drive is allocated to this request, and the data set is not opened during execution, Step Termination will fail to catalog because the density of the data set, which is required for cataloging, cannot be determined unless the data set is opened. The following messages will ensue:

```
IEF287I   USER1.TP1                         NOT CATLGD 7
IEF287I   VOL SER NOS= 000327
IEF285I   ICFCAT.VTECH01                    KEPT
IEF285I   VOL SER NOS= TECH01
```

In the example above, cataloging would be successful if the **DEN** subparameter were coded in the DCB parameter. The same **DD** statement would successfully catalog the data set, even it is not opened, if 3480 tape were used.

Example 3:

```
//OUTA   DD   DSN=USER1.TP1,DISP=(,CATLG,DELETE),UNIT=TAPE,
//            DCB=(BLKSIZE=32000,LRECL=100,RECFM=FB)
```

If the data set is not opened during execution, step termination
will fail to catalog the data set because the request is nonspecific and
the volume serial cannot be determined without an open. However,
no message will appear to that effect. Step termination does not inform the user that the cataloging failed — or rather, that it could not
be attempted without a volume serial.

Figure 6.3 expands on Examples 3 and 4, showing where
DISP=(,CATLG) is (or is not) dependent on opening the data set.

Note that disk data sets will always be cataloged (assuming no
unusual conditions, such as duplicate entries, exist) whether or not
they are opened. Tape data sets, considering that Case C is by far
the most common way to create a tape data set, are often not
cataloged if not opened. This in neither surprising nor undesirable.
When the DD statement has NEW disposition, unless opened for output, the tape data set does not exist. Therefore, for Cases E and F it
would be preferable that the data set not be cataloged if not opened.
In both cases, a data set that does not exist becomes cataloged, a fact
that can lead to an S813-04 ABEND failure (see Section 7.3.2 in
Chapter 7).

6.6 CATALOGING AN EXISTING DATA SET

Cataloging when the data set is created by using DISP=(,CATLG) is
very common and strongly recommended. However, it is not mandatory. For example, DISP=(,KEEP) will cause the data set to be
created but not cataloged. Also, as discussed before, DISP=(,CATLG)
may be specified but the cataloging operation fails. In such cases,
cataloging can be performed after the data set already exists.

There are several ways to catalog an existing data set:

• Using JCL

```
//SA   EXEC   PGM=IEFBR14
//D1   DD     DSN=USER1.FSET,DISP=(SHR,CATLG),UNIT=SYSDA,
//            VOL=SER=PACK32
```

There are several dangers inherent in this operation:
— There is little or no protection against supplying the wrong
   DSN. Neither the allocation nor the step termination routines

```
CASE A. //DD1   DD  DSN=USER1.DSK1,DISP=(,CATLG),UNIT=SYSDA,
        //          DCB=(BLKSIZE=23400,LRECL=100,RECFM=FB),
        //          SPACE=(CYL,(10,2),RLSE)),VOL=SER=PACK03


CASE B. //DD2   DD  DSN=USER1.DSK2,DISP=(,CATLG),UNIT=SYSDA,
        //          DCB=(BLKSIZE=23400,LRECL=100,RECFM=FB),
        //          SPACE=(CYL,(10,2),RLSE))


CASE C. //DD3   DD  DSN=USER1.TAP1,DISP=(,CATLG),UNIT=TAPE,
        //          DCB=(BLKSIZE=23400,LRECL=100,RECFM=FB)


CASE C. //DD4   DD  DSN=USER1.TAP2,DISP=(,CATLG),UNIT=TAPE,
        //          DCB=(BLKSIZE=23400,LRECL=100,RECFM=FB),
        //          VOL=SER=000224


CASE D. //DD5   DD  DSN=USER1.TAP3,DISP=(,CATLG),UNIT=TAPE,
        //          DCB=(BLKSIZE=23400,LRECL=100,RECFM=FB,
        //          DEN=4),VOL=SER=000907


CASE E. //DD6   DD  DSN=USER1.TAP4,DISP=(,CATLG),UNIT=CART,
        //          DCB=(BLKSIZE=23400,LRECL=100,RECFM=FB),
        //          VOL=SER=001357
```

	DATA SET OPENED	DATA SET NOT OPENED
CASE A	CATALOGED	CATALOGED
CASE B	CATALOGED	CATALOGED
CASE C	CATALOGED	NO ACTION-NO MESSAGE
CASE D*	CATALOGED	NOT CATLGD 7
CASE E	CATALOGED	CATALOGED
CASE F**	CATALOGED	CATALOGED

*   Dual density 3420 tape device allocated
** 3480 tape device allocated

Figure 6.3 Dependence of cataloging on open for new data sets.

verifies that the data set resides on the alleged volume (see Section 7.3.1 in Chapter 7), and the data set will be cataloged even if it doesn't exist. There is only one protection: If the high qualifier of the wrong data set name is not an alias of a user catalog and neither STEPCAT nor JOBCAT is used, the system will attempt to add the entry in the master catalog. For the majority of users, who have no write authority to the master catalog, such an attempt will fail.

— If the wrong volume serial is supplied in the VOL parameter, and such a volume exists, again the data set will be cataloged for the same reasons as in the previous case. If the wrong volume serial does not exist, the operator will be forced to cancel the job and no cataloging will take place.

If the data set to be cataloged is on tape, there are additional considerations:

```
//SA   EXEC  PGM=IEFBR14
//D1   DD    DSN=USER1.TSET,DISP=(OLD,CATLG),UNIT=(TAPE,,DEFER),
//            VOL=SER=002952
```

If TAPE describes 3420 tape and the device allocated is dual density, the cataloging will fail as described in Example 2 of Section 6.5 of this chapter.

```
IEF287I   USER1.TSET                              NOT CATLGD 7
IEF287I   VOL SER NOS= 002952
```

If the DEN subparameter in the DCB parameter is added or if TAPE describes 3480 tape, the cataloging will be successful.

However, in all cases, a tape device must be allocated just to add an entry to the catalog. In some cases this will be inadvisable.

• Using the IEHPROGM utility

```
//SC   EXEC  PGM=IEHPROGM
//SYSPRINT  DD  SYSOUT=*
//SYSIN     DD  *
   CATLG  DSNAME=USER1.FSET,VOL=SYSDA=PACK32
/*
```

This is even more dangerous than cataloging via JCL.

— If the wrong name is supplied in DSNAME, the wrong data set can easily be cataloged. The utility does not verify that the data set resides on the specified volume.

— If the wrong volume serial is supplied in the VOL parameter, again the data set will be cataloged whether or not the wrong volume exists.

— If the wrong device type is supplied in the VOL parameter, again the data set will be cataloged but only if the device is a valid one. The validity of the device is the only thing the utility checks. It does not check if it is the appropriate device for the volume.

— The use of a generated name (e.g., SYSDA) in the VOL parameter can cause a problem. When cataloging via JCL, a parameter like UNIT=SYSDA will never cause a problem. The allocation routines (see Figure 1.7) determine what type of device the allocated volume resides on and the catalog entry will eventually contain not SYSDA, but the exact device type, such as 3380. The IEHPROGM utility, however, has nothing comparable to the allocation routines and provides a device description indicative of SYSDA in the catalog entry. Upon reconfiguration, such a catalog entry can become invalid. It is, therefore, recommended that if IEHPROGM is used to provide an entry in the catalog, a generic name be used in the VOL parameter as opposed to a generated name.

```
CATLG   DSNAME=USER1.FSET,VOL=3380=PACK32
```

Actually, considering all the dangers stated above, it may be best to avoid using IEHPROGM for cataloging.

When an existing tape data set must be cataloged, IEHPROGM holds an advantage over cataloging via JCL. It does not allocate a tape device in order to catalog.

```
CATLG   DSNAME=USER1.TSET,VOL=3480=010267
```

• Using IDCAMS (Access Method Services)

```
//SI   EXEC   PGM=IDCAMS
//SYSPRINT  DD   SYSOUT=*
//SYSIN     DD   *
   DEFINE   (NAME(USER1.FSET) DEVT(3380) VOL(PACK32))
/*
```

What was said for cataloging using IEHPROGM can also be said for IDCAMS. Exactly the same dangers exist.

It should be noted that IDCAMS, just like IEHPROGM, will not allocate a tape device in order to catalog a tape data set.
- Using TSO/ISPF Options 3.2 or 3.4

TSO/ISPF is 100% safe when cataloging disk data sets. Inaccurate or invalid entries in the catalog are impossible. Of course, TSO/ISPF is an interactive facility and may be impractical or impossible to use in a batch environment. Also, TSO/ISPF cannot catalog tape data sets or multivolume disk data sets.

Sometimes DISP=(OLD,CATLG) or (MOD,CATLG) is used for a data set that is already cataloged. In the example below, data set USER1.EXT5 is being extended:

```
//S1    EXEC  PGM=COPYX
//OUT   DD    DSN=USER1.EXT5,DISP=(MOD,CATLG)
```

If the extended data set does not go into additional volumes, a message will appear:

```
IEF287I  USER1.EXT5                              NOT RECTLGD 2
IEF287I  VOL SER NOS= 004911
IEF285I  ICFCAT.VTECH01                          KEPT
IEF285I  VOL SER NOS= TECH01
```

If the extended data set goes into an additional volume, let's say 000286, a message will appear:

```
IEF285I  USER1.EXT5                              RECATALOGED
IEF285I  VOL SER NOS= 004911 000286
IEF285I  ICFCAT.VTECH01                          KEPT
IEF285I  VOL SER NOS= TECH01
```

The "RECATALOGED" message means that the existing entry in the catalog was updated to contain up-to-date volume information. The "NOT RECTLGD 2" and the "NOT CATLGD 2" messages have a similar meaning. However, the first message is benign and the second can cause serious problems, as discussed earlier in this chapter.

These messages appear with DISP=(MOD,CATLG) as well as with (OLD,CATLG) or (SHR,CATLG) whether the data set is tape or disk. It should be noted that if DD statement OUT describes a disk data set that allocates a single device, the "NOT RECTLGD 2" message is not particularly meaningful since the data set cannot possibly extend into additional volumes. By the same token, a "RECATALOGED" message is impossible for this data set. It would be possible if the DD statement identified multiple volumes or devices:

```
//OUT  DD    DSN=USER1.EXT5,DISP=(MOD,CATLG),VOL=SER=(PACK02,
//           PACK05),UNIT=SYSDA
```

or

```
//OUT  DD    DSN=USER1.EXT5,DISP=(MOD,CATLG),UNIT=(,2)
```

or

```
//OUT  DD    DSN=USER1.EXT5,DISP=(MOD,CATLG),VOL=(,,,2)
```

If the data set is not opened, the message will always be "NOT CATLDG 2" as opposed to "NOT RECTLDG 2."

6.7 UNCATALOGING A TAPE DATA SET

A data set can be uncataloged in several ways:

• Using JCL — DISP=(OLD,UNCATLG)
• Using IDCAMS — The DELETE command
• Using IEHPROGM — The UNCATLG control statement

This section will focus on uncataloging tape data sets. Disk data sets can be uncataloged in comparable ways, but they are usually deleted as they are uncataloged. This is covered in Section 7.3.4 of Chapter 7.

Consider a tape data set which must be uncataloged in the first step of a job in production. This is necessary so that the same data set can be cataloged in a subsequent step. IEFBR14, or any other program which does not open the data set, can be used.

```
//S1  EXEC  PGM=IEFBR14
//D1  DD    DSN=FED.TRAN1,DISP=(OLD,UNCATLG),UNIT=(,,DEFER)
```

This JCL will work but has two problems:

1. It will allocate a tape device. Even though a mount message to the operator console will not appear — DEFER is used and

IEFBR14 does not open the data set — the device will still be allocated. This may not be a problem, since a tape device will be used again later to create the like-named data set.

2. If the data set is already uncataloged, a "DATA SET NOT FOUND" JCL error will be the result.

There are several ways to resolve problem 2:

• Using MOD

```
//S1  EXEC  PGM=IEFBR14
//D1  DD    DSN=FED.TRAN1,DISP=(MOD,UNCATLG),
//          UNIT=(TAPE,,DEFER)
```

If the data set is cataloged, MOD defaults to an existing data set (much like OLD) and the data set will be uncataloged. If the data set is not cataloged, MOD defaults to "NEW" avoiding a JCL error. The DD statement appears to be creating a tape data set but, since there is no open, the data set is never actually created (see Section 8.3 in Chapter 8). No uncataloging can be performed — the data set was not cataloged.

• Using VOL. This method eliminates the possibility for getting the JCL error of the previous method.

```
//S1  EXEC  PGM=IEFBR14
    //D1  DD    DSN=FED.TRAN1,DISP=(OLD,UNCATLG),
    //          UNIT=(TAPE,,DEFER),VOL=SER=000134
```

The data set will be retrieved without the catalog and an attempt will be made to uncatalog it whether or not it is cataloged. The volume serial specified in the VOL=SER is arbitrary. It will never be called for, since there will be no open and DEFER is used. The possible problem of this method is that, like the previous one, a tape device will be allocated. If cataloged, the data set will be uncataloged. If not cataloged, the following harmless message will appear:

```
IEF287I  FED.TRAN1                         NOT UNCTLGD 2
IEF287I  VOL SER NOS= 000134
```

• By using VOL and UNIT=SYSDA, the possibility for JCL error is eliminated and no tape device is allocated, taking care of problem 1:

```
//S1    EXEC   PGM=IEFBR14
//D1    DD     DSN=FED.TRAN1,DISP=(OLD,UNCATLG),
//             UNIT=SYSDA,VOL=SER=PROD12
```

The data set will be retrieved without the catalog and an attempt will be made to uncatalog it whether or not it exists or is cataloged. The volume serial coded in the VOL parameter, however, must exist. If it does not, the operator will be forced to cancel the job. Selecting an existing volume is easy if the JCL is to be run once or only over a short period of time. For a production job running for years, however, an exposure exists. The volume used may be eliminated or change serial number. For such jobs, the volume must be carefully selected. A good technique would be to use VOL=REF referring to a cataloged disk data set which is likely to be always present. A model DSCB used for GDGs (or a system data set like SYS1.LINKLIB, if permissible) is a good choice since it will always be present and changing the volume on which it resides will have no negative effect.

```
//S1    EXEC   PGM=IEFBR14
//D1    DD     DSN=FED.TRAN1,DISP=(OLD,UNCATLG),
//             VOL=REF=PROD.GDGMODEL
```

These DD statements are admittedly strange. The data set to be uncataloged is on tape and yet the DD statements describe disk. The method works because the allocation routines do not verify if the data set exists on the volume (see Section 7.3.1 in Chapter 7). It does not, of course, but this creates no problem because IEFBR14 does not open the data set. If cataloged, the data set will be uncataloged. If not cataloged, the following harmless message will appear:

```
IEF287I   FED.TRAN1                              NOT UNCTLGD 2
IEF287I   VOL SER NOS= FED002
```

If this method is used, it is advisable to provide comments explaining how it works, or risk confusing others.

The IEHPROGM utility can also be used to uncatalog the data set.

```
//S1         EXEC PGM=IEHPROGM
//SYSPRINT   DD   SYSOUT=*
//SYSIN      DD   *
```

```
        UNCATLG  DSNAME=FED.TRAN1
/*
```

If the data set is cataloged, it will be uncataloged. If not,
IEHPROGM will issue a warning message and a return code of 4.
This is normally no problem because a return code of 4 is considered
benign. Note that no tape device will be allocated.

IDCAMS can also be used to uncatalog the data set.

```
//S1         EXEC PGM=IDCAMS
//SYSPRINT   DD    SYSOUT=*
//SYSIN      DD    *
   DELETE   FED.TRAN1   NOSCRATCH
/*
```

If the data set is cataloged, it will be uncataloged. If not, IDCAMS
will issue a warning message and a return code of 8. This can be a
problem because a return code of 8 is considered questionable. This
will cause a subsequent step using COND=(4,LT) not to be executed
while there is really nothing wrong. This problem can be eliminated
by using IDCAMS execution control commands IF/THEN and the
SET command:

```
//S1         EXEC PGM=IDCAMS
//SYSPRINT   DD    SYSOUT=*
//SYSIN      DD    *
   DELETE   FED.TRAN1   NOSCRATCH
   IF LASTCC=8 THEN -
   SET MAXCC=4 (or SET MAXCC=0, if preferable)
```

The IF and SET commands will change the return code from 8 to 4
(or 0), thus eliminating the problem.

Note that no tape device will be allocated.

Retrieving Data Sets

The purpose of a DD statement (except when DUMMY or DSN=NULFILE is coded) is to create or retrieve a data set.

This chapter will discuss the logic the system uses in retrieving disk and tape data sets and some of its unexpected results, the various ways a data set can be retrieved, the function of the catalog, and the various peculiarities and problems that can be encountered when retrieving.

7.1 DEFINITION

The system "retrieves" a data set by means of a DD statement. The DD statement must describe an existing data set (DISP of SHR, OLD, or MOD) and include sufficient information so that the volume on which the data set resides and the device on which this volume is supposed to be mounted can be determined. In essence, the system needs to have four basic pieces of information available in order to successfully retrieve a data set:

- The data set name — to identify the data set to be retrieved.
- The DISP parameter — to denote the existing status of the data set. Note that if DISP is omitted, DISP=(NEW,DELETE) is the default.
- Volume information — to identify the volume serial on which the data set resides.

• Unit information — to identify the device type on which the volume is (or, for tape, will be) mounted.

If any of these elements of information is unavailable or inaccurate, the result will be a JCL error, an ABEND failure, or, possibly, the retrieval of the wrong data set.

7.1.1 Required and Optional Parameters for Retrieval

This section will describe which parameters are required, which are optional, and, if optional, under what circumstances they must be specified.

DSN: Required. It can be omitted only for an NL tape data set (not recommended).

DSN may be omitted in certain special DD statements used only by Utilities (and IDCAMS):

```
//DD1  DD  UNIT=SYSDA,VOL=SER=PROD31,DISP=OLD
```

This DD statement, rather than describing a data set, describes a volume. An ordinary program cannot use such a DD statement.

DISP: Required. The default is (NEW DELETE) — inappropriate for retrieving.

UNIT: Optional. It must be coded, however, if:

• The data set is neither cataloged nor passed and VOL=REF is not used.
• UNIT=AFF is needed.
• More than one device must be allocated.
• Deferred mounting must be used.
• The description of the device in the catalog is too broad and a subset must be supplied (very rare).
• A multivolume disk data set is created using a nonspecific request.

VOL: Optional. It must be coded, however, if:

• The data set is neither cataloged nor passed.
• RETAIN is needed.

- A multivolume cataloged data set must be processed beginning with a volume other than the first one.
- A cataloged data set is expected to extend to a specific new volume.

SPACE: Optional. It must be coded, however, if:

- A secondary allocation different than the one specified when the data set was created is desired.
- All unused space is to be freed when the data set is closed.

LABEL: Optional. It must be coded, however, if:

- The (tape) data set is not SL.
- The (tape) data set is SL, it is not cataloged, and its sequence is greater than one.

   Note: The LABEL parameter may be required for TMS or TLMS.

DCB: Optional. It must be coded, however, if:

- Any DCB values for BLKSIZE, LRECL, amd RECFM are not hard-coded (see Section 7.10 in Chapter 7) and data set is not SL.
- There is a need to code OPTCD, EROPT, or BUFNO.
- A new GDG generation using a relative name is created and a cataloged model DSCB is in use.

FREE: Optional. It must be coded, however, if:

- The (tape) device needs to be deallocated at close time.
- The disk data set needs to be freed from exclusive usage and made available to other jobs, at close time.

7.2 RETRIEVAL WITH AND WITHOUT THE CATALOG

```
//IN  DD   DSN=USER1.FAY,DISP=SHR,VOL=SER=PACK01,UNIT=SYSDA
```

   The DD statement above will be retrieved without the use of the catalog because it contains VOL=SER. The user here must supply the four pieces of information (DSN, DISP, VOL, and UNIT) required for retrieval.

```
//IN  DD   DSN=USER1.FAX,DISP=SHR
```

The DD statement above will be retrieved using the catalog because it contains neither VOL=SER nor VOL=REF (see Section 6.3 in Chapter 6). Unit and volume information will come from the data set's entry in the catalog. The main contents of this data set's catalog entry are:

```
DSN             VOL        UNIT
---------------------------------
| USER1.FAX     | PACK00  | 3380 |
---------------------------------
```

It is important to note here that while a generated unit name, such as UNIT=SYSDA, may have been used while creating and cataloging the data set, the catalog identifies the actual device where volume PACK00 is mounted, in this case 3380. SYSDA is an installation-generated name which could include all 3380s or a subset of them or possibly a combination of different devices (like 3380 and 3350). The meaning of SYSDA is completely up to the installation.

Now consider several examples of retrieval assuming that SYSDA is a subset of 3380. The same cataloged data set, USER1.FAX, whose catalog entry was shown above, will be retrieved in most examples:

Example 1:

```
//D1  DD  DSN=USER1.FAX,DISP=SHR,VOL=SER=PACK00
```

This is a JCL error. The presence of VOL=SER negates the search of the catalog and the DD statement does not include a UNIT parameter. Since there is no default for UNIT, a JCL error results:

```
IEF210I  jobname stepname ddname - UNIT FIELD SPECIFIES INCORRECT
                                   DEVICE NAME
```

This message is a bit misleading since no device at all was specified. It actually means that UNIT information is missing. To correct such a problem, the UNIT parameter must be added if the data set is not cataloged. If it is, the VOL parameter should be removed.

Example 2:

```
//D1  DD  DSN=USER1.FAX,DISP=SHR,VOL=REF=USER1.SETX
```

VOL=REF always supplies both volume and unit information. The catalog will not be used. A UNIT parameter is unnecessary and if supplied it would be ignored unless it describes a subset of the device type supplied by VOL=REF.

Example 3:

```
//D1   DD   DSN=USER1.FAX,DISP=SHR,UNIT=TAPE
```

The catalog will be searched in this example (the presence of the UNIT parameter in the DD statement does not impact the search of the catalog). The catalog entry for data set USER1.FAX contains a unit of 3380, which contradicts the UNIT=TAPE in the DD statement. No warning or error message will appear. Simply the unit in the catalog prevails and the unit provided by the DD statement is ignored. It should be noted, however, that the UNIT parameter can contain two additional subparameters, number of devices to allocate and DEFER. They will not be ignored.

In essence, the unit parameter here appears to be harmless. True, but it also conveys some false information to whoever sees it.

Example 4:

```
//D1   DD   DSN=USER1.FAX,DISP=SHR,UNIT=3380
```

In this example the unit in the catalog and DD statement agree completely, so it makes no difference which is used. Actually, the unit in the catalog is used.

Example 5:

```
//D2   DD   DSN=USER1.TAP,DISP=OLD,UNIT=AFF=D1
```

The catalog will be used for this DD statement, but only to extract volume information. UNIT=AFF will always prevail over the unit in the catalog.

Example 6:

```
//D1   DD   DSN=USER1.FAX,DISP=SHR,UNIT=SYSDA
```

In this example SYSDA is coded in the unit parameter and because SYSDA is a subset of 3380, it will be used while the unit in the catalog will be ignored.

For disk data sets, coding the UNIT parameter when retrieving through the catalog is never useful and potentially dangerous. In Example 6, PACK00 is a 3380 volume, and using the unit from the catalog will never cause a problem. Coding UNIT=SYSDA will cause a JCL error if the device address of PACK00 is not included in the installation's description of SYSDA:

```
IEF702I  jobname stepname ddname - UNABLE TO ALLOCATE
```

Therefore, it is best to avoid the UNIT parameter in the DD statement.

If the data set is on tape, the situation is basically the same except a scenario exists where using the UNIT parameter can help solve a problem. The scenario is an unusual one. A mainframe with most of its peripheral devices is located on the 8th floor of a building. Some of its 3480 tape drives, however, are located on the 6th floor where operators mount tapes for certain applications. Two generated unit names are used: UNIT=TAPE8, which includes only 8th floor tape devices, for 8th floor runs; UNIT=TAPE6, which includes only 6th floor tape devices, for 6th floor runs.

For creating data sets on the 6th floor, the DD statement below will always call for a 6th floor tape device,

```
//OUT  DD   DSN=USER1.TP1,DISP=(,CATLG,DELETE),UNIT=TAPE6,
//           DCB=(LRECL=100,BLKSIZE=23400,RECFM=FB)
```

and it will create a catalog entry:

```
    DSN            VOL       UNIT
-----------------------------------
| USER1.TP1    | 000371   | 3480 |
-----------------------------------
```

Note that the catalog entry identifies the device as 3480, not TAPE6.

When the data set is retrieved via the catalog using DD statement

```
//IN   DD   DSN=USER1.TP1,DISP=OLD
```

the system can select any 3480 device, on either floor, creating a serious problem. The DD statement below solves the problem:

```
//IN   DD   DSN=USER1.TP1,DISP=OLD,UNIT=TAPE6
```

TAPE6, being a subset of 3480, will be used, resulting in the selection of only a 6th floor tape device.

7.3 THE LOGIC OF ALLOCATION, PROGRAM EXECUTION, AND STEP TERMINATION FOR RETRIEVAL

The allocation routines (Figure 1.7) are responsible for retrieving a data set. This is also frequently referred to as "allocating" the data set. Both terms are actually misnomers, because retrieving (or allocating) a data set does not include determining the actual location of the data set or even verifying that the data set exists on the volume. These functions are the responsibility of the open routines, not the allocation routines.

Let us examine what happens during the process of allocation, program execution, and step termination (Figure 1.7) when retrieving a data set.

The process is different for disk as opposed to tape, so each will be discussed separately.

7.3.1 Disk Data Set Retrieval

Consider the DD statement:

```
//IN   DD   DSN=USER1.SET8,DISP=SHR,UNIT=SYSDA,VOL=SER=PACK33
```

(The discussion that follows also applies to the DD statement

```
//IN   DD   DSN=USER1.SET8,DISP=SHR
```

except here unit and volume information are supplied by the catalog. In JES2 the catalog is searched by the allocation routines, whereas in JES3 it is searched before the job begins execution and, when that is impossible, also by the allocation routines.)

The allocation routines will determine if volume PACK33 is mounted on a device whose address is included in what the installation has defined as unit "SYSDA." If so, it will be allocated and assigned a "use count" of one. If already allocated, the "use count" of the device is increased by one. And that's all. No attempt is made to verify that data set USER1.SET8 actually exists on volume PACK33. As mentioned before, this is not the responsibility of the allocation routines. If the data set does not exist, no indication of any nature will be given during this process.

If volume PACK33 is not mounted on any device, the system initiates an "allocation recovery" on the operator console. Given the fact that volumes are nonremovable, "recovery" is virtually impossible and the operator has no other option but to cancel the job.

If volume PACK33 is mounted on a disk device whose address is not included in what the installation has defined as unit "SYSDA," the result will be JCL error:

```
IEF702I  jobname stepname ddname - UNABLE TO ALLOCATE
```

If volume PACK33 is found to be mounted on a tape device, the result will be a different JCL error:

```
IEF245I  jobname stepname ddname - INCONSISTENT UNIT NAME AND
                                   VOLUME SERIAL
```

If the allocation process is successful, program execution begins. When (and if) the program opens the data set during execution, the open routines search the VTOC of volume PACK33 to locate the DSCB entry for data set USER1.SET8 in preparation for the read (or write) instructions that will follow. If the data set does not reside on the volume, the program will ABEND with a S213-04 completion code. So, an error condition that went unnoticed by the allocation routines will now be caught by the open routines. The S213-04 ABEND is the true "data set does not exist" condition, rather than the "DATA SET NOT FOUND" JCL error (see Section 6.3 in Chapter 6). If the program does not open the data set, no S213-04 ABEND can occur (since all Sx13 ABEND failures happen during the open process) and no other indication will be given that data set USER1.SET8 does not exist.

Step termination is the process that always follows program execution, whether on not the program ABENDs, and it is responsible for disposition processing. DISP=SHR defaults to DISP=(SHR,KEEP). A message will be issued:

```
IEF285I USER1.SET8                                      KEPT
IEF285I VOL SERS PACK33
```

This message will appear under all possible circumstances:

1. Data set USER1.SET8 exists on volume PACK33 and it is opened successfully.
2. Data set USER1.SET8 exists on volume PACK33 and it is not opened.
3. Data set USER1.SET8 does not exist on volume PACK33 and it is not opened.

4. Data set USER1.SET8 does not exist on volume PACK33, it is opened and ABENDs with a completion code S213-04.

The reason for this rather surprising fact is that, in response to a DISP request to "KEEP" the data set, the step termination routines do absolutely nothing. The data set is assumed to exist, and by doing nothing it will continue to exist. All other DISP requests result in some action by step termination: CATLG — an entry is added to the catalog; DELETE — a DSCB is removed from the VTOC, etc. A DISP request to KEEP results in no action whatsoever. As a result, a "NOT KEPT" message will never appear.

Some of these cases are worth examining further, especially #3 and #4.

• In case #3, the data set USER1.SET8 does not exist:
  — There is no indication of this fact during the allocation process.
  — There is no indication of this fact during program execution because there is no open.
  — Step termination issues a message indicating that the nonexistent data set is "kept." The system is actually *lying*, although it is unaware of it.
    It is very easy, in such a case, to assume a data set exists when it does not, an assumption that can lead to considerable confusion.
• In case #4, the data set USER1.SET8 again does not exist:
  — There is no indication of this fact during the allocation process.
  — Program execution attempts to open and ABENDs with an S213-04 (which means that the data set does not exist).
  — Step termination totally contradicts the S213-04 ABEND by claiming the data set was "kept."
    Which of the conflicting signals is to be trusted? The S213-04 ABEND or the "kept" message? Unless one knows that the data set was opened during execution and there was no S213-04 ABEND, the "kept" message cannot be trusted. The S213-04 ABEND is always accurate.

Under unusual conditions it may become necessary to supply two DD statements in the same step, one that creates and one that retrieves the same data set.

```
//CRE  DD   DSN=USER1.SETX,DISP=(,CATLG),UNIT=SYSDA,VOL=SER=PACK05,
//          DCB=(LRECL=80,RECFM=FB,BLKSIZE=23440),SPACE=(CYL,(10,3))
//RET  DD   DSN=USER1.SETX,DISP=OLD,UNIT=SYSDA,VOL=SER=PACK05
```

This JCL may appear illogical but, based on the way a data set is allocated, it will work fine as long as the use of the catalog when retrieving is avoided. DD statement RET will have no problem going through allocation. When it is opened, the data set will exist, having been created by DD statement CRE. Interestingly, the two DD statements can be provided in any sequence.

7.3.2 Tape Data Set Retrieval

Consider the DD statement below in a JES2 environment (JES3 works differently, as will be pointed out later):

```
//IN  DD   DSN=USER1.TAP1,DISP=OLD,UNIT=TAPE,VOL=SER=000236
```

LABEL not supplied — the default is (1,SL).
(The discussion that follows also applies to the DD statement

```
//IN  DD   DSN=USER1.TAP1,DISP=OLD
```

except here the unit, volume and sequence information are supplied by the catalog during allocation processing.)

The allocation routines will select a device whose address is included in what the installation has defined as unit "TAPE," allocate it, and issue a mount message to the operator console

```
*IEF233A M ddd,000236,SL,jobname,stepname,dsn
```

(where ddd is the device address) but do not wait for the operator to mount the tape volume requested.

Program execution begins, and when the data set is opened, the volume serial and data set name will be verified:

- The volume serial is taken from the volume label (first 80-byte record on a SL tape) and compared against the volume coded in the DD statement (or the volume that was supplied by the catalog). If they do not match, the tape volume will be unloaded and the mount message repeated. If they match, the volume is accepted.
- Then the data set name is taken from the data set label (HDR1) and compared against the DSN in the DD statement (actually only the last 17 characters are compared because that is all the label has room for). If they match, the data set is accepted. If they do not, the result is an S813-04 ABEND failure. This is the logical equivalent of the S213-04 ABEND for disk.

It is interesting to note that in the DD statement below,

```
//IN   DD   DSN=USER1.TAPI,DISP=OLD,UNIT=TAPE,VOL=SER=000238,
//           LABEL=2
```

misspelling the data set name, the volume serial, or the sequence can cause the very same ABEND: S813-04.

If NL or BLP is used in the LABEL, neither the volume nor the data set name can be verified (see discussion later in Section 7.6 of this chapter).

JES3 works a little differently than JES2. JES3 will preallocate (before the job begins execution) a "high water mark" of tape devices for the job, will issue mount messages for the first volume to be used on each tape device, and perform volume verification. If a given tape device is used again in a later step, the volume verification will be done by the open routines as is in JES2. The data set name verification works the same in both subsystems.

7.3.3 Tape Data Set Retrieval with Deferred Mounting

A variation of tape data set retrieval using deferred mounting is shown below. The discussion again pertains to JES2, with JES3 differences to be pointed out later.

```
//IN   DD   DSN=USER1.TAP1,DISP=OLD,UNIT=(TAPE,,DEFER),VOL=SER=000236
```

LABEL not supplied — the default is (1,SL).
(The discussion that follows also applies to the DD statement

```
//IN   DD   DSN=USER1.TAP1,DISP=OLD,UNIT=(,,DEFER)
```

except here the unit, volume, and sequence information are supplied by the catalog.)

When DEFER is used, the allocation routines do not issue the mount message to the operator console. The message is issued when the data set is opened during execution. A common misunderstanding is that the allocation of the device is postponed. This is not true! The device is allocated whether or not DEFER is used. Only the mount message is postponed. The message, when issued by the open routines, has the same basic content as when issued by the allocation routines except that its message prefix begins with IEC instead of IEF.

```
*IEC501A M 982,000236,SL,,USER1B,STEP2,USER1.TAP1
```

where 982 is the device address, USER1B is the jobname, and
STEP2 is the stepname.

If the data set is opened, DEFER is of no value and actually
counterproductive. Without DEFER, the mount message is issued by
the allocation routines. Since the open occurs later, the operator has
a chance to mount the tape and avoid or minimize the wait state
that results if the open finds the tape not mounted and ready. With
DEFER, the mount message and the wait state occur at the same
time, since they are both functions of the open routines. The operator
has no chance to avoid the wait state. When the mount message
appears on the console, the program is already in a wait state.

DEFER should normally be avoided unless the data set is not
opened. Not opening a data set means that there will no I/O and,
clearly, volume mounting is unnecessary. Yet, if DEFER is not used,
the mount message will appear, the operator will attempt to mount
the volume, and often be confused when the step terminates before
the tape is mounted (no open — no wait state). DEFER causes the
mount message not to appear when there is no open.

Some programs may open a data set only under certain conditions
(Example: a data set is opened on a weekend run but not during
weekday runs). Using DEFER in such situations can also be beneficial.

DEFER should never be used with disk, since disk volumes are
nonremovable and mount messages should never appear.

In JES3, when tape volumes are premounted before the job begins
execution, DEFER is ignored. For those tape volumes, however, that
are not premounted, DEFER works the same as in JES2.

7.3.4 Retrieving and Deleting Data Sets

One of the main responsibilities of the step termination routines is to
satisfy the normal and abnormal disposition of the DISP parameter.
Chapter 6 discusses CATLG and UNCATLG. Chapter 9 discusses
PASS. KEEP was discussed earlier in this chapter. This section will
discuss DELETE.

Consider the examples below:

```
1. //D1 DD DSN=USER1.DSK1,DISP=(OLD,DELETE) DISK DATA SET
2. //D2 DD DSN=USER1.DSK2,DISP=(OLD,DELETE),UNIT=SYSDA,
   //      VOL=SER=PACK01
```

3. `//D3 DD DSN=USER1.TAP1,DISP=(OLD,DELETE) TAPE DS`
4. `//D4 DD DSN=USER1.DSK2,DISP=(OLD,DELETE),UNIT=TAPE,`
   `//      VOL=SER=000219`
5. `//D5 DD DSN=USER1.PDS1(M3),DISP=(OLD,DELETE) PDS+MEMEBER`

In example 1, these messages will appear:

```
                                              UNCATALOGED
IEF285I USER1.DSK1
IEF285I VOL SER NOS=PACK21
IEF285I USER1.DSK1                            DELETED
IEF285I VOL SER NOS=PACK21
```

Although uncataloging was not specifically requested, it is performed, along with deleting, because the catalog was used during retrieval.

If data set USER1.DSK1 does not exist on volume PACK01, the data set will not be uncataloged because the delete also fails:

```
                                              NOT DELETED 8
IEF283I USER1.DSK1
IEF283I VOL SER NOS=PACK21
```

In example 2, these messages will appear:

```
                                              DELETED
IEF285I USER1.DSK2
IEF285I VOL SER NOS=PACK01
```

The catalog was not used during retrieval, so the data set is only deleted. If this data set is cataloged, the result is an entry in the catalog for a data set which does not exist. This is a totally undesirable situation and must be avoided. It is likely to cause future problems, most likely a S213-04 ABEND.

In example 3, these messages will appear:

```
                                              UNCATALOGED
IEF285I USER1.TAP1
IEF285I VOL SER NOS=000294
IEF285I USER1.TAP1                            DELETED
IEF285I VOL SER NOS=000294
```

The data set is uncataloged; however, it is not deleted. The DELETE disposition for tape is meaningless, as tape data sets cannot be deleted until written over. DISP=(OLD,UNCATLG) would have provided the same result though not the same messages.

In example 4, these messages will appear:

```
IEF285I USER1.TAP2                              DELETED
IEF285I VOL SERS 000219
```

As in example 3, the DELETED message is meaningless.

Example 5 will produce the same messages as Example 1. Note that the entire PDS is deleted, not just the member. There is no way to delete a member of a PDS through JCL.

The member can be deleted by using the IEHPROGM utility:

```
//PRG       EXEC  PGM=IEHPROGM
//SYSPRINT  DD    SYSOUT=*
//DD1       DD    UNIT=SYSDA,VOL=SER=PACK03,DISP=OLD
//SYSIN     DD    *
     SCRATCH  DSNAME=USER1.PDS1,MEMBER=M3,VOL=SYSDA=PACK03
/*
```

IDCAMS can also be used to delete the member:

```
//IDC       EXEC  PGM=IDCAMS
//SYSPRINT  DD    SYSOUT=*
//SYSIN     DD    *
     DELETE    USER1.PDS1(M3)
/*
```

Using IDCAMS is preferable to IEHPROGM. IEHPROGM cannot use the catalog and requires an additional DD statement, DD1. For IDCAMS to be used, however, the PDS must be cataloged.

TSO/ISPF can also delete a member.

It is a common practice to delete and uncatalog a disk data set in the first step of a job so that the same data set can be created and cataloged later in the job. Which one (or ones) of the several available ways to accomplish this is (or are) the best? Certainly, not the way shown below, since it deletes without uncataloging, as discussed earlier.

```
//S1  EXEC PGM=IEFBR14
//D2  DD   DSN=USER1.DSK2,DISP=(OLD,DELETE),UNIT=SYSDA,
//         VOL=SER=PACK01
```

Even if a second DD statement is added to provide uncataloging,

```
//S1   EXEC  PGM=IEFBR14
//D2   DD    DSN=USER1.DSK2,DISP=(OLD,DELETE),UNIT=SYSDA,
//           VOL=SER=PACK01
//D3   DD    DSN=USER1.DSK2,DISP=(OLD,UNCATLG),UNIT=SYSDA,
//           VOL=SER=PACK01
```

this method is of questionable value because it is volume dependent, and volume dependence is an undesirable feature. Also, if the volume is not known, this method cannot be used.

The method below appears to accomplish the desired goal of deleting and uncataloging, as discussed before:

```
//S1   EXEC  PGM=IEFBR14
//D2   DD    DSN=USER1.DSK2,DISP=(OLD,DELETE)
```

However, it has one weakness. If the data set has already been deleted and uncataloged, the result will be a "DATA SET NOT FOUND' JCL error. That would be unacceptable, especially in a production environment.

The possibility of a JCL error can be eliminated if MOD rather than OLD were used:

```
//S1   EXEC  PGM=IEFBR14
//D2   DD    DSN=USER1.DSK2,DISP=(MOD,DELETE),UNIT=SYSDA,
//           SPACE=(TRK,0)
```

If the data set is cataloged, MOD becomes identical to OLD (positioning to the end of data occurs during the open and IEFBR14 does not open), and the data set will be deleted and uncataloged. The SPACE parameters will be ignored. UNIT=SYSDA must be carefully checked so that it does not create the "UNABLE TO ALLOCATE" JCL error discussed earlier in Section 7.3.1. If the data set is not cataloged, MOD defaults to NEW and the data set will be created and deleted, eliminating the JCL error.

If JCL (IEFBR14) is to be used for deleting a data set, the last method is the recommended one. However, IDCAMS can also be used to achieve equally successful results:

```
//S1       EXEC  PGM=IDCAMS
//SYSPRINT DD    SYSOUT=*
//SYSIN    DD    *
   DELETE  USER1.DSK2
```

This will cause the data set to be deleted and uncataloged. ID-CAMS can never delete without uncataloging. Unfortunately, again there is a weakness. If the data set has already been deleted and uncataloged, the DELETE will issue a return code of 8, which may become the return code of the step. This is normally treated as a questionable return code and will cause a subsequent step using COND=(4,LT) or COND=(0,LT), not to be executed while there is really nothing wrong. This problem can be eliminated by using ID-CAMS execution control commands IF/THEN:

```
//S1        EXEC PGM=IDCAMS
//SYSPRINT  DD   SYSOUT=*
//SYSIN     DD   *
   DELETE   USER1.DSK2
   IF LASTCC=8 THEN -
   SET MAXCC=4 (or SET MAXCC=0)
```

The IF and SET commands will change the return code from 8 to 4 (or 0), thus eliminating the problem.

Either of the last two methods is recommended. The IEHPROGM utility, which can also delete and uncatalog a data set, is not recommended (see Section 13.4 in Chapter 13).

7.4 RETRIEVING PARTITIONED DATA SETS

A Partitioned Data Set (PDS) can be retrieved in two different ways:

- //IN1 DD DSN=USER1.PDS1(MEMBER5),DISP=SHR
- //IN2 DD DSN=USER1.PDS1,DISP=SHR

These two DD statements are very different from one another. In the first example, a particular member, MEMBER5, is requested within PDS USER1.PDS1. If a program opens for this DD statement, it can process the member using an ordinary sequential access method, such as QSAM (Queued Sequential Access Method), and the program is confined to the specified member only.

In the second example, the entire PDS is requested. If a program opens for this DD statement, it can add, delete, or modify as many members as it wishes. However, the program must use BPAM (Basic Partitioned Access Method). This access method is mostly used by vendor-written programs (such as Utilities, IDCAMS, etc.) and rarely by user-written programs. Most high-level languages (COBOL, for example) cannot use BPAM.

When dealing with a PDS and a given member within it, the relationship between the DSN and DISP parameters is not obvious and carries certain dangers. Consider the example below:

```
//DD1   DD   DSN=USER1.LIB2(Z32),DISP=(OLD,DELETE,KEEP)
```

An interesting question arises here. What do the various fields of the DISP parameter pertain to? The PDS or the member? The answer is consistent: All of them pertain to the PDS, none to the member. It is an OLD PDS and, as discussed in Section 7.3.4, the PDS, not just the member, will be deleted.

What about the member? Is it an OLD or a NEW member? The DISP parameter, unless NEW is coded (in which case the member must also be NEW), provides no such information for the member.

How a member is handled depends on whether or not it exists and on whether the program opens for input or output. A summary of all possibilities is presented below:

```
//S1   EXEC   PGM=P1
//D1   DD     DSN=USER1.LIBA(M12),DISP=SHR   (or DISP=OLD)
```

- Member M12 exists:
  — If program P1 opens for input and reads, member M12 will be read.
  — If program P1 opens for output and writes, member M12 will be replaced (but not in-place).
  — If program P1 does not open, nothing happens.
- Member M12 does not exist:
  — If program P1 opens for input and reads, the result will be a S013-18 ABEND failure.
  — If program P1 opens for output and writes, member M12 will be created.
  — If program P1 does not open, nothing happens.

If DISP=MOD is used (defaulting to an existing status rather than NEW), it will have the same effect as DISP=OLD except when the member exists and the program opens for output. Rather than replacing the member, MOD will cause an SB14 ABEND failure (see Section 7.8).

7.5 DISP=OLD vs DISP=SHR

Both OLD and SHR are used to describe an existing data set (retrieval). However, OLD demands exclusive usage, whereas SHR allows the data set to be shared.

For tape data sets DISP=OLD is appropriate since tape is a non-sharable device. DISP=SHR will basically work the same way as DISP=OLD for tape and will provide a benefit only under very unusual conditions. Example: Two jobs need to use two different tape data sets residing on different volumes but which have the same data set name (this is a poor practice and should be avoided). To be able to run concurrently, both jobs must use DISP=SHR in the DD statements describing the two data sets.

For disk data sets, DISP=SHR is appropriate if the data set is opened for input, DISP=OLD, if opened for output. Using DISP=OLD for input data sets can cause loss of throughput to the entire system. Consider a DD statement in the 14th step of a job:

```
//STEP14   EXEC   PGM=HA1
//D1       DD     DSN=USER1.INSET,DISP=OLD
```

Assume that data set USER1.INSET is not referenced anywhere else in the job. From the beginning of this job's execution until STEP14 has terminated, no other job that refers to the same data set name in any step (regardless of DISP) can begin execution. The fact that the first 13 steps of the job do not use the data set makes no difference. After STEP14 the data set will be freed.

For two jobs to run together using the same data set, both must use SHR. Any other combination of DISP (not only OLD, but MOD and NEW as well) will stop the jobs from running concurrently.

This is an inefficient method of providing sharability, and for this reason the user must be careful. When retrieving a disk data set, SHR should always come to mind first. In the great majority of cases, it will be appropriate. This is because a data set being retrieved is apt to be read (input) much more often than written to (output). If, of course, the data set is being updated, DISP=OLD should be used to protect its integrity. DISP=SHR could be dangerous because another job may also be using DISP=SHR and updating the same data set. If these two jobs run concurrently, there is a possibility that the data set will be destroyed.

7.6 RETRIEVING WITH NL, BLP, AND LTM

Nonlabeled tape data sets are seldom used. Given the fact that no labels exist, neither the volume serial nor the data set name can be verified. As a result, when a mount is requested for an NL input data set, any NL volume and any data set on it is accepted. This makes the use of NL very dangerous and most installations avoid using it. Normally, SL is used unless the tape volume is either to be sent to or comes from an installation which does not use MVS.

The following DD statement retrieves an NL data set:

```
//IN   DD   DSN=USER1.NLTP,DISP=OLD,UNIT=TAPE,VOL=SER=004911,
//          LABEL=(,NL),DCB=(LRECL=100,BLKSIZE=32000,RECFM=FB)
```

Any DSN and VOL can be used. The effect of supplementary tape management packages, such as TMS or TLMS, is not considered. If they are used, LABEL=(,NL,EXPDT=98000) may be needed to allow the data set to be processed outside TMS (or TLMS) control. NL data sets normally are not cataloged.

As mentioned before, in response to the mount message from a DD statement for NL tape, any NL tape volume can be mounted and accepted. However, an SL tape volume is rejected. The open routines check the first record on the volume and if it is a volume label, reject the volume and repeat the mount message.

This raises an interesting question: What if one wishes to process an SL data set but cannot use (or default to) SL. If, for example, the volume serial or data set name is not known, SL cannot be used. NL also cannot be used since the volume is SL, as explained in the preceding paragraph. Using BLP will solve the problem. To understand how BLP works, note a similarity between the first data set on an SL volume ("SL DATA SET # 1" in the diagram below) and the second data set on an NL volume ("NL DATA SET # 2" in the diagram below).

SL

| VOL | HDR1 | HDR2 | TM | SL DATA SET #1 | TM | EOF1 | EOF2 | TM | | TM | |

NL

| NL DATA SET #1 | TM | NL DATA SET #2 | TM | | TM | |

TM stands for tape mark.

In either case, the volume contains several records, a tape mark, and then several more records. The only difference is that for SL the beginning records happen to be labels.

The second NL data set can be retrieved using LABEL=(2,NL) But, as discussed before, the same parameter will fail if the SL volume is mounted in an attempt to get to the second physical file on the volume, which is the data of the first SL data set. However, it will work if LABEL=(2,BLP) is used instead of LABEL=(2,NL). BLP and NL work almost identically with one major exception: when NL is requested, an NL volume must be mounted; if BLP is requested, any type of volume can be mounted, including SL. In essence, when BPL is used, any group of records preceding a tape mark is treated as a physical file (first file is an exception as it is not preceded by a tape mark) and labels are not recognized.

The complete DD statement using BLP is shown below. Keep in mind that, if an installation uses TMS or TLMS, EXPDT=98000 may also have to be included in the LABEL parameter, as discussed before for NL.

```
//IN   DD   DSN=USER1.BLTP,DISP=OLD,UNIT=TAPE,VOL=SER=000195,
//           LABEL=(2,BLP),DCB=(LRECL=100,BLKSIZE=32000,RECFM=FB)
```

If BLP is to be used to access the second data set on an SL volume, LABEL=(5,BLP) must be used. Using the formula below, any SL data set can be accessed using BLP:

$$n = 3s - 1$$

where n is the number to be used with BLP and s is the number that would be used for SL. Example: To access the 11th SL data set using BLP, $n = 3 \times 11 - 1 = 32$, LABEL=(32,BLP).

The use of BLP should be treated as a last resort. If neither SL or NL will work, then it is acceptable to use BLP. Some installations disallow the use of BLP in a production environment.

LABEL=(2,NL) can be used to process the first data set on a DOS/VSE NL tape. This is due to the fact the DOS NL tapes begin with a tape mark, while MVS/XA NL tapes do not. Using LABEL=(,LTM) is an alternative technique to accomplish the same goal. Both work equally well for a single volume data set. LABEL=(,LTM) can also retrieve a multivolume data set while LABEL=(2,NL) reverts to (1,NL) on the second volume, encounters the leading tape mark and terminates, failing to process the remaining volumes (and failing to give any error indication). DOS/VSE SL tapes can be processed under MVS/XA using LABEL=(,SL) as long as the DCB parameter is included to supply all needed subparameters. If this presents a problem, LABEL=(2,BLP) can be used.

7.7 RETRIEVING MULTIVOLUME DATA SETS

Retrieving multivolume data sets using the catalog is as simple as retrieving single-volume data sets.

```
//INV  DD  DSN=USER1.MVSET,DISP=SHR
```

The catalog supplies the volumes where the data set resides.

If processing must begin with a volume other than the first one (let us say the second), then VOL=(,,2) must be included in the DD statement.

For multivolume *disk* data sets, there is no need to supply multiple devices, such as UNIT=(SYSDA,3) or UNIT=(SYSDA,P). Whether the volumes are explicitly stated in the VOL parameter or they come from the catalog, the system will allocate as many devices as there are volumes (this is exactly what UNIT=(SYSDA,P) does). The system automatically allocates as many disk devices as there are volumes because there is no way for two or more nonremovable volumes to be mounted on a single device.

For multivolume *tape* data sets,the system will not allocate more than one device unless it is requested. UNIT=(TAPE,2) can be used to enhance processing multivolume data sets. When only one device is allocated (default), and a volume reaches its end, it rewinds, unloads, and a request appears on the console to mount the next volume on the same device. For each volume, a minute or more can be wasted while going from one volume to the next. If UNIT=(TAPE,2) is used, two devices are allocated, and while a volume is being processed on one device, the operator can be mounting the next volume on the other device. This eliminates delays after the first volume is mounted.

The technique discussed in the preceding paragraph may not always be advantageous. Considering the fact that most installations are short of tape devices, it can backfire. It may speed up one job's execution, while another job either cannot begin or suspends its execution for want of tape devices. So, UNIT=(TAPE,2) should be used only if it is warranted and always with operations management approval. Allocating more than two tape devices can seldom be justified and should be avoided. UNIT=(TAPE,P) — commonly known as a parallel mount — must also be avoided for tape, especially when retrieving a cataloged data set for which the number of volumes may not be known. The system will attempt to allocate as many tape devices as there are volumes. This is too dangerous! If there are many volumes, there is a good chance that allocation will fail. And if it succeeds, the entire environment may suffer.

7.8 RETRIEVING USING MOD

Retrieving a sequential data set using the MOD subparameter of the DISP parameter allows the data set to be extended. When the program opens the data set for output, the read/write mechanism of the device will be positioned over the end-of-file marker at the end of the data set. As new blocks are written, the data set will be extended. The program issuing the open and write instructions is unaware that the data set is being extended. JCL controls where the data is written. The read/write mechanism is positioned to the beginning of the data set if DISP=OLD is used and to the end if DISP=MOD is used. MOD is only meaningful for output. If the program opens for input, MOD will be treated the same as OLD.

Consider the DD statement below:

```
//EXT   DD   DSN=USER1.SEQ1,DISP=(MOD,KEEP)
```

The system, during the Allocation process, assumes that USER1.SEQ1 is an existing data set and attempts to determine the volume serial on which the data set resides. Such information will be found if:

• The DD statement contains VOL=SER or VOL=REF (for a disk data set, VOL=REF cannot be a referback to a nonspecific new request for another data set).
• The data set is passed.
• The data set is cataloged.

If volume serial is found, the system will treat MOD the same as it does OLD until the data set is opened, at which time it will position to the end of the data set.

In the example above, if data set USER1.SEQ1 is neither passed nor cataloged, MOD will default to NEW, resulting in JCL error caused by the fact that no UNIT parameter has been included.

If data set USER1.SEQ1 is passed or cataloged, MOD will default to an existing data set, which will be extended when opened for output.

If USER1.SEQ1 is a tape data set, a danger exists. If the first volume is exhausted while writing, the system will issue a mount message to the operator for a new volume to be mounted (five volumes are available by default), so that the data set can continue into the new volume. However, since DISP=(MOD,KEEP) was used, the catalog entry of the data set will not be updated to contain the new volume serial. And if subsequently the data set is retrieved using the catalog, the last volume will not be called for, resulting in loss of data. Furthermore, no message will appear to warn the user of this problem. This danger can be eliminated if the DD statement is changed to.

```
//EXT   DD   DSN=USER1.SEQ1,DISP=(MOD,CATLG)
```

Now, if the data set extends to a new volume, the catalog will be updated to contain the new volume serial and the following Step Termination message will appear:

```
IEF285I   USER1.SEQ1                          RECATALOGED
IEF285I   VOL SER NOS= 000551,003864
```

The word "Recataloged" can easily be misunderstood to mean that the catalog entry was replaced. A catalog entry cannot be replaced. Rather, it is updated to contain accurate volume serial information.

If a new volume is not added, the message will be

```
IEF287I   USER1.SEQ1                          NOT RECTLGD 2
IEF287I   VOL SER NOS= 000551
```

This message is benign, indicating that the catalog entry remained unaltered and, of course, accurately describes the data set.

One more point can be made here, although it represents an unusual situation. Assume that a multivolume cataloged data set consisting of two volumes, 000228 and 000771, is to be extended.

```
//OUT   DD   DSN=USER1.MSET,DISP=(MOD,CATLG)
```

The allocation routines treat MOD as OLD and request the mounting of the first volume (000228). This is clearly the wrong volume. The open routines rectify the error by eliminating the previous mount message and issuing a new mount message for the correct volume (000771). However, the operator has already seen the first message and may even have mounted the incorrect volume (000228). This is not dangerous, as ultimately only the second mount takes effect. But it creates unnecessary work for the operator and possible confusion. The double message can be eliminated in two different ways. The first way takes advantage of DEFER:

```
//OUT   DD   DSN=USER1.MSET,DISP=(MOD,CATLG),UNIT=(,,DEFER)
```

DEFER causes the Allocation routines not to issue a mount message. The message will be issued by the open routines, which, as discussed before, will call for the correct volume.

The other way uses the volume sequence subparameter of the VOL parameter:

```
//EXT   DD   DSN=USER1.SEQ1,DISP=(MOD,CATLG),VOL=(,,2)
```

Here, the Allocation routines issue the mount message for the correct volume (000771) because (,,2) in the VOL parameter requests that processing of the data set begin with the second volume. This method is the least advantageous of the two, because the user must know the number of volumes contained in the catalog entry. Using DEFER eliminates the need to know. With DEFER, the last volume will be called for, regardless of how many volumes the data set consists of.

When retrieving a PDS, MOD is seldom needed. Extending a PDS with new members does not require the use of MOD. When adding members to a PDS, MOD and OLD work identically, but while OLD can be used to replace members, MOD cannot. Consider the DD statement below:

```
//DD1   DD   DSN=USER1.PDSA(M35),DISP=(MOD,KEEP)
```

- If member M35 does not exist within the PDS and the program opens for output, member M35 will be created. DISP=(OLD,KEEP), of course, would accomplish exactly the same goal.
- If member M35 exists within the PDS and the program opens for output, the result will be an SB14 ABEND and no replacement of the member will take place.
- If the program opens for input (whether member M35 exists or not), MOD will do exactly what OLD does and, actually, neither is a good choice. SHR would be preferable.

So the only situation where MOD can be useful with a PDS is when a member must be added but replacing an identically named member must be avoided. With that exception, MOD is best not used because it may appear to imply that a member is being extended. A member of a PDS cannot be extended by using MOD. If extending a member is necessary, the member must be copied to a sequential data set, the data set can be extended using MOD and then copied back into the PDS, replacing the original member.

7.9 ALTERING SECONDARY ALLOCATION AND RELEASING UNUSED SPACE

Consider the following DD statements, all of which open for output:

```
//DD1   DD   DSN=USER1.PDS1(M7),DISP=OLD

//DD2   DD   DSN=USER1.EXT1,DISP=(MOD,KEEP)

//DD3   DD   DSN=USER1.OVR1,DISP=OLD
```

In all of the DD statements, if available disk space is exhausted while adding or replacing a member (first example), extending a sequential data set (second example), or overlaying an existing data set (third example), the system checks the data set's DSCB in the VTOC and tries to provide whatever secondary allocation was coded in the SPACE parameter when the data set was created.

Now consider the same DD statements, each with a SPACE parameter and each opened for output:

```
//DD1   DD   DSN=USER1.PDS1(M7),DISP=OLD,SPACE=(CYL,(15,5))

//DD2   DD   DSN=USER1.EXT1,DISP=(MOD,KEEP),SPACE=(CYL,(15,5))

//DD3   DD   DSN=USER1.OVR1,DISP=OLD,SPACE=(CYL,(15,5))
```

An out-of-space condition will now will be handled differently. The system will try to provide the secondary allocation that appears in the SPACE parameter.

The presence of the SPACE parameter does not change what has been recorded in the data set's DSCB in the VTOC pertaining to the original secondary allocation. It simply forces the system to provide the secondary allocation of the SPACE parameter and ignore the

VTOC. Let us say, for example, that DD1 exhausted space and, because of the SPACE parameter, five cylinders of disk space were supplied. If later the same DD statement is used again but without the SPACE parameter and again an out-of-space condition is encountered, the system will now use the VTOC to determine what secondary allocation the data set is entitled to, based on the DD statement that created the data set.

In all examples above, the primary allocation is ignored. However, a value must be supplied (0 is acceptable) for syntactical reasons. SPACE=(CYL,(,5)) will result in a JCL error.

Suppose the SPACE parameter does not contain secondary allocation:

```
//DD1   DD   DSN=USER1.PDS1(M7),DISP=OLD,SPACE=(CYL,15)

//DD2   DD   DSN=USER1.EXT1,DISP=(MOD,KEEP),SPACE=(CYL,15)

//DD3   DD   DSN=USER1.OVR1,DISP=OLD,SPACE=(CYL,15)
```

Now, if available space is exhausted, the result will be a SD37-04 ABEND failure. Coding SPACE=(CYL,15) is the same as coding SPACE=(CYL,(15,0)), and this requests that no secondary allocation be provided, regardless of how the data set was initially created.

In addition to the secondary allocation, the RLSE subparameter is also meaningful if the SPACE parameter appears with a DISP other than NEW and the data set is opened for output. All other subparameters in the space parameter are ignored. If the data set is opened for input, the entire SPACE parameter is always ignored.

```
//DD1   DD   DSN=USER1.PDS1(M7),DISP=OLD,SPACE=(CYL,0,RLSE)
```

If the above DD statement is opened for output, all unused space will be released when the data set is closed.

Consider an existing sequential data set USER.SS3 whose excess space must be released. The IEBGENER utility can be used to provide the open for output (SYSUT2).

```
//GEN       EXEC   PGM=IEBGENER
//SYSPRINT  DD     SYSOUT=*
//SYSIN     DD     DUMMY
//SYSUT1    DD     DUMMY,DCB=(BLKSIZE=80,LRECL=80,RECFM=FB)
//SYSUT2    DD     DSN=USER1.SS3,DISP=(MOD,KEEP),SPACE=(TRK,0,RLSE)
```

IEBGENER opens SYSUT2 for output, positioning the read/write head over the existing EOF marker (because of MOD), writes no records (because SYSUT1 is DUMMY), and closes writing an EOF marker over the existing one. RLSE will cause all unused space to be released. It should be noted that if DISP=OLD were used instead of MOD, the EOF marker would be written at the beginning of the data set, effectively destroying it.

If the data set whose space to be released were partitioned, again IEBGENER can be used as follows:

```
//GEN       EXEC  PGM=IEBGENER
//SYSPRINT  DD    SYSOUT=*
//SYSIN     DD    DUMMY
//SYSUT1    DD    DUMMY,DCB=(BLKSIZE=80,LRECL=80,RECFM=FB)
//SYSUT2    DD    DSN=USER1.PD4(MX),DISP=OLD,SPACE=(TRK,0,RLSE)
```

IEBGENER opens SYSUT2 for output, creates member MX, and writes no records (because SYSUT1 is DUMMY). The close will cause all unused space to be released. The empty member can be eliminated later using ISPF, IDCAMS, or IEHPROGM (but not JCL).

7.10 DCB CONSIDERATIONS FOR RETRIEVAL

When retrieving a standard labeled data set, the DCB parameter in the DD statement is seldom required.

Compare the two DD statements below, both of which can be considered technically correct:

```
//IN1  DD  DSN=USER1.FIL1,DISP=SHR

//IN2  DD  DSN=USER1.FIL2,DISP=SHR,
//         DCB=(LRECL=80,RECFM=FB,BLKSIZE=6000)
```

In DD statement IN1, any DCB attributes not hard-coded in the program (possibly LRELC and RECFM and frequently BLKSIZE) will be supplied by the standard label of the data set (SL is the default). This is almost always desirable, given the fact that the label normally supplies correct information.

In DD statement IN2, any DCB attributes not hard-coded in the program will be supplied by the DCB parameter, and, of course, accuracy cannot be guaranteed. Suppose that the BLKSIZE specified in DCB parameter is incorrect. If it is a data set opened for input, there are several possibilities:

- BLKSIZE in the DCB parameter is larger than the actual blocksize of the data set and a multiple of the LRECL. No problem! The system accepts the larger BLKSIZE because the buffers acquired based on the wrong blocksize are large enough to contain the actual blocks.
- BLKSIZE in the DCB parameter is smaller than the actual blocksize of the data set and a multiple of the LRECL. The result will be an S001-4 ABEND failure because the buffers acquired based on the wrong blocksize are too small to contain the actual blocks.
- BLKSIZE in the DCB parameter is smaller or greater than the actual blocksize of the data set but not a multiple of the LRECL. The result will be an S013-20 ABEND failure because, for RECFM=FB, the BLKSIZE must be a multiple of the LRECL (SYSOUT is an exception).

It is obvious that supplying any of the three DCB subparameters when retrieving an SL data set is practically always unnecessary and downright dangerous. And since the vast majority of tape data sets and all disk data sets are SL, the DCB parameter should seldom be used, unless other DCB subparameters not supplied by the label are required (the label can supply BLKSIZE, LRECL, RECFM DSORG, OPTCD, RKP, and KEYLEN — the last three are ISAM-related).
Example:

```
//IN2   DD  DSN=USER1.FIL2,DISP=SHR,
//            DCB=(BUFNO=50,EROPT=SKP)
```

Since neither of the DCB subparameters above can be supplied by the label, they must be specified in the DCB parameter. BUFNO is usually not recommended if the data set has an adequate blocksize (i.e., 4K and above) because the five buffers that are available by default normally suffice. A large BUFNO may be recommended if the data set being retrieved contains very small blocks (i.e., 80 bytes). EROPT=SKP requests that, in the event of an I/O error, the block where the error occurred be skipped. This, of course, puts the integrity of the data set in question, and it is seldom used.

When a data set is retrieved and opened for output, supplying a DCB parameter can be even more dangerous. Here are two examples:

```
//OUT1  DD  DSN=XX.PDS1(M4),DISP=OLD,
//            DCB=(LRECL=80,RECFM=FB,BLKSIZE=4000)
```

```
//OUT2   DD DSN=XX.SSET,DISP=(MOD,KEEP),
//          DCB=(LRECL=80,RECFM=FB,BLKSIZE=4000)
```

In both DD statements, if the data set is opened for output (in the first example adding or replacing a member and in the second extending the data set) and the BLKSIZE coded in the DCB parameter is smaller than the actual blocksize of the data set, no failure will occur, but the BLKSIZE value supplied in the DCB parameter will overlay the proper BLKSIZE in the label of the data set. Future S001-4 ABEND failures are now likely to occur when the data set is retrieved and the label is used to supply DCB information.

When NL, BLP, or LTM is used in the LABEL parameter, the DCB parameter must provide information not hard-coded in the DCB of the program. If a tape coded in ASCII is to be read, OPTCD=Q must be coded in the DCB parameter. This will cause ASCII information to be automatically translated to EDCDIC.

It should be noted that the DEN subparameter in the DCB parameter is never needed when inputting tape data sets. For 3420 tape, the density will automatically adjust. For 3480 tape, only one density exists, 38,000 BPI, and the DEN subparameter is meaningless (and ignored).

Example:

```
//INA   DD  DSN=USER1.FILA,DISP=OLD,LABEL=(,NL),
//          UNIT=TAPE,VOL=SER=00293,DCB=(BLKSIZE=2000,
//          LRECL=80,RECFM=FB,OPTCD=Q)
```

Since the data set is NL, all needed subparameters not hard-coded in the program must be supplied in the DCB parameter.

7.11 USING UNIT AFFINITY AND FREE=CLOSE

```
//SA        EXEC   PGM=PG3
//IN1       DD  DSN=PROD.OLDMST1,DISP=OLD
//IN2       DD  DSN=PROD.OLDMST2,DISP=OLD
```

In the step above, if PROD.OLDMST1 and PROD.OLDMST2 are tape data sets, two tape devices will be needed. Assuming that both data sets' density can be provided by the same tape device, UNIT=AFF can be used to allocate the same device to both data sets, thus keeping the other device available.

```
//SA        EXEC  PGM=PG3
//IN1       DD   DSN=PROD.OLDMST1,DISP=OLD
//IN2       DD   DSN=PROD.OLDMST2,DISP=OLD,UNIT=AFF=IN1
```

Tape devices cannot be shared, and, as a result, a serious restriction exists. Both data sets cannot be open at the same time. If PROD.OLDMST1 is not closed before PROD.OLDMST2 is opened, an S413-04 ABEND failure will be the result. How data sets open and close during the execution of a program is not obvious, and, therefore, careful examination of documentation is recommended before UNIT=AFF is used.

UNIT=AFF is useful only for tape data sets since its purpose is to increase availability of nonsharable devices. It should never be used with disk data sets. Disk is sharable, and the use of this parameter can cause problems without providing any benefit.

The FREE=CLOSE parameter can also have an effect on tape device utilization. It causes the allocated device to deallocate at close time rather than step termination or possibly much later for JES3. It also causes a data set to be freed from an exclusive usage status and become available to other jobs.

```
//IN1        DD   DSN=PROD.OLDMST1,DISP=OLD,FREE=CLOSE
```

This parameter can be of value to the user if *all* of the following conditions exist:

- The program closes the data set (some programs do not, in which case the step termination does).
- The close occurs a considerable time before step termination (the longer this time, the greater the benefit).
- The data set is not opened more than once. Since FREE=CLOSE deallocates the device, if there is an open, a close (device is now deallocated) and a second open, message

```
IEC130I  IN1 - DD STATEMENT MISSING
```

will be issued by the open routines. Although processing continues, an attempt to read or write will cause an unpredictable failure, most likely a program check (S0Cx ABEND failure). This failure may not occur if the close was coded in Assembly Language with LEAVE or REWIND.
- The data set is on tape. Using FREE=CLOSE with a disk data set is pointless from a device utilization standpoint (disk is shareable) and still dangerous in the event of multiple opens.

For a disk data set, FREE=CLOSE will have a second effect. The data set will be released from exclusive usage and made available to other jobs at close time. This may or may not be desirable and can be potentially dangerous, if the data set will be used for output later in the job

Using FREE=END has the same effect as not supplying the FREE parameter.

7.12 RETRIEVING CONCATENATED DATA SETS

The JCL below shows a concatenation:

```
//S1   EXEC  PGM=PCA
//IN   DD    DSN=USER1.SET1,DISP=OLD
//     DD    DSN=USER1.SET2,DISP=OLD
//     DD    DSN=USER1.SET3,DISP=OLD
```

Concatenations and their rules are fully discussed in Section 10.10 of Chapter 10.

Concatenated DD statements are allocated the same way as independent DD statements. During execution, the first concatenated DD statement behaves the same way as any other input DD statement. Beginning with the second DD statement, however, certain ABEND failures will be different with concatenations as opposed to other DD statements. Consider the JCL shown above, assuming that the concatenations describe tape data sets. If the data set name in the first concatenation does not match with the data set name in the label, the result is a S813-04 ABEND failure, the same as an independent DD statement. If the same problem, however, occurs with the second (or any subsequent) DD statement, the ABEND failure will be a S237-08. This difference is due to the fact that the data set name verification for the first concatenation is performed by the open routines (SVC 13), whereas the same verification for the concatenations that follow is performed by the end-of-volume routines (SVC 37) which simulate the open functions. Message IEC0231 which gives details about this failure, identifies the failing concatenation as "+n" where n is its sequence. For example, the second concatenation would be identified as "+2."

A similar situation exists for disk concatenations:

```
//S1   EXEC  PGM=PCA
//IN   DD    DSN=USER1.FIL1,DISP=SHR,UNIT=SYSDA,VOL=SER=PACK35
```

```
//      DD    DSN=USER1.FIL2,DISP=SHR,UNIT=SYSDA,VOL=SER=PACK16
//      DD    DSN=USER1.FIL3,DISP=SHR
```

If data set USER1.FIL1 of the first concatenation does not reside on volume PACK35, the result will be a S213-04 ABEND failure. If data set USER1.FIL2 of the second concatenation does not reside on volume PACK16, the result will be a S737-04 ABEND failure. Message IEC0271 which gives details about this failure, will identify the failing concatenation as "+2."

As is explained in Section 10.10 of Chapter 10, for tape concatenations it is imperative to code UNIT=AFF in order to avoid allocating as many tape devices as there are concatenations.

```
//IN    DD    DSN=USER1.TAP1,DISP=OLD
//      DD    DSN=USER1.TAP2,DISP=OLD,UNIT=AFF=IN
//      DD    DSN=USER1.TAP3,DISP=OLD,UNIT=AFF=IN
//      DD    DSN=USER1.TAP4,DISP=OLD,UNIT=AFF=IN
//      DD    DSN=USER1.TAP5,DISP=OLD,UNIT=AFF=IN
```

However, when there are many concatenations, it may be desirable to allocate two tape devices, comparable to UNIT=(TAPE,2) with a multivolume data set (see Section 7.7 in this chapter), in order to avoid loss of time while mounting volumes. Allocating two tape devices appears to be no problem. The first two concatenations in the JCL below will allocate a device each.

```
//IN    DD    DSN=USER1.TAP1,DISP=OLD
//      DD    DSN=USER1.TAP2,DISP=OLD
//      DD    DSN=USER1.TAP3,DISP=OLD,UNIT=AFF=IN
//      DD    DSN=USER1.TAP4,DISP=OLD,UNIT=AFF=IN
//      DD    DSN=USER1.TAP5,DISP=OLD,UNIT=AFF=IN
```

What remains to be done is to have the third concatenation allocate the same device as the first, the fourth concatenation the same device as the second and so on. UNIT=AFF=IN accomplishes this in the third concatenation. But the fourth concatenation cannot refer to the second because it has no ddname.

An extraneous DD statement can be introduced here to provide a reference point and accomplish the desired goal:

```
//XTRA DD    UNIT=(TAPE,,DEFER)
//IN    DD    DSN=USER1.TAP1,DISP=OLD
//      DD    DSN=USER1.TAP2,DISP=OLDUNIT=AFF=XTRA
```

```
//      DD      DSN=USER1.TAP3,DISP=OLD,UNIT=AFF=IN
//      DD      DSN=USER1.TAP4,DISP=OLD,UNIT=AFF=XTRA
//      DD      DSN=USER1.TAP5,DISP=OLD,UNIT=AFF=IN
```

DD statement XTRA (the ddname is arbitrary) is not used by the executing program. Its only purpose is to provide an additional device in a DD statement that can be referenced. This example demonstrates a good use of DEFER. The data set will not be opened and the operator will not see a mount message.

A similar problem can arise if one of the sort packages which allow unlike device concatenation, as discussed in Section 10.10 of Chapter 10, uses several concatenations in the SORTIN DD statement the first of which is on disk and the rest on tape. If the sequence of the concatenations cannot be altered, the tape concatenations cannot be allocated to the same device because they canot refer to each other. The concatenation below will result in the allocation of three tape devices. This is normally unacceptable.

```
//SORTIN DD     DSN=USER1.DISKDS1,DISP=SHR        DISK DATA SET
//      DD      DSN=USER1.TAPEDS1,DISP=OLD        TAPE DATA SET
//      DD      DSN=USER1.TAPEDS2,DISP=OLD        TAPE DATA SET
//      DD      DSN=USER1.TAPEDS3,DISP=OLD        TAPE DATA SET
```

An extraneous DD statement can again be introduced to provide a reference point.

```
//DUM    DD     UNIT=(TAPE,,DEFER)
//SORTIN DD     DSN=USER1.DISKDS1,DISP=SHR        DISK DATA SET
//      DD      DSN=USER1.TAPEDS1,DISP=OLD,UNIT=AFF=DUM
//      DD      DSN=USER1.TAPEDS2,DISP=OLD,UNIT=AFF=DUM
//      DD      DSN=USER1.TAPEDS3,DISP=OLD,UNIT=AFF=DUM
```

DD statement DUM is not used by the sort program. Its only purpose is to provide a ddname for all tape concatenations to refer to.

7.13 RETRIEVING VSAM DATA SETS

Retrieving a VSAM data set is basically no different than retrieving a cataloged non-VSAM data set.

```
//VIN    DD DSN=USER1.VS1,DISP=SHR              VSAM DS
```

VSAM data sets (often referred to as clusters) are always cataloged, and the catalog must always be used in retrieving them. DISP=SHR may be used even if the data set is to be updated, because the integrity of a VSAM data set is often best protected by VSAM's share options rather than DISP=OLD. The only acceptable disposition field for VSAM data sets in KEEP. If any other disposition is coded, it will be changed to KEEP. No message will be given to indicate that the DISP parameter was changed.

The only other parameter that may appear in a DD statement retrieving a VSAM data set is the AMP parameter:

```
//SIN    DD   DSN=USER1.VS1,DISP=SHR,AMP='BUFND=8'
```

In this example, the number of data buffers will be 8 rather than the default 2, providing enhancement for sequential processing. This is applicable to all types of clusters, KSDS (Key Sequenced Data Set — or Indexed), ESDS (Entry Sequenced Data Set — or Nonindexed), and RRDS (Relative Record Data Set — or Numbered).

```
//DIN    DD   DSN=USER1.VS1,DISP=SHR,AMP='BUFNI=4'
```

In this example, the number of index buffers will be 4 rather than the default 1, providing enhancement for direct processing. It is only applicable to KSDS clusters.

8

Creating Data Sets

The purpose of a DD statement (except when DUMMY or DSN=NULFILE is coded) is to create or retrieve a data set.

This chapter will discuss the logic the system uses in creating disk and tape data sets, SPACE parameter considerations, the various ways a data set can be created, public/private considerations, and problems that can be encountered when creating data sets.

8.1 DEFINITION

The system "creates" a data set by means of a DD statement. Such a DD statement must specify "NEW" in the DISP parameter or default to it.

8.1.1 Required and Optional Parameters for Creating

This section will describe which parameters are required and under what circumstances.

No single parameter can actually be described as required. Under varying conditions, each parameter can be omitted:

DSN: Optional. It must be coded, however, if the data set is non-temporary.

DISP: Optional. It must be coded, however, if DISP other than (NEW,DELETE) is needed.

UNIT: Optional. It must be coded, however, if:

* VOL=REF is not coded in the DD statement.
* More than one device must be allocated for tape.
* Deferred mounting is required for tape.
* More than one device must be allocated for a nonspecific disk request.

Note: The UNIT parameter is the most often used parameter when creating data sets.

VOL: Optional. It must be coded, however, if:

* The data set must be created on a particular volume.
* RETAIN is needed to keep a tape volume mounted between steps.
* Tape data set being created will exceed five volumes.

SPACE: Optional. It must be coded, however, if the data set being created is on disk and does not use Virtual I/O (VIO).

Note: The SPACE parameter is practically always used when creating a disk data set.

LABEL: Optional. It must be coded, however, if:

* The data set being created is on tape and its sequence on the volume other than 1.
* A data set being created is not SL
* An expiration date is needed.

DCB: Optional. It must be coded, however, if:

* All DCB values for BLKSIZE, LRECL, and RECFM are not hard-coded (see section 8.4 in this chapter).
* There is a need to code OPTCD, EROPT or BUFNO.
* For 3420 tape, a data set is to have a density other than the highest available on the allocated device.
* A (+n) generation of a GDG is being created using a cataloged model DSCB (see Section 11.4 in Chapter 11).

FREE: Optional. It must be coded, however, if:

* A (tape) device needs to be deallocated when the data set is closed.

• A disk data set needs to be freed from exclusive usage and made available to other jobs.

8.2 THE LOGIC OF ALLOCATION FOR CREATING DISK DATA SETS

The allocation routines (Figure 1.7) are responsible for creating a disk data set. This is also occasionally referred to as "allocating" the data set. However, the word "allocate" can also be used for an existing data set (retrieval), and as a result the term becomes ambiguous and should be avoided.

8.2.1 Creating Nontemporary Sequential Disk Data Sets

Consider the DD statement below:

```
//IN   DD   DSN=USER1.SET2,DISP=(,CATLG),UNIT=SYSDA,VOL=SER=PACK13,
//           SPACE=(CYL,(25,10)),DCB=(LRECL=80,RECFM=FB,BLKSIZE=23440)
```

This DD statement is known as a specific request (volume serial is specified). The Allocation routines will determine if volume PACK13 is mounted on a device whose address is included in what the installation has defined as unit "SYSDA." If so, and the device is not allocated, it will be allocated and assigned a "use count" of one. If already allocated, the use count of the device is increased by one. Then the data set name will be checked for uniqueness. If a data set by the same name resides on the volume, the result will be a JCL error:

```
IEF253I   jobname stepname ddname - DUPLICATE NAME ON DIRECT ACCESS
                                     VOLUME
```

If the data set name is unique, volume PACK13 is searched for the smallest possible extent equal to or greater than 25 cylinders, the primary allocation. If no such extent is found, the volume is searched for two extents that add up to 25 cylinders. If not available, three, then four, and finally five extents can be used to provide the needed space.

Sufficient space having been found, a Format 1 DSCB is generated in the VTOC and the data set now exists. If more than three extents are needed, a Format 3 DSCB is also generated in the VTOC to contain the addresses of extent 4 and beyond (Format 1 has room for only three extents).

If the requested primary allocation is not available (even by combining five extents), the result is a JCL error:

```
IEF257I  jobname stepname ddname - SPACE REQUESTED NOT AVAILABLE
```

If volume PACK33 is not mounted on any device, the system initiates an "allocation recovery" on the operator console. Given the fact that the volumes on today's disk devices (such as 3380) are nonremovable, recovery is virtually impossible and the operator has no other option but to cancel the job.

If volume PACK33 is mounted on a disk device whose address is not included in the installation's description of unit "SYSDA," the result is a JCL error:

```
IEF702I  jobname stepname ddname - UNABLE TO ALLOCATE
```

If volume PACK33 is found to be mounted on a tape device, the result is a JCL error:

```
IEF245I  jobname stepname ddname - INCONSISTENT UNIT NAME AND
                                   VOLUME SERIAL
```

The DD statement below is known as a nonspecific request (no volume is given):

```
//IN1  DD  DSN=USER1.SET3,DISP=(,CATLG),UNIT=SYSDA,
//          SPACE=(CYL,(10,5)),DCB=(LRECL=80,RECFM=FB,BLKSIZE=23440)
```

For such a request the allocation routines will determine if any devices whose addresses are included in the installation's description of unit "SYSDA' contain volumes with the "use" attribute of "STORAGE" (see discussion on public/private considerations in Section 8.2.7 in this chapter). If several such volumes exist (as is normally the case) that can satisfy the primary allocation (10 cylinders), the one with the least number of allocated data sets is selected. If the volume is found to already contain a data set by the same name, another volume will be used. The rest of the allocation process is the same as the specific request discussed earlier. The only difference is that if none of the "STORAGE" volume can accommodate the primary allocation, the result is a JCL error:

```
IEF246I  jobname stepname ddname - INSUFFICIENT SPACE ON STORAGE
                                    VOLUMES
```

If no "STORAGE" volumes are mounted on any SYSDA devices, the system initiates an "allocation recovery" on the operator console and, as explained before, cancellation of the job will follow.

Nonspecific/nontemporary requests are always assigned by the system to "STORAGE" volumes, and several such volumes are usually available. If, however, the data sets assigned to them are allowed to remain there indefinitely, the volumes will eventually fill up. For this reason, most installations will periodically (often on a daily basis) empty out these volumes. An installation's standards should be consulted to determine the life expectancy of such data sets.

8.2.2 Creating Temporary Sequential Disk Data Sets

The two DD statements below represent the most common ways of creating temporary data sets:

```
//WK01   DD   DSN=&&TEMP,DISP=(,PASS),UNIT=SYSDA,
//            SPACE=(9000,(500,200),RLSE),
//            DCB=(LRECL=100,RECFM=FB,BLKSIZE=9000)

//WK02   DD   UNIT=SYSDA,SPACE=(CYL,(30,10))
```

In WK01, the temporary data set is created and passed. It is expected that it will be received in a subsequent step (see Section 9.2 in Chapter 9).

In WK02, the temporary data set is created and deleted within the same step. Its name is assigned by the system and DISP=(NEW,DELETE) is assumed as a default. DD statements of this sort are often used by vendor software packages (such as the SORT), and DCB is usually not required.

Both of the DD statements work similarly to the one for a nonspecific nontemporary request discussed earlier, with the following differences:

• With temporary requests only PASS or DELETE can be specified. Any attempt to specify KEEP, CATLG, or even UNCATLG (the last one would make no sense) will cause the system to substitute PASS and issue a message: IEF648I INVALID DISP FIELD —

PASS SUBSTITUTED Ultimately all temporary data sets will be deleted either during the job's execution or during job termination.

- Temporary requests can be assigned (by the system) to either a "STORAGE" or a "PUBLIC" volume ("PUBLIC" volumes may not be available — see Section 8.2.7 in this chapter).

A temporary request is seldom, if ever, specific:

```
//WK01   DD   DSN=&&TEMP,DISP=(,PASS),UNIT=SYSDA,
//             SPACE=(9000,(500,200),RLSE),VOL=SER=WORK04,
//             DCB=(LRECL=100,RECFM=FB,BLKSIZE=9000)
```

Although technically acceptable, the DD statement above is not recommended. Since a temporary data set seldom has a good reason for residing on a particular volume, even if it is a "STORAGE" or "PUBLIC" volume, it is best to omit the VOL parameter allowing the system to determine the best volume selection. Assigning a temporary data set to a "PRIVATE" volume is a very poor practice and often forbidden.

A temporary data set name can be generated in two ways: by omitting the DSN parameter or by coding DSN=&&name (or DSN=&name). Which DSN is better for which usage?

If a temporary data set will be used again in a subsequent step after being created, omitting the DSN parameter is acceptable but inconvenient.

```
//STEP001  EXEC  PGM=PA
//WRK0001  DD     DISP=(,PASS),UNIT=SYSDA,
//                SPACE=(9000,(500,200),RLSE),
//                DCB=(LRECL=100,RECFM=FB,BLKSIZE=9000)
//STEP002  EXEC  PGM=PB
//RECTDS   DD     DSN=*.STEP001.WRK0001,DISP=(OLD,DELETE)
```

A referback must be used in DD statement RECTDSand:

- The syntax of a referback is cumbersome. Also, unless the two steps are near each other, it can be difficult to find the step and ddname being referenced.
- Referbacks are generally not encouraged by most installations. Using the DSN=&&name format would be more appropriate.

```
//STEP001  EXEC  PGM=PA
//WRK0001  DD     DSN=&&TT,DISP=(,PASS),UNIT=SYSDA,
//                SPACE=(9000,(500,200),RLSE),
```

```
//             DCB=(LRECL=100,RECFM=FB,BLKSIZE=9000)
//STEP002   EXEC  PGM=PB
//RECTDS    DD    DSN=&&TT,DISP=(OLD,DELETE)
```

If a temporary data set is used only once, using DSN=&&name is acceptable but, obviously, not useful at all. Also, there is a remote danger of duplication if another data set by the same DSN parameter is created later in the job. Here it would be best to omit the DSN parameter.

```
//STEP03   EXEC  PGM=PC
//WRK001   DD    UNIT=SYSDA,SPACE=(TRK,(40,15),RLSE)
```

8.2.3 Creating Partitioned Data Sets

Creating a partitioned data set (or PDS) is very similar to creating a sequential one except that the SPACE parameter must contain a directory quantity. A PDS can be created with a member:

```
//PD1   DD  DSN=USER1.PDS1(X13),DISP=(,CATLG),UNIT=SYSDA,
//          SPACE=(23440,(300,80,20)),VOL=SER=DEV001,
//          DCB=(LRECL=80,RECFM=FB,BLKSIZE=23440)
```

or without a member:

```
//PD2   DD  DSN=USER1.PDS2,DISP=(,CATLG),UNIT=SYSDA,
//          SPACE=(CYL,(30,10,40)),VOL=SER=DEV001,
//          DCB=(LRECL=80,RECFM=FB,BLKSIZE=23440)
```

These two DD statements will accomplish the same result if the data set is not opened: create and catalog a PDS with no members. If the data set is opened for output, the two are very different.

In the first DD statement the open will result in the creation of a single member, X13, using an ordinary sequential access method (QSAM or BSAM). As far as the executing program is concerned, it is the same as writing to a sequential data set.

In the second DD statement many members can be created, but it is the executing program's responsibility to place their entries in the directory (by using, for example, macros such as STOW). BPAM (Basic Partitioned Access Method) must be used here. BPAM is seldom used in user-written programs, and it is not available to many high-level languages, such as COBOL. If the program were to use a sequential access method, the data set would be written to sequentially, without preserving the directory area. The result would be a sequential data set and not a PDS.

When creating a PDS, the directory quantity must be supplied (there is no default value) in the SPACE parameter. If absent, the first attempt to add a member to the PDS will result in an S013-14 ABEND failure. The directory quantity value identifies the number of 256-byte blocks to be set aside for directory use. Member entries vary in size, and approximately six of them can be placed into a single directory block. When estimating the number of directory blocks needed, divide the maximum number of members expected by six and then increase the result by at least 50%. Being generous with the directory is a good idea because, while the part of the PDS that contains the members data is dynamically expandable (via secondary allocations), the directory is static. When the available directory space is exhausted, the result is an S013-14 ABEND failure. Now the PDS must be copied to another PDS with a larger directory. Note that compressing a PDS will not reclaim any directory space because directory member entries are reuseable.

Here is a directory block estimate example: A PDS is expected to have a maximum of 240 members. 240/6 = 40. A directory quantity of at least 60 should be used (50% higher than 40).

When using TRK or CYL, the directory space is taken away from the beginning of the primary allocation. SPACE=(TRK,(100,20,25)). twenty-five 256-byte blocks will be taken away from the beginning of the 100-track primary. When using the blocksize method, however, this is not true. SPACE=(15000,(400,100,30)). First, the amount of space in (tracks) needed to accommodate 400 15000-byte blocks is calculated by the system, then the same is done for 30 256-byte blocks. The two values added become the primary allocation.

Partitioned data sets are seldom temporary. The SYSLMOD DD statement in Compile-Linkedit-Go procedures is one of the rare places where such a data set will be found.

```
//SYSLMOD   DD  DSN=&&GODATA(RUN),DISP=(,PASS),UNIT=SYSDA,
//              SPACE=(TRK,(10,5,1))
```

8.2.4 Creating Direct Data Sets

Direct (also referred to as random) data sets are not as commonly used as sequential or partitioned. When they are used, frequently they are part of a database.

Creating a direct data set is very similar to creating a sequential with the following exceptions:

- A direct data set should be created with no secondary allocation. Direct data sets are preformatted (dummy records are written into the data set before the real records). After preformatting, the data set will not get secondary allocations, since there is no attempt to write beyond the last record.
- The CONTIG subparameter of the SPACE parameter, practically never recommended for sequential data sets, may be advisable. Direct data sets are often used in online systems and may be used heavily. Under such conditions, multiple extents can cause significant disk arm movement resulting in degradation. CONTIG would guarantee a single extent primary, minimizing disk arm movement.
- A small blocksize is acceptable for a direct data set which is mostly processed directly (as opposed to sequentially), as in an online system environment. Large blocks degrade rather enhance performance for direct processing. A direct data set can only have F (or FB) record format. V, VB, or U cannot be used.

```
//DA1    DD   DSN=CICS.RFILE,DISP=(,CATLG),UNIT=SYSDA,
//             SPACE=(CYL,75,,CONTIG),VOL=SER=DEV001,
//             DCB=(LRECL=260,RECFM=F,BLKSIZE=260,DSORG=DA)
```

8.2.5 SPACE Parameter Considerations

There are four ways to supply the SPACE parameter:

- Absolute track allocation. Example:

```
SPACE=(ABSTR,(500,352))
```

This requests that 500 tracks be allocated beginning with track #353 (track 0 is the first track used by the system), before the step begins execution. No more space will be available. This method is almost never used. It is dangerous — one almost never knows which extents are available. Also, there is seldom reason for requesting disk space in a particular location. In all the other methods that follow, it is the system that decides where to place the requested amount of disk space, not the user.
- Track allocation. Example:

```
SPACE=(TRK,(200,50))
```

This requests that 200 tracks (primary allocation, or primary quantity) be allocated on a requested (or system-selected) volume, before the step begins execution. If 200 tracks are available in one extent (contiguous), they will be allocated. If not, the system attempts to combine two extents totaling 200 tracks. If not possible, then three, four, and finally five extents will be tried, as discussed in Section 8.2.1. If the system succeeds in providing the primary quantity, execution begins. If this space is exhausted (while writing), then the system attempts to supply the secondary allocation (or quantity), 50 tracks in this case. This is done in exactly the same way as the primary allocation: in one extent if possible and in as many as five extents if necessary. If the secondary allocation is exhausted, the system tries for another secondary. The system will always provide the secondary allocation unless:
— No space is available on the volume to satisfy the secondary allocation.
— The secondary allocation, if supplied, would cause the data set to exceed 16 extents on a volume.

Unless the data set can extend into another volume (see Section 8.2.6), either of the conditions above will result in a SB37-04 ABEND failure. For a PDS this can also be a SE37-04, and its meaning is basically the same as the SB37-04.

The amount requested in the secondary allocation is recorded in the data set's DSCB, and it is available for the life of the data set as long as the conditions above are not encountered.

The primary allocation is mandatory (no default exists). Secondary allocation is optional (the default is 0).

SPACE=(TRK,300) — this can also be coded as SPACE=(TRK,(300)) or SPACE=(TRK,(300,0)).

In the example above, if the primary is exhausted, the result will be a SD37-04 ABEND failure.

Directory quantity, SPACE=(TRK,(300,100,40)), is optional (the default is 0) and is only needed for creating partitioned data sets.

Track allocation is device dependent. When migrating from a device to another with different track capacity, the SPACE parameter must be changed.

• Cylinder allocation. Example:

```
SPACE=(CYL,(50,10))
```

This requests a primary allocation of 50 cylinders and a secondary of 10. The mechanism is identical to that of track allocation.

One primary allocation before the step begins execution, and as many secondary allocations as needed provided that the space is available and 16 extents for the data set are not exceeded on the volume.

An interesting question arises as to why one would wish to allocate in cylinders as opposed to tracks and vice versa. Compare two SPACE parameters, SPACE=(TRK,150) and SPACE=(CYL,10), for a 3380 volume:

— In terms of capacity the two are identical. Appendix A shows that a 3380 cylinder contains 15 tracks.
— From a performance standpoint, cylinder allocation will be slightly advantageous for sequential processing. There are two reasons for this:

Based on the design of a disk device (see Figure 8.1), the read/write heads of a volume are always positioned over a full cylinder, and this tends to reduce arm movement. This movement, also known as "seek time," has an average duration of 11 to 17 milliseconds for 3380 (depending on model), and is the single most time-consuming element of disk I/O.

The second reason lies in the fact that an entire cylinder can be read from or written to without checking for extents, since all the tracks of a cylinder are always together. With track allocation, ex-

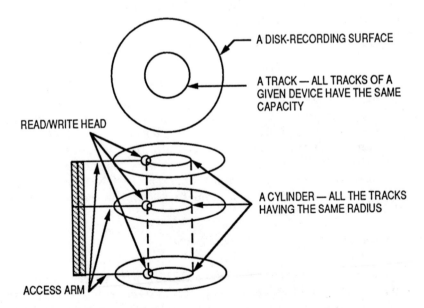

Figure 8.1 Disk tracks and cylinders.

tent checking is more frequent, resulting in some degradation. For direct (random) processing, cylinder allocation offers no performance advantage.

— Track allocation provides better availability. Each cylinder must begin at the top and end at the bottom recording surface, and this restriction makes cylinders more difficult to allocate. It is, for example, possible for a 3380 volume to have 150 tracks available but not 10 cylinders.

— Accuracy of allocation favors tracks. Suppose 151 tracks are needed. If cylinders are specified, this must be coded as SPACE=(CYL,11). SPACE=(TRK,151) gives the exact amount, but SPACE=(CYL,11) gives 14 tracks too many.

— Active volumes where many data sets are often created and deleted (such as STORAGE and PUBLIC volumes) tend to get "fragmented." A fragmented volume contains many noncontiguous extents causing difficulty in allocating and possible inability to use some small extents. Cylinder allocation when used consistently will tend to minimize fragmentation.

None of the above considerations are of great importance. Installations will sometimes provide guidelines for track vs. cylinder usage.

Cylinder allocation is device dependent. When migrating from a device to another with different cylinder capacity, the SPACE parameter must be changed.

• Block allocation. Example:

```
SPACE=(23440,(300,100))
```

This requests that the system determine the amount of tracks needed to contain 300 blocks, 23440 bytes each, and provide that as the primary allocation. Secondary allocations will be based on the amount of tracks needed to contain 100 blocks of the actual blocksize being used. The primary/secondary mechanism is identical to the track or cylinder allocation. The ROUND subparameter can be used to cause the system to allocate in cylinders rather than tracks. Example:

```
SPACE=(23440,(300,100),,,ROUND)
```

The blocksize value coded in the SPACE parameter should identify the correct blocksize. If not, the system will not inform the user of the discrepancy. During the allocation process, the incorrect blocksize will be used to calculate the number of tracks or cylinders needed for the primary allocation. This happens before the beginning of execution and since data set has not been opened yet, the system does not know the true blocksize. Even if a DCB BLKSIZE is coded in the DD statement, the system will not reconcile the two values. However, for the secondary allocation (which always occurs after the open), the system switches to the correct blocksize to compute the needed space. This can produce unexpected results. If, for example, SPACE=(23440,(300,100)) used and the true blocksize was 80, the primary allocation will be based on 300 23440-byte blocks, which (using Appendix B) is 150 tracks. Secondary allocations, however, will be based on 100 80-byte blocks, which is 2 tracks, much less than the expected 100 23440-byte blocks or 50 tracks. A SB37-04 ABEND can easily be the result.

The blocksize value in the SPACE parameter is never used by the system to provide DCB information. It is used only for primary allocation space calculations. The BLKSIZE value in the DCB parameter can be used for space calculations but only for secondary allocations.

Block allocation is device independent. When migrating from one device to another with different track/cylinder capacity, the SPACE parameter need not be changed, provided that the blocksize is appropriate for both devices (see Section 8.5).

Determining the proper SPACE parameter when creating a data set is of great importance. The often used method, guessing, is really not advisable. It can result in underallocating, causing SB37-04 ABEND failures, or overallocating, abusing the installation's disk space resources.

Most SB37-04 ABEND failures are preventable. They are frequently the result of poor planning and failure to understand how the SPACE parameter works.

Let us consider a few examples:

```
//OUT1   DD  DSN=USER1.SET1,DISP=(,CATLG,DELETE),UNIT=SYSDA,
//           VOL=SER=PROD12,SPACE=(TRK,(50,10)),
//           DCB=(LRECL=80,RECFM=FB,BLKSIZE=9040)
```

If volume PROD12 is nearly empty, each allocation (primary and secondary) will be given in a single extent. The maximum number of tracks that can be acquired is one primary allocation (50 tracks) plus 15 secondary allocations (10 tracks each) for a total of 200 tracks. However, the minimum number of tracks, assuming the step begins

212 Expert MVS/XA JCL

execution, is 50. If the volume is nearly full, it may be impossible to get even one secondary allocation. Unless one is thoroughly familiar with the contents of the volume being used (impossible under normal conditions), it is risky to depend heavily on secondary allocations. As many as 15 and as few as none may be available. When the volume is fragmented, even if it contains considerable free space, the results can be just as unpredictable. Consider a volume containing 3000 free tracks in 300 10-track extents (see Figure 8.2). Although a volume is unlikely to become fragmented in such symmetrical fashion, the example will be used to help demonstrate the volatility of the SPACE parameter under adverse conditions. The primary allocation will be given in five 10-track extents, leaving only 11 more extents available. Despite the considerable amount of free space on the volume, the maximum possible number of tracks is now reduced to 160.

Assume data set USER1.SET1 needs 170 tracks. The SPACE parameter above becomes a risky one and for repetitive executions, such as production jobs, a virtual time bomb. To reach 170 tracks, 12 secondary allocations are needed, and there is no guarantee that they will always be available. It may work once or several times, but eventually an SB37-04 ABEND becomes inevitable. The old saying that "if it works once it will work twice" does not apply here. Secondary allocations are completely dependent on the condition of the allocated volume, and, since that is practically never known to the user, they are unpredictable. It is, therefore, advisable to supply a primary allocation that satisfies the needs of the data set thus avoiding dependence on secondary allocations. Clearly, the primary allocation may also be unavailable. However, failure to get the primary is a JCL error that stops the step from executing, as opposed to an SB37-04 ABEND caused by the unavailability of a secondary which may occur well into the execution of the step, resulting in loss of time and potential restart complications. It is always a good idea to code a secondary allocation, just to be on the safe side, but not to be dependent on it.

Depending mostly or only on the primary allocation is what is normally recommended. However, this recommendation can backfire

10 TRKS FREE	OCCU- PIED	10 TRKS FREE	OCCU- PIED	10 TRKS FREE	OCCU- PIED	10 TRKS FREE	....more..

Figure 8.2 Example of disk volume with fragmented space.

when the primary gets so large that it becomes an invitation to a JCL error (such as "SPACE REQUESTED NOT AVAILABLE"). Multivolume allocation (discussed in Section 8.2.6) can be used to alleviate this problem.

Another example can be used to demonstrate the volatility and even the possible paradoxical nature of the SPACE parameter.

```
//TOUT   DD   DSN=&&TEMP,DISP=(,PASS),SPACE=(TRK,(50,40)),
//             UNIT=SYSDA,DCB=(LRECL=100,RECFM=FB,BLKSIZE=9000)
```

Based on the discussion above, if execution begins, the SPACE parameter can ideally provide a maximum of 650 tracks (50 + 15 x 40). But when the allocated volume is badly fragmented,the maximum can be drastically different, even if the volume has considerable free space. On the volume as shown in Figure 8.2, the primary allocation must be given in five 10-track extents and each secondary in four 10-track extents, using up extents rapidly. As shown in Figure 8.3, only two secondary allocations are possible because a third one would result in 17 extents, one over the limit of 16. The maximum in this case is only 130 tracks, a far cry from 650 tracks. Keep in mind, the same SPACE parameter was used in both cases and both volumes contained a considerable number of available tracks.

At this point a paradox can be shown. If both the primary and the secondary were to be reduced to 10 tracks,

```
//POUT   DD   DSN=&&TEMP,DISP=(,PASS),SPACE=(TRK,(10,10)),
//             UNIT=SYSDA,DCB=(LRECL=100,RECFM=FB,BLKSIZE=9000)
```

ALLOCATION	TRACKS	EXTENTS USED	EXTENTS USED TOTAL
PRIMARY	50	5	5
SECONDARY #1	40	4	9
SECONDARY #2	40	4	13
TOTAL	130	13	13

Figure 8.3 Allocating space on a fragmented disk volume.

the maximum would be higher, 160 tracks (one 10-track primary and 15 10-track secondaries). In other words, less was requested but more was provided. Normally, of course, the higher the primary and/or secondary values, the more space is likely to be allocated. But under unusual and adverse conditions, the opposite can also occur. This example is intended to demonstrate the unpredictable and occasionally surprising results one can get when secondary allocations are heavily depended on.

The same DD statement with a different secondary allocation can be used to demonstrate that higher quantities may not necessarily provide more space:

```
//TOUT   DD   DSN=&&TEMP,DISP=(,PASS),SPACE=(TRK,(50,60)),
//            UNIT=SYSDA,DCB=(LRECL=100,RECFM=FB,BLKSIZE=9000)
```

In this case only the primary will be given. No secondary can be provided because 60 tracks can only become available in six extents, one more than allowed. Increasing the primary allocation may fare no better. For example, coding SPACE=(TRK, (60,40)), will cause a JCL error because now even the primary allocation is not available.

The question arises: What does one do when a SB37-04 ABEND occurs? Unfortunately, there is no answer that will work 100% of the time. Increasing the primary allocation appropriately will normally take care of the problem. But given the possible unusual situations just discussed and the fact that disk space is a finite resource, no guarantees can be given. Increasing the secondary allocation is acceptable, but that implies a dependence on it that is undesirable. Also, as shown in the previous two examples, decreasing either or both quantities can solve the problem under the right conditions.

As mentioned before, supplying a primary allocation large enough to contain all the records of the data set will have the effect of minimizing SB37-04 ABEND failures. How to determine the size of this allocation will be discussed below.

Determining the primary allocation for data sets with fixed blocked format (RECFM=FB) is simple. Needed information is the blocksize and the number of blocks. When using the block allocation method, the SPACE parameter can be coded if two values are known: blocksize and the number of blocks for the primary.

```
SPACE=(blocksize,(# of blocks primary,# of blocks secondary))
```

If not readily available, these two values can be derived from other data attributes, such as the logical second length, the number of logical records, and the blocking factor. The two formulas below can be used:

blocksize = (logical second length) x (blocking factor)

$$\text{\# of blocks} = \frac{\text{\# of logical records \#}}{\text{blocking factor}}$$

Consider a data set using a record format FB which will contain 90,000 100-byte logical records blocked at 90 (this means that the blocking factor is 90 or that 90 logical records will be placed in each block). Using the formulas above,

blocksize = 100 x 90 = 9000
# of blocks = 90000 / 90 = 1000

SPACE=(9000,1000) (secondary allocation not supplied)

The result of this SPACE parameter will be the number of tracks needed (computed by the system) to contain 1000 9000-byte blocks, regardless of device being used. If it is desired to use the SPACE parameter using track allocation, then the device must be known and the calculation must be performed by the user. Assume a 3380 device.

Step 1: Based on the known blocksize, determine the number of blocks that will fit into a 3380 track. To find this out, consult Appendix B. Observe that the value for the blocksize, 9000, lies between the values of 9076 and 7476 that appear in the left hand column (lines 5 and 6). Take the first of these two lines and move horizontally to the next column on the right where 5 appears. This means that five 9000-byte blocks will fit into a 3380 track.

Step 2: If a track will contain five blocks, then 1000 blocks will require 1000/5 = 200 tracks.

SPACE=(TRK,200)   (secondary allocation not supplied)

Cylinder allocation can easily be derived from the track allocation. Since there are 15 tracks in a 3380 cylinder, the number of cylinders needed is 200/15 = 13.33 or 14 (rounded to the next integer).

SPACE=(CYL,14)   (secondary allocation not supplied)

Note that for a different device (such as 3350), Appendix D would have to be used, yielding different values: SPACE=(TRK,500) or SPACE=(CYL,17).

Calculating the primary allocation for data sets with variable blocked (RECFM=VB) or undefined format (RECFM=U — rarely used except in load libraries) requires the approximation of an average blocksize and the number of blocks.

In the example, an exact number of records was used. In the real world, an exact number is seldom realistic. In a production environment, variations are frequently based on business activity. For example, in a brokerage firm, the size of a data set may depend on the number of transactions in a given day. In a situation like this:

- Estimate the maximum number of records possible for current activity.
- Add an increment based on estimated growth over a period of time.
- Add another increment for unexpected and unusual situations.
- The sum of the above is the basis for the primary allocation. A secondary allocation (an arbitrary value, normally considerably smaller than the primary) should also be provided. SB37-04 ABEND failures should now be infrequent. They cannot be eliminated, but with the proper planning they can be greatly minimized.

A proper SPACE parameter can be provided without calculations. A test can be executed with a representative number of records using a large SPACE parameter with the RLSE subparameter. When the execution ends, the size of the data set (easily found via ISPF Option 3.2) represents the needed primary allocation, after adjustments for growth, etc., are made.

The discussion thus far has focused on ways to avoid SB34-04 ABEND failures. However, a JCL error resulting from the unavailability of primary allocation can be nearly as problematic. It is preferable to an SB37-04 ABEND failure because it occurs before the step begins execution, as opposed to during execution for the ABEND, and so it can be considered the lesser of the two evils. This type of JCL error, however, is detected during the allocation process, a fact that allows previous steps to execute, potentially resulting in significant delays. Consider the JCL below:

```
//PROD551A  JOB   XH76,'JOB 551A'CLASS=P,MSGCLASS=K
//S1        EXEC  PGM=P1
.............................................
//S12       EXEC  PGM=P12
```

```
//OUT1       DD    DSN=GL3,MASTER,DISP=(,CATLG,DELETE),UNIT=SYSDA,
//                 VOL=SER=PROD34,SPACE=(CYL,(125,30),RLSE),
//                 DCB=(LRECL=23472,RECFM=VB,BLKSIZE=23476)
```

If the 125 cylinders needed for the primary allocation are not available on volume PROD34, a (SPACE REQUESTED NOT AVAILABLE) JCL error will occur at the beginning of step S12 after all previous steps have executed. This can result in delays and possible restart difficulties. To avoid this problem, a step can be introduced at the beginning of the job intended to simply create and catalog an empty data set.

```
//PROD551A  JOB   XH76,'JOB 551A'CLASS=P,MSGCLASS=K
//ALLOC     EXEC  PGM=IEFBR14
//DD1       DD    DSN=GL3.MASTER,DISP=(,CATLG),UNIT=SYSDA,
//                VOL=SER=PROD34,SPACE=(CYL,(125,30)),
//                DCB=(LRECL=23472,RECFM=VB,BLKSIZE=23476)
//S1        EXEC  PGM=P1
..............................................
//S12       EXEC  PGM=P12
//OUT1      DD    DSN=GL3.MASTER,DISP=(OLD,KEEP,DELETE),
//                SPACE=(CYL,0,RLSE)
```

Now if the primary allocation is unavailable, the resulting JCL error will be encountered at the beginning of the job. In step S12, program P12 will open and write to the empty data set. Note that the abnormal disposition DELETE is not coded in DD statement DD1 (IEFBR14 cannot ABEND as it consists of only two instructions) but coded in DD statement OUT1. Also, RLSE is not coded in DD statement DD1 (it would be useless since IEFBR14 neither opens nor closes the data set), but is coded in DD statement OUT1 where it will provide the intended benefit.

The DCB parameter can be coded in DD statement DD1, as shown above, or in DD statement OUT1.

When track, cylinder, or blocksize allocation is used, the system determines how and where a data set is placed on a given volume. For either primary or secondary allocations, the system always allocates using the least number of extents possible, as discussed earlier. When the number of extents is established for an allocation, and there are several extents that can be chosen, the system will allocate in such a way as to preserve the largest available extents. Consider an example where a volume contains the following extents:

EXTENT #1: 295 TRKS
EXTENT #2: 150 TRKS
EXTENT #3: 190 TRKS
EXTENT #4: 50 TRKS
EXTENT #5: 20 TRKS
EXTENT #6: 20 TRKS
EXTENT #7:   5 TRKS

For a SPACE=(TRK,40) parameter, extent #4 (40 of the 50 tracks) will be used. For a SPACE=(TRK,300) parameter, extents #2 and #3 (150 of the 190 tracks) will be used, thus preserving the largest #1 extent. When several candidate extents of the same size are available, the first found will be used. For a SPACE=(TRK,20) parameter, extent #5 will be used.

8.2.6 Creating Multivolume Disk Data Sets

For certain data sets, using multiple volumes is necessary or desirable. Clearly, a data set whose space requirements exceed the capacity of a single volume must be multivolume. Consider a data set which will require 3000 cylinders, and double density 3380 volumes are available. A single volume provides only 1770 cylinders (see Appendix A), and two volumes must be used:

```
//TALR   DD   DSN=USER1.MSET,DISP=(,CATLG),SPACE=(CYL,(1650,1350)),
//            UNIT=SYSDA,DCB=(LRECL=100,RECFM=FB,BLKSIZE=23400),
//            VOL=SER=(PROD11,PROD14)
```

Volume PROD11 will be used for the primary allocation. When that is exhausted, the secondary allocation, which cannot be contained on the same volume, will go to volume PROD14. Note that it is not necessary to use UNIT=(SYSDA,2) or UNIT=(SYSDA,P). 3380 volumes are nonremovable, and the system will allocate as many devices as there are volumes.

Multivolume allocation can also be used effectively to alleviate the problem of a very large, though not impossible, primary allocation. In the previous section it was recommended that, in order to avoid SB37-04 ABEND failures, the primary allocation be large enough to satisfy the needs of the data set. This, of course, can backfire when the primary allocation is so large as to invite a JCL error, as discussed earlier in this chapter. What is considered large will depend on the amount of space the volume to be used normally has available. Consider a temporary data set, to be used in a production job, which will need 800 cylinders. Assume that the "STORAGE" (and "PUBLIC," if any) volumes are double density 3380.

```
//OUT   DD   DSN=&&TEMP,DISP=(,PASS),SPACE=(CYL,(800,20),RLSE),
//           UNIT=SYSDA,DCB=(LRECL=200,RECFM=FB,BLKSIZE=23400)
```

The SPACE parameter requests a primary allocation about half of a volume's capacity. In most installations this is unreasonably large, resulting in frequent JCL errors. If the primary allocation is reduced, as in the DD statement below, frequent SB37-04 ABEND failure can be expected. Ten secondary allocations will be needed (200+10x60=800) to reach 800 cylinders, and they must come on a volume that has already given up 200 cylinders to the primary.

```
//OUT   DD   DSN=&&TEMP,DISP=(,PASS),SPACE=(CYL,(200,60),RLSE),
//           UNIT=SYSDA,DCB=(LRECL=200,RECFM=FB,BLKSIZE=23400)
```

This is far too risky. If, however, the data set is allowed to extend to a second volume, the secondary allocation becomes far more reliable because 16 more extents are now available on the second volume. The data set can now have as many as 32 extents.

```
//OUT   DD   DSN=&&TEMP,DISP=(,PASS),SPACE=(CYL,(200,60),RLSE),
//           UNIT=(SYSDA,2),DCB=(LRECL=200,RECFM=FB,BLKSIZE=23400)
```

Since two devices are requested, two (STORAGE or PUBLIC) volumes will be allocated. The primary/secondary allocation on the first volume works the same as the previous single-volume example. But now if the first volume can no longer provide a secondary allocation, rather than causing a SB37-04 ABEND failure, the system continues into the second volume acquiring secondary allocations for another maximum of 16 extents (the primary allocation is not repeated). The second volume will not be used if the first volume supplies all the needed space. The possibility of getting a SB37-04 ABEND is now much reduced. If a third volume is added, with a total of 48 extents available, SB37-04 ABEND failures are likely to become rare.

```
//OUT   DD   DSN=&&TEMP,DISP=(,PASS),SPACE=(CYL,(200,60),RLSE),
//           UNIT=(SYSDA,3),DCB=(LRECL=200,RECFM=FB,BLKSIZE=23400)
```

If the second or third volume does not have enough space to satisfy even one secondary allocation, the result will be an SE37-08 ABEND failure.

The multivolume technique can also be used for data sets whose space requirements vary widely from one execution to the next. Rather than providing a primary allocation to accommodate the maximum possible space requirement and potentially wasting considerable space, a smaller primary, accommodating an average space requirement, can be used. Secondary allocations spread over more than one volume will now be counted on to provide the maximum when it is needed. Whereas it is inadvisable to depend heavily on secondary allocations when a single volume is allocated, secondary allocations become much more reliable for a multivolume data set.

What was said thus far for temporary/nonspecific data sets applies to all data sets. They all work exactly the same way. In the DD statement below, data set USER1.SETM will continue getting secondary allocations of 25 cylinders each on the second volume, PACK25, when the first volume, PACK08, can no longer provide any.

```
//DD4   DD   DSN=USER1.SETM,DISP=(,CATLG,DELETE),UNIT=SYSDA,
//           VOL=SER=(PACK08,PACK25),SPACE=(CYL,(50,25)),
//           DCB=(BLKSIZE=23400,LRECL=200,RECFM=FB)
```

Note that it is difficult to distribute a multivolume data set evenly across two or more volumes. If this is desirable for a nontemporary/specific data set, the following steps must be followed (assume data set PROD.TWOSET needs 700 cylinders to be split evenly between volumes PROD22 and PROD17):

Step 1: Create a dummy data set (or more than one if necessary) on each of the two volumes in such a way so that less than 700 cylinders remain available on each.

Step 2: Execute step that writes to data set PROD.TWOSET, coding DD statement:

```
//OUT   DD   DSN=PROD.TWOSET,DISP=(,CATLG,DELETE),
//           UNIT=SYSDA,VOL=SER=(PROD22,PROD17),
//           SPACE=(CYL,(350,350)),
//           DCB=(LRECL=120,RECFM=FB,BLKSIZE=23400)
```

Note that the second volume will not be used unless the 350 cylinders in the first volume are exhausted. There is no way to create a data set occupying space on more than one volume by executing PGM=IEFBR14.

Step 3: Delete all dummy data sets created in step 1.

The same would be extremely difficult, if not impossible, to accomplish for a nonspecific request. Such requests allocate on "STORAGE" and "PUBLIC" volumes which are not under the control of any individual user.

Using the multivolume technique, it is recommended that one always check with the installation's technical management to ensure that the necessary resources will be available. If not available, the result will be job cancellation by the operator (following an allocation recovery attempt), or perhaps the use of unauthorized resources.

Partitioned data sets cannot be multivolume. They are confined to only one volume.

8.2.7 Public/Private Considerations

In an MVS/XA environment disk volumes are assigned one of three possible "use" attributes: PRIVATE, STORAGE or PUBLIC. The user has no control over the "use" attribute of any given volume. A volume is assigned its attribute in one of two ways:

- During the Initial Program Load (IPL) process. The system looks up the Volume Attribute Table (VAT) in SYS1.PARMLIB and assigns to each listed volume the attribute indicated.
- If a volume is not listed in the VAT or it is varied offline (a VARY OFFLINE command causes a volume to loose its attributes), the MOUNT command can be used by the console operator to assign the desired attribute.

The reader should be reminded, as discussed in Section 5.5 of Chapter 5, that the PRIVATE subparameter of the VOL parameter is basically incapable of assigning the PRIVATE attribute to any nonremovable volume.

The meaning of the various attributes is as follows:

PRIVATE: A PRIVATE volume does not accept the allocation of new requests if they're nonspecific (neither VOL=SER nor VOL=REF coded). A PRIVATE volume accepts only specific (VOL=SER or VOL=REF coded) new requests, temporary or non temporary. The majority of volumes in an average installation are PRIVATE.

PUBLIC: A PUBLIC volume accepts all new requests except those that are both nonspecific and nontemporary. Many installations do not use PUBLIC volumes, using STORAGE volumes to satisfy all nonspecific requests.

STORAGE: A STORAGE volume accepts all new requests, specific or nonspecific, temporary or nontemporary. An average installation normally has several STORAGE volumes. Note that it is the only type of volume which accepts nonspecific/nontemporary NEW requests. Rarely, an installation with a great number of users — such as a university — may have no STORAGE volumes and all nontemporary requests must be directed to particular volumes.

STORAGE and PUBLIC volumes are often called "scratch packs," "work packs," "scratch volumes," or "work volumes."

Examples of the different types of NEW requests are given below:

A. SPECIFIC/NONTEMPORARY

```
//SNT1 DD   DSN=USER1.PERM,DISP=(,CATLG),SPACE=(CYL,(20,10),RLSE),
//          UNIT=SYSDA,DCB=(LRECL=100,RECFM=FB,BLKSIZE=23400),
//          VOL=SER=TEST32

//SNT2 DD   DSN=USER1.MAPL,DISP=(,CATLG),SPACE=(TRK,(50,20),RLSE),
//          VOL=REF=USER1.AA,DCB=(LRECL=100,RECFM=FB,BLKSIZE=23400)
```

Specific/nontemporary requests are very common.

B. SPECIFIC/TEMPORARY

```
//ST1 DD    DSN=&&TT,DISP=(,PASS),SPACE=(CYL,(20,10),RLSE),
//          UNIT=SYSDA,DCB=(LRECL=100,RECFM=FB,BLKSIZE=23400),
//          VOL=SER=TEST32

//ST2 DD    SPACE=(TRK,(75,25),RLSE),UNIT=SYSDA,VOL=SER=WORK03
```

Specific/temporary requests are not recommended and should be seldom, if ever, used. Temporary requests are normally nonspecific.

C. NONSPECIFIC/TEMPORARY

```
//NST1 DD   DSN=&&AB,DISP=(,PASS),SPACE=(CYL,(25,10),RLSE),
//          UNIT=SYSDA,DCB=(LRECL=100,RECFM=FB,BLKSIZE=23400)

//NST2 DD   SPACE=(TRK,(75,25),RLSE),UNIT=SYSDA
```

Nonspecific/temporary requests are very common.

D. NONSPECIFIC/NONTEMPORARY

```
//NSNT1 DD    DSN=USER1.NT1,DISP=(,CATLG),SPACE=(CYL,(15,5),RLSE),
//            UNIT=SYSDA,DCB=(LRECL=80,RECFM=FB,BLKSIZE=23440)

//NSNT2 DD    DSN=USER1.NT2,DISP=(,PASS),SPACE=(TRK,(25,5),RLSE),
//            UNIT=SYSDA,DCB=(LRECL=80,RECFM=FB,BLKSIZE=23440)
```

Note that a nontemporary data set name and DISP=(,PASS) will be treated as a nontemporary request despite the fact that new passed data sets are often deleted before the job terminates.

Non-specific/nontemporary requests are very common in the great majority of installations. Rarely, however, when STORAGE volumes are not used, they will be disallowed.

Figure 8.4 summarizes this discussion. A PRIVATE volume is the most restrictive, a STORAGE volume the most permissive. A specific request will allocate on any volume; a nonspecific/ nontemporary request is restricted to only STORAGE volumes. The discussion above does not take software security into consideration.

Disk volumes are also assigned "mount" attributes:

RESERVED: A RESERVED volume remains available unless it is unloaded or varied offline (using the UNLOAD or VARY OFFLINE commands). A volume becomes RESERVED either via the VAT (vol-

	Use Attribute		
Type of new request	PRIVATE	PUBLIC	STORAGE
SPECIFIC/NONTEMPORARY	YES	YES	YES
SPECIFIC/TEMPORARY	YES	YES	YES
NONSPECIFIC/TEMPORARY	NO	YES	YES
NONSPECIFIC/NONTEMPORARY	NO	NO	YES

Figure 8.4 Allocating on PRIVATE, PUBLIC, and STORAGE volumes.

ume attribute table) during IPL or via the MOUNT operator command.

PERMANENTLY RESIDENT: A PERMANENTLY RESIDENT volume must always be online. It cannot be unloaded or varied offline. A volume becomes PERMANENTLY RESIDENT either via the VAT during IPL or by containing certain system data sets of major importance (such as SYS1.SVCLIB).

"Mount" attributes are basically transparent to the user. The great majority of an average installation's disk volumes are RESERVED. PERMANENTLY RESIDENT volumes tend to be system residence volumes which are normally unavailable to the average user.

8.3 THE LOGIC OF ALLOCATION, OPEN, AND CLOSE FOR CREATING TAPE DATA SETS

Creating data sets under JES2 is somewhat different than under JES3. The discussion that follows is for JES2. Later in the chapter the differences for JES3 will be explained.

When a step is executed, the allocation routines (Figure 1.7) are responsible for allocating the device(s), where the volume(s) which will contain the new data set will be mounted. If no DEFER is used, they are also responsible for issuing a mount message (or messages) informing the operator what tape volume(s) to mount on what device(s). When the mount message is issued, the allocation routines do not wait for the operator to respond to the request. Program execution follows and when the data set is opened, volume verification will take place (if needed) and HDR1/HDR2 labels will be created. At this point it can be said that the data set exists. The allocation routines, which are responsible for creating a disk data set, aside from allocating the needed device(s) and (optionally) issuing a mount message, do not directly contribute to the creation of a tape data set. In essence, a new tape data set does not exist unless it is opened for output. Consider the DD statement below:

```
//OUTT   DD  DSN=USER1.TP1,DISP=(,CATLG),UNIT=TAPE,
//            DCB=(BLKSIZE=32720,LRECL=80,RECFM=FB)
```

This DD statement contains no volume serial information, and it is known as a nonspecific request.

The allocation routines will allocate a device that is included in the installation's definition of "TAPE" (assume address 582) and will issue the message:

```
*IEF233A M 582,PRIVAT,SL,USER1A,STEP2,USER1.TP1
```

USER1A is the jobname; STEP2 is the stepname; USER1.TP1, the data set name, may or may not appear depending on whether the MONITOR DSNAMES operator command was issued at a prior point.

The operator is expected to mount any SL scratch volume (an SL volume whose contents are of no value to anyone) on device address 582. The step will begin execution whether or not the tape volume is mounted. When the data set is opened, the device must be ready or the step will go into a "wait state." A step enters a wait state when it cannot use the CPU, even if it is available. If the wait state lasts a long time, the result will be an S522 ABEND failure. This is usually called "a job timing out" and the allowed duration of the wait state is installation defined (usually 10 to 20 minutes). When the operator readies the device, the open routines read the first record on the volume (the first 80-byte record on an SL volume is the volume label) to verify that it is an SL volume. If the volume is NL, message IEC704A may appear if the installation permits the operator to label the volume by supplying the volume serial on the console. If the installation disallows this practice, the volume will be unloaded and message IEF233A will be repeated. If the mounted volume is SL and is expired, it is accepted and its volume serial is saved for later use. HDR1 and HDR2 labels are created by the open routines. EOF1 and EOF2 labels are created by the close routines (see Figure 8.6). Normally, when all I/O activity for a data set ends, the program closes the data set. If the program does not (it does not have to), the step termination routines, which always follow program execution, do.

The program actually is unaware of labels. Looking at Figure 8.6, the volume label is created by the installation; HDR1/HDR2 and the tape mark that follows are created by the OPEN routines; the program writes the records of the data set; EOF1/EOF2 (often referred to as Trailer1/Trailer2) and the tape mark that follows are created by the close routines; the last tape mark shown is created by the end-of-volume routines, which are called by the close routines, and it is meant to indicate that there are no other data sets on this volume. The program writes only the data. And since it is not concerned with labels, the same program can create SL as well as NL data sets.

An alternative way of creating a tape data set is to include volume serial information in the DD statement.

```
//OUTS   DD   DSN=USER1.TP2,DISP=(,CATLG),VOL=SER=000294,
//             UNIT=TAPE,DCB=(BLKSIZE=32720,LRECL=80,RECFM=FB)
```

This DD statement is known as a specific request. The message issued to the operator console will be:

```
*IEF233A M 948,000294,SL,USER1B,STEP3,USER1.TP2
```

The operator now must mount tape with volume serial 000294 on device address 948. No other volumes are acceptable. Since there is seldom a reason for requesting a particular volume for creating a data set, specific requests for tape are far less common than nonspecific ones, especially in a production environment. This DD statement will be treated basically the same way as the previous one, except that the open will verify that the volume requested, in this case serial 000294, is mounted. Any other volume will be rejected and a message basically identical to IEF233A will be issued:

```
*IEC501A M 948,000294,SL,6250,USER1B,STEP3,USER1.TP2
```

This message is issued by the open routines, has a different identifier (IEC indicates Data Management), and also contains density information, 6250 BPI.

When creating a tape data set, which is not opened, the normal (or abnormal) field of the DISP parameter may not take effect:

• If it is a nonspecific request CATLG, PASS or KEEP will be ignored.
• If it is a specific request, DISP=(,CATLG) is coded, a dual density 3420-type tape device is allocated, and the DEN subparameter in the DCB is not coded, cataloging will fail with a "NOT CATLGD 7" message. Without the open, density cannot be determined, and without density information included in the DD statement cataloging cannot be performed (see Section 6.5 in Chapter 6) for a 3420 tape data set.

In all other cases, as mentioned above, even without an open, what is requested in the DISP will be performed, as the example below demonstrates:

```
//OUTP   DD  DSN=USER1.TPP,DISP=(,PASS),VOL=SER=003487,
//              UNIT=TAPE,DCB=(BLKSIZE=32700,LRECL=100,RECFM=FB)
```

The data set will be passed even if there is no open. This is unfortunate because the data set being passed does not exist, as explained earlier in this chapter. If the data set is received in a subsequent step, the result will be a S813-04 ABEND failure. Volume 003487 contains a data set whose data set name does not match USER1.TPP.

As with retrieval, a DELETE request in the DISP parameter is meaningless for tape. A tape data set cannot be deleted through the DISP parameter. However, a message will still appear indicating the data set was deleted.

```
IEF285I data set name                           DELETED
IEF285I VOL SER NOS=volume ser
```

This message should be ignored.

JES3 works a little differently than JES2. JES3 will preallocate (before the job begins execution) a "high water mark" of tape devices for the job, will issue mount messages for the first volume to be used on each tape device, and (when needed) perform volume verification. If a given tape device is used again in a later step, any needed volume verification will be done by the open routines as in JES2.

8.3.1 Creating Tape Data Sets with Deferred Mounting

A variation of creating a tape data set using deferred mounting is shown below.

```
//OUT  DD  DSN=USER1.TAPZ,DISP=(,CATLG),UNIT=(TAPE,,DEFER),
//          DCB=(BLKSIZE=32720,LRECL=80,RECFM=FB)
LABEL not supplied — the default is (1,SL)
```

DEFER accomplishes only one thing: It postpones the mount message to the operator shown below until open time.

```
*IEC501A M 581,PRIVAT,SL,6250,USER1A,STEP4,USER1.TAPZ
```

where 581 is the device address, 6250 is the density, USER1A is the jobname, and STEP4 is the stepname. For 3480 tape the density would not appear.

In Section 7.3.3 of Chapter 7, DEFER was fully discussed in relation to retrieving tape data sets. Anything to be said here about DEFER would be a repetition. Remember, if the data set is opened, DEFER seldom serves a useful purpose. If the data set is not opened, DEFER is recommended because it eliminates an unnecessary mount message to the operator.

8.3.2 Creating Nonlabeled Tape Data Sets

Nonlabeled tape data sets are seldom used. Although creating an NL
tape data set is a fairly safe process, retrieval is dangerous because
neither the volume serial nor the data set name can be verified. Normally, an NL volume is sent to an installation which does not use
MVS. This is how this section will treat NL volumes.

The following DD statement creates an NL data set:

```
//OUT   DD   DSN=USER1.NLTP,DISP=(,KEEP),UNIT=TAPE,
//           LABEL=(,NL),DCB=(LRECL=100,BLKSIZE=32000,RECFM=FB)
```

Normally, DISP=(,KEEP) is avoided. In this case it is acceptable
since the volume is to be sent to another installation and cataloging
is useless. The following message will appear on the operator console:

```
*IEF233A M 787,PRIVAT,NL,USER1A,STEP2,USER1.TPNL
```

787 is the device address, USER1A is the jobname, STEP2 is the
stepname; USER1.TP1, the data set name, may or may not appear
depending on whether the MONITOR DSNAME operator command
was issued at a prior point.

The operator is expected to mount any NL scratch volume (an NL
volume whose contents are not of value to anyone) on device address
787. If the volume mounted is SL, the open routines may issue message IEC534D if the installation permits the operator to destroy the
label, thus making an SL into an NL volume. If the installation disallows this practice, the volume will be dismounted and message
IEC501A, which is basically identical to message IEF233A, will be
issued. If the mounted volume is NL, it is accepted and a volume
serial Lnnnnn (where nnnnn is a number — example L00001) is generated by the system for future use. If VOL=SER were included in
the DD statement above, the IEF233A message would contain that
volume serial in place of PRIVAT, but still no volume verification
would take place. No labels of any sort will be created by the open
routines.

In some installations using the TMS or TLMS software package,
coding LABEL=(,NL,EXPDT=98000) may be required. This permits
the data set to be created outside TMS or TLMS control.

BLP should never be used when creating data sets. Since BLP
does not recognize the existence of labels, it can easily destroy them
and most installations are likely to forbid its use.

8.3.3 Creating Multivolume Tape Data Sets

Tape volumes have considerably less capacity than disk volumes. For example, a single density 3380 volume has a (theoretical) capacity of 630 megabytes. A 6250 tape volume with all 2400 feet available and using a blocksize of 32760 has an approximate capacity of 170 megabytes. A 3480 volume, similarly blocked, has a capacity of a little over 200 megabytes.

It is not unusual for a tape data set to extend into additional volumes. This is almost always the case when dumping a disk volume to tape. A tape data set can extend into five volumes by default.

```
//OUT   DD   DSN=USER1.TAPL,DISP=(,CATLG),UNIT=TAPE,
//           DCB=(BLKSIZE=32720,LRECL=80,RECFM=FB)
```

If the first volume is exhausted, a mount message will appear requesting a second scratch volume on the same device. If the data set attempts to extend into a sixth volume, the result will be a SE37-04 or a S837-08 ABEND failure. To go beyond the fifth volume the volcount subparameter must be supplied in the VOL parameter.

```
//OUT   DD   DSN=USER1.TAPL,DISP=(,CATLG),UNIT=TAPE,VOL=(,,,43),
//           DCB=(BLKSIZE=32720,LRECL=80,RECFM=FB)
```

Now as many as 43 volumes (actually 50, as discussed in Section 5.5 of Chapter 5) can be used. The maximum is 255 volumes. If VOL=SER is used to supply multiple volumes, the volcount subparameter is unnecessary.

```
//OUT   DD   DSN=USER1.TAPL,DISP=(,CATLG),UNIT=TAPE,
//           VOL=SER=(000125,002099,002950,000021,000998,007737),
//           DCB=(BLKSIZE=32720,LRECL=80,RECFM=FB)
```

When multivolume data sets are created, the system will not allocate more than one device unless asked to. When a volume reaches the end, it rewinds, unloads and a request appears on the console to mount the next volume on the same device. For each volume, a minute or more can be wasted. If UNIT=(TAPE,2) is used, two devices are allocated and while a volume is being processed on one device, the operator can be mounting the next volume on the other device. This eliminates delays beyond the first volume. However, considering the fact that most installations are short of tape devices, this technique can be counterproductive. It may speed up one job's execution, while another job either cannot begin or cannot continue its execution due to the unavailability of a tape device. So, UNIT=(TAPE,2) should be used only if it is warranted and always with operations management approval. Allocating more than two tape devices can seldom be justified and should be avoided.

8.3.4 Creating Multifile Tape Volumes

In the vast majority of cases, a tape volume is likely to contain only one data set. However, under certain conditions many data sets (maximum 9999) can reside on the same tape volume. Typically, a production job which updates several VSAM clusters may save them on tape at the beginning of the job so that if any of them are destroyed during execution, they can be recovered. It is a common practice to put such data sets on a single tape volume.

The JCL below is an example for four such files.

```
//PROD1111  JOB  ........
//S1        EXEC  PGM=IDCAMS
//SYSPRINT  DD   SYSOUT=*
//IN        DD   DSN=PROD.CLUST1,DISP=SHR
//OUT       DD   DSN=PROD.SAVE1,DISP=(,CATLG,DELETE),UNIT=TAPE,
//               VOL=(,RETAIN),          NO LABEL DEFAULTS TO (1,SL)
//               DCB=(BLKSIZE=32760,LRECL=32756,RECFM=VB)
//SYSIN     DD   *
     REPRO  INFILE(IN)  OUTFILE(OUT)
/*
//S2        EXEC  PGM=IDCAMS,COND=(4,LT)
//SYSPRINT  DD   SYSOUT=*
//IN        DD   DSN=PROD.CLUST2,DISP=SHR
//OUT       DD   DSN=PROD.SAVE2,DISP=(,CATLG,DELETE),
//               VOL=(,RETAIN,REF=*.S1.OUT),LABEL=2,
//               DCB=(BLKSIZE=32760,LRECL=32756,RECFM=VB)
//SYSIN     DD   *
     REPRO  INFILE(IN)  OUTFILE(OUT)
/*
//S3        EXEC  PGM=IDCAMS,COND=(4,LT)
//SYSPRINT  DD   SYSOUT=*
//IN        DD   DSN=PROD.CLUST3,DISP=SHR
//OUT       DD   DSN=PROD.SAVE3,DISP=(,CATLG,DELETE),
//               VOL=(,RETAIN,REF=*.S2.OUT),LABEL=3,
//               DCB=(BLKSIZE=32760,LRECL=32756,RECFM=VB)
```

```
//SYSIN     DD   *
    REPRO   INFILE(IN)   OUTFILE(OUT)
/*
//S4        EXEC  PGM=IDCAMS,COND=(4,LT)
//SYSPRINT  DD   SYSOUT=*
//IN        DD   DSN=PROD.CLUST4,DISP=SHR
//OUT       DD   DSN=PROD.SAVE4,DISP=(,CATLG,DELETE),
//               VOL=(,RETAIN,REF=*.S3.OUT),LABEL=4,
//               DCB=(BLKSIZE=32760,LRECL=32756,RECFM=VB)
//SYSIN     DD   *
    REPRO   INFILE(IN)   OUTFILE(OUT)
/*
```

The use of the VOL parameter is very important in this example. Observe that in step S2 the VOL makes reference to the volume of the preceding step, S1. In S3, similarly, reference is made to S2 and so on. This is essential. If all steps after S1 made reference to S1 — using VOL=(,RETAIN,REF=*.S1.OUT) — an ABEND failure might occur.

This requires careful analysis. If VOL=REF=*.S1.OUT were coded in steps S2 to S4 and if all data sets fit on a single volume, there is no danger of an ABEND. If the last (4th) data set extends into a second volume, still no problem. But if it is the 3rd data set that extends, the result will be an SA13-18 ABEND failure in step S4.

Figure 8.5 shows why. DD statement OUT in step S4 refers to S1 — VOL=(,RETAIN,REF=*.S1.OUT). This translates to VOL#1, which has no room left, rather than VOL#2, which S4 needs. This causes the SA13-18 ABEND failure. If, however, the VOL of each step after the first refers to the volume used in the preceding step (as in the example above), the VOL of OUT in S4 will reference the

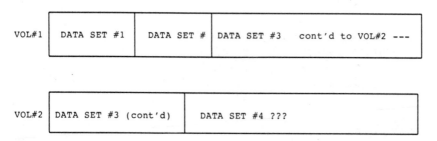

Figure 8.5 Multifile tape volumes.

VOL of OUT in S3, which consists of two volumes (VOL#1 and VOL#2). When VOL=REF refers to a multivolume tape data set, only the last volume will be supplied. This last volume is the right one (VOL#2). Using this JCL, many volumes can be used with no problems.

This JCL still has a different problem, however. It does not allow for restart. If, for example, the first three steps execute successfully but the fourth fails, the job cannot be restarted at the fourth step without changing JCL. VOL=REF=*.S3.OUT makes reference to step S3, which will not be executed during restart, thus creating a JCL error. To resolve this problem, VOL=REF can be replaced by VOL=SER in the restart run, requiring a JCL change.

This problem can be eliminated if VOL=REF=referback is replaced with VOL=REF=dsname.

```
//PROD1111   JOB  ........
//S1         EXEC  PGM=IDCAMS
//SYSPRINT   DD   SYSOUT=*
//IN         DD   DSN=PROD.CLUST1,DISP=SHR
//OUT        DD   DSN=PROD.SAVE1,DISP=(,CATLG,DELETE),UNIT=TAPE,
//                VOL=(,RETAIN),             NO LABEL DEFAULTS TO (1,SL)
//                DCB=(BLKSIZE=32760,LRECL=32756,RECFM=VB)
//SYSIN      DD   *
     REPRO  INFILE(IN)  OUTFILE(OUT)
/*
//S2         EXEC  PGM=IDCAMS,COND=(4,LT)
//SYSPRINT   DD   SYSOUT=*
//IN         DD   DSN=PROD.CLUST2,DISP=SHR
//OUT        DD   DSN=PROD.SAVE2,DISP=(,CATLG,DELETE),
//                VOL=(,RETAIN,REF=PROD.SAVE1),LABEL=2,
//                DCB=(BLKSIZE=32760,LRECL=32756,RECFM=VB)
//SYSIN      DD   *
     REPRO  INFILE(IN)  OUTFILE(OUT)
/*
//S3         EXEC  PGM=IDCAMS,COND=(4,LT)
//SYSPRINT   DD   SYSOUT=*
//IN         DD   DSN=PROD.CLUST3,DISP=SHR
//OUT        DD   DSN=PROD.SAVE3,DISP=(,CATLG,DELETE),
//                VOL=(,RETAIN,REF=PROD.SAVE2),LABEL=3,
//                DCB=(BLKSIZE=32760,LRECL=32756,RECFM=VB)
//SYSIN      DD   *
     REPRO  INFILE(IN)  OUTFILE(OUT)
/*
```

```
//S4          EXEC  PGM=IDCAMS,COND=(4,LT)
//SYSPRINT    DD    SYSOUT=*
//IN          DD    DSN=PROD.CLUST4,DISP=SHR
//OUT         DD    DSN=PROD.SAVE4,DISP=(,CATLG,DELETE),
//                  VOL=(,RETAIN,REF=PROD.SAVE3),LABEL=4,
//                  DCB=(BLKSIZE=32760,LRECL=32756,RECFM=VB)
//SYSIN       DD    *
     REPRO  INFILE(IN)   OUTFILE(OUT)
/*
```

Now restart is possible without changing JCL. If, for example, S4 fails, the job can be restarted at S4. The VOL parameter in S4 refers to data set PROD.SAVE3, which was cataloged during the first run.

There is still one more possible complication. If the DSN in the OUT DD statements were to represent new generations of GDGs, then the previous example would not work. VOL=REF=gdgindex(+1) is invalid and using absolute names, such as VOL=REF= gdgindex.G0028V00, would be self-defeating since the absolute name would require constant changes. A 100% solution does not exist. But JCL can be set up to allow restart with minimal JCL changes.

```
//PROD1111    JOB   ........
//S1          EXEC  PGM=IDCAMS
//SYSPRINT    DD    SYSOUT=*
//IN          DD    DSN=PROD.CLUST1,DISP=SHR
//OUT         DD    DSN=PROD.SV1(+1),DISP=(,CATLG,DELETE),UNIT=TAPE,
//                  VOL=(,RETAIN),         NO LABEL DEFAULTS TO (1,SL)
//       .          DCB=(BLKSIZE=32760,LRECL=32756,RECFM=VB)
//SYSIN       DD    *
     REPRO  INFILE(IN)   OUTFILE(OUT)
/*
//S2          EXEC  PGM=IDCAMS,COND=(4,LT)
//SYSPRINT    DD    SYSOUT=*
//IN          DD    DSN=PROD.CLUST2,DISP=SHR
//DUM         DD    DSN=PROD.SV1(+1),DISP=OLD,UNIT=(,,DEFER)
//OUT         DD    DSN=PROD.SV2(+1),DISP=(,CATLG,DELETE),
//                  VOL=(,RETAIN,REF=*.DUM),LABEL=2,
//                  DCB=(BLKSIZE=32760,LRECL=32756,RECFM=VB)
//SYSIN       DD    *
     REPRO  INFILE(IN)   OUTFILE(OUT)
/*
//S3          EXEC  PGM=IDCAMS,COND=(4,LT)
//SYSPRINT    DD    SYSOUT=*
```

```
//IN          DD   DSN=PROD.CLUST3,DISP=SHR
//DUM         DD   DSN=PROD.SV2(+1),DISP=OLD,UNIT=(,,DEFER)
//OUT         DD   DSN=PROD.SV3(+1),DISP=(,CATLG,DELETE),
//                 VOL=(,RETAIN,REF=*.DUM),LABEL=3,
//                 DCB=(BLKSIZE=32760,LRECL=32756,RECFM=VB)
//SYSIN       DD   *
     REPRO    INFILE(IN)  OUTFILE(OUT)
/*
//S4          EXEC  PGM=IDCAMS,COND=(4,LT)
//SYSPRINT    DD   SYSOUT=*
//IN          DD   DSN=PROD.CLUST4,DISP=SHR
//DUM         DD   DSN=PROD.SV3(+1),DISP=OLD,UNIT=(,,DEFER)
//OUT         DD   DSN=PROD.SV4(+1),DISP=(,CATLG,DELETE),
//                 VOL=(,RETAIN,REF=*.DUM),LABEL=4,
//                 DCB=(BLKSIZE=32760,LRECL=32756,RECFM=VB)
//SYSIN       DD   *
     REPRO    INFILE(IN)  OUTFILE(OUT)
/*
```

In this example, a DD statement DUM is added in each step. Its only use is to supply a reference for the VOL=REF parameter. VOL=REF=dsname will not work and VOL=REF= *.stepname.

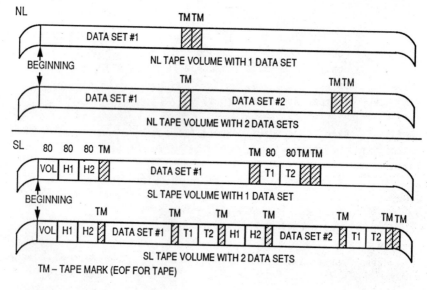

Figure 8.6 SL and NL tape volumes.

ddname causes restart problems, as discussed before. VOL=REF=*.ddname works well but a DD statement must be available to refer to. DUM serves that purpose. A small change, however, will be needed to restart. If, for example, S3 fails, the job can be restarted at S3 but the dsn in DUM must be changed to DSN=USER1.SV2(0) because DSN=USER1.SV2(+1) is invalid with DISP=OLD unless the (+1) generation was created in a previous step of the same job. Note that the change is necessary only for the re-starting step. The remaining JCL remains unchanged.

8.3.5 Using Unit Affinity and FREE=CLOSE

As discussed in Section 7.11 of Chapter 7, UNIT=AFF can be used to reduce tape device utilization, when the appropriate conditions exist. In the JCL below, both DD statements will allocate to the same tape device:

```
//SA        EXEC  PGM=PG3
//IN        DD  DSN=PROD.OLDMST,DISP=OLD
//OUT       DD  DSN=PROD.NEWMST,DISP=(,CATLG,DELETE),UNIT=AFF=IN,
//            DCB=(BLKSIZE=32700,LRECL=100,RECFM=FB)
```

Since two data sets cannot physically use the same nonshareable device at the same time, the data set described in DD statement IN must close before the data set described in DD statement OUT opens. Failure to adhere to this rule will cause an S413-04 ABEND failure. Most user-written programs seldom provide the appropriate open/close conditions for using UNIT=AFF.

There are, however, three software packages — DFSORT (developed by IBM), SYNCSORT (developed by Syncsort), and CASORT (developed by Computer Associates) — where UNIT=AFF can safely be used. All three are sort/merge software packages with many similarities in their use. The required SORTIN (input to be sorted) and SORTOUT (sorted output) DD statements are never open at the same time. UNIT=AFF=SORTIN can always be used in the SORTOUT DD statement.

UNIT=AFF is useful only for tape data sets since its purpose is to save a non-shareable device. It should never be used with disk data sets. Disk is shareable and the use of this parameter can cause problems without providing any benefit.

The FREE=CLOSE parameter can also have an effect on tape device utilization. It causes an allocated device to deallocate at close time rather than step termination. It also causes a data set to be freed from an exclusive usage status and become available to other jobs.

```
//OUT1    DD  DSN=PROD.NEWMST,DISP=(,CATLG,DELETE),UNIT=TAPE,
//              DCB=(BLKSIZE=32700,LRECL=100,RECFM=FB),FREE=CLOSE
```

The FREE=CLOSE parameter can be of value to the user if *all* of the following conditions exist:

- The program closes the data set (some programs do not, in which case the step termination does).
- The close occurs a considerable time before step termination (the longer this time, the greater the benefit).
- The data set is not opened more than once. Since FREE=CLOSE deallocates the device, if there is an open, a close (device is now deallocated) and a second open, message

```
IEC130I  IN1 - DD STATEMENT MISSING
```

will be issued by the open routines. Although processing continues, an attempt to read or write will cause an unpredictable failure, most likely a program check (S0Cx ABEND failure). This failure may not occur if the close was coded in Assembly Language with LEAVE or REWIND.
- The data set is on tape. Using FREE=CLOSE with a disk data set is pointless from a device utilization standpoint (disk is shareable) and still dangerous in the event of multiple opens.

Coding FREE=CLOSE can have a second effect. The data set will be released from exclusive usage and made available to other jobs at close time. This is likely to have no effect on tape data sets in view of the fact that tapes are nonshareable devices. It can have an effect on disk data sets and it should be used with great care.

Using FREE=END has the same effect as not supplying the FREE parameter.

8.4 DCB CONSIDERATIONS FOR CREATING DATA SETS

The DCB parameter in a DD statement creating a data set is needed if:

- One or more of the values for BLKSIZE, LRECL, and LRECL are not hard-coded in the DCB inside the program (they were not supplied by the program).
- Additional values or attributes which normally are not (or cannot be) hard-coded (such as, DEN, OPTCD, EROPT, or BUFNO) are required.
- A new generation of a GDG is created and a cataloged model DSCB must be used (see Section 11.4 in Chapter 11).

It is possible to omit the DCB parameter when creating a data set. If all the values for BLKSIZE, LRECL, and LRECL are hard-coded and the defaults for other values are acceptable,the DCB parameter can be omitted (for a new GDG generation, a noncataloged model DSCB must be in use). The DCB parameter shown below has the following meaning:

```
//S1     EXEC   PGM=PT3
//OUT    DD     DSN=USER1.SELECT,DISP=(,CATLG,DELETE),UNIT=SYSDA,
//              SPACE=(CYL,(30,10),RLSE),VOL=SER=TEST55,
//              DCB=(BLKSIZE=23400,LRECL=100,RECFM=FB)
```

If any of the values for BLKSIZE, LRECL, or RECFM are not hard-coded in the program, then the values in the DCB parameter will be used. Any values hard-coded will always be used, causing the respective values in the DCB parameter to be ignored. The DCB parameter in the example above is intended to "fill in" what was not hard-coded in the program, not "replace" already existing values.

In essence, one cannot speculate about the attributes of the data set being created by just looking at the DD statement, unless one is familiar with how the executing program was coded. If the program hard-coded all the values, the DCB parameter shown above would be completely ignored (it would be, however, syntactically checked). No messages appear to tell the user which subparameters are being used, which are being ignored, and what values are hard-coded and, consequently, in effect. The user is kept in the dark, and wrong assumptions can easily be made here. This reluctance of the system to provide the user with essential information makes the DCB one of the most ambiguous parameters in JCL.

The DCB parameter can contain many subparameters. The three shown above are the most common. It is important to understand which of these often-used subparameters are normally hard-coded and which are not:

- BLKSIZE — Seldom hard-coded. Many installations' standards disallow hard-coding the BLKSIZE for sequential and partitioned data sets. If QSAM is used for sequential processing (it is used far more often than BSAM), the BLKSIZE is unrelated to the logic of the program and hard-coding its value would cause unnecessary program changes whenever the BLKSIZE changed. There is seldom justification for hard-coding the BLKSIZE. In COBOL, BLOCK CONTAINS 0 RECORDS must be coded to avoid hard-coding the BLKSIZE. In Assembly Language, the BLKSIZE must be omitted from the DCB macro. Omitting the BLOCK CONTAINS clause will cause a default of 1 to be used. The result will be a hard-coded BLKSIZE equal to the LRECL. This is practically always undesirable for sequential and partitioned data sets (it is OK for SYSOUT and possibly for direct data sets).
- LRECL — Frequently hard-coded. The logic of an ordinary program is dependent on the LRECL and, as a result, the LRECL cannot be changed without changing the logic of the program. Many high-level languages (like COBOL) always hard-code the LRECL. Vendor-written programs, such as utilities, in order to provide maximum flexibility, often do not hard-code the LRECL.
- RECFM — Frequently hard-coded. The logic of an ordinary program is dependent on the REFCM and, as a result, the RECFM cannot be changed without changing the logic of the program. Many high-level languages (like COBOL) always hard-code the RECFM. Vendor-written programs, such as utilities, in order to provide maximum flexibility, often do not hard-code the RECFM.

If values for BLKSIZE or LRECL are not supplied by any source (hard-coded or the DCB parameter), the result will be an S013-34 ABEND failure. If RECFM is not supplied by any source, RECFM=U (seldom used except in load libraries) is the default.

Other ABEND failures are possible when supplying inconsistent values:

- S013-20 ABEND when RECFM=FB is used but the LRECL is not an exact multiple of the BLKSIZE.
- S013-34 ABEND when RECFM=FB is used and the LRECL is greater than the BLKSIZE.
- S013-34 ABEND when RECFM=VB is used and the LRECL is greater than the BLKSIZE-4.

In addition to BLKSIZE, LRECL, and RECFM there are several other DCB subparameters that can appear in an everyday environment. They are seldom hard-coded, and it is expected that, when coded in the DCB parameter of the DD statement, they will take effect.

- BUFNO — Specifies the number of buffers to be built by the open routines. The default of 5 is often adequate, if the BLKSIZE is not too small. If the BLKSIZE is small, a large number of buffers can enhance I/O performance. When increasing the number of buffers, the REGION parameter may also have to be increased.

```
//OUT   DD    DSN=USER1.SBSET,DISP=(,CATLG,DELETE),UNIT=SYSDA,
//            SPACE=(CYL,(40,10),RLSE),DCB=BUFNO=100
```

In the example above, the BLKSIZE is hard-coded at 80 bytes. DCB=BUFNO=100 will significantly enhance the speed of I/O.
- DEN — Only needed for 3420 tape when the desired density is other than the highest available (6250 BPI). If DEN is omitted, the default for 3420 tape will be the highest available density on the allocated devive (usually 6250 BPI). For 3480 tape, the DEN subparameter is meaningless and is ignored.

```
//OUT   DD    DSN=USER1.MBF, DISP=(,CATLG,DELETE),UNIT=TAPE,
//            DCB=(BLKSIZE=32700,LRECL=100,RECFM=FB,DEN=3)
```

DD statement above will create a 1600 BPI density data set.
- OPTCD — From the many possible options, OPTCD=Q is the most often used. It is needed when EBCDIC to ASCII conversion is required when writing (or ASCII to EBCDIC conversion when reading). ASCII is used by much of non-IBM equipment as the native code. In the example below, a tape (to be sent to another installation) will be written in ASCII code:

```
//OUT   DD    DSN=USER1.ASCII,DISP=(,KEEP),UNIT=TAPE,LABEL=(,NL),
//            DCB=(BLKSIZE=2000,LRECL=100,RECFM=FB,OPTCD=Q)
```

Note: BLKSIZE is limited to 2048 for ASCII tapes.
- EROPT — If an unrecoverable I/O error occurs, EROPT=SKP instructs the system to skip the block causing the error. EROPT=ACC instructs the system to accept the block causing the error. Both are rarely used, as neither guarantees the integrity of the data set. The default EROPT=ABE, which often results in an S001 ABEND failure, is normally used.

```
//OUT   DD    DSN=USER1.IOE, DISP=(,CATLG,DELETE),UNIT=TAPE,
//            DCB=(BLKSIZE=32700,LRECL=100,RECFM=FB,EROPT=ACC)
```

The DSORG subparameter is almost never needed in the DCB parameter. It is almost impossible to write a program without hardcoding the organization of the data set. If coded, the DSORG is normally ignored.

The DCB parameter can use a referback, DCB=*.stepname.ddname, or DCB=*.ddname. This referback uses the same syntax as the referback in the DSN or VOL=REF parameters, but has a different meaning. DSN=*.S1.D1 requests that the same data set name be used as the one in DD statement D1 of step S1. D1 need not contain a DSN parameter, the name will still be supplied. Similarly, VOL=REF=*.S1.D1 requests that the same volume be allocated as the one in D1 of S1. A volume will be supplied even if the VOL parameter does not appear in D1. DCB=*.S1.D1 requests that the DCB parameter be copied from D1 of S1. This is very different from the other two. If D1 contains no DCB parameter, the DCB referback supplies no information. Again, no messages appear to inform the user of this fact.

DCB=(*.stepname.ddname,subparams) or DCB=(*.ddname,subparams) can also be used to override some of the attributes supplied in the referback.

Modeling after the attributes of an existing cataloged disk data set can be accomplished by using what is known as a model DSCB: DCB=model or DCB=(model,subparams).

```
//OUT   DD    DSN=USER1.MLIB,DISP=(,CATLG,DELETE),UNIT=SYSDA,
//            SPACE=(CYL,(20,5,30)),VOL=SER=TSO002,
//            DCB=(USER2.MODL,BLKSIZE=9040)
```

In the example above, the system, using the catalog, finds the DSCB of (disk) data set USER2.MODL, extracts its attributes (BLKSIZE, LRECL, RECFM, DSORG, OPTCD, KEYLEN, and RKP — the last three are basically ISAM-related subparameters), overrides the BLKSIZE with 9040, and fills those values which are not hard-coded. The model DSCB also supplies the expiration date even though that is part of the LABEL, not the DCB, parameter.

8.5 SELECTING A PROPER BLOCKSIZE

The LRECL and RECFM values are always program dependent. The logic of the program determines their values.

The BLKSIZE is seldom dependent on the logic of the program. It is if access method BSAM is used for reading or writing sequential data sets or members of libraries. BSAM, however, is seldom used. QSAM is much more often used, and then the BLKSIZE is unrelated to the logic of the program.

Figure 8.7 shows what happens when a program reads a sequential data set using QSAM. During the open the DCB is checked for completeness and consistency. If the DCB has inconsistent values or it remains incomplete after all sources of DCB information are used,

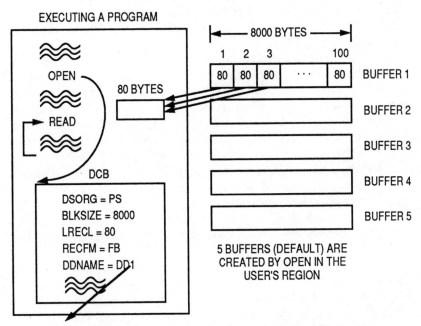

//DD1   DD   DSN=CP.DSETX,DISP=SHR,UNIT=SYSDA,VOL=SER=CP0001

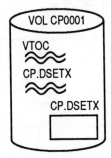

Figure 8.7 Reading logical records.

the result will be an ABEND failure (S013). Otherwise, the open routines create buffers in storage, inside the REGION but outside the code of the program, each equal to the BLKSIZE of the DCB. The number of buffers defaults to five, unless the the BUFNO DCB subparameter is coded with a different value.

The first instruction to read a logical record (into a buffer inside the program) follows the open. The data management routines (which perform the physical I/O operations on behalf of the program) will read the first five blocks of the data set into the five buffers. Rather than performing the expected five I/O operations to read in the five blocks, the system reads them all in one I/O operation by "chaining I/O instructions." Note that the first request by the program to read one 100-byte logical record has resulted in 5 x 234 or 1170 logical records to be read into storage. The first logical record is then placed in the 100-byte buffer inside the program and this completes the program's first read operation. The record is processed and the second logical record is requested by the program. The system provides the second record. No physical I/O takes place because the record is already in storage. The move is storage-to-storage. This continues until most of the buffers are "emptied" of their records. Then the system proceeds to fill the "empty" buffers with new blocks with a single I/O operation which is asynchronous with the program's requests for logical records. This continues until all the logical records of the data set have been supplied to the program, at which point the system passes control to the program's end-of-file routine.

Writing works basically the same way, with the system writing out the large buffers when several of them are filled with logical records.

Note that the I/O operation statistics (often referred to as EXCPs) that usually appear at the end of a step's messages are not accurate. The number of I/O operations shown equals the number of blocks read or written (label processing adds one or two I/Os). Actually, considerably fewer I/O operations have occurred. This "chaining" of I/O operations accounts for the significantly better performance realized when small blocks are used and a BUFNO subparameter with a large value is coded in the DCB.

As mentioned before, the LRECL and RECFM are often decided by those who design the application long before the program is even tested. The BLKSIZE can be decided at the last minute by someone who knows nothing of the application except the LRECL and the RECFM.

For RECFM=FB, the BLKSIZE can be any value up to 32760 that is a multiple of the LRECL. If BLKSIZE=23400 is coded, it means that all the blocks, except the last one, will contain 23400 bytes. RECFM=F need not be used. It indicates that the LRECL and the BLKSIZE are the same size. This will seldom be the case and, even if it is (for a direct data set, for example), RECFM=FB can be used for the same purpose.

For RECFM=VB, which indicates that the blocks and logical records can be of variable size, the BLKSIZE can also be any value up to 32760. If BLKSIZE=23476 is coded, it indicates that the blocksize cannot exceed 23476. The LRECL can be no bigger than 4 bytes less than the BLKSIZE. RECFM=V need not be used. It indicates that the LRECL is exactly 4 bytes less than the BLKSIZE. This will seldom be the case and, even if it is, RECFM=VB can be used for the same purpose. RECFM=VBS indicates that the LRECL can span more than one block, and it is rarely used. With VBS, LRECL can be larger than BLKSIZE.

For RECFM=U, the BLKSIZE can be any value up to 32760 and the LRECL will always be 0 (there are no logical records). Only blocks exist. If BLKSIZE=23476 is coded, it indicates that the blocksize cannot exceed 23476. With the exception of load libraries whose RECFM is always U, it is rarely used.

Clearly, the value that can be assigned to the BLKSIZE has a broad range. It appears that the user can choose any blocksize as long as the basic rules are followed. This is only partly true. BLKSIZE severely affects I/O performance for sequential processing as well as space utilization, and it must be carefully selected.

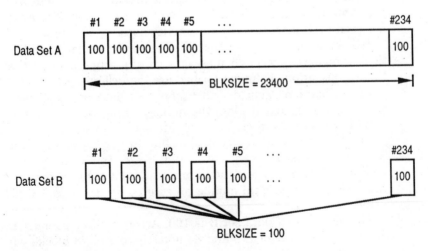

Figure 8.8 A blocked and an unblocked data set.

Small blocksizes will cause major inefficiencies in both areas. It is easy to demonstrate both:

1. I/O performance. Consider two data sets both containing the same number of 100-byte logical records, 234. Data set A has a blocksize of 23400 and data set B a blocksize of 100 (see Figure 8.8). To read into storage all the records for data set A, one I/O operation is needed. A much greater number of I/O operations will be needed to read in the same number of records for data set B, as many as 234 if BUFNO=1 were coded. The difference in time spent doing I/O will be tremendous, even though the same number of bytes is transferred in both cases. Each disk I/O operation, before any data is transferred, will sometimes require a movement of the disk access arm (11 to 17 milliseconds average, depending on 3380 model) and will always require a rotational delay (8.3 milliseconds average). Both of these delays constitute disk I/O overhead which is blocksize independent. The time it takes to transfer the data will be exactly the same for both data sets (7.8 msec — the transfer rate of 3380 is 3 megabytes/second), since they both contain the same amount of data.

   Processing data set B will take much longer than data set A even with I/O chaining. For the small number of records used in this example, the difference is insignificant. For a large number of records, however, the difference can be gigantic.

   Similar inefficiencies can be expected for tape data sets with very small blocksizes. Arm movement and rotational delay do not exist on tape but start-stop activity does.

   It is significant to note that the system will give no indication whatsoever (through messages or any other means) that the I/O operations being performed are inefficient.

2. Space utilization. Consider the same two data sets discussed above. It is easy to calculate the number of logical records that will fit in one 3380 track for each data set.

   The blocksize of data set A is 23400. According to Appendix B, this value is between 23476 and 15476 (left column) and, therefore, two blocks will fit in one track. Each block contains 234 records, so the total number of records per track is 2 x 234 = 468.

   The blocksize of data set B is 100. According to Appendix B, this value is between 116 and 84 and, therefore, 78 blocks will fit in one track. Each block contains 1 record, so the total number of records per track is 78.

The difference is again great. Data set B will require six times (468/78 = 6) more space than data set A for the same number of logical records.

Small blocks on tape cause similar inefficiencies. A 2400-foot 6250 BPI tape volume can contain approximately 166 megabytes if the blocksize is 23400, and 8.8 megabytes if the blocksize is 100. In the second case, about 95% of the tape volume would be occupied by interblock gaps, which constitute overhead.

Obviously, small blocks are extremely detrimental to sequential I/O performance and space utilization. They must be avoided for sequential and partitioned data sets containing a significant number of records.

When using small blocksizes, one would expect some tradeoff to offset the poor performance and space utilization. In essence, there is none. The only conceivably positive consideration is the fact that small blocksizes result in small buffers requiring a smaller REGION. In view of the fact that virtual storage is readily available, this consideration is of no great importance. There is basically only one excuse for using a small blocksize for a sequential or partitioned data set with a large number of records: ignorance.

Large blocksizes must be used. In the author's opinion, a blocksize smaller than 4K is small. Can any large blocksize then be used with good results? For tape, the answer is yes. The maximum blocksize, 32760, can be used for tape to provide optimum performance and medium utilization. For disk, however, the answer must be qualified.

Consider a data set on 3380 disk using a blocksize of 32,760. Performance will be excellent, but space utilization will be questionable. The 3380 track capacity is 47,476 bytes. When a 32,760-byte block is written on a 47,476-byte track, it leaves 14,716 bytes free. These free bytes cannot be used and will be wasted, resulting in only 69% space utilization. IBM documentation mentions a feature called "track overflow" which can be requested by using T in the RECFM subparameter (i.e., RECFM=FBT). This feature would allow a second 32,670-byte block to use the remaining bytes on the track and continue (overflow) into the following track. This feature, however, is not supported for 3380, or any of the other most recent disk devices.

Appendix B can be used in selecting a blocksize which provides good performance and good space utilization. The values appearing on the left column, beginning with the second line, 23476, and stopping with 4276 can be considered target blocksizes. Which one should be used depends on an installation's guidelines. If no guidelines exist, 23476 can be used as the optimum value. Equaling the selected target blocksize would be ideal and that can always be done with RECFM=VB and RECFM=U. It is, however, difficult with RECFM=FB, in view of the fact that the blocksize must be a multiple of the logical record length. In this case, the value for blocksize should as close as possible to the target blocksize without exceeding it.

A simple formula can be used to compute the blocksize. Here is an example:

The logical record length of a data set is 80. Using 23476 as the target blocksize, determine the best blocksize.

Divide the target blocksize by the logical record length and drop the decimal from the answer. This number is the blocking factor. The blocking factor multiplied by the logical record length yields the blocksize: (blocking factor) x (logical record length) = blocksize
23476/80 = 293.45   293 (decimal dropped) is the blocking factor
293 x 80 = 23440 — optimum blocksize

For tape data sets the same formula can be used with 32760 as the target blocksize.

Assume the logical record length of a tape data set to be 133. The optimum blocksize can be calculated as follows:

32760/133 = 246.315   246 (decimal dropped) is the blocking factor
246 x 133 = 32718 — optimum blocksize

Some installations provide their technical staff with a TSO CLIST which, when given the logical record length, provides the blocksize.

8.6 CREATING USING MOD

DISP of NEW is normally used to create a data set. However, MOD can also be used. Consider the DD statement below (it is the output statement of the IEBGENER utility):

```
//SYSUT2   DD   DSN=USER1.MTW,DISP=(MOD,CATLG),UNIT=TAPE,
//              DCB=(BLKSIZE=32700,LRECL=100,RECFM=FB)
```

When this DD statement is used for the first time, MOD will default to NEW (unfortunately, no message will appear to indicate this). MOD defaults to NEW when both of the conditions below are met:

• No VOL=SER or VOL=REF is coded in the DD statement.

and

• The data set is neither passed nor cataloged.

During the first execution, the data set will be created and cataloged. During the second (or any subsequent) execution, the very same DD statement will have a different meaning. Since the data set is now cataloged, MOD will default to OLD, with the proper positioning to the end of the data, allowing records to be added. The UNIT parameter will be ignored (or used if TAPE describes a subset of the unit supplied by the catalog). If the added records have not caused the data set to extend to a second volume, DISP=(MOD,CATLG) will result in a step termination message:

```
IEF287I   USER1.MTW                                    NOT RECTLGD 2
IEF285I   VOL SER NOS= 001468
```

This is a benign message indicating that the entry for USER1.MTW in the catalog was not altered.

If the added records have caused the data set to extend to a second volume, DISP=(MOD,CATLG) will result in a step termination message:

```
IEF287I   USER1.MTW                                    RECATALOGED
IEF285I   VOL SER NOS= 001468,000053
```

This message indicates that the entry for USER1.MTW was updated to contain the new volume serial, 000053.

MOD should be used to create data sets only when there is a need to sometimes create and sometimes extend a sequential data set without changing JCL, as demonstrated above.

9

Passing and Receiving Data Sets

Section 5.3 in Chapter 5 provided a basic description of PASS in the DISP parameter. This chapter will expand upon the details, benefits, and, mostly, the dangers of passing.

9.1 DEFINITIONS

To PASS a data set means to request that the system create and save an entry in memory containing the data set's name plus related volume and unit information. This information is intended for later use when the data set is *"received."* Also, if the data set is on tape, its volume is to remain mounted so that it can be used later in the job without operator intervention. PASS is performed by the step termination routines of the Initiator (see Figure 1.7). A data set is said to be passed if it has such an in-memory entry.

To "receive" a passed data set means to provide a DD statement describing the data set using DISP=OLD, SHR, or MOD (not defaulting to NEW) and *omitting specific volume information (VOL=SER or VOL=REF)*. The absence of this information forces the system to search and locate the entry that was saved during passing, use the volume and unit information from it and then remove the entry from memory. Receiving is only meaningful for a passed data set, and it is performed by the allocation routines of the initiator.

9.2 PASSING AND RECEIVING

Passing provides a facility that, to a degree, mimics that of cataloging but with an important number of differences. When a data set is cataloged, it can be retrieved using basically just two parameters:

```
//IN2   DD   DSN=USER1.FILEA,DISP=SHR
```

As explained in Section 6.3 of Chapter 6, the absence of specific volume information causes the system to search the catalog, find the entry for USER1.FILEA, and extract the needed unit and vol information. The system, being in possession of (the required) DSN, DISP, UNIT, and VOL information, can now retrieve the data set.

When a data set is passed, the system places an entry in an in-memory table, to be known hitherto as the *passed data set queue*, which resides in the job's own region and is created by the system when (and if) a data set is first passed during the job's execution. If more data sets are passed, their entries will be added to the same passed data set queue. Each executing job (that passes at least one data set) will have its own passed data set queue.

Consider the following JCL:

```
//S1     EXEC  PGM=P1
//OUT1   DD    DSN=USER1.SET1,DISP=(,PASS),UNIT=SYSDA,
//             SPACE=(TRK,(100,20),RLSE),
//             DCB=(LRECL=100,BLKSIZE=23400,RECFM=FB)
//S2     EXEC  PGM=P2,COND=(4,LT)
//IN2    DD    DSN=USER1.SET1,DISP=(OLD,KEEP)
```

When step S1 terminates, the system creates the passed data set queue and places an entry in it for data set USER1.SET1. Keep in mind, this resides in memory as opposed to disk, where catalog entries reside. The contents of this entry are very similar (though not identical) to those of the catalog.

Assuming the data set was allocated on 3380 volume PACK24, the entry provides the following basic information:

```
PASSED DATA SET QUEUE
-----------------------------------------
| dsn              | vol    | unit |
-----------------------------------------
| USER1.SET1       | PACK24 | 3380 |   Passed Data Set Queue entry
-----------------------------------------
```

During the allocation of step S2, the system analyzes DD statement IN2. It describes an existing data set (OLD) and contains no specific volume information (VOL=SER or VOL=REF). This means that the catalog must be searched. However, before searching the catalog,the system *must* search the passed data set queue, where the entry will be found. The system extracts the needed vol and unit information and then **removes** the entry from the passed data set queue. The passed data set is now said to have been "received." For this reason, if a data set is passed once, it can be received only once. If the entry were not found, the system would have continued the search into the catalog.

Suppose that the JCL shown above contained a third step, as follows:

```
//USER1A JOB    FF78,PTEST,CLASS=R
//S1     EXEC  PGM=P1
//OUT1   DD     DSN=USER1.SET1,DISP=(,PASS),UNIT=SYSDA,
//              SPACE=(TRK,(100,20),RLSE),
//              DCB=(LRECL=100,BLKSIZE=23400,RECFM=FB)
//S2     EXEC  PGM=P2,COND=(4,LT)
//IN2    DD     DSN=USER1.SET1,DISP=(OLD,KEEP)
//S3     EXEC  PGM=P3,COND=(4,LT)
//IN3    DD     DSN=USER1.SET1,DISP=(OLD,KEEP)
```

The data set USER1.SET1 was received during step S2 and, as a result, its entry has been removed from the job's passed data set queue. In step S3, the system will again attempt but fail to locate the entry in the passed data set queue, continue the search into the catalog, and, unable to find the entry there, terminate the job with a JCL error:

```
IEF212I  USER1A S3 IN3 - DATA SET NOT FOUND
```

A pass can be followed by only one receive. This does not mean, of course, that a passed data set cannot be received more than once during the execution of a job. If the data set is passed again in DD statement IN2 of step S2, then its entry is written back into the passed data set queue and now it can be received one more time as shown below:

```
//USER1A JOB    FF78,PTEST,CLASS=R
//S1     EXEC  PGM=P1
//OUT1   DD     DSN=USER1.SET1,DISP=(,PASS),UNIT=SYSDA,
```

```
//              SPACE=(TRK,(100,20),RLSE),
//              DCB=(LRECL=100,BLKSIZE=23400,RECFM=FB)
//S2     EXEC   PGM=P2,COND=(4,LT)
//IN2    DD     DSN=USER1.SET1,DISP=(OLD,PASS)
//S3     EXEC   PGM=P3,COND=(4,LT)
//IN3    DD     DSN=USER1.SET1,DISP=(OLD,KEEP)
```

As long as the number of passes and the number of receives are equal, a data set can be passed and received a maximum of 254 times within a job. When an attempt is made to receive a data set more times than it has been passed, the result is the "DATA SET NOT FOUND" JCL error mentioned above, unless the data set is cataloged. The example below shows how this error may not occur:

```
//USER1A JOB    FF78,PTEST,CLASS=R
//S1     EXEC   PGM=P1
//OUT1   DD     DSN=USER1.SET1,DISP=(,PASS),UNIT=SYSDA,
//              SPACE=(TRK,(100,20),RLSE),
//              DCB=(LRECL=100,BLKSIZE=23400,RECFM=FB)
//S2     EXEC   PGM=P2,COND=(4,LT)
//IN2    DD     DSN=USER1.SET1,DISP=(OLD,CATLG)
//S3     EXEC   PGM=P3,COND=(4,LT)
//IN3    DD     DSN=USER1.SET1,DISP=(OLD,KEEP)
```

In this example, the data set USER1.SET1 is received in DD statement IN2 of step S2 and cataloged. At the end of step S2, the entry in the passed data set queue has been removed (as the result of receiving) and an entry for it has been added to the catalog. DD statement IN3 of step S3 appears to be attempting to receive the data set for a second time and the system will fail to find the entry in the passed data set queue; however, the system continues the search into the catalog where an entry for the data set exists, resulting in the successful retrieval of the cataloged data set. No error will occur in this case.

9.3 PASSING WITHOUT RECEIVING

Whenever a data set is passed, the system expects it to be received and, unless passed again, assigned a "final" disposition. Final means anything other than pass. Pass is an interim and not a final disposition, meaningful only while the job is executing. After the job terminates, it makes no sense to say that a data set is still passed since the passed data set queue, which contained its entry, was in the job's memory (region) and, after job end, no longer in existence. It stands to reason, then, that if the user does not receive a passed data set and give it a final disposition, someone else will. That someone else is the job termination routines (see Figure 1.7).

The job termination routines, which get control after the last step of the job has been executed, scan the passed data set queue for entries. If an entry is found, it always means that a data set was passed but was not received and given a final disposition. Such an entry is called an "unsatisfied (or unreceived) pass" and the job termination routines determine what is to be done with the data set.

Here is the logic used by the job termination routines in disposing of a data set whose entry is an unsatisfied pass:

1. If a data set was created and passed during the execution of the job and was never kept or cataloged while being received, it will be deleted. In essence, the data set is returned to the status it had before the job began execution: nonexistent (see Example 1 below).

   Most data sets being passed are created during the execution of the job. Therefore, having a passed data set deleted during job termination is a common occurrence.

2. A data set was created and passed during the execution of the job and was kept or cataloged while being received. If this data set is passed again in a subsequent step and its entry remains an unsatisfied pass, it will be kept (see Example 2 below).

   This is not likely to happen frequently.

3. If the data set was created and passed during the execution of the job and was kept or cataloged without being received, the results are difficult to predict (see Examples 3A and 3B below).

   Retrieving a passed data set without receiving it is a very poor practice that can cause serious problems as Example 3B and other examples will demonstrate. It must *always* be avoided.

4. If the passed data set was in existence before the job began execution, it will be kept. In essence, the data set is returned to the existing status it had before the job began execution: (see Example 4 below).

   This happens moderately often.

Several examples will be used to demonstrate the action taken by the job termination routines in response to an unsatisfied pass. The number of each example relates to the numbers above. A note should be made here that some of the examples may contain questionable or even bad JCL — explanations will be given.

Example 1:

```
//S1     EXEC  PGM=P1
//OUT1   DD    DSN=USER1.SET1,DISP=(,PASS),UNIT=SYSDA,
//             SPACE=(TRK,(100,20),RLSE),
//             DCB=(LRECL=100,BLKSIZE=23400,RECFM=FB)
//S2     EXEC  PGM=P2,COND=(4,LT)
//IN2    DD    DSN=USER1.SET1,DISP=(SHR,CATLG)
```

If both steps of this example are executed, there will be no unsatisfied pass. At the end of step S1 an entry for data set USER1.SET1 will be added to the passed data set queue. IN2 in step S2 receives (removing the entry from the passed data set queue) and catalogs the data set. job termination finds no unsatisfied passes and, therefore, takes no action.

Now assume that step S1 issued a return code of 12. Step S2 will not be executed and the data set will not be received. The entry remains in the passed data set queue; it is found by job termination, which will delete the data set, returning it to the nonexistent status it had before the job began execution.

Example 2:

```
//S1     EXEC  PGM=P1
//OUT1   DD    DSN=USER1.SET1,DISP=(,PASS),UNIT=SYSDA,
//             SPACE=(TRK,(100,20),RLSE),
//             DCB=(LRECL=100,BLKSIZE=23400,RECFM=FB)
//S2     EXEC  PGM=P2,COND=(4,LT)
//IN2    DD    DSN=USER1.SET1,DISP=(SHR,CATLG)
//S3     EXEC  PGM=P3,COND=(4,LT)
//IN3    DD    DSN=USER1.SET1,DISP=(SHR,PASS)
```

As in Example 1 (when both steps are executed), USER1.SET1 is passed in S1, received and cataloged in S2. No entry remains in the passed data set queue. Step S3 retrieves the cataloged data set and passes it again, creating an unsatisfied pass. This data set will be kept by job termination because it was given a permanent status (cataloged) while being received in step S2.

Example 3A:

```
//S1     EXEC  PGM=P1
//OUT1   DD    DSN=USER1.SET1,DISP=(,PASS),UNIT=SYSDA,
```

```
//              SPACE=(TRK,(100,20),RLSE),
//              DCB=(LRECL=100,BLKSIZE=23400,RECFM=FB)
//S2     EXEC   PGM=P2,COND=(4,LT)
//IN2    DD     DSN=USER1.SET1,DISP=(OLD,PASS),
//              VOL=REF=*.S1.OUT1
//S3     EXEC   PGM=P3,COND=(4,LT)
//IN3    DD     DSN=USER1.SET1,DISP=(SHR,CATLG)
```

This example contains what must be considered *bad* JCL. The user here is fortunate to escape without a serious problem. To ensure that the reader fully understands, it will be analyzed in greater detail than the previous examples.

At the end of step S1 an entry will exist in the passed data set queue:

```
PASSED DATA SET QUEUE
---------------------------------------
| dsn            | vol    | unit |
---------------------------------------
| USER1.SET1     | PACK24 | 3380 | <--Passed Data Set Queue entry
---------------------------------------
```

DD statement IN2 in S2 contains a VOL=REF parameter. Not only is this parameter completely unnecessary, but it causes the data set not to be received (to receive, VOL=SER or VOL=REF must be omitted — see definition). However, because all the required parameters are included (DSN, DISP, UNIT, and VOL — VOL=REF supplies both UNIT, and VOL), the system successfully retrieves the data set. Note that *"receive"* and *"retrieve"* do not have the same meaning!

The data set was not received and its entry is still in the passed data set queue. And now it is being passed again in step S2. While the catalog can never have duplicate entries, the passed data set queue can. A second entry, with identical information as the first, will be added.

```
PASSED DATA SET QUEUE
----------------------------------------
| dsn            | vol    | unit |
----------------------------------------
| USER1.SET1     | PACK24 | 3380 | <--- Entry #1 created by S1
| USER1.SET1     | PACK24 | 3380 | <--- Entry #2 created by S2
----------------------------------------
```

If multiple entries for the same data set name exist in the passed data set queue, the first will always be used when receiving the data set. DD statement IN3 in step S3 (which contains neither VOL=SER nor VOL=REF) receives the data set, using (and, in the process, removing) the first of the two entries, and catalogs it.

The second entry remains in the passed data set queue. Job termination finds it, but it does not recognize the data set as being the same one that was created and passed in the first step of the job because DD statement IN2 did not receive the data set. It will be treated as a data set that existed before the job began execution and will be *kept*. The user has escaped unscathed even though the JCL being used is downright dangerous. Not so in the example that follows.

Example 3B:

```
//S1      EXEC  PGM=P1
//OUT1    DD    DSN=USER1.SET1,DISP=(,PASS),UNIT=SYSDA,
//              SPACE=(TRK,(100,20),RLSE),
//              DCB=(LRECL=100,BLKSIZE=23400,RECFM=FB)
//S2      EXEC  PGM=P2,COND=(4,LT)
//IN2     DD    DSN=USER1.SET1,DISP=(SHR,CATLG),
//              VOL=REF=*.S1.OUT1
```

The JCL in this example is worse than the previous one. The user here is not so fortunate, as will be seen.

At the end of step S1, an entry will exist in the Passed Data Set Queue:

```
PASSED DATA SET QUEUE
-----------------------------------
| dsn              | vol    | unit |
-----------------------------------
| USER1.SET1       | PACK24 | 3380 |  <--- Passed Data
-----------------------------------                Set Queue entry
```

DD statement IN2 in S2, as explained in Example 3A, does not receive, because of the presence of VOL=REF, but it does retrieve the data set and ultimately catalogs it.

Since the data set was not received, its entry is still in the passed data set queue. Job termination will find it and the data set will be deleted. As if that were not enough, the catalog entry will not be removed, a fact that can certainly cause problems later. VOL=REF, which was called unnecessary in the previous example, is far worse than that now. It is destructive, since its presence is causing the unwanted (and, most likely, unexpected) deletion of a data set while leaving its catalog entry behind.

Note that if the VOL parameter were to be removed from DD statement IN2, the JCL becomes perfectly normal.

When a passed data set is retrieved without being received, unpredictable (and mostly unpleasant) events can occur. Yet, in some cases, no problems will result. For example, if the data set being passed were on tape, the delete performed by job termination would be meaningless and benign since tape data sets cannot be deleted. Also, if the data set being passed were temporary (as often is the case), there would be no problem. A temporary data set cannot be cataloged (or kept) and will always be deleted by the time the job ends.

Example 4:

```
//S1     EXEC   PGM=P1
//IN1    DD     DSN=USER1.SETA,DISP=(SHR,PASS),UNIT=SYSDA,
//              VOL=SER=TEST22
//S2     EXEC   PGM=P2,COND=(4,LT)
//IN2    DD     DSN=USER1.SETA,DISP=(SHR,PASS)
```

In this example, data set USER1.SETA was in existence before the job began execution. Step S1 retrieves and passes it in DD statement IN1 placing an entry in the passed data set queue. In step S2 the data set is received (entry removed) and passed again (entry placed back again). Job termination finds the entry and keeps the data set, giving it the same (existing) status it had before the job executed.

Please note that when job termination disposes of a data set because of an unsatisfied pass being found, it uses only two of the available dispositions: DELETE or KEEP.

9.4 OTHER PROBLEMS WITH PASSING

When passing a data set, several seemingly unexpected things can happen, especially as it relates to the DISP parameter.

Unusual defaults for DISP=SHR, DISP=OLD, and DISP=MOD   DISP=SHR and DISP=OLD are very frequently coded without the second field of the DISP parameter. There exists a very common belief that DISP=SHR always defaults to DISP=(SHR,KEEP) and DISP=OLD always to DISP=(OLD,KEEP). These defaults will actually be in effect in the vast majority of cases — but *not always*.

If a data set is being received, DISP=SHR and DISP=OLD can end up with different defaults: DELETE or PASS in addition to KEEP. When DISP=OLD becomes DISP=(OLD,DELETE):

```
//S1      EXEC  PGM=PA
//OUT1    DD    DSN=USER1.SETX,DISP=(,PASS),UNIT=SYSDA,
//              SPACE=(CYL,(10,5),RLSE),
//              DCB=(LRECL=100,BLKSIZE=23400,RECFM=FB)
//S2      EXEC  PGM=PB,COND=(4,LT)
//IN2     DD    DSN=USER1.SETX,DISP=OLD
```

In the example above, DISP=OLD will default to DISP=(OLD, DELETE), perhaps to the surprise of many. Although DISP=(OLD,KEEP) is the normal default, the system will *never* keep while receiving a passed data set which was created during the execution of the job unless KEEP (or CATLG) is *specifically* requested. Neither was requested here, and the system opts to delete the data set.

When DISP=OLD becomes DISP=(OLD,PASS)

```
//S1      EXEC  PGM=PA
//OUT1    DD    DSN=&&TEMP,DISP=(,PASS),UNIT=SYSDA,
//              SPACE=(CYL,(10,5),RLSE),
//              DCB=(LRECL=100,BLKSIZE=23400,RECFM=FB)
//S2      EXEC  PGM=PB,COND=(4,LT)
//IN2     DD    DSN=&&TEMP,DISP=OLD
```

In the example above, DISP=OLD will default to DISP=(OLD,PASS). Actually, this has nothing to do with the fact that the temporary data set is passed. Rather, it has to do with the fact that the system is unable to honor the normal default (OLD,KEEP) because the data set is temporary (a temporary data set can only be passed or deleted). A warning message will appear:

```
IEF648I  INVALID DISP FIELD - PASS SUBSTITUTED
```

DISP=OLD has been changed to DISP=(OLD,PASS).
When DISP=OLD becomes DISP=(OLD,KEEP):

```
//S1      EXEC  PGM=P1
//IN1     DD    DSN=USER1.SETA,DISP=(SHR,PASS)
//S2      EXEC  PGM=P2,COND=(4,LT)
//IN2     DD    DSN=USER1.SETA,DISP=SHR
```

In the example above, the data set was not created during the job, and DISP=SHR will default to DISP=(SHR,KEEP) as it usually does. Whatever was said about DISP=OLD in the preceding examples can also be said about DISP=SHR.

Using DISP=MOD Using DISP=MOD is less safe than the other two. It has exactly the same peculiarities as DISP=SHR or DISP=OLD whenever MOD defaults to an existing data set. However, it can also become DISP=(NEW,DELETE) if MOD defaults to NEW. To avoid any nasty surprises, it is recommended that DISP=(MOD,KEEP) be coded whenever needed, rather than coding DISP=MOD and depending on getting KEEP as a default.

When PASS is the second field of DISP:

```
//S1     EXEC  PGM=P1
//DD1    DD    DSN=USER1.FILE1,DISP=(,CATLG,DELETE),
//             UNIT=SYSDA,SPACE=(CYL,(10,5),RLSE),
//             DCB=(LRECL=100,BLKSIZE=23400,RECFM=FB)
```

The DISP parameter shown above requests that the data set USER1.FILE1 be cataloged if the step does not ABEND and deleted if the step ABENDs. In either case, the action will be performed by Step Termination. This is true if the second (normal) disposition field is KEEP, CATLG, UNCATLG, or DELETE.

If, however, PASS is used in the second field, step termination does not take care of the abnormal disposition field. Rather, it passes the data set whether or not an ABEND occurs. If an ABEND does occur, it is job termination that will try to perform the abnormal disposition (third field), provided that an unsatisfied pass entry for the data set is found for the passed data set queue.

```
//S1     EXEC  PGM=P1
//DD1    DD    DSN=USER1.FILE1,DISP=(,PASS,CATLG),
//             UNIT=SYSDA,SPACE=(CYL,(10,5),RLSE),
//             DCB=(LRECL=100,BLKSIZE=23400,RECFM=FB)
```

In the example above, step S1 ABENDs. Step termination will pass the data set. If none of the following steps are executed, as is usually the case, an unsatisfied pass will be found by job termination. In this case, rather than delete the data set, job termination performs the requested abnormal disposition, CATLG. However, if a step following the ABENDing step is executed and receives the data set (assigning to it a final disposition), then job termination will find no unsatisfied pass and the abnormal disposition of CATLG will be ignored. The example below, which is admittedly an unusual situation, demonstrates this point:

```
//S1     EXEC   PGM=P1
//DD1    DD     DSN=USER1.FILE1,DISP=(,PASS,CATLG),
//              UNIT=SYSDA,SPACE=(CYL,(10,5),RLSE),
//              DCB=(LRECL=100,BLKSIZE=23400,RECFM=FB)
//S2     EXEC   PGM=P2,COND=EVEN
//DD2    DD     DSN=USER1.FILE1,DISP=(OLD,KEEP)
```

Assume step S1 ABENDs. Data set USER1.FILE1 will be passed. One would expect the data set to be cataloged by job termination. Step S2, however, is executed (because of COND=EVEN) and the data set is received and kept. Since job termination finds no unsatisfied pass, no action will be taken and the data set will not be cataloged.

DISP=(,PASS,CATLG) is of marginal usefulness. It is best to avoid it.

9.5 PASSING TEMPORARY DATA SETS

Many of the preceding examples showed data sets with nontemporary names being passed. Such data sets best demonstrate the problems that can occur when passed data sets are retrieved without being received.

In a real environment, most passed disk data sets are likely to be temporary. A temporary data set must be passed if it is to be used in more than one step. Here is a perfectly normal example of passing and receiving a temporary data set.

```
//S1     EXEC   PGM=PA
//OUT1   DD     DSN=&&XYZ,DISP=(,PASS),UNIT=SYSDA,
//              SPACE=(CYL,(10,5),RLSE),
//              DCB=(LRECL=80,RECFM=FB,BLKSIZE=23440)
//S2     EXEC   PGM=PB,COND=(4,LT)
//IN2    DD     DSN=&&XYZ,DISP=(OLD,PASS)
//S3     EXEC   PGM=PB,COND=(4,LT)
//IN3    DD     DSN=&&XYZ,DISP=(OLD,DELETE)
```

Step S1 creates and passes a temporary data set. Step S2 receives and passes it again. Step S3 receives it for the last time and deletes it. No unsatisfied passes — no work for job termination.

If the pass/receive combination is used improperly, given the fact that temporary data sets cannot be saved beyond the end of a job, the problems that are likely to occur with nontemporary data sets may diminish or disappear with temporary ones. Consider the example below:

```
//S1     EXEC  PGM=PA
//OUT1   DD    DSN=&&XYZ,DISP=(,PASS),UNIT=SYSDA,
//             SPACE=(CYL,(10,5),RLSE),
//             DCB=(LRECL=80,RECFM=FB,BLKSIZE=23440)
//S2     EXEC  PGM=PB,COND=(4,LT)
//IN2    DD    DSN=&&XYZ,DISP=(OLD,PASS),VOL=REF=*.S1.OUT1
//S3     EXEC  PGM=PB,COND=(4,LT)
//IN3    DD    DSN=&&XYZ,DISP=(OLD,DELETE)
```

Clearly, there is absolutely no justification for using VOL=REF in DD statement IN2. Let's see if this will cause any problems.

Step S1 creates and passes the temporary data set. During step termination an entry is added to the newly built passed data set queue.

```
PASSED DATA SET QUEUE
-----------------------------------------------------
| dsn                                | vol    | unit |
-----------------------------------------------------
| SYS89220.T123928.RA000.USER1B.XYZ | WORK01 | 3380 |<=Passed Data
--------------------------------------------------- Set Queue entry
```

Step S2 retrieves without receiving the data set and passes it again. A new entry with the same information will be added to the passed data set queue.

```
PASSED DATA SET QUEUE
-----------------------------------------------------
| dsn                                | vol    | unit |
-----------------------------------------------------
| SYS89220.T123928.RA000.USER1B.XYZ | WORK01 | 3380 |<- Passed Data
--------------------------------------------------- Set Queue entry #1
| SYS89220.T123928.RA000.USER1B.XYZ | WORK01 | 3380 |<- Passed Data
--------------------------------------------------- Set Queue entry #2
```

Step S3 receives the data set (using and removing the first of the two entries) and deletes it. There still remains the second entry in the passed data set queue and job termination finds it. Because the DD statement (IN2) that generated this entry did not receive the data set but rather retrieved it using all the required information (DSN, DISP UNIT, and VOL — VOL and UNIT come from VOL=REF), the system assumes that the data set existed before the job began execution and, surprisingly, attempts to keep it, even though it is temporary. Since the system practically never rejects an attempt to keep (it never checks the VTOC of the appropriate volume to verify that the data set actually exists), the following unusual message will be issued:

```
IEF285I   SYS89220.T123928.RA000.USER1B.XYZ                    KEPT
IEF285I   VOL SER NOS= WORK01
```

Since the data set was already deleted in step S2, this message is meaningless and harmless, albeit confusing. Despite the poor JCL, no harm was caused (though one may be hard pressed to explain the message above, which, in addition to being highly unusual for a temporary data set, also directly contradicts the "DELETED" message for the same data set issued by step termination of step S2).

Is it then safe to assume that using the pass/receive combination improperly will always be harmless for temporary data sets? The answer to this question is: "Often but not always."

The following example is taken from an actual occurrence in a nameless installation, as are most examples in this book.

A procedure containing JCL similar to the example just discussed will be used.

PROCEDURE L33

```
//S1     EXEC   PGM=PA
//OUT1   DD     DSN=&&XYZ,DISP=(,PASS),UNIT=SYSDA,
//              SPACE=(CYL,(10,5),RLSE),
//              DCB=(LRECL=80,RECFM=FB,BLKSIZE=23440)
//S2     EXEC   PGM=PB,COND=(4,LT)
//IN2    DD     DSN=&&XYZ,DISP=(OLD,PASS),VOL=REF=*.S1.OUT1
//S3     EXEC   PGM=PB,COND=(4,LT)
//IN3    DD     DSN=&&XYZ,DISP=(OLD,DELETE)
```

When the procedure was executed once,

```
//PROD55A JOB   ZZ19,PROD55A,CLASS=P
//PR1     EXEC  L33
```

everything seemed to work well. Since the temporary data set was created and deleted inside the execution of the procedure, there appeared to be no reason why the procedure could not be safely executed twice in the same job.

```
//PROD55A JOB    ZZ19,PROD55A,CLASS=P
//PR1     EXEC   L33
//PR2     EXEC   L33
```

When procedure L33 is executed twice, something very strange happens. The job executes successfully about 20% of the time and fails with an S213-04 ABEND the rest of the time. Let's follow the events carefully and observe the insidious effects of passing and retrieving without receiving.

The first execution of procedure L33 is identical for both jobs and it was discussed in detail a few paragraphs earlier. At the end of step S3, there exists an entry in the passed data set queue while the temporary data set has been deleted.

```
PASSED DATA SET QUEUE
-----------------------------------------------------
| dsn                             | vol    | unit |
-----------------------------------------------------
| SYS89234.T040533.RA000.PROD55A.XYZ | WORK01 | 3380 |< Passed Data
-----------------------------------------------------  Set entry
```

Aside from an unusual message as it was seen earlier, this entry creates no problems when the procedure is executed once.

When executed twice, during the second execution of the procedure, in step S1 a new temporary data set, with exactly the same name as the previous one, is created on a volume most likely different than volume WORK01 (which was assigned by the system during the first execution of the procedure), say WORK05. This data set is passed, resulting in a second entry in the passed data set queue.

```
PASSED DATA SET QUEUE
-----------------------------------------------------
| dsn                             | vol    | unit |
-----------------------------------------------------
| SYS89234.T040533.RA000.PROD55A.XYZ | WORK01 | 3380 |< Passed Data
-----------------------------------------------------  Set entry #1
| SYS89234.T040533.RA000.PROD55A.XYZ | WORK05 | 3380 |< Passed Data
-----------------------------------------------------  Set entry #2
```

Step S2 retrieves without receiving the data set, removing none of the existing entries and, by passing again, adding yet a third one identical to the second.

```
PASSED DATA SET QUEUE

-----------------------------------------------------------
| dsn                                    | vol    | unit |
-----------------------------------------------------------
| SYS89234.T040533.RA000.PROD55A.XYZ | WORK01 | 3380 |< Passed Data
----------------------------------------------------------- Set entry #1
| SYS89234.T040533.RA000.PROD55A.XYZ | WORK05 | 3380 |< Passed Data
----------------------------------------------------------- Set entry #2
| SYS89234.T040533.RA000.PROD55A.XYZ | WORK05 | 3380 |< Passed Data
----------------------------------------------------------- Set entry #3
```

Step S3 receives the data set, using and removing the first of the three entries. Unfortunately, this entry points to volume WORK01 while the data set actually resides on volume WORK05. The result is an S213-04 ABEND failure.

Step termination for step S3 attempts but is unable to delete the data set, since it does not reside on the volume issuing the message:

```
IEF283I   SYS89234.T040533.RA000.PROD55A.XYZ        NOT DELETED 8
IEF283I   VOL SER NOS= WORK01
```

Job termination finds two unsatisfied pass entries in the passed data set queue, and the following messages will appear:

```
IEF285I   SYS89234.T040533.RA000.PROD55A.XYZ        DELETED
IEF285I   VOL SER NOS= WORK05

IEF285I   SYS89234.T040533.RA000.PROD55A.XYZ        KEPT
IEF285I   VOL SER NOS= WORK05
```

This job failed with a S213-04 ABEND about 80% of the time. The intermittent nature of this failure can be easily explained by the fact that the installation was using five "STORAGE" volumes. During the first execution of procedure L33, the system allocated one of them for the temporary data set. During the second execution of L33, there is approximately a 20% probability that the same volume will be allocated, in which case the job completes successfully without an

ABEND. Approximately 80% of the time a different volume will be allocated, resulting in the ABEND failure discussed above.

The villain, of course, is the VOL parameter which stops the data set from being received. Without it the job would run successfully 100% of the time.

It would be of interest to note that, for a long time, the installation, unable to explain the intermittent failure, kept running the job (it was of short duration) until it worked.

9.6 WHEN TO USE PASS

By now it should be obvious that passing can be treacherous if one is unfamiliar with its many peculiarities. Why then pass? Pass should be used only when it is necessary or advantageous:

- If a temporary data set is to be used in more than one step of a job, passing becomes necessary because a temporary data set can only be passed or deleted. If any other DISP field (CATLG, KEEP, or UNCATLG) is used, the system will issue a warning message, "INVALID DISP FIELD — PASS SUBSTITUTED," and pass the data set.
- If an existing cataloged data set is to be used many times in different steps of a job, pass can offer a small performance advantage. Consider the JCL below where the data set USER1.PLAYX is retrieved via the catalog in each of many steps.

```
//S1     EXEC   PGM=SIG1
//IN1    DD     DSN=USER1.PLAYX,DISP=SHR
//S2     EXEC   PGM=SIG2,COND=(4,LT)
//IN1    DD     DSN=USER1.PLAYX,DISP=SHR
. . . . . . . . . . . . . . . . . . . . . . . . . . . . . . . . . . . .
//SN     EXEC   PGM=SIGN,COND=(4,LT)
//IN1    DD     DSN=USER1.PLAYX,DISP=SHR
```

Nothing wrong with this JCL. However, for each retrieval of the data set USER1.PLAYX, the catalog will be used, generating I/O activity on the master catalog and one of the user catalogs.

If the data set were to be retrieved via the catalog in the first step, and passed and received in all the subsequent steps, given the fact that the passed data set queue resides in memory, some I/O activity would be eliminated and the job would run a little faster.

```
//S1     EXEC   PGM=SIG1
//IN1    DD     DSN=USER1.PLAYX,DISP=(SHR,PASS)
//S2     EXEC   PGM=SIG2,COND=(4,LT)
//IN1    DD     DSN=USER1.PLAYX,DISP=(SHR,PASS)
. . . . . . . . . . . . . . . . . . . . . . . . . . . . . . . . . . . . . . . . . . . . . . .
//SN     EXEC   PGM=SIGN,COND=(4,LT)
//IN1    DD     DSN=USER1.PLAYX,DISP=(SHR,KEEP)
```

- A tape data set is to be used in several steps of the same job. When a tape data set is passed, the system will attempt to keep the volume (where the data set resides) mounted so that when the data set is received the volume is found mounted, avoiding operator intervention. Passing is one of two ways available to keep a tape volume mounted between steps of a job. VOL=(,RETAIN) can also be used to accomplish the same. Actually, in view of the potential restart difficulties posed by passing (see the following section), RETAIN used in conjunction with the catalog is preferable.

Whenever a data set is passed, JCL should exist in a subsequent step to receive it. It makes little sense to pass a data set with no intention of receiving it. Remember to balance passes and receives. Even though the action that will be taken by job termination may be predictable, it is usually a poor practice to deliberately let job termination dispose of a data set. Consider the example below:

```
//S1     EXEC   PGM=PA
//OUT1   DD     DSN=&&TEMP,DISP=(,PASS),UNIT=SYSDA,
//              SPACE=(CYL,(60,20),RLSE),
//              DCB=(LRECL=80,RECFM=FB,BLKSIZE=23440)
//S2     EXEC   PGM=PB,COND=(4,LT)
//IN2    DD     DSN=&&TEMP,DISP=(OLD,PASS)
//    . . . . . . . . . . . . . . . . . . . . . . . . . . . . . . . . . . . . .
//    . . . . . . . . . . . . . . . . . . . . . . . . . . . . . . . . . . . . .
```

Assume that step S2 is not the last step in the job and none of the subsequent steps receive the temporary data set. Obviously, the temporary data set will be deleted when the job terminates, so why bother deleting it? The reason is that this data set will continue to occupy space (maximum 360 cylinders) until the end of the job, while this space could have been freed at the end of step S2 if DISP=(OLD,DELETE) instead of DISP=(OLD,PASS) were used.

Here is a good rule of thumb: When a data set is received for the last time in the job, assign to it the desired disposition. And do it explicitly, since defaults are often hard to predict.

If passing and receiving were coded properly and all the steps in a job were executed, there would never be unsatisfied passes to be resolved by job termination. However, sometimes steps will not be executed due to previous ABEND failures or bad return codes. A step that does not execute cannot receive a passed data set. So, even with the best of JCL, unsatisfied passes will be a common occurrence when a job passes data sets and does not complete normally.

9.7 PASS AND RESTART RECOVERY

When a step fails, it is often desirable to restart the job with the step that failed so as to avoid repetitive processing. This is especially needed in a production environment. Passing can seriously handicap the ability to restart.

Passing data sets that were not created during the execution of a job is acceptable. As was seen before, such data sets, if they become unsatisfied passes, will not be deleted by job termination, remaining available for restart purposes.

```
//S1     EXEC   PGM=PG1
//IN1    DD     DSN=USER1.FA,DISP=(SHR,PASS)
//S2     EXEC   PGM=PG2,COND=(0,LT)
//IN2    DD     DSN=USER1.FA,DISP=(SHR,PASS)
//S3     EXEC   PGM=PG3,COND=(0,LT)
//IN2    DD     DSN=USER1.FA,DISP=(SHR,KEEP)
```

If step S2 fails, data set USER1.FA will be kept by job termination, making restart possible.

Passing new data sets makes job restart very difficult, if not impossible. As discussed before, when a failure occurs, subsequent steps often are not executed, causing new passed data sets not to be received and resulting in their ultimate deletion by job termination. Therefore, if restart is needed, passing new data sets must be avoided. Cataloging rather than passing is the recommended alternative.

Here is an example of passing and the resulting restart problems.

```
//S1     EXEC   PGM=PA
//OUT1   DD     DSN=USER1.F1,DISP=(,PASS),UNIT=SYSDA,
//              SPACE=(CYL,(10,5),RLSE),
//              DCB=(LRECL=80,RECFM=FB,BLKSIZE=23440)
//S2     EXEC   PGM=PB,COND=(4,LT)
```

```
//IN2    DD      DSN=USER1.F1,DISP=(SHR,PASS)
//S3     EXEC    PGM=PC,COND=(4,LT)
//IN3    DD      DSN=USER1.F1,DISP=(SHR,CATLG))
```

If step S2 fails, data set USER1.F1 will be deleted by job termination, making restart impossible. The abnormal disposition can be used here to good purpose.

```
//S1     EXEC    PGM=PA
//OUT1   DD      DSN=USER1.F1,DISP=(,PASS),UNIT=SYSDA,
//               SPACE=(CYL,(10,5),RLSE),
//               DCB=(LRECL=80,RECFM=FB,BLKSIZE=23440)
//S2     EXEC    PGM=PB,COND=(4,LT)
//IN2    DD      DSN=USER1.F1,DISP=(SHR,PASS,CATLG))
//S3     EXEC    PGM=PC,COND=(4,LT)
//IN3    DD      DSN=USER1.F1,DISP=(SHR,CATLG))
```

Here if step S2 ABENDs, data set USER1.F1 will be cataloged by job termination, thus permitting restart. This technique, of course, does not take into account a bad return code. If step S2 issues a bad return code and step S3 is not executed, data set USER1.F1 will not be received and, therefore, is deleted by job termination. An additional step at the end of the job may help.

```
//S1     EXEC    PGM=PA
//OUT1   DD      DSN=USER1.F1,DISP=(,PASS),UNIT=SYSDA,
//               SPACE=(CYL,(10,5),RLSE),
//               DCB=(LRECL=80,RECFM=FB,BLKSIZE=23440)
//S2     EXEC    PGM=PB,COND=(4,LT)
//IN2    DD      DSN=USER1.F1,DISP=(SHR,PASS,CATLG))
//S3     EXEC    PGM=PC,COND=(4,LT)
//IN3    DD      DSN=USER1.F1,DISP=(SHR,CATLG))
//S4     EXEC    PGM=IEFBR14,COND=(0,LE,S3)
//DD1    DD      DSN=USER1.F1,DISP=(SHR,CATLG))
```

This example appears to cover both possibilities, ABEND or bad return code. An ABEND works was explained before. A bad return code from step S2 which would cause step S3 not to be executed would also cause step S4 to be executed — COND=(0,LE,S3) will be ignored if step S3 is not executed — cataloging the data set. If step S3 is executed, no matter what return code it issues, step S4 will not be executed, which is fine because the data set was received and cataloged in step S3. So this appears to allow passing and still permit restart. It does, but it has a weakness. If step S2 fails with a S322 ABEND (CPU availability based on the TIME parameter of the JOB statement is exhausted), or if the operator cancels the job during the execution of step S2 (S222 or S122 ABEND), step S4 cannot be executed and data set USER1.F1 will be deleted by job termination Even if this weakness is ignored, the JCL is simply too complicated and confusing. The JCL below is preferable and simpler.

```
//S1      EXEC  PGM=PA
//OUT1    DD    DSN=USER1.F1,DISP=(,CATLG,DELETE),UNIT=SYSDA,
//              SPACE=(CYL,(10,5),RLSE),
//              DCB=(LRECL=80,RECFM=FB,BLKSIZE=23440)
//S2      EXEC  PGM=PB,COND=(4,LT)
//IN2     DD    DSN=USER1.F1,DISP=SHR
//S3      EXEC  PGM=PC,COND=(4,LT)
//IN3     DD    DSN=USER1.F1,DISP=SHR
```

If step S2 fails, data set USER1.F1 remains cataloged and available for restart.

Here is another example where a temporary data set is used.

```
//S1      EXEC  PGM=PA
//OUT1    DD    DSN=&&TEMP1,DISP=(,PASS),UNIT=SYSDA,
//              SPACE=(CYL,(20,5),RLSE),
//              DCB=(LRECL=80,RECFM=FB,BLKSIZE=23440)
//S2      EXEC  PGM=PB,COND=(4,LT)
//IN2     DD    DSN=&&TEMP1,DISP=(OLD,PASS)
//S3      EXEC  PGM=PC,COND=(4,LT)
//IN3     DD    DSN=&&TEMP1,DISP=(OLD,DELETE)
```

Note that in this example the temporary data set makes restart impossible. Again, the JCL below is preferable.

```
//S1      EXEC  PGM=PA
//OUT1    DD    DSN=USER1.TEMP,DISP=(,CATLG,DELETE),UNIT=SYSDA,
//              SPACE=(CYL,(20,5),RLSE),
//              DCB=(LRECL=80,RECFM=FB,BLKSIZE=23440)
//S2      EXEC  PGM=PB,COND=(4,LT)
//IN2     DD    DSN=USER1.TEMP,DISP=OLD
//S3      EXEC  PGM=PC,COND=(4,LT)
//IN3     DD    DSN=USER1.TEMP,DISP=OLD
//S4      EXEC  PGM=IEFBR14,COND=(4,LT)
//DD1     DD    DSN=USER1.F1,DISP=(OLD,DELETE)
```

In this example, if step S2 or S3 ABENDs or issues a bad return code, data set USER1.TEMP remains cataloged (because step S4 will not be executed) allowing for restart. If all three steps execute well, step S4 will be executed and data set USER1.TEMP will be deleted and uncataloged (as a temporary data set would always be deleted). This JCL, however, may require manual intervention to delete and uncatalog the data set under certain conditions. If, for example, step S1 issues a bad return code, the data set will remain cataloged. This potential problem can be eliminated by adding a step at the beginning of the job similar to the one at the end. Its purpose will be to delete and uncatalog the data set if the last step of the previous run failed to do so (see Section 7.3.4 in Chapter 7).

```
//S0     EXEC  PGM=IEFBR14
//DD1    DD    DSN=USER1.F1,DISP=(MOD,DELETE),UNIT=SYSDA,
//             SPACE=(TRK,0)
//S1     EXEC  PGM=PA
//OUT1   DD    DSN=USER1.TEMP,DISP=(,CATLG,DELETE),UNIT=SYSDA,
//             SPACE=(CYL,(20,5),RLSE),
//             DCB=(LRECL=80,RECFM=FB,BLKSIZE=23440)
//S2     EXEC  PGM=PB,COND=(4,LT)
//IN2    DD    DSN=USER1.TEMP,DISP=OLD
//S3     EXEC  PGM=PC,COND=(4,LT)
//IN3    DD    DSN=USER1.TEMP,DISP=OLD
//S4     EXEC  PGM=IEFBR14,COND=(4,LT)
//DD1    DD    DSN=USER1.F1,DISP=(OLD,DELETE)
```

10

Special DD Statements and Parameters

This chapter will discuss DD statements and DD statement parameters that are out of the ordinary:

- DD statements which are not opened by the executing program. Instead, they are used by the system to accomplish certain goals.
- DD statements which, when included in a step, the system provides additional services to the user.
- DD statement parameters where the ordinary rules for creating and retrieving data sets do not hold.
- DD statement parameters which cause a DD statement to be under complete or partial JES2/JES3 control.

There is a number of DD statement parameters that are meaningful only when used in conjunction with the type of parameter mentioned above. They will be discussed in this chapter rather than Chapter 5.

10.1 DD * AND DD DATA — SUPPLYING SYSIN DATA

The input stream submitted to the system for execution consists of two possible parts:

- JCL. This a mandatory part of the input stream.

• Data mixed in with JCL in the input stream. This data is known as *sysin data* or *input stream data*. It is an optional part of the input stream and always has a logical record length of 80. Any records encountered in the input stream which are not JCL statements will be treated as sysin data.

Sysin data must be preceded by a DD statement such as:

```
//INPUT  DD  *
-- data --
```

Sysin data encountered by JES2 or JES3 following a DD * statement will be saved on the SPOOL volume for future use. This is known as input spooling. The sysin data is delimited (the spooling operation stops) by:

• A /* (delimiter) statement found.
• A valid JCL statement.
• An end-of-file condition on the reading device.

The asterisk (*) is a positional parameter, but it is practically always the only one coded in the parameter field. DD * is a special statement, which is under complete JES2 or JES3 control. Most DD statement parameters cannot be coded in it. Some parameters are allowed, but realistically none are ever used (in JES3 the system may add DCB=BLKSIZE=80 after the asterisk).

SYSIN is a very common ddname used by many vendor-written programs.

```
//SYSIN  DD  *
```

A complication arises if the sysin data must consist of JCL statements. They cannot be read in as data using DD * because any JCL statement delimits sysin data. To accomplish this, DD DATA instead of DD * must be used:

```
//SYSUT1  DD  DATA
```

DD DATA and DD * work alike with one exception: A JCL statement does not delimit sysin data when DD DATA is used. Unless the sysin data is at the very end of the input stream, a /* statement must be used to delimit it. Failure to supply a /* will cause serious problems. JCL statements following DD DATA will unintentionally become part of sysin data.

A further complication can arise if the JCL statements in the sysin data contains a /*. The /* will cause premature delimiting of the sysin data with all of the following records being treated as JCL, rather than data, or being ignored. To avoid this problem, the DLM parameter must be used:.

```
//SYSUT1  DD   DATA,DLM=')('
-- data and JCL (including /*) --
)(
```

The two characters that are coded in the DLM parameter (apostrophes must be used for special characters) will act as a delimiter for this DD statement, and /* will be treated as data. Any two characters can be used. However, characters that are likely to appear in the first two positions of any data record must be avoided.

If sysin data not preceded by DD * or DD DATA is found in the input stream, the system will generate a statement and place it in front of the sysin data:

```
//SYSIN  DD  *      GENERATED STATEMENT
```

The user can take advantage of this feature, as //SYSIN DD * is a very common DD statement. It need never be supplied by the user.

If this generated DD statement appears unexpectedly in the output, it means that data records were accidentally included with JCL. A line with blanks is the most common offender. It is invisible to the user but it will be treated as data by the system. This may or may not cause a problem. To understand when it does, consider the following JCL where such an accidental record exists.

```
//S3     EXEC  PGM=FRA
//D1     DD    DSN=USER1.FILE1,DISP=SHR
//D2     DD    SYSOUT=*
-- unintended data record --
//D3     DD    DSN=USER1.CNTL1,DISP=SHR
```

The system will provide the generated statement.

```
//S3     EXEC  PGM=FRA
//D1     DD    DSN=USER1.FILE1,DISP=SHR
//D2     DD    SYSOUT=*
//SYSIN  DD  *      GENERATED STATEMENT
  -- unintended data record --
//D3     DD    DSN=USER1.CNTL1,DISP=SHR
```

In this case, since the program FRA does not use a DD statement named SYSIN, the generated statement is simply an additional and unnecessary DD statement which causes no harm. But suppose that the program does require a DD statement named SYSIN and it is coded before the generated statement.

```
//S3      EXEC  PGM=FRA
//SYSIN   DD    DSN=USER1.FILE1,DISP=SHR
//D2      DD    SYSOUT=*
//SYSIN   DD  *      GENERATED STATEMENT
-- unintended data record --
//D3    DD    DSN=USER1.CNTL1,DISP=SHR
```

Now there are two DD statements by the same name in the same step. This is not an error condition. When the program opens for SYSIN the first of the two will be used. The other will be allocated and ignored. Again, no problem exists, since the unintentional statement will be ignored. As the last possibility, suppose the required SYSIN DD statement is coded after the generated one.

```
//S3      EXEC  PGM=FRA
//D2      DD    SYSOUT=*
//SYSIN   DD  *      GENERATED STATEMENT
-- unintended data record --
//D3    DD    DSN=USER1.CNTL1,DISP=SHR
//SYSIN   DD    DSN=USER1.FILE1,DISP=SHR
```

Clearly, this is a problem. When the program opens for SYSIN, the accidental record will be read in and the good data set will be ignored.

10.2 THE SYSOUT PARAMETER

Print records generated by a program are not normally routed directly to a physical printer (theoretically it is possible, but in practice it is seldom done). Instead, they are written on the SPOOL pack and saved there for later viewing on a terminal or printing (or both). This is called output spooling, and it is under the control of JES2 or JES3 which later can use one of their print routines to print the data set. These print routines must schedule the data sets for printing, and classes are used for this purpose. All printer routines (called printers or writers) are associated with one or more classes (maximum 36) and each data set to be printed must also be assigned a class. The printer routines select data sets for printing in a very similar way as initiators select jobs for execution.

An external writer can also be used to route such print data sets to a printer. However, external writers are normally used to output such data sets to disk or tape. They are used infrequently.

The SYSOUT parameter can assign this class, known as sysout or output class, to a data set. Such data sets are called sysout or output data sets.

General Syntax

```
SYSOUT=(class|*[,writer|INTRDR][,form])        keyword parameter
```

or

```
SYSOUT=(,)
```

class — Identifies the sysout class of the data set from A to Z and 0 to 9.

```
SYSOUT=A
```

* — Indicates that the same class used in the MSGCLASS parameter of the JOB statement (or the installation-defined default, if the MSGCLASS parameter is omitted) is to be used.

```
SYSOUT=*
```

writer — Identifies the routine which will be used to print the sysout data set. Seldom used. Normally JES2 or JES3 (or external writer) routines do the printing.

```
SYSOUT=(X,MYWTR)
```

INTRDR — Identifies a system internal reader. When this subparameter is coded, records written to the DD statement will be submitted to JES2 or JES3 as input stream.

The JCL below demonstrates how INTRDR can be used:

```
//GEN        EXEC  PGM=IEBGENER
//SYSPRINT   DD    SYSOUT=*
```

```
//SYSIN    DD     DUMMY
//SYSUT1   DD     DATA
//PROD222  JOB    PJ44,GENL,CLASS=D
//STEP1    EXEC   PGM=GL1
//IN       DD     DSN=GLX.MAS,DISP=SHR
//  .   .   .   .   .   .   .   .   .
//  .   .   .   .   .   .   .   .   .
/*
//SYSUT2   DD     SYSOUT=(A,INTRDR)
```

The IEBGENER utility will read in the sysin data in DD statement SYSUT1, which is JCL for job PROD222 and output it to a system internal reader. Internal readers are logical (not physical) readers. One of these readers is always used when the SUBMIT command is used in TSO or ISPF (as well as other time-sharing systems). There are many internal readers in the system.

The result of executing the JCL above is to submit job PROD222 for execution.

form — Identifies the print from to be used for the sysout data set, if the form required is different than the default print form of the installation.

(,) — This unusual notation omits the sysout class, allowing it to be supplied through an OUTPUT statement. If an OUTPUT statement fails to supply the sysout class, SYSOUT=(,) defaults to SYSOUT=*.

10.2.1 Parameters Used With SYSOUT

A sysout data set is mostly under JES2 or JES3 control. As a result, there are several parameters that cannot be coded in a sysout DD statement: DSN, VOL, DISP, LABEL, and DDNAME. If any of them are coded, the result will be a JCL error.

The UNIT and SPACE parameters, if coded, will be ignored and not generate a JCL error. A long time ago both of these parameters were meaningful in a sysout DD statement. For compatibility reasons their presence is accepted but ignored.

A step can have many sysout DD statements (the limit is the same as for DD statements per step, 3273), frequently specifying the same class:

```
//S4       EXEC  PGM-RR1
//REPRT1   DD    SYSOUT=F
//REPRT2   DD    SYSOUT=F
//REPRT3   DD    SYSOUT=F
```

Normally the three reports produced by the three sysout DD statements shown above will be printed together, or will be displayed together on a CRT screen after the job terminates. The sequence in which the reports appear is independent of the sequence of the DD statements within the step. It is determined by the sequence of opening. The data set opened first will appear first, and so on. If, therefore, the sequence of sysout reports is not satisfactory, rearranging JCL will have no effect. Programming changes will be required.

Many parameters can be coded in a sysout DD statement. Most of them are meaningful only for sysout. An explanation of the most commonly used of these parameters follows:

10.2.1.1 The DCB Parameter

In some ways, the DCB parameter is treated the same for sysout as for ordinary data sets. If LRECL and RECFM are not hard-coded in the program, they must be coded in the DCB parameter (RECFM will default to U, which is rarely used). BLKSIZE, however, need not be coded, even if it is not hard-coded. JES2 or JES3 will compute a BLKSIZE from the LRECL. If the BLKSIZE is coded in the DCB parameter, any valid size is acceptable, even if it is not a multiple of LRECL (for RECFM=FB). Also, coding a small BLKSIZE will have no negative effect on either performance or space utilization.

```
//PRINT   DD   SYSOUT=*,DCB=(LRECL=133,RECFM=FBA,BLKSIZE=133)
```

The "A" in the RECFM subparameter informs the system that the first character of each print line is not to be printed. Rather, it is to be used as a carriage control character.

10.2.1.2 The FREE Parameter

The FREE parameter, when coded in a sysout DD statement, makes a sysout data set available for printing before the job terminates.

General Syntax

```
FREE={CLOSE|END}                    keyword parameter
```

CLOSE — Indicates that printing can begin when the data set is closed, rather than waiting for job termination.

END — Indicates that printing can begin after the job terminates.

If the FREE parameter is used for many SYSOUT data sets in the same job, it becomes a logistical problem for the operator to collect all the printouts together as a job, without losing some.

It should be used only when it is essential that printing begin before the job terminates.

Defaults:

If the FREE parameter is omitted, FREE=END is the default.

```
//PRINT   DD   SYSOUT=*,FREE=CLOSE
```

10.2.1.3 The COPIES Parameter

The COPIES parameter is used when multiple copies of a sysout data set are required.

General Syntax

```
COPIES=([number][,number-per-page])        keyword parameter
```

number — Specifies the number of copies of the data set to be printed, from 1 to 255 (254 for JES3).

number-per-page — Specifies the number of copies for each page to be printed before proceeding with the printing of the next page. The value is from 1 to 255 (254 for JES3). This subparameter is only valid for 3800 printer output. For 3800 output, if this value is coded, the first value will be ignored.

The COPIES parameter neither overrides nor is overridden by the COPIES parameter in the /*JOBPARM JES2 statement or the subparameter of the accounting information parameter in the JOB statement which identifies the number of copies for the entire job's output.

Defaults:

If the COPIES parameter is omitted, the default is one copy.

```
//PRINT   DD   SYSOUT=*,COPIES=3
```

10.2.1.4 The OUTLIM Parameter

The OUTLIM parameter is used to limit the number of records (print lines) of a sysout data set.

General Syntax

```
OUTLIM=number                    keyword parameter
```

number — Specifies the number of lines the sysout data set is permitted to output from 1 to 16777215.

If the number of lines coded in the OUTLIM parameter is exceeded, the result normally is an S722 ABEND failure. An installation, however, can supply a user-written routine which can determine a different course of action.

The OUTLIM parameter is basically used for testing when the programmer wishes to avoid writing an excessive number of lines (possibly filling up the spool pack) in the event of a write-loop in the program.

Defaults:

If the OUTLIM parameter is omitted, for JES2 there is no limit beyond the available capacity of the spool pack(s). For JES3, an installation-defined default exists.

```
//PRINT   DD   SYSOUT=*,OUTLIM=7000
```

10.2.1.5 The FCB Parameter

The FCB (Forms Control Buffer) parameter is used to provide a guide for printing when installation-defined defaults are not appropriate. The FCB parameter basically specifies the number of lines per inch and the form length. For the 3800 laser printer, it can also provide graphic capabilities.

General Syntax

```
FCB=fcb                 keyword parameter
```

fcb — Specifies a name from 1 to 4 alphabetic, numeric, or national characters. The name identifies an FCB image which is a member of system library SYS1.IMAGELIB. The last 4 characters of the member name are the same as the name that is coded in the FCB parameter.

IBM supplies two standard FCBs: STD1 (6 lines per inch on 8.5-inch paper) and STD2 (6 lines per inch on 11-inch paper). Most FCBs are user-defined to serve the needs of the installation.

Note: In some old printers, such as the 1403 printer, a carriage control tape with holes in it serve the same purpose as an FCB.

Defaults:

If the FCB parameter is omitted, an installation-defined default FCB will be used.

```
//PRINT  DD  SYSOUT=*,FCB=IM10
```

10.2.1.6 The UCS Parameter

The UCS (Universal Character Set) parameter is used to provide a different print train on an impact printer than the print train used by default.

General Syntax

```
UCS=ucs                 keyword parameter
```

ucs — Identifies the print train to be used (from 1 to 4 characters). Before the sysout data set begins to print, the operator will be asked to mount the requested print train and the corresponding UCS image will be loaded into the printer's buffer.

The UCS parameter is ignored for a 3800 laser printer.

Before coding this parameter, the user must confirm that the desired print train is physically available in the installation. This parameter is seldom used.

Defaults:

If the UCS parameter is omitted, an installation-defined default will be used.

```
//PRINT  DD  SYSOUT=*,UCS=HN
```

10.2.1.7 The HOLD Parameter

The HOLD parameter is used when it is desired that a sysout data set not be printed until the operator releases it.

General Syntax

```
HOLD={YES|NO}                            keyword parameter
```

YES — It indicates that the sysout data set is to be held. Operator intervention is required (a release command) to allow the data set to be printed. This subparameter can also be coded as Y.

NO — It indicates that the sysout data set is to be processed normally. This subparameter can also be coded as N. HOLD=NO has the same effect as omitting the HOLD parameter.

Defaults:

If the HOLD parameter is omitted, HOLD=NO will be the default.

```
//PRINT  DD  SYSOUT=*,HOLD=YES
```

10.2.1.8 The DEST Parameter

The DEST parameter is used to route a sysout data set to a remote or local destination.

General Syntax

```
DEST=destination                    keyword parameter
```

destination — It identifies the destination where the sysout data set will be routed. Many formats are available:

For JES2:

Rnnnn
RMnnnn
RMTnnnn
name
Uddd
LOCAL
Nnnnn
NnnnnRmmmm

For JES3:

dev-name
address
group
node
ANYLOCAL

JES2

- Rnnnn — Identifies the RJE (Remote Job Entry) or local station where the data set will be routed. It can also be coded as RM or RMT instead of R. From 0 to 4000.
     DEST=R0 means the same as DEST=LOCAL.

```
//PRINT   DD   SYSOUT=*,DEST=R15
```

- name — Identifies the local or RJE station by an installation-defined name where the data set will be routed. From 1 to 8 alphabetic, numeric, or national characters

```
//PRINT   DD   SYSOUT=*,DEST=SANFRAN
```

- Uddd — ddd identifies a three-digit hexadecimal device address where the data set will be routed.

```
//PRINT   DD   SYSOUT=*,DEST=U00F
```

- LOCAL — Indicates that any local device can print the sysout data set.

```
//PRINT   DD   SYSOUT=*,DEST=LOCAL
```

- Nnnnn — Identifies a node where the data set will be routed. From 1 to 1000

```
                  //PRINT   DD   SYSOUT=*,DEST=N7
```

- NnnnnRmmmm — Identifies a node and an RJE or local station within that node where the data set will be routed. From 1 to 4000 for nnnn and 1 to 1000 for mmmm. n and m together cannot exceed 6 digits.

```
//PRINT   DD   SYSOUT=*,DEST=N3R35
```

JES3
- dev-name — Identifies the local or RJE station by an installation-defined name where the data set will be routed. From 1 to 8 alphabetic, numeric, or national characters.

```
//PRINT   DD   SYSOUT=*,DEST=BKLYN
```

- address — Identifies a three-digit hexadecimal device address where the data set will be routed.

```
//PRINT   DD   SYSOUT=*,DEST=010
```

- group — Identifies an RJE station or a group of RJE stations or a group of local stations by an installation-defined name where the data set will be routed. From 1 to 8 alphabetic, numeric, or national characters.

```
//PRINT   DD   SYSOUT=*,DEST=LA12
```

- node — Identifies an installation-defined name of a node where the data set will be routed.

```
//PRINT   DD   SYSOUT=*,DEST=CHICAGO
```

• ANYLOCAL — Indicates that any local device can print the sysout data set.

```
//PRINT   DD   SYSOUT=*,DEST=ANYLOCAL
```

Defaults:

If the DEST parameter is omitted, the sysout data set will be routed to the default destination of the device used to submit the job. JES2 and JES3 control statements can also be used to route the entire job's output or part of it. Such statements are not discussed in this book.

10.2.1.9 The BURST Parameter

The BURST parameter is used to request that the continuous form paper be burst into separate sheets. This parameter is valid only with a 3800 printer. It is ignored with impact printers.

General Syntax

```
BURST={YES|NO}                         keyword parameter
```

YES — Requests that the output be burst into separate pages. This subparameter can also be coded as Y.

NO — Indicates that the output remain continuous. This subparameter can also be coded as N. BURST=NO has the same effect as omitting the BURST parameter.

Defaults:

If the BURST parameter is omitted, BURST=NO will be the default.

```
//PRINT   DD   SYSOUT=*,BURST=YES
```

10.2.1.10 The CHARS Parameter

The CHARS parameter is used to request a particular character-type table for the sysout data set. This parameter is valid only with a 3800 printer. It is ignored with impact printers.

General Syntax

```
CHARS=character-type-table                keyword parameter
```

character-type-table — Identifies the character-type table to be used for printing the sysout data set.

Defaults:

If the CHARS parameter is omitted, an installation-defined default will be used.

```
//PRINT  DD  SYSOUT=*,CHARS=GU12
```

10.2.1.11 The FLASH Parameter

The FLASH parameter is used to request that a forms overlay (like a transparency) be used in printing the sysout data set. This parameter is valid only with a 3800 printer. It is ignored with impact printers.

General Syntax

```
FLASH={(overlay[,count])|NONE}                keyword parameter
```

overlay — Identifies the name of the forms overlay which must be inserted into the printer before the printing begins. This name will appear in a message to the operator. From 1 to 4 alphabetic, numeric or national characters.

count — Specifies the number of copies for each page to flash. From 0 to 255 (254 for JES3). If 0 is coded all copies will be flashed. The same will happen if the count is omitted.

NONE — No flashing is to be done. FLASH=NONE has the same effect as omitting the FLASH parameter.

Defaults:

If the FLASH parameter is omitted, no flashing is performed. If the count is omitted, all copies will be flashed.

```
//PRINT  DD  SYSOUT=*,FLASH=OVR2
```

10.2.1.12 The OUTPUT Parameter

The OUTPUT parameter is used to request that the parameters
coded in one or more OUTPUT statements be combined with the
parameters coded in the SYSOUT DD statement. When multiple
OUTPUT statements are used, each OUTPUT statement's parameters combine with the single SYSOUT DD statement's parameters to
generate multiple reports with the same data but each with possibly
different characteristics.

General Syntax

```
OUTPUT=(referback[,referback]....)                keyword parameter
```

referback — this can have three formats:

— *.outname — Refers to a previous OUTPUT statement found in
the same step, or to an OUTPUT statement placed before the
first EXEC statement.

```
//PRNT  DD  SYSOUT=*,OUTPUT=*.OUTA
```

— *.stepname.outname — Refers to an OUTPUT statement found
in a previous step "stepname."

```
//PRNT  DD  SYSOUT=*,OUTPUT=(*.OUTA,*.S2.OUTE)
```

— *.procexec.stepname.outname — Refers to an OUTPUT statement found in previous step "stepname" found within a procedure "procexec" (name of EXEC statement invoking the procedure).

```
//PRNT  DD  SYSOUT=*,OUTPUT=*.PR1.STEP5.OUTB
```

The OUTPUT parameter can reference a maximum of 128 OUT-
PUT statements. The order of the referenced OUTPUT statements is
not important.
```
// PRNT DD SYSOUT=*,OUTPUT=(*.OUTX,*.S3.OUTY,*.OUTF)
```
Defaults:

If the OUTPUT parameter is omitted, the SYSOUT DD statement
will use the parameters of any OUTPUT statements found at a prior

point in the same step, provided they contain the DEFAULT=YES parameter (see Sections 10.3.2 and 10.3.3 later in this chapter for an explanation of the DEFAULT parameter). If no such OUTPUT statements are found, the SYSOUT DD statement will use the parameters of any OUTPUT statements found between the JOB and first EXEC statement, provided they also contain the DEFAULT=YES parameter. If no such OUTPUT statements are found, the SYSOUT DD statement will use only its own parameters.

10.3 THE OUTPUT STATEMENT

The OUTPUT statement contains parameters identifying sysout processing options. These options can be used only if a SYSOUT DD statement refers to the OUTPUT statement explicitly (via the OUTPUT parameter) or implicitly by default, as will be explained in Section 10.3.3).

Syntactically, an OUTPUT JCL statement appears similar to a DD statement. It can be found within a step, and when inside a procedure, the rules for overriding it are the same as those for a DD statement. However, an OUTPUT statement can also be placed between the JOB and first EXEC statement. Without a SYSOUT DD statement making explicit or implicit reference to it, an OUTPUT statement is of no value.

General Syntax

```
//name   OUTPUT [COPIES=([number][,number-per-page])   ]
                [FCB=fcb                                 ]
                [DEST=destination                        ]
                [UCS=ucs                                 ]
                [BURST={YES|NO                           ]
                [CHARS=character-type-table              ]
                [FLASH={(overlay[,count])|NONE}          ]
                [CLASS=class|*                           ]
                [WRITER=writer                           ]
                [FORMS=form                              ]
                [CONTROL={PROGRAM|SINGLE|DOUBLE|TRIPLE}  ]
                [DEFAULT={YES|NO}                        ]
                [JESDS={JCL|MSG|LOG|ALL}                 ]
                [LINECT=number                           ]
                [GPOUPID=output group                    ]
```

The above is a list of selected OUTPUT statement parameters. All parameters in the OUTPUT statement are keyword.

The majority of the parameters in the OUTPUT statement and SYSOUT DD statement are identical. Some parameters can exist only in the OUTPUT statement, others only in the SYSOUT DD statement. And yet others can exist in both but with different syntax.

Selected parameters common to both SYSOUT DD and OUTPUT statements:

- The COPIES parameter
- The FCB parameter
- The UCS parameter
- The DEST parameter
- The BURST parameter
- The CHARS parameter
- The FLASH parameter

Section 10.2.1 in this chapter contains a discussion of these parameters and it will not be repeated here. When a parameter appears in both SYSOUT and OUTPUT, the one from the SYSOUT DD statement will prevail.

Selected parameters available only in the SYSOUT DD statement:

- The DCB parameter
- The FREE parameter
- The OUTLIM parameter
- The HOLD parameter
- The OUTPUT parameter

Section 10.2 in this chapter contains the discussion of these parameters and it will not be repeated here.

10.3.1 Parameters Common to Both SYSOUT DD and OUTPUT Statements but with Different Syntax

These are:

- The CLASS parameter
- The WRITER parameter
- The FORMS parameter

When a parameter appears in both SYSOUT and OUTPUT, the one from the SYSOUT DD statement will prevail.

10.3.1.1 The Class Parameter

The CLASS parameter is used to identify the sysout class of the data set.

General Syntax

```
CLASS=class|*
```

class — Identifies the sysout class of the data set. From A to Z and 0 to 9

* — It indicates that the same class used in the MSGCLASS parameter of the JOB statement (or the installation-defined default, if the MSGCLASS parameter is omitted) is to be used.

Defaults:

If the CLASS parameter is omitted and SYSOUT=(,) is coded in the SYSOUT DD statement, SYSOUT=* is the default.

```
//OUTA   OUTPUT   CLASS=T
```

10.3.1.2 The Writer Parameter

The WRITER parameter is used to identify a routine other than JES2 or JES3 (or the program provided by the external writer) to print the sysout data set.

General Syntax

```
WRITER=writer
```

writer — Identifies the routine which will be used to print the sysout data set. Seldom used. Normally JES2 or JES3 (or external writer) routines do the printing.

Defaults:

If the WRITER parameter is omitted and no writer is coded in the SYSOUT DD statement, the JES2 or JES3 (or external writer) routines will be used.

```
//OUTA   OUTPUT   WRITER=YOURWTR
```

10.3.1.3 The FORMS Parameter

The FORMS parameter is used to identify the print forms to be used for the data set, when the default print forms are not appropriate.

General Syntax

```
FORMS=form
```

form — Identifies the print form to be used for the sysout data set.

Defaults:

If the FORMS parameter is omitted and no form is coded in the SYSOUT DD statement, an installation-defined default form will be used.

```
//OUTA   OUTPUT   FORMS=3PLY
```

10.3.2 Selected Parameters Available only in the OUTPUT Statement

These are:

- The CONTROL parameter
- The DEFAULT parameter
- The JESDS parameter
- The LINECT parameter
- The GROUPID parameter

10.3.2.1 The CONTROL Parameter

The CONTROL parameter is used to specify that each print line begins with a carriage control character or to force single, double or triple spacing.

General Syntax

```
CONTROL={PROGRAM|SINGLE|DOUBLE|TRIPLE}
```

PROGRAM — Indicates that the first character of each print line is a control character and will be used for print carriage control.

SINGLE — Indicates that single spacing is to be forced and carriage control characters, if any, are to be ignored.

DOUBLE — Indicates that double spacing is to be forced and carriage control characters, if any, are to be ignored.

TRIPLE — Indicates that triple spacing is to be forced and carriage control characters, if any, are to be ignored.

Defaults:

If the CONTROL parameter is omitted and the program does not use carriage control characters, then:

- In JES2 an installation-defined default can be assumed or supplied by an operator command. Normally the default is single spacing.
- In JES3 an installation-defined default is assumed. Normally the default is single spacing.

```
//OUTA    OUTPUT   CONTROL=DOUBLE
```

10.3.2.2 The DEFAULT Parameter

The DEFAULT parameter is used when it is desired to assign the print options of the OUTPUT statement to one or more SYSOUT DD statements which do not contain the OUTPUT parameter.

General Syntax

```
DEFAULT={YES|NO}   or  DEFAULT={Y|N}
```

YES or Y — For an OUTPUT statement within a step, it requests that the print options of the OUTPUT statement be assigned to any SYSOUT DD statement which follows the OUTPUT statement in the same step and omits the OUTPUT parameter.

For an OUTPUT statement found between the JOB and first EXEC statement, it requests that the print options of the OUTPUT statement be assigned to any SYSOUT DD statement in the job which:

- omits the OUTPUT parameter

and

- is not preceded, in the same step, by any OUTPUT statement containing a DEFAULT=YES parameter

  NO or N — Indicates that the print options of the OUTPUT statement be assigned to a SYSOUT DD statement only if it contains an OUTPUT parameter making reference to the OUTPUT statement.

Defaults:

If the DEFAULT parameter is omitted, the default is NO.

```
//OUTA   OUTPUT   DEFAULT=YES,DEST=R12
```

10.3.2.3 The JESDS Parameter

The JESDS parameter requests that some or all system-managed sysout data sets (those not created by a program) in the job be processed using the print options of the OUTPUT statement.

An OUTPUT statement which contains the JESDS parameter must be placed between the JOB and first EXEC statement. Anywhere else, it will result in a JCL error.

General Syntax

```
JESDS={JCL|MSG|LOG|ALL}
```

JCL — Requests that JCL, JES2 or JES3 statements and associated messages be processed according to the options of the OUTPUT statement

MSG — Requests that all system messages (such as Allocation and Termination messages) are to be processed according to the options of the OUTPUT statement

LOG — Requests that the JES2 or JES3 log is to be processed according to the options of the OUTPUT statement. The log contains all information that appears or is entered into the operator console, associated with the executed job. The log follows the separator page in the output.

ALL — Requests that all of the above are to be processed according to the options of the OUTPUT statement

Defaults:

If the JESDS parameter is omitted, the system-managed sysout data sets will not use the options of the OUTPUT statement.

```
//OUTA    OUTPUT  DEFAULT=YES,JESDS=ALL,COPIES=3
```

10.3.2.4 The LINECT Parameter

This parameter is valid for JES2 only.

The LINECT parameter is used to identify the number of lines per output page, if the JES2 default number is not appropriate.

General Syntax

```
LINECT=number
```

number — It specifies the maximum number of lines per page. From 1 to 255.

LINECT=0 will stop JES2 from ejecting to a new page regardless of the number of lines printed.

Defaults:

If the LINECT parameter is omitted, and the print lines contain no carriage control character in the first position, the value coded in the LINECT parameter of the /*JOBPARM JES2 statement will be used. If this is also omitted, the value coded in the JOB statement accounting information will be used. If this is also omitted, an installation-defined default will be used (usually around 60).

Caution: A program which outputs print lines that contain a carriage control character in the first position usually counts lines, establishing its own lines-to-print-before-ejecting number.

If the number supplied by the LINECT parameter is smaller than the line count of the program, JES2 will cause a page eject before the program does. The program will count a few more lines and eject again, resulting in erroneous carriage control.

```
//OUTA    OUTPUT  LINECT=52
```

10.3.2.5 The GROUPID Parameter

This parameter is valid for JES2 only.

The GROUPID parameter is used to identify the sysout data set as being a part of a JES2 output group. Grouped data sets should have the same class and destination. JES2 will print such data sets together.

General Syntax

```
GROUPID=group-name
```

group-name — Specifies the name of the output group. The name (which has the same syntax as other names used in JCL) is selected by the user. It is not installation-defined.

Defaults:

If the GROUPID parameter is omitted, JES2 may still group a sysout data set with others which have similar characteristics. If not, the data set will be handled by JES2 individually.

```
//OUTA    OUTPUT   GROUPID=G38
```

10.3.3 Examples of the OUTPUT Parameter and the OUTPUT Statement

To best explain the relationship between the OUTPUT parameter in the SYSOUT DD statement and the OUTPUT statement, the JCL of two jobs with several examples will be discussed:

```
//TESTA111  JOB      FJ09,'TEST OUTPUT',CLASS=A,MSGCLASS=F
//OUTJ1     OUTPUT   DEST=DOWNT,DEFAULT=YES,JESDS=ALL,
//          CLASS=K
//OUTJ2     OUTPUT   DEST=LA,COPIES=2
//S1        EXEC     PGM=PG1
//OUTSA     OUTPUT   DEST=LOCAL,DEFAULT=YES,FCB=FC10,
//          CLASS=K,LINECT=54
//OUTSB     OUTPUT   DEST=BKLYN,DEFAULT=YES,COPIES=3
//OUTSC     OUTPUT   DEST=NEWARK,COPIES=2
//PRINT1    DD       SYSOUT=*,FCB=FC01
//S2        EXEC     PGM=PG2,COND=(4,LT)
//OUTSD     OUTPUT   DEST=LOCAL,CLASS=E
//PRINT2    DD       SYSOUT=W,FCB=FC08
```

```
//PRINT3    DD      SYSOUT=(,)
//S3        EXEC    PGM=PG3,COND=(4,LT)
//OUTSE     OUTPUT  DEST=FRANCE,CLASS=X,CONTROL=SINGLE,DEFAULT=YES
//PRINT4    DD      SYSOUT=(,),OUTPUT=(*.OUTSE,*.S2.OUTSD,
//                  *.S1.OUTSB,*.OUTJ2)


//TESTA222  JOB     FJ02,'TEST OUTPUT',CLASS=A,MSGCLASS=G
//S1        EXEC    PGM=PG1
//OUTSX     OUTPUT  DEST=GREECE
//PRINT5    DD      SYSOUT=*,FCB=FC12
```

1. SYSOUT DD statement PRINT1.

   DD statement PRINT1 does not contain an OUTPUT parameter. There are three OUTPUT statements, OUTSA, OUTSB and OUTSC preceding it in the same step. OUTPUT statement OUTSC does not contain DEFAULT=YES and cannot be used. The other two do, and will be used to supply print options to DD statement PRINT1.

   As a result of the two OUTPUT statements, two reports with identical data will be generated. The first (based on OUTSA) will be routed to a local device, use a line count of 54, an FCB FC01, and an output class F (from the MSGCLASS parameter). Note that FCB and the output class came from the SYSOUT DD statement, not the OUTPUT statement OUTSA. The second (based on OUTSB) will be routed to a remote station named BKLYN, use an FCB=FC01, output class F, and will be repeated three times.

2. SYSOUT DD statement PRINT2.

   DD statement PRINT2 does not contain an OUTPUT parameter. There is one OUTPUT statement, OUTSD, preceding it in the same step. This OUTPUT statement does not contain DEFAULT=YES and cannot be used. The system checks for OUTPUT statements between the JOB and first EXEC statement. Two of them exist, OUTJ1 and OUTJ2. OUTPUT statement OUTJ2 does not contain DEFAULT=YES and cannot be used. The other does and will be used to supply print options to DD statement PRINT2.

   As a result, an output (based on OUTSA) will be routed to a remote station named DOWNT, use an FCB=FC08, and an output class W (the CLASS parameter of the OUTPUT statement will be ignored). All the system-managed sysout data sets will be assigned the same print options as the output data set.

3. SYSOUT DD statement PRINT3.

DD statement PRINT3 will work exactly the same way as PRINT2, except a default FCB will be assumed and its sysout class will be K (supplied by OUTPUT statement OUTJ1).

4. SYSOUT DD statement PRINT4.

DD statement PRINT4 makes explicit reference to four OUTPUT statements, causing four reports with identical data to be generated, each based completely on the print options of each of the four referenced statements. Since DD statement PRINT4 contains no options, all options will be supplied by the OUTPUT statements. Statements OUTSE and OUTSB do not contain the CLASS parameter and SYSOUT=* will be assumed.

5. SYSOUT DD statement PRINT5.

DD statement PRINT5 makes no explicit reference to any OUTPUT statements. The OUTPUT statement OUTSX, which precedes the DD statement, cannot be used because it does not contain DEFAULT=YES. There are no OUTPUT statements between the JOB and first EXEC statement. The print options of the PRINT5 SYSOUT DD statement will come only from its own parameter field and defaults. In this case, OUTPUT statement OUTSX serves no useful purpose.

10.4 THE DUMMY PARAMETER

A DD statement that contains the DUMMY parameter will allocate no devices. Also, an attempt by the executing program to perform input or output operations for that DD statement will be ignored.

When a DD statement which is opened for input is dummied, the first read instruction issued by the program will cause an end-of-file condition to be encountered. When the dummied DD statement is opened for output, the system goes through the motions of writing, but since there is no allocated device, no data will be transferred.

General Syntax

```
//ddname  DD  DUMMY                    positional parameter
```

DUMMY is a valuable and commonly used parameter. Since DD statements that are opened by the program cannot be removed,

DUMMY provides a safe way to eliminate I/O activity when required.

Only DD statements using sequential (QSAM or BSAM) or VSAM organization can be dummied. For VSAM, the dummied DD statement must contain the AMP parameter:

```
//VSAMDD  DD   DUMMY,AMP=AMORG
```

Direct organization is also acceptable but only for sequential loading, not random access. Partitioned data sets cannot be dummied. If the original DD statement to be dummied is

```
//LIB  DD   DSN=TEST.LIBA,DISP=SHR
```

where TEST.LIBA is a PDS, then coding

```
//LIB  DD   DUMMY
```

will cause an S013-64 ABEND failure. If, however, a DD statement using DSN=TEST.LIBA(membername) is used, no failure will occur. DSN=pdsname(membername)is treated as a sequential data set.

An alternate way to dummy a DD statement is to code DSN=NULLFILE. This parameter works the same as DUMMY (except DUMMY is positional and DSN is not).

All parameters, except DCB, which follow DUMMY or are combined with DSN=NULFILE will be syntactically checked and ignored.

The DCB parameter may be required when coding DUMMY. If all or some of the values for LRECL, RECFM, and BLKSIZE are not hard-coded inside the program, omitting the corresponding values in the DCB parameter may cause an S013-10 ABEND failure. Sometimes this failure does not occur. It is difficult to understand and remember under what conditions the failure will occur. Therefore, it is always best and safe to code the needed DCB subparameters when DUMMY or DSN=NULLFILE is used.

```
//OUT  DD   DUMMY,DCB=(LRECL=80,RECFM=FB,BLKSIZE=80)
```

In the event the blocksize is not known, the same value as the LRECL can be given to the BLKSIZE, if RECFM=FB is used. If RECFM=VB is used, the BLKSIZE can be coded as 4 bytes larger than the LRECL. When coding DUMMY, small blocksizes cannot result in inefficiencies, since there is no allocation and no I/O activity.

10.5 THE DDNAME PARAMETER

The DDNAME parameter allows one to postpone the definition of a
data set until a DD statement later in the same step provides that
definition.

It is basically a convenience rather than a necessity.

General Syntax

```
DDNAME=ddname
```

ddname identifies the name of the DD statement which, when supplied later in the same step, will provide the data set definition. If
such a DD statement is not supplied, the DDNAME parameter will
have the same effect as DUMMY.

It is best to describe how this parameter works through examples:
Example 1:

```
//S1      EXEC   PGM=P1
//DD1     DD     DDNAME=IN
.  .       .       .    .    .    .
.  .       .       .    .    .    .
//IN      DD     DSN=USER1.FILE2,DISP=SHR
```

The definition of the data set in DD statement DD1 is postponed
until DD statement IN is found later in the same step. When it is
found, the data set defined in IN will also be defined in DD1. It is as
if DD statement DD1 borrows the parameter field from DD statement IN.

The ddname IN is arbitrary. Any name can be used in the
DDNAME parameter as long as the same name is used later in the
DD statement where it is referenced. The IN DD statement is only
used for reference purposes. It will not be opened by the program.
The JCL below is equivalent to the JCL in Example 1.

```
//S1      EXEC   PGM=P1
//DD1     DD     DSN=USER1.FILE2,DISP=SHR
.  .       .       .    .    .    .
.  .       .       .    .    .    .
```

Example 2:

```
//LKED    EXEC   PGM=IEWL
//SYSLIN  DD     DDNAME=SYSIN
```

```
. .     .     .    .    .    .
. .     .     .    .    .    .
//SYSIN    DD       *
```

This is typically the JCL used in Linkage Editor procedures. The SYSLIN DD statement is inside the procedure. The SYSIN DD statement is normally provided as an overriding additional DD statement in the form:

```
//LKED.SYSIN    DD    *
```

This a convenience. The SYSLIN DD statement could be overridden or added, providing the same result:

```
//LKED.SYSLIN    DD    *
```

However, this can be inconvenient, especially because SYSLIN normally describes concatenations. Coding DDNAME=SYSIN and later adding a //SYSIN DD * statement is easier.

The JCL of Example 2 is equivalent to the JCL below:

```
//LKED      EXEC   PGM=IEWL
//SYSLIN    DD       *
. .     .     .    .    .    .
. .     .     .    .    .    .
```

Example 3:

```
//LKED      EXEC   PGM=IEWL
//SYSLIN    DD      DDNAME=SYSIN
. .     .     .    .    .    .
. .     .     .    .    .    .
```

No SYSIN DD statement is coded. SYSLIN is DUMMY.
The JCL of Example 3 is equivalent to the JCL below:

```
//LKED      EXEC   PGM=IEWL
//SYSLIN    DD      DUMMY
. .     .     .    .    .    .
. .     .     .    .    .    .
```

The only parameter that can be coded with the DDNAME parameter is DCB (only some of the subparameters). It should be avoided.

The DDNAME parameter provides the only forward reference in JCL.

10.6 THE JOBLIB AND STEPLIB DD STATEMENTS

There are four ways to tell the system in which library, or libraries, the program to be executed in a step is expected to reside.

1. Using the referback in the PGM parameter (see Section 2.2.1 in Chapter 2).

```
//S1    EXEC   PGM=*.LKED.SYSLMOD
```

The library to be used will be the one defined in DD statement SYSLMOD in step LKED. This method is rarely used except in Compile-Linkedit-Go procedures.

If the SYSLMOD DD statement defines the member within the library,

```
//SYSLMOD   DD   DSN=&&LOAD(PG13),DISP=(,PASS),UNIT=SYSDA,
//                SPACE=(CYL,(5,2))
```

program PG13 will be executed.

If the SYSLMOD DD statement defines only the library and no member,

```
//SYSLMOD   DD   DSN=&&LOAD,DISP=(,PASS),UNIT=SYSDA,
//                SPACE=(CYL,(5,2))
```

the first program found in the library will be executed.
2. Using a JOBLIB DD statement to determine the library, or libraries, to be searched for the entire job.
3. Using a STEPLIB DD statement to determine the library, or libraries, to be searched for the step
4. Using no referback, no JOBLIB, and no STEPLIB. The system searches an installation-defined list of default libraries. There is one library, SYS1.LINKLIB, that is always part of this list. All utilities, IDCAMS, the Linkage Editor, and many other IBM-written programs reside in this library. In some installations, certain libraries are made part of this list, thus eliminating the need for JOBLIB or STEPLIB for programs residing in these libraries. If the program is not found in any of the default libraries, the result will be an S806-04 ABEND failure.

Special DD Statements and Parameters   301

10.6.1 The JOBLIB DD Statement

The JOBLIB DD statement identifies the program library where the programs to be executed throughout the job reside.

It must be placed between the JOB and the first EXEC statement. If found in a different location, the result will be a JCL error.

```
//PROD213   JOB    SH21,'PAYROL RUN',CLASS=P
//JOBLIB    DD     DSN=PROD.LOADLIB,DISP=SHR
//S1        EXEC   PGM=PROGA
//S2        EXEC   PGM=PROGB
//S3        EXEC   PGM=PROGC
```

Program PROGA is expected to reside in PROD.LOADLIB as a member of the library and the system searches the directory. If the program is found, it is executed. If not found, the system extends the search into the default libraries. If the program is not found there either, the result will be S806-04 ABEND failure.

The same process is repeated for programs PROGB and PROGC.

A JOBLIB DD statement can have several concatenations (maximum: 16).

```
//JOBLIB    DD   DSN=TEST.LOADLIB,DISP=SHR
//         DD   DSN=TEST.MYLIB,DISP=SHR
//         DD   DSN=PROD.LOADLIB,DISP=SHR
```

All concatenations may be searched to locate a program. If, however, the program is found in a concatenation other than the last one, the other concatenations will not be used. When duplicate member names exist in different concatenations, the user can decide which one is to be executed, by determining the sequence of the concatenations.

If an installation uses Data Facility Product (DFP) Version older than 2.3 and the blocksizes of the concatenations are not the same, the concatenations must be arranged in such a way so that the blocksize of the first concatenation is not exceeded by the blocksizes of those that follow. If the needed sequence violates this rule, a DCB parameter can be added to the first concatenation specifying the largest blocksize. Suppose that the blocksize of the first two concatenations is 19069 and the last one 23476.

```
//JOBLIB    DD   DSN=TEST.LOADLIB,DISP=SHR,DCB=BLKSIZE=23476
//         DD   DSN=TEST.MYLIB,DISP=SHR
//         DD   DSN=PROD.LOADLIB,DISP=SHR
```

This blocksize discrepancy is relatively rare, because the blocksize to a load library is usually assigned by the Linkage Editor, resulting in consistent blocksizes.

If an installation uses Data Facility Product (DFP) Version 2.3 or later, the concatenations can be arranged in any order regardless of blocksizes.

The JOBLIB DD statement has two peculiarities. One is its unusual location. If placed anywhere else than between the JOB statement and the first EXEC statement of the job, the result will be a JCL error:

```
IEF606I MISPLACED DD STATEMENT
```

The other peculiarity is related to the DISP parameter. When retrieving a data set, DISP=SHR defaults to DISP=(SHR,KEEP). This often used default does not apply to JOBLIB, where DISP=SHR defaults to DISP=(SHR,PASS). The user can code DISP=(SHR,PASS) or DISP=SHR. Coding DISP=(SHR,KEEP) in a JOBLIB DD statement can cause a serious problem. The program of the first step will be found, but none of the other programs will, even though they may reside in the library described by JOBLIB, resulting in S806-04 ABEND failures. Unless a job has only one step, coding DISP=(SHR,KEEP) in the JOBLIB DD statement must be avoided.

The same argument can be made for DISP=OLD. However, JOBLIB always describes a read-only data set and coding DISP=OLD, which disallows shareability, is inappropriate.

The library (or libraries) described in a JOBLIB DD statement will not be searched for a given step, if the step contains a STEPLIB DD statement (see next section).

Defaults:

If a JOBLIB DD statement is omitted, and a STEPLIB DD statement is also omitted, the default libraries only will be used to locate the program.

10.6.2 The STEPLIB DD Statement

The STEPLIB DD statement identifies the program library where the program to be executed for the step where STEPLIB is found resides.

There is no special location for STEPLIB. It can be placed anywhere in a step.

```
//PROD213   JOB    SH21,'PAYROL RUN',CLASS=P
//S1        EXEC   PGM=PROGA
//STEPLIB   DD     DSN=TEST.LOADLIB1,DISP=SHR
//S2        EXEC   PGM=PROGB
//STEPLIB   DD     DSN=TEST.LOADLIB2,DISP=SHR
//S3        EXEC   PGM=PROGC
//STEPLIB   DD     DSN=TEST.LOADLIB3,DISP=SHR
```

Program PROGA is expected to reside in PROD.LOADLIB as a member of the library and the system searches its directory. If the program is found, it is executed. If not found, the system extends the search into the default libraries. If the program is not found there either, the result will be an S806-04 ABEND failure.

The same process is repeated for programs PROGB and PROGC using libraries TEST.LOADLIB2 and TEST.LOADLIB3, respectively.

A STEPLIB DD statement can have as many as 16 concatenations.

```
//S3        EXEC PGM=P13
//STEPLIB   DD   DSN=TEST.LOADLIB,DISP=SHR
//          DD   DSN=TEST.MYLIB,DISP=SHR
//          DD   DSN=PROD.LOADLIB,DISP=SHR
```

All concatenations may be searched to locate a program. If, however, the program is found in a concatenation other than the last one, the other concatenations will not be used. When duplicate member names exist in different concatenations, the user can decide which one is to be executed by determining the sequence of the concatenations.

If an installation uses a Data Facility Product (DFP) version older than Version 2.3 and the blocksizes of the concatenations are not the same, the concatenations must be arranged in such a way that the blocksize of the first concatenation is not exceeded by the blocksizes of those that follow. If the needed sequence violates this rule, a DCB parameter can be added to the first concatenation specifying the largest blocksize. Suppose that the blocksize of the first two concatenations is 19069 and the last one 23476.

```
//S3        EXEC PGM=P13
//STEPLIB   DD   DSN=TEST.LOADLIB,DISP=SHR,DCB=BLKSIZE=23476
//          DD   DSN=TEST.MYLIB,DISP=SHR
//          DD   DSN=PROD.LOADLIB,DISP=SHR
```

This blocksize discrepancy is relatively rare, because the blocksize to a load library is usually assigned by the Linkage Editor, resulting in consistent blocksizes.

If an installation uses Data Facility Product (DFP) Version 2.3 or later, the concatenations can be arranged in any order regardless of blocksizes.

DISP=OLD should be avoided in STEPLIB. STEPLIB always describes a read-only data set, and coding DISP=OLD, which disallows shareability, is inappropriate.

A STEPLIB DD statement has the effect of negating the JOBLIB DD statement (if one exists) for a particular step. See the example below, where only step S2 contains a STEPLIB:

```
//PROD213   JOB    SH21,'PAYROL RUN',CLASS=P
//JOBLIB    DD     DSN=PROD.LOADLIB,DISP=SHR
//S1        EXEC   PGM=PROGA
//S2        EXEC   PGM=PROGB
//STEPLIB   DD     DSN=TEST.LOADLIB1,DISP=SHR
//S3        EXEC   PGM=PROGC
```

To locate program PROGA, JOBLIB will be used.

To locate program PROGB, STEPLIB only will be used. If TEST.LOADLIB1 (described in STEPLIB) does not yield PROGB, the default libraries will be searched. TEST.LOADLIB (described in JOBLIB) will not be searched.

To locate program PROGC, JOBLIB will be used.

Defaults:

If a STEPLIB DD statement is omitted, the JOBLIB DD statement will be used. If JOBLIB DD is also omitted, the default libraries will be used to locate the program.

10.7 THE JOBCAT AND STEPCAT DD STATEMENTS

The use of JOBCAT and STEPCAT DD statements is disallowed or restricted in most installations. The JOBCAT/STEPCAT facility is dangerous, and, with few exceptions, it is unnecessary. If the high qualifier of a data set name is an alias name for a used catalog, no JOBCAT or STEPCAT is needed.

For a complete discussion of how the catalog operates, including JOBCAT and STEPCAT, see Section 6.3 in Chapter 6.

10.8 THE SYSUDUMP, SYSMDUMP, AND SYSABEND DD STATEMENTS

When a step encounters an ABEND failure, it is often advantageous to request a virtual storage dump, which can be helpful in determining the cause of the ABEND.

To request such a dump, one of three DD statements must be included in the JCL for the step:

• A SYSUDUMP DD statement
• A SYSMDUMP DD statement
• A SYSABEND DD statement

10.8.1 The SYSUDUMP DD Statement

When a SYSUDUMP DD statement is included in a step which ABENDs, a formatted virtual storage dump will be provided.

```
//SYSUDUMP   DD   SYSOUT=*
```

SYSUDUMP usually writes to sysout. It can, however, write to a disk data set, providing a way to preserve the SYSUDUMP information for later viewing and analysis.

```
//SYSUDUMP   DD   DSN=USER1.DUMP1,DISP=(,DELETE,CATLG),UNIT=SYSDA,
//                SPACE=(CYL,(0,5),RLSE)
```

Note that the DISP parameter will cause the data set to be cataloged if there is an ABEND failure and deleted if the step completes successfully. Also note the SPACE parameter. No disk space will be allocated for the primary allocation, and if there is no ABEND, zero space will be used for the data set. If there is an ABEND, writing will immediately cause a request for secondary allocation where the SYSUDUMP information will be stored. No DCB parameter is needed.

10.8.2 The SYSMDUMP DD Statement

When a SYSMDUMP DD statement is included in a step which ABENDs, a nonformatted virtual storage dump will be provided containing only information about the failed step. This type of dump is very difficult to analyze unless it is saved on disk or tape and then processed by the PRDUMP service aid, as shown below.

```
//STEP2      EXEC   PGM=NFC
//SYSMDUMP   DD     DSN=USER1.MDUMP,DISP=(,DELETE,CATLG),UNIT=SYSDA,
//                  SPACE=(CYL,(0,5),RLSE)
//PRDMP      EXEC   PGM=IKJEFT01,PARM=AMDPRDMP,COND=ONLY
//SYSUT1     DD     DSN=USER1.MDUMP,DISP=(OLD,DELETE)
//PRINTER    DD     SYSOUT=*
//SYSIN      DD     *
     FORMAT
     LOGDATA
     END
/*
```

SYSMDUMP is seldom used.

10.8.3 The SYSABEND DD Statement

When a SYSABEND DD statement is included in a step which ABENDs, a formatted virtual storage dump will be provided. This dump will include information about the failed step, as well as most of the MVS storage-resident information. The result is voluminous output, most of which is unnecessary for the average user. The output provided by SYSUDUMP normally suffices. SYSABEND is intended for system programming use. Average users must avoid it.

```
//SYSABEND  DD   SYSOUT=*
```

If neither a SYSUDUMP nor a SYSMDUMP nor a SYSABEND statement is coded within the JCL of an ABENDing step, a small amount (about 1/4 of a print page) of information is provided. This information is seldom useful in resolving the problem that caused the ABEND failure.

If more than one of the above statements is included in the JCL of a step, only the last one will be used. The previous ones will be ignored.

```
//STEP5     EXEC  PGM=STRILE
//SYSABEND  DD    SYSOUT=*
//SYSUDUMP  DD    SYSOUT=*
```

There is never a need to code more than one of these statements in a step. Knowing that the last one will be used, however, is important. To explain why, consider a procedure which contains a SYSABEND DD statement in a step.

Procedure PR19

```
.    .    .    .    .    .    .

.    .    .    .    .    .    .

//STEP7      EXEC  PGM=PG7
//SYSABEND   DD    SYSOUT=*

.    .    .    .    .    .    .

.    .    .    .    .    .    .
```

and SYSABEND must be overridden by SYSUDUMP. Since the two ddnames are not identical, one cannot override the other. But if a SYSUDUMP DD statement is added, it will be the last one in the step and the desired result will be accomplished.

```
//AA                EXEC  PR19
//STEP7.SYSUDUMP    DD    SYSOUT=*
```

10.9 VIRTUAL I/O (VIO)

A temporary data set, rather than residing on disk, can also reside on virtual storage and take advantage of the Virtual Input/Output (VIO) facility of MVS.

Consider a DD statement describing a temporary data set on disk:

```
//WK01  DD   DSN=&&TEMP,DISP=(,PASS),UNIT=SYSDA,SPACE=(TRK,(300,50),
//           RLSE),DCB=(BLKSIZE=23440,LRECL=80,RECFM=FB)
```

Only one change is needed to make this a VIO request:

```
//WK01  DD   DSN=&&TEMP,DISP=(,PASS),UNIT=VIO,SPACE=(TRK,(300,50),
//           RLSE),DCB=(BLKSIZE=23440,LRECL=80,RECFM=FB)
```

Instead of UNIT=SYSDA, UNIT=VIO was coded. VIO is a generated device name defined by the installation to describe virtual I/O. Any valid generated name can be used, but VIO is very common. RLSE when VIO is used will be ignored.

The use of virtual I/O is transparent to the executing program and the access method being used (the vast majority of temporary data sets are sequential — QSAM). To them, the data set appears to be on whatever device UNIT=VIO has been generated to simulate.

Advantages of VIO:

- Writing and reading operations for the data set will be at the speed of virtual storage rather than that of a disk device. This may not always be an advantage. Depending on the hardware configuration (i.e., availability of CPUs with expanded storage, disk control units with cash storage, etc.), the size of the VIO data set, and amount of paging activity in the system, the number of paging data sets available, etc. using VIO excessively can result in slower I/O and cause overall system degradation.
- A VIO data set occupies no disk space and no space in the user's private address space. Theoretically, a VIO data set has the availability of an entire simulated volume. However, large VIO data sets can cause the type of problems discussed in the preceding paragraph, and they are discouraged.
- Fifteen secondary allocations are guaranteed, if needed, unless the capacity of the simulated volume is exceeded. Rarely can such a guarantee be given for a disk data set.

Disadvantages of VIO:

- The first two advantages stated above can become disadvantages under the right conditions.
- Only temporary sequential and partitioned data sets can use VIO. VSAM data sets cannot.
- Because of the possible problems of VIO, many installations restrict its use and may not always be available.

Notes on DD statement parameters with VIO:

- SPACE
  - Track, cylinder, or blocksize allocation in the SPACE parameter will be treated the same way for a VIO data set.
  - The subparameters RLSE, CONTIG, and ROUND in the SPACE parameter for a VIO data set will be ignored.
  - If the SPACE parameter is omitted when creating a VIO data set, SPACE=(1000,(10,50)) will be used as a default. Note the a disk data set has no SPACE default.
- DSN
  - Only coding DSN=&&name or omitting the dsn parameter is acceptable.
- DISP
  Since all VIO data sets are temporary, only PASS and DELETE are acceptable in th second and third field.

- UNIT
  - A generated unit name defining VIO must be used when creating a VIO data set. When receiving a passed VIO data set the UNIT parameter need not be coded, as with any other passed data set.
  - The device count and the DEFER subparameters are ignored.
- VOL
  All fields in the VOL parameter are either invalid or ignored. Do not code VOL.
- DCB
  Same as an ordinary data set.

Before using VIO, the user should check installation guidelines. As mentioned earlier in this section, the use of VIO may be restricted.

10.10 CONCATENATION

Concatenation is a very useful feature of MVS/XA. It allows a program which normally inputs one data set to input several data sets with comparable DCB characteristics without programming changes.

Only sequential and partitioned data sets can be concatenated. Also VSAM or ICF user catalogs can be concatenated in the JOBCAT or STEPCAT DD statement (see Section 6.3 in Chapter 6).

For sequential data sets, the maximum number of concatenations is 255. For partitioned data sets, the maximum number of concatenations is 16.

Consider the JCL below for a step, executing program PAL which opens DD statement IN and reads using QSAM. QSAM is by far the most commonly used non-VSAM sequential access method — the other seldom used alternative is BSAM.

```
//S1   EXEC   PGM=PAL
//IN   DD     DSN=USER1.SAP1,DISP=SHR
```

When the program issues "read" instructions, the system performs the physical I/O operations and provides the program with the requested logical records. When the last record has been read in and the program attempts one more read, the system will give control to the program's end-of-file routine.

Now consider the JCL below:

```
//S1   EXEC   PGM=PAL
//IN   DD     DSN=USER1.SAP1,DISP=SHR
```

```
//              DSN=USER1.SAP2,DISP=SHR
//              DSN=USER1.SAP3,DISP=SHR
```

Two additional DD statements are coded after the DD statement IN. These two DD statements have no ddnames, and they will be treated as concatenations of the first DD statement.

What this means is the following. First, it is important to note that program PAL has not been modified. It opens DD statement IN, and reads logical records. In this case, however, when the system encounters an end-of-file condition for data set USER1.TAP1, it continues reading data set USER1.TAP2, the second concatenation, without informing the program. Since data set names are unknown to the program, the program continues to receive records, unaware that they are coming from the second data set. Actually, a program is always unaware of and unconcerned about where records are being read from or written to. That is controlled by JCL and the access method.

The system will keep on reading one data set in the concatenation after another. The EOF routine of the program will be given control only when the data set of the last concatenation encounters an EOF condition.

In this particular example, the program has read three sequential data sets (it could be as many as 255) as though it were only one data set.

There are a number of rules and restrictions for concatenations:

1. Syntactically, the ddname must be omitted from a DD statement in order to be treated as concatenated to the preceding one. The first concatenation is the only one with a ddname.
2. The logical record length and the record format of concatenated data sets must be the same. However, the blocksizes need not be.

    In MVS/XA systems not yet using Data Facility Product (DFP) Version 2.3, the blocksize of the first concatenation must be greater than or equal to the blocksizes of all subsequent concatenations. If a concatenation violates this rule, the result will be an S001-4 ABEND failure (this ABEND may not appear with certain utility functions which intercept the ABEND and issue a bad condition code, usually 12)

    If it is necessary to concatenate data sets in a sequence which violates this rule, the DCB parameter can be coded in the first concatenation to specify a blocksize equal to the largest blocksize of all the concatenations. Assume that in the JCL below, the first concatenation has a blocksize of 15400, the second a blocksize of 9000 and the third a blocksize of 23400.

```
//IN  DD     DSN=USER1.SET1,DISP=SHR,DCB=BLKSIZE=23400
//           DSN=USER2.SET1,DISP=SHR
//           DSN=USER3.SET1,DISP=SHR
```

The blocksize coded in the DCB parameter, rather than the correct blocksize, as it appears in the label, will be used by the program. The buffers created by open are 23400 bytes each, large enough to contain the largest block.

In MVS/XA systems using Data Facility Product (DFP) Version 2.3 or later, the sequence of concatenations is independent of the blocksize of each concatenation.

3. Both sequential data sets and partitioned data sets can be concatenated, but not with each other — sequential with sequential and partitioned with partitioned only.

This rule may need further clarification. Consider the concatenation

```
//IN1  DD  DSN=TEST.LIB3(MEMBER8),DISP=SHR
//    DD  DSN=USER1.SEQDS,DISP=SHR          SEQUENTIAL DS
```

At first glance this concatenation appears to violate the rule. However, when DSN=pdsname(membername) is coded, it will be treated as a sequential data set. As a result, the concatenation is perfectly valid (assuming LRECL and RECFM are the same). If the membername is removed,

```
//IN1  DD  DSN=TEST.LIB3,DISP=SHR
//    DD  DSN=USER1.SEQDS,DISP=SHR
```

the concatenation is invalid.

For the same reason, the concatenation below is also invalid if the second concatenation describes a partitioned data set.

```
//IN1  DD  DSN=TEST.LIB3(MEMBER8),DISP=SHR
//    DD  DSN=USER1.LIB1,DISP=SHR           PARTITIONED DS
```

4. Disk as well as tape data sets can be concatenated, but not with each other. Only like devices should be concatenated, disk with disk and tape with tape. There are no other restrictions. For example, a 6250 BPI tape SL data set can be concatenated

with a 3480 tape SL data set and a 1600 BPI NL tape data set. Also, a 3350 disk data set can be concatenated with a 3380 disk data set of any density (single, double, or triple). If this rule is violated, the result will an S637-0C ABEND failure.

Actually, a program written in Assembly Language has a way of circumventing this restriction. This is very seldom done. There are, however, three software packages available on the market that take advantage of this facility and allow unlike device concatenation. These are the sort packages, DFSORT, SYNCSORT and CASORT. The SORTIN DD statement in all of them allows unlike device concatenation.

```
//SORTIN  DD   DSN=USER1.DISKDS,DISP=SHR        DISK DATA SET
//        DD   DSN=USER1.TAPEDS,DISP=OLD        TAPE DATA SET
```

5. Despite the fact that concatenated data sets act as one, they allocate independently. The three tape concatenations below will allocate three tape devices, seriously affecting tape device availability, or failing to allocate the needed devices.

```
//IN   DD    DSN=USER1.TAP1,DISP=OLD
//     DD    DSN=USER1.TAP2,DISP=OLD
//     DD    DSN=USER1.TAP3,DISP=OLD
```

UNIT=AFF must be used to eliminate this problem.

```
//IN   DD    DSN=USER1.TAP1,DISP=OLD
//     DD    DSN=USER1.TAP2,DISP=OLD,UNIT=AFF=IN
//     DD    DSN=USER1.TAP3,DISP=OLD,UNIT=AFF=IN
```

Now all concatenations will be allocated to the same tape device. When using UNIT=AFF with two independent (not concatenated) DD statements, if the DD statement being referenced is not closed before the one containing UNIT=AFF opens, the result will be an S413-04 ABEND. With concatenated DD statements, only one open is issued and consequently, no such failure can occur. UNIT=AFF is always safe to use and practically always recommended for tape concatenations.

See Section 7.12 in Chapter 7 for additional techniques on the use of UNIT=AFF with concatenations.

6. A DD statement using DUMMY must not be placed in the middle of a concatenation. If it is, it will cause all concatenations following the DUMMY to be treated as DUMMY also. Even

though they allocate their respective devices (DUMMY allocates no devices), they cannot be used, because DUMMY causes an EOF condition to be given to the program, giving the same effect as DUMMY.

7. Concatenation is intended for input data sets only. Output concatenations are acceptable syntactically, but no concatenation will be used beyond the first one.

8. The maximum number of concatenations for sequential data sets is 255. The maximum number of concatenations for partitioned data sets is 16. For the reasons mentioned earlier, for the concatenation below, the maximum number of concatenations is 255, not 16.

```
//IN1   DD   DSN=TEST.LIB3(CNTLA),DISP=SHR
//      DD   DSN=TEST.LIB1(GENR),DISP=SHR
```

If the membernames were removed, then the maximum would be 16.

```
//IN1   DD   DSN=TEST.LIB3,DISP=SHR
//      DD   DSN=TEST.LIB1,DISP=SHR
```

11

Generation Data Groups

A Generation Data Group (frequently referred to by the acronym GDG, and occasionally also called a Generation Data Set) is used when JCL must remain unchanged and yet the name of an output and/or input data set must be different for different executions.

This chapter will discuss the many peculiarities and features of GDGs, how they operate, how to initiate them, how to change their characteristics, and how to recover when they fail.

11.1 HOW GDGS WORK

Consider an application in daily production where the output of Monday's run becomes the input to Tuesday's run and so on. The JCL below would work on Monday, but on Tuesday the DSN parameters must be changed.

```
//IN    DD   DSN=PROD.MONDAY,DISP=SHR
//OUT   DD   DSN=PROD.TUESDAY,DISP=(,CATLG,DELETE),UNIT=SYSDA,
//           VOL=SER=PROD31,SPACE=(CYL,(10,5),RLSE),
//           DCB=(BLKSIZE=23440,LRECL=80,RECFM=FB)
```

Using GDGs, JCL can remain unchanged while the data set names change with every execution. To explain the GDG mechanism, the JCL used by a GDG already in operation will be analyzed. Consider the JCL below:

```
//IN    DD   DSN=PROD.DAY(0),DISP=SHR
//OUT   DD   DSN=PROD.DAY(+1),DISP=(,CATLG,DELETE),UNIT=SYSDA,
//           VOL=SER=PROD31,SPACE=(CYL,(10,5),RLSE),
//           DCB=(PROD.GDGMODEL,BLKSIZE=23440,LRECL=80,RECFM=FB)
```

This JCL looks ordinary except for the (0) and (+1) in the DSN parameter.

If one looked at the catalog, a number of entries would be found whose names all begin with the same qualifiers as those that pre-cede the left parenthesis of the DSN parameter in both the IN and OUT DD statements.

```
ENTRIES IN THE CATALOG
-----------------------
```

DSN	VOL	UNIT
PROD.DAY.G0031V00	PROD31	3380
PROD.DAY.G0032V00	PROD31	3380
PROD.DAY.G0033V00	PROD31	3380
PROD.DAY.G0034V00	PROD31	3380
PROD.DAY.G0035V00	PROD31	3380

When the JCL above is submitted, the system recognizes PROD.DAY(0) to represent a generation of a GDG whose base (or index) is PROD.DAY. It scans the catalog and translates PROD.DAY(0) to PROD.DAY.G0035V00, the latest generation. This is normally the generation with the largest number after the "G" in the last level of the data set name (an exception exists when the number goes past 9999 — it will be discussed later in Section 11.7). In response to PROD.DAY(+1), the system finds the latest entry in the catalog, adds the number which appears in parentheses, +1, to the number that follows the "G" and generates a new name, PROD.DAY. G0036V00. This is the name of the data set that will be cataloged during Step Termination. The first portion of the data set name (PROD.DAY) is provided by the user and can be as long as 35 characters. The last portion (G0036V00 — affectionately referred to as the "goovoo" level) is provided by the system and is always 8 char-acters.

PROD.DAY(0) and PROD.DAY(+1) are known as *"relative"* names, PROD.DAY.G0035V00 and PROD.DAY.G0036V00 as *"absolute"* names. The absolute names are the actual names of the data sets.

Since the catalog is the main tool used by the system in translat-ing relative to absolute names, cataloging new generations of a GDG is mandatory. Surprisingly, DISP=(,KEEP) or DISP=(,PASS) are permitted with GDGs. They should be avoided.

It can easily be seen that if a job containing the same JCL is executed again, PROD.DAY(0) will be translated to PROD.DAY.G0036V00 and PROD.DAY(+1) to PROD.DAY.G0037V00. This JCL will always provide the previous run's output as this run's input. This is one of the basic objectives of GDGs.

Consider the catalog as it appeared originally (generations 31 to 35) and a variation of the JCL used before:

```
//IN    DD   DSN=PROD.DAY(-1),DISP=SHR
//OUT   DD   DSN=PROD.DAY(+2),DISP=(,CATLG,DELETE),UNIT=SYSDA,
//           VOL=SER=PROD31,SPACE=(CYL,(10,5),RLSE),
//           DCB=(PROD.GDGMODEL,BLKSIZE=23440,LRECL=80,RECFM=FB)
```

Any number can theoretically be used inside the parentheses between -254 and +254, with 0 and +1 the most common by far. In the example above, PROD.DAY(-1) will become PROD.DAY.G0034V00 and PROD.DAY(+2), PROD.DAY.G0037V00 (0035+2=0037). The negative numbers do not work the same as the positive. PROD.DAY(-1) simply means go one back from the latest, or (0), generation and use whichever generation is found, regardless of its name. The system does not subtract for the negative numbers as it adds for the positive ones.

The examples shown thus far are disk GDGs. This is not to imply that tape GDGs are not used. On the contrary, they are probably more common than disk. Actually, the generations of a GDG need not all be on disk or all on tape, although this is normally what happens. The JCL below shows an example of a tape GDG:

```
//IN    DD   DSN=MAIN.WKK(0),DISP=OLD
//OUT   DD   DSN=MAIN.WKK(+1),DISP=(,CATLG,DELETE),UNIT=CART,
//           DCB=(PROD.GDGMODEL,BLKSIZE=32720,LRECL=80,RECFM=FB)
```

All generations of a disk GDG tend to reside on the same volume. If space limitations make this impractical, it is possible to have generations alternate between two volumes:

```
//FLIP  DD   DSN=DEV.TUES(-1),DISP=SHR
//IN    DD   DSN=DEV.TUES(0),DISP=SHR
//OUT   DD   DSN=DEV.TUES(+1),DISP=(,CATLG,DELETE),
//           VOL=REF=*.FLIP,SPACE=(CYL,(10,5),RLSE),
//           DCB=(PROD.GDGMODEL,BLKSIZE=23440,LRECL=80,RECFM=FB)
```

This JCL cannot be executed unless at least two generations already exist. Assume that two generations have been created, each on a different volume.

```
ENTRIES IN THE CATALOG
----------------------
DSN                     VOL           UNIT
---                     ---           ----
DEV.TUES.G0001V00       DEV004        3380
DEV.TUES.G0002V00       DEV009        3380
```

OUT creates (and catalogs) data set DEV.TUES.G0003V00 on volume DEV004, the same volume as the (-1) generation, DEV.TUES.G0001V00. Next time the JCL above is executed, OUT will create (and catalog) data set DEV.TUES.G0004V00 on volume DEV009, the same volume as the (-1) generation, DEV.TUES. G0002V00. The generations will alternate between volumes DEV004 and DEV009.

11.2 PREPARING FOR A GDG

Before a DD statement using DSN=gdgbase(+1) with a NEW disposition can be used, the catalog must be primed. The method for accomplishing this varies depending on whether ICF (Integrated Catalog Facility), VSAM, or CVOL catalogs are used. As of the writing of this book, the vast majority of installations are in an ICF catalog environment. The few that are not use a dual catalog environment: VSAM catalogs (normally intended for VSAM data set entries — but also capable of containing non-VSAM data set entries) and CVOL catalogs (intended for non-VSAM data set entries — including GDGs). Eventually, it is expected that all MVS installations will come under an ICF environment.

If an installation is under ICF, IDCAMS must be used to "DEFINE" the GDG base to the catalog. Here is an example of how the GDG being discussed would be defined:

```
//S1        EXEC   PGM=IDCAMS
//SYSPRINT  DD     SYSOUT=*
//SYSIN     DD     *
     DEFINE  GDG   (NAME(PROD.DAY) LIMIT(5) SCRATCH)
/*
```

The NAME parameter identifies the GDG base, LIMIT can be given a value up to 255. It identifies the maximum number of generations available at any point in time. The very first generation created using (+1) will have the absolute name PROD.DAY.G0001V00. When PROD.DAY.G0006V00 is created, the limit of five has been exceeded and, as PROD.DAY.G0006V00 is cataloged during step termination, PROD.DAY.G0001V00 will be uncataloged and, if SCRATCH was specified in the DEFINE command, deleted. Thus the number of generations is maintained at the limit of 5. Every time a new generation is created, the oldest one is eliminated. Note that if SCRATCH were omitted from the DEFINE command the default is NOSCRATCH and the data sets being uncataloged will not be deleted. This is OK for tape GDGs (tape data sets cannot be deleted via JCL), but it is seldom recommended for disk GDGs.

It should also be noted here that the new generation is created during the allocation process (see Figure 1.7), while the oldest generation is deleted at step termination. Between the two, there will be a generation present beyond the limit. When working with disk GDGs, this must be taken into consideration in disk space estimates.

The EMPTY parameter is also available in the DEFINE command:

```
DEFINE  GDG  (NAME(PROD.DAY) LIMIT(5) SCRATCH EMPTY)
```

EMPTY will cause all previous generations to be uncataloged (and deleted) when the limit is exceeded. EMPTY is of questionable value and very seldom used. If omitted, NOEMPTY is the default.

If an installation is not under ICF, there is a good chance CVOL catalogs are used for GDGs. Instead of IDCAMS, the IEHPROGM utility must be used.

```
//S1        EXEC  PGM=IEHPROGM
//SYSPRINT  DD    SYSOUT=*
//SYSIN     DD    *
      BLDG  INDEX=PROD.DAY,ENTRIES=5,DELETE
/*
```

IEHPROGM and IDCAMS use parameters with different spelling which have the same meaning: INDEX and NAME; ENTRIES and LIMIT; DELETE and SCRATCH. The EMPTY parameter is the only one spelled the same way for both.

In the unlikely event that a VSAM catalog is used to contain a GDG, IDCAMS must be used the same way as with ICF catalogs.

IDCAMS can define a GDG base only in an ICF or VSAM catalog. IEHPROGM can do the same only in a CVOL catalog. They cannot be used interchangeably for GDGs.

Note that after defining the GDG index, no (0) generation exists yet and using DSN=PROD.DAY(0) would result in a JCL error.

```
IEF212I jobname stepname ddname - DATA SET NOT FOUND
```

Surprisingly, the same JCL error will result if an attempt is made to create a (+1) generation before the GDG base has been defined.

11.3 CHANGING THE CHARACTERISTICS OF A GDG

It sometimes becomes necessary to change the characteristics of a GDG, such as LIMIT, SCRATCH, or EMPTY, after several generations have been created.

Changing NOSCRATCH to SCRATCH and EMPTY to NOEMPTY (or vice versa) can be done easily by using the ALTER command of IDCAMS (ICF or VSAM catalogs only).

The JCL below will execute IDCAMS to change a GDG base defined with NOSCRATCH and EMPTY, to SCRATCH and NOEMPTY.

```
//S1         EXEC  PGM=IDCAMS
//SYSPRINT   DD    SYSOUT=*
//SYSIN      DD    *
      ALTER   PROD.DAY SCRATCH NOEMPTY
/*
```

Changing the LIMIT is much more complicated. To accomplish this, the GDG base must be deleted and then redefined. Assume that the limit of five must be increased to seven for the GDG with generations PROD.DAY.G0031V00, PROD.DAY.G0032V00, PROD.DAY. G0033V00, PROD.DAY.G0034V00, and PROD.DAY.G0035V00

Step 1: Uncatalog (but do not delete) all generations. This can be done easily by using the following JCL:

```
//S1  EXEC PGM=IEFBR14
//UNC DD   DSN=PROD.DAY,DISP=(OLD,UNCATLG)
```

Step 2: Delete the GDG index:

```
//S1          EXEC  PGM=IDCAMS
//SYSPRINT    DD    SYSOUT=*
//SYSIN       DD    *
    DELETE   PROD.DAY
/*
```

Steps 1 and 2 can be combined by using the DELETE command with the FORCE parameter, which causes all the generations to be uncataloged (but not deleted) before the base is removed from the catalog.

```
//S1          EXEC  PGM=IDCAMS
//SYSPRINT    DD    SYSOUT=*
//SYSIN       DD    *
    DELETE   PROD.DAY   FORCE
/*
```

Step 3: Using IDCAMS, define again the GDG index with the desired limit of seven.

Step 4: Using any available method, catalog back all the generations (see Section 6.6 in Chapter 6).

11.4 USING A GDG MODEL

A model DSCB (sometimes referred to as a GDG model) must be supplied when a new generation is created using a relative name. There are two methods available.

Method 1: A model DSCB is specified in the DCB parameter. If this model (which must be a cataloged disk data set residing on an online volume) contains all the needed DCB attributes, no other DCB subparameters are necessary: DCB=USER1.MODL. Most installations use this method and, rather than allowing all users to create various models, a single model is provided for everyone's use. This model is likely to be protected against accidental deletion and have an entry in the master catalog (which is write-protected). Such a model could not possibly satisfy the DCB needs of all GDGs, and normally it contains no DCB attributes at all. Then the DCB parameter must contain the needed subparameters following the model name.

```
//OUT  DD   DSN=PROD.DAY(+1),DISP=(,CATLG,DELETE),UNIT=SYSDA,
//          VOL=SER=PROD31,SPACE=(CYL,(10,5),RLSE),
//          DCB=(PROD.GDGMODEL,BLKSIZE=23440,LRECL=80,RECFM=FB)
```

One may wonder what the usefulness of the model DSCB is, since it supplies either the wrong DCB attributes or, usually, none at all. The answer is almost humorous: It provides no useful information, but if not specified, the result is a JCL error:

```
IEF218I  jobname stepname ddname - PATTERN DSCB RECORD NOT FOUND
                             IN VTOC
```

It has, in essence, a negative usefulness: It stops a JCL error.

Method 2. A different model DSCB must be supplied for every GDG. Such a model:

- Must have the same name as the GDG base and cannot be cataloged (the catalog does not allow a GDG base and a data set name to be identical).
- It must reside on the same volume as the user catalog that contains the base.

For the GDG under discussion, such a model DSCB can be created as follows:

```
//S1 EXEC PGM=IEFBR14
//MDL DD   DSN=PROD.DAY,DISP=(,KEEP),UNIT=SYSDA,
//             VOL=SER=SYS201,SPACE=(TRK,0), VOL SYS201 CONTAINS USER CATALOG
//             DCB=(BLKSIZE=23440,LRECL=80,RECFM=FB)
```

Now the DCB parameter can be completely omitted from the output DD statement.

```
//OUT  DD   DSN=PROD.DAY(+1),DISP=(,CATLG,DELETE),UNIT=SYSDA,
//             VOL=SER=PROD31,SPACE=(CYL,(10,5),RLSE)
```

This method is seldom used with good reason. When many GDGs are used, the models (one per GDG), even though they occupy no space, tend to clutter the VTOCs of volumes that contain user catalogs. It is also difficult to protect against the accidental deletion of the numerous models, an event that would cause the "PATTERN DSCB RECORD NOT FOUND IN VTOC" JCL error mentioned earlier. This method is also less user-friendly since it is the user who becomes responsible for creating the model.

Absolute names can be used in JCL, although they are normally avoided. If the absolute name is used while creating a new generation, two interesting facts can be observed:

- A model DSCB is not required.
- The oldest generation will not be eliminated when the new one is created. The total number of generations will be adjusted to what the LIMIT parameter supplied when a new generation is created using a relative name.

```
//OUT   DD   DSN=PROD.DAY.G0036VOO,DISP=(,CATLG,DELETE),
//           VOL=SER=PROD31,SPACE=(CYL,(10,5),RLSE),UNIT=SYSDA,
//           DCB=(BLKSIZE=23440,LRECL=80,RECFM=FB)
```

The system is actually unaware that the data set being created is a generation of a GDG and treats it as an ordinary data set. The catalog is alphabetically organized and, as a result, the new entry is placed in the right position and it becomes part of the GDG.

11.5 PECULIARITIES OF GDGS

GDGs have several peculiarities, some of which are difficult to fathom. Consider the JCL below:

```
//S1    EXEC PGM=P1
//IN    DD   DSN=PROD.DAY(0),DISP=SHR
//OUT   DD   DSN=PROD.DAY(+1),DISP=(,CATLG,DELETE),UNIT=SYSDA,
//           VOL=SER=PROD31,SPACE=(CYL,(10,5),RLSE),
//           DCB=(PROD.GDGMODEL,BLKSIZE=23440,LRECL=80,RECFM=FB)
//IN1   DD   DSN=PROD.DAY(-2),DISP=SHR
//S2    EXEC PGM=P2
//D1    DD   DSN=PROD.DAY(0),DISP=SHR
//D2    DD   DSN=PROD.DAY(+1),DISP=SHR
//S3    EXEC PGM=P3
//D3    DD   DSN=PROD.DAY(0),DISP=(OLD,DELETE)
//D4    DD   DSN=PROD.DAY(+1),DISP=(OLD,DELETE)
//D5    DD   DSN=PROD.DAY(-1),DISP=(OLD,DELETE)
//S4    EXEC PGM=P4
//D6    DD   DSN=PROD.DAY(+2),DISP=(,CATLG,DELETE),UNIT=SYSDA,
//           VOL=SER=PROD31,SPACE=(CYL,(10,5),RLSE),
//           DCB=(PROD.GDGMODEL,BLKSIZE=23440,LRECL=80,RECFM=FB)
//D7    DD   DSN=PROD.DAY(+1),DISP=(,CATLG,DELETE),UNIT=SYSDA,
//           VOL=SER=PROD31,SPACE=(CYL,(10,5),RLSE),
//           DCB=(PROD.GDGMODEL,BLKSIZE=23440,LRECL=80,RECFM=FB)
//S5    EXEC PGM=P5
//D8    DD   DSN=PROD.DAY(-1),DISP=SHR
//S6    EXEC PGM=P5
//D9    DD   DSN=PROD.DAY(0),DISP=SHR
```

This JCL is, to say the least, highly unusual and it is very unlikely that it will be used in a real environment. It is used only to demonstrate the GDG mechanism and some of its peculiarities.

Assume the catalog initially appears as follows:

```
ENTRIES IN THE CATALOG
----------------------

DSN                      VOL            UNIT
---                      ---            ----
PROD.DAY.G0044V00        PROD31         3380
PROD.DAY.G0045V00        PROD31         3380
PROD.DAY.G0046V00        PROD31         3380
PROD.DAY.G0047V00        PROD31         3380
PROD.DAY.G0049V00        PROD31         3380
```

In step S1, DD statement IN will retrieve data set PROD.DAY. G0049V00, OUT will create (and catalog) data set PROD.DAY. G0050V00, and IN1 will retrieve data set PROD.DAY.G0046V00. Data set PROD.DAY.G0044V00 will be eliminated (a LIMIT of five is assumed).

At the end of S1 the catalog will appear as follows:

```
ENTRIES IN THE CATALOG
----------------------

DSN                      VOL            UNIT
---                      ---            ----
PROD.DAY.G0045V00        PROD31         3380
PROD.DAY.G0046V00        PROD31         3380
PROD.DAY.G0047V00        PROD31         3380
PROD.DAY.G0049V00        PROD31         3380
PROD.DAY.G0050V00        PROD31         3380
```

In step S2, D1 will retrieve data set PROD.DAY.G0049V00 and D2 will retrieve data set PROD.DAY.G0050V00. This represents one of the most well-known quirks of GDGs. It may be logical to assume that DSN=PROD.DAY(0) will retrieve the latest available generation, PROD.DAY.G0050V00. This not true! DSN=PROD.DAY(0) will always retrieve whichever was the latest generation before the job (not the step) began execution, no matter where the DSN parameter appears in the job. By the same token, DSN=PROD.DAY(+1) will always be assigned an absolute name whose "G" number is one more than the (0) generation no matter where the DSN parameter appears in the job. The (0) and (+n) generations can never change absolute names during the execution of a job. So when a (+1) generation is created, to retrieve it in a subsequent step of the same job, (+1) must again be used in the DSN parameter. After the job terminates, (0) and (+1) in a new job will be assigned different absolute names . . . (0) is the latest generation, etc.

At the end of S2 the catalog remains unaltered.

In step S3, D3 will retrieve (and delete) data set PROD.DAY.G0049V00, D4 will retrieve (and delete) data set PROD.DAY.G0050V00, and D5 will retrieve (and delete) data set PROD.DAY.G0047V00.

At the end of S3 the catalog will appear as follows:

```
ENTRIES IN THE CATALOG
-----------------------

DSN                     VOL             UNIT
---                     ---             ----
PROD.DAY.G0045V00       PROD31          3380
PROD.DAY.G0046V00       PROD31          3380
```

In step S4, D6 and D7 will create (and catalog) data sets PROD.DAY.G0051V00 and PROD.DAY.G0050V00, respectively (not G0048V00 and G0047V00, as one may incorrectly assume). No old generation will be eliminated because the total number of generations is four, one below the limit.

At the end of S4 the catalog will appear as follows:

```
ENTRIES IN THE CATALOG
-----------------------

DSN                     VOL             UNIT
---                     ---             ----
PROD.DAY.G0045V00       PROD31          3380
PROD.DAY.G0046V00       PROD31          3380
PROD.DAY.G0050V00       PROD31          3380
PROD.DAY.G0051V00       PROD31          3380
```

In step S5, D8 will retrieve data set PROD.DAY.G0046V00, the generation preceding the (0) generation, even though the (0) generation does not exist. Note that in S3, D5 specified (-1) and got generation PROD.DAY. G0047V00. When using (-n), it is possible to have different absolute names assigned for the same relative name (in JES3 the catalog is searched before the job begins execution and (-n) in this example may be assigned the same absolute name, PROD.DAY.G0046V00). For (0) or (+n) generations, the same absolute name will always be assigned to a given relative name within a job's execution.

At the end of S5 the catalog remains unaltered.

In step S6, D9 will attempt to retrieve data set PROD.DAY. G0049V00 (not PROD.DAY.G0051V00, as one may erroneously assume). JCL error "DATA SET NOT FOUND" will be the result.

There are restrictions as to what DISP parameter (first field) can be used with GDGs:

- If DSN=gdgindex(0) or DSN=gdgindex(-n) is used, only DISP of OLD, SHR, or MOD (not defaulting to NEW) is acceptable. Using DISP=(NEW,...) will result in a JCL error:

```
IEF286I  jobname stepname ddname - DISP FIELD INCOMPATIBLE
                                             WITH DSNAME
```

- If DSN=gdgindex(+n) is used, all DISP fields are acceptable. However, if OLD, SHR, or MOD (not defaulting to NEW) is used, DSN=gdgindex(+n) must have been created and cataloged in a previous step of the same job. Otherwise, the result will be the same JCL error just mentioned.

11.6 CONCATENATING GENERATIONS OF A GDG

The generations of a GDG can be concatenated by using a DD statement that specifies the GDG base in the DSN parameter:

```
//D1    DD  DSN=PROD.DAY,DISP=SHR
```

This DD statement will result in the concatenation of all existing generations beginning with the latest one and going to the oldest one. Note that if no generations exist, the result will be a JCL error:

```
IEF212I jobname stepname D1 - DATA SET NOT FOUND
```

A daily production job could be creating a new generation each workday of the week. A weekly job could retrieve all the data contained within the five generations by using a DD statement as the one discussed above. And note that JCL would remain the same for both the daily as well as the weekly runs.

If the data sets of a GDG were on tape, this type of concatenation will allocate one tape device, eliminating the need for the UNIT=AFF parameter needed for ordinary tape concatenations.

The DD statement below will cause all generations to be uncataloged and deleted:

```
//D5    DD   DSN=PROD.DAY,DISP=(OLD,DELETE)
```

The DD statement below will cause all generations to be uncataloged

```
//D6    DD   DSN=PROD.DAY,DISP=(OLD,UNCATLG)
```

11.7 GENERATION 9999

Until fairly recently, reaching a generation with G9999V00 meant trouble. No longer. When the latest generation is G9999V00, the (+1) generation will be assigned an absolute name with G0000V00. This is the only time that such a generation can exist. Note that the first generation is G0001V00. The system keeps careful control during this wrap-around, and no JCL changes should be required.

11.8 USING DIFFERENT VERSIONS OF A GDG GENERATION

A GDG generation can have as many as 100 different versions, V00 to V99. Versions can be made available by varying the number that follows the "V" in the last level of the data set name. This can be accomplished only by using absolute names. Assume that the latest generation is PROD.DAY.G0035V00.

```
//OUT   DD   DSN=PROD.DAY.G0035V01,DISP=(,CATLG,DELETE),UNIT=SYSDA,
//           VOL=SER=PROD31,SPACE=(CYL,(10,5),RLSE),
//           DCB=(BLKSIZE=23440,LRECL=80,RECFM=FB)   NO MODEL NEEDED
```

The DD statement above will create the second version (V01) of generation 35. The addition of new versions does not result in the removal of old generations. When generation 35 becomes the over-the-limit generation, all the versions within it will be removed together. Versions are marginally useful in providing a way to have a greater number of entries in a GDG than the limit permits.

Generally, versions are neither practical nor useful and, as a result, they are very seldom used.

11.9 RECOVERING FROM A BAD GENERATION

Consider an application in production using a GDG as follows:

```
//IN    DD   DSN=PROD.DAY(0),DISP=SHR
//OUT   DD   DSN=PROD.DAY(+1),DISP=(,CATLG,DELETE),UNIT=SYSDA,
//           VOL=SER=PROD31,SPACE=(CYL,(10,5),RLSE),
//           DCB=(PROD.GDGMODEL,BLKSIZE=23440,LRECL=80,RECFM=FB)
```

and the catalog containing the entries below.

DSN	VOL	UNIT
---	---	----
PROD.DAY.G0045V00	PROD31	3380
PROD.DAY.G0046V00	PROD31	3380
PROD.DAY.G0047V00	PROD31	3380
PROD.DAY.G0048V00	PROD31	3380
PROD.DAY.G0049V00	PROD31	3380

PROBLEM 1: Generation PROD.DAY.G0049V00 is bad and must be recreated.

SOLUTION:

Step 1: Eliminate the cause for the bad generation. Note that the cause was not an ABEND failure. In an ABEND, the abnormal disposition of DELETE would have resulted in the data set's deletion, and no cataloging would have taken place.

Step 2: Delete and uncatalog the bad generation. It is essential that both be done. If the data set were on tape, only uncataloging would be required.

Step 3: Rerun the JCL with no changes. Since the bad generation has been removed, DSN=PROD.DAY(0) will be converted to PROD.DAY.G0048V00, the generation that must be used as input. DSN=PROD.DAY(+1) will be converted to PROD.DAY.G0049V00, recreating the bad generation.

When dealing with the last generation, recovering a bad generation is a fairly simple matter. There are several other possible solutions, but none as good and straightforward as the one discussed.

PROBLEM 2: Generation PROD.DAY.G0047V00 is bad and must be recreated. Given the cyclical nature of this JCL, if this generation was bad initially, all the subsequent generations would be bad also. It is then assumed that this generation was good initially, but has since been contaminated or deleted. This problem is more complex than the previous one. Several solutions can be provided.

SOLUTION 1: This solution will work whether the bad generation exists or has been deleted.

Step 1: If the bad generation exists, delete and uncatalog it. If the generation is already deleted, skip step 1.

Step 2: Change JCL as follows:

```
//IN    DD  DSN=PROD.DAY(-2),DISP=SHR
//OUT   DD  DSN=PROD.DAY.GOO47V00,DISP=(,CATLG,DELETE),
//          VOL=SER=PROD31,SPACE=(CYL,(10,5),RLSE),
//          DCB=(BLKSIZE=23440,LRECL=80,
//          RECFM=FB),UNIT=SYSDA
```

PROD.DAY(-2) will be converted to PROD.DAY.G0046V00, the generation that must be used as input. The OUT DD statement supplies the absolute name, recreating the bad generation.

SOLUTION 2: This solution will also work whether the bad generation exists or has been deleted.

Step 1: If the bad generation exists, delete and uncatalog it. If the generation is already deleted, skip step 1.

Step 2: Uncatalog generations PROD.DAY.GOO48V00 and PROD.DAY.GOO49V00 without deleting them.

Step 3: Rerun JCL with no changes. DSN=PROD.DAY(0) will be translated to PROD.DAY.G0046V00, the generation that must be used as input. DSN=PROD.DAY(+1) will be translated to PROD.DAY.G0047V00, recreating the bad generation.

Step 4: Catalog back generations PROD.DAY.GOO48V00 and PROD.DAY.GOO49V00.

Solution 2 has the advantage of avoiding JCL changes. However, step 4 requires considerable manual intervention, and, therefore, it is not recommended.

SOLUTION 3: This solution can be used only if the bad generation exists but is contaminated.

Step 1: Change JCL as follows:

```
//IN    DD  DSN=PROD.DAY(-3),DISP=SHR
//OUT   DD  DSN=PROD.DAY(-2),DISP=OLD
```

PROD.DAY(-3) will be translated to PROD.DAY.G0046V00, the generation that must be used as input. PROD.DAY(-2) will be translated to PROD.DAY.G0047V00, the bad generation, which will now be overlaid.

This solution, if it applies (note that the bad generation must exist), is probably the easiest and safest.

11.10 USING BLP WITH GDGS

Under certain rare conditions, BLP may have to be used to access the data of a tape GDG generation. The DD statement below seems to contain all the needed information, but it will not work.

```
//IN    DD   DSN=PROD.TPG(0),DISP=OLD,
//.          VOL=SER=000481,UNIT=TAPE,LABEL=(2,BLP),
//           DCB=(BLKSIZE=32720,LRECL=80,RECFM=FB)
```

The problem here is that, despite the presence of VOL=SER, the catalog will still be used. The relative name PROD.TPG(0) must be translated into an absolute name and this can be done only through the catalog which supplies sequence number for tape data sets. For this data set this number in the catalog is 1. The LABEL parameter ends up supplying BLP only. The 2 from the LABEL parameter will be ignored. The result is (1,BLP), instead of the needed (2,BLP). To eliminate the problem, the relative name must be removed from the DSN parameter and replaced by the absolute name. Actually, considering that with BLP there is no data set name (or volume) verification, any data set name can be used.

```
//IN    DD   DSN=PROD.TPG.G0037V00,DISP=OLD,
//           VOL=SER=000481,UNIT=TAPE,LABEL=(2,BLP),
//           DCB=(BLKSIZE=32720,LRECL=80,RECFM=FB)
```

AVOIDING AN EMPTY GENERATION

Under certain conditions, it is possible to cause the creation of an empty disk GDG generation. Consider the JCL below:

```
//SDW     EXEC PGM=DAYWEEK
//OUT     DD   DSN=PROD.DW(+1),DISP=(,CATLG,DELETE),UNIT=SYSDA,
//             VOL=SER=PROD31,SPACE=(CYL,(10,5),RLSE),
//             DCB=(PROD.GDGMODEL,BLKSIZE=23440,LRECL=80,RECFM=FB)
```

If no ABEND occurs, a new generation will be created and cataloged. This generation, however, will be an empty one if program DAYWEEK does not open and write to it. In most cases such a generation is undesirable and should be eliminated. This can be accomplished by adding two more steps to the jobstream:

```
//SDW       EXEC PGM=DAYWEEK
//OUT       DD   DSN=PROD.DW(+1),DISP=(,CATLG,DELETE),UNIT=SYSDA,
//          VOL=SER=PROD31,SPACE=(CYL,(10,5),RLSE),
//          DCB=(PROD.GDGMODEL,BLKSIZE=23440,LRECL=80,RECFM=FB)
//AMS       EXEC PGM=IDCAMS
//D1        DD   DSN=PROD.DW(+1),DISP=OLD
//SYSPRINT DD SYSOUT=*
//SYSIN     DD *
    PRINT INFILE(D1) COUNT(1)
/*
//BR14      EXEC PGM=IEFBR14,COND=(8,GE,AMS)
//D2        DD   DSN=PROD.DW(+1),DISP=(OLD,DELETE)
```

If the new generation is opened and data written to it, the PRINT command of IDCAMS in step AMS will work well, issuing a return code of 0, and step BR14 will not be executed (is 8 greater than or equal to 0? Yes!). If the new generation is not opened, an empty data set will be cataloged. The PRINT command of IDCAMS will fail with a return code of 12, step BR14 will be executed (Is 8 greater than or equal to 12? No!) deleting the empty generation.

The same problem is unlikely to occur for a new tape generation:

```
//OUT       DD   DSN=PROD.DW(+1),DISP=(,CATLG,DELETE),UNIT=TAPE,
//          DCB=(PROD.GDGMODEL,BLKSIZE=32720,LRECL=80,RECFM=FB)
```

This is a nonspecific (no VOL=SER or VOL=REF) request, as the great majority of tape requests are. If the new generation is not opened, no cataloging will take place (see Section 6.5 in Chapter 6) and the problem will not occur.

If a specific tape request is used, the same problem experienced with disk can also occur.

```
//OUT       DD   DSN=PROD.TP(+1),DISP=(,CATLG,DELETE),
//          VOL=SER=00287,UNIT=TAPE,
//          DCB=(PROD.GDGMODEL,BLKSIZE=32720,LRECL=80,RECFM=FB)
```

If the device allocated for this DD statement is 3480 (cartridge) or 3420 single density, the new generation will be cataloged even if it is not opened (see Section 6.5 in Chapter 6). In this case the generation is not just empty, it does not exist at all (a new tape data set does not exist until it is opened for output). The same technique shown

above for disk can be used again to eliminate the unwanted catalog
entry.

```
//SDW       EXEC PGM=DAYWEEK
//OUT       DD   DSN=PROD.TP(+1),DISP=(,CATLG,DELETE),UNIT=TAPE,
//               VOL=(,RETAIN,SER=000287),
//               DCB=(PROD.GDGMODEL,BLKSIZE=32720,LRECL=80,RECFM=FB)
//AMS       EXEC PGM=IDCAMS
//D1        DD   DSN=PROD.TP(+1),DISP=OLD
//SYSPRINT  DD SYSOUT=*
//SYSIN     DD *
    PRINT INFILE(D1) COUNT(1)
/*
//BR14      EXEC PGM=IEFBR14,COND=(8,GE,AMS)
//D2        DD   DSN=PROD.TP(+1),DISP=(OLD,UNCATLG),UNIT=(,,DEFER)
```

If the new generation is opened and data written to it, the PRINT
command of IDCAMS in step AMS will work well, issuing a return
code of 0, and step BR14 will not be executed. If the new generation
is not opened, a nonexisting generation will be cataloged. This will
cause an S813-04 ABEND failure during the execution of the PRINT
command. IDCAMS will intercept this ABEND and issue a return
code of 12 which will allow step BR14 to be executed removing the
unwanted entry from the catalog.

The technique discussed in this section will actually work with any
data set, not just GDGs, disk or tape.

12

Using Procedures

A procedure is basically "prepackaged" JCL. It is usually JCL needed by many different users (like Compile-Linkedit-Go), JCL that is executed on a repetitive basis over a time interval (like JCL for a daily production job), or JCL that is often repeated within the execution on a single job.

This chapter will discuss how a procedure is invoked, the use of overrides and symbolic parameters, the use of commonly used procedures, and considerations when coding a procedure.

12.1 GENERAL

There are two types of procedures:

• Cataloged procedures
• In-stream procedures

A cataloged procedure is a member of a PDS, which is often referred to as procedure library or proclib.

The word "cataloged" should not be confused with the same word when it describes a data set. A cataloged data set is one that has an entry in the catalog. The word "cataloged" when used for a procedure means that the procedure is a member of a PDS.

An in-stream procedure is contained within a job's input stream.

The two types of procedures obey the same rules and, with some minor exceptions relating to the PROC and PEND statements (discussed later), they work identically. Until the last three sections of this chapter, the discussion and various examples will refer to cataloged procedures. The reader should be aware that whatever is being discussed pertains to both, keeping in mind that one is a member of a PDS, while the other is part of the input stream of a job. Specifics about in-stream procedures, such as coding and placement, will be discussed in Sections 12.16, 12.17 and 12.18 in this chapter.

For expediency, in this book a cataloged procedure will be referred to simply as a procedure. An in-stream procedure will be referred to by its full name.

12.2 THE USE OF PROCEDURE LIBRARIES

A (cataloged) procedure, as mentioned above, is a member of a procedure library (see Figure 12.1). An installation normally uses several procedure libraries. They are defined as concatenations in the JCL that is used to start JES2 or JES3. Once the subsystem in use is

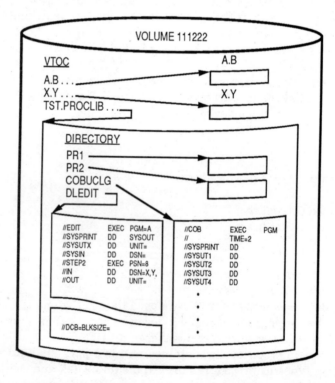

Figure 12.1 A procedure library.

initialized, the user has limited or no control over which procedure libraries will be used. SYS1.PROCLIB (an IBM-provided proclib) is normally available, as are several installation-provided test and production procedure libraries. Some installations add DD statements in the JCL of JES2 or JES3 defining a different proclib or a different concatenation of proclibs, giving the user some choice as to which proclib(s) will be used in her or his job. In JES2, this can be accomplished by supplying the PROCLIB parameter in the JOBPARM JES2 control statement.

```
//USER1A    JOB   DR55,MC...
/*JOBPARM   PROCLIB=PROC01
```

PROC01 is a DD statement included in the JCL of JES2 defining a proclib or a concatenation of proclibs which will be used by job USER1A. In JES3, the PROC parameter in the MAIN JES3 control statement must be supplied.

```
//USER1B    JOB   XK34,MD.......
//*MAIN     PROC=01
```

01 is a number representing the last two digits of a DD statement included in the JCL of JES3 defining a proclib or a concatenation of proclibs which will be used by job USER1B.

In some installations, the job class coded in the CLASS parameter of the JOB statement may determine the proclib, or proclibs, to be used. There are also other-vendor (non-IBM) software packages available on the market that can provide much more flexibility in choosing proclibs. This book generally avoids the discussion of software packages.

12.3 INVOKING A PROCEDURE

Invoking (or executing) a procedure can be achieved by using an EXEC statement,

```
//PR   EXEC   ABC
```

or

```
//PR   EXEC   PROC=ABC
```

where ABC is the name of a procedure. The parameter ABC or PROC=ABC (they work identically) is positional. When this type of EXEC statement is found during the reading of a job, the system searches the directory of the proper proclib(s) for member ABC. If not found, the result will be a JCL error:

```
IEF612I PROCEDURE NOT FOUND
```

If found, the system takes the contents of procedure ABC and submits its contents to the JES2 or JES3 input facilities. It is as if the EXEC statement which invoked the procedure is replaced with the contents of the procedure.

12.4 RESTRICTIONS

The number of steps in a procedure cannot exceed 255.
   The following are not permitted to reside in a procedure:

- A JOB statement.
- A EXEC statement invoking a procedure. This restriction can be rephrased to say: All EXEC statements inside a procedure must use PGM as a positional parameter.
- A JOBLIB DD statement.
- A JOBCAT DD statement.
- A DD * statement.
- A DD DATA statement.
- A /* (delimiter) statement.
- A // (null) statement.
- Input stream (sysin) data.
- A PEND statement (for cataloged procedures only. For in-stream procedures, it is a required statement).

If any of the above is included in a procedure, there will be a JCL error when the procedure is executed:

```
IEF601I INVALID STATEMENT IN PROCEDURE
```

12.5 OVERRIDING PROCEDURES

If the JCL in a procedure is exactly what the user needs, then the EXEC statement that invokes the procedure is all that is required.

Often, however, the JCL in the procedure may not completely satisfy the user's needs and some changes are required. These changes are nondestructive, involve read-only operations, and they never affect the contents of a procedure. They are on-the-fly changes, and they are known as *overrides*.

Terminology can be confusing in this area. Many documents often use the work *"modify"* to describe an *"override."* This will be avoided in this book because the word modification implies permanence (i.e., to modify a data set — the data set is permanently updated). Words such as "alter," "update," "change" will also not be used in place of "override." Updates to a procedure are certainly possible and very common. One of the most popular ways of updating a procedure is to use Option 2 of TSO/ISPF (the Edit Option). Updating is a process totally unrelated to the topic of this section.

Overriding does not alter, either permanently or temporarily, the contents of a procedure. Simply, as the system reads a procedure, it changes some of its parameters, based on the user-supplied overrides, but never writes the changed procedure back. Several people could be using the same procedure with different overrides and none of them would have any effect on the others.

The are two types of overrides:

* A regular override.
* A symbolic override.

The word "regular" is not an official term. It will be used when it is necessary to differentiate between the two types of overrides. Unless otherwise stated, the word override will imply "regular' override. A symbolic override will be referred to by its full name. Symbolic parameters and symbolic overrides will be discussed in Sections 12.12, 12.13 and 12.14 later in this chapter.

Overriding can:

* Add, replace, or nullify any EXEC statement parameter, except PGM.
* Add, replace, or nullify any DD statement parameter.
* Add an entire DD statement.

The method to supply overrides for EXEC statements is totally different from the one for DD statements. The best way to demonstrate the two mechanisms for overriding is to provide a sample procedure, LAM (see Figure 12.2), invoke it, and override it.

Procedure LAM is to be executed with the following overrides:

```
------------------------------------------------------------------
Procedure LAM

//S1        EXEC  PGM=ED,PARM=(A,B,C,E),REGION=900K,TIME=(5,30)
//STEPLIB   DD   DSN=DEV.LOADLIB,DISP=SHR
//IN1       DD    DSN=USER1.FILE2,DISP=OLD
//IN2       DD    DSN=EXTER.FILEX,DISP=OLD,UNIT=TAPE,
//               VOL=SER=000101
//REP       DD    SYSOUT=*,DEST=R4
//OUT       DD    DSN=USER1.PLA,DISP=(,CATLG,DELETE),UNIT=SYSDA,
//               VOL=SER=DEV003,SPACE=(CYL,(20,5),RLSE),
//               DCB=(BLKSIZE=4000,LRECL=80,RECFM=FB)
//S2        EXEC  PGM=FORM,REGION=900K
//INA       DD    DSN=USER1.PLA,DISP=SHR
//          DD    DSN=USER1.F226,DISP=SHR
//          DD    DSN=USER1.F232,DISP=SHR
//          DD    DSN=USER1.F118,DISP=SHR
//OUTA      DD    DSN=USER1.VAT(+1),DISP=(,CATLG,DELETE),UNIT=TAPE,
//               VOL=(,RETAIN),
//               DCB=(TEST.MODEL,BLKSIZE=32700,LRECL=100,RECFM=FB)
//PRNT      DD    SYSOUT=*,COPIES=2
//S3        EXEC  PGM=REPO,REGION=400K,COND=(0,LT)
//IN3       DD    DSN=USER1.VAT(+1),DISP=OLD
//OUT3      DD    DSN=USER1.TRAIL,DISP=(,CATLG,DELETE),UNIT=SYSDA,
//               VOL=SER=DEV012,SPACE=(CYL,(50,15),RLSE),
//               DCB=(BLKSIZE=23440,LRECL=80,RECFM=FB)
//OT3    OUTPUT   DEST=R7,LINECT=50,COPIES=3
//OT4    OUTPUT   DEST=N4,CLASS=C
//PRNT      DD    SYSOUT=(,),OUTPUT=(*.OT3,*.OT4)
------------------------------------------------------------------
```

Figure 12.2 Procedure LAM.

1. In step S1:
   a. The value of the PARM parameter must be (A,B,C,D) and the TIME parameter must be nullified.
   b. In DD statement IN1, DSN must be USER1.FILE3.
   c. DD statement IN2 must retrieve data set USER1.FILEX as a cataloged data set.
   d. In DD statement REP, FCB=FCB8 must be added.
   e. In DD statement OUT, BLKSIZE must be 23440.
2. In step S2:

   a. COND=(0,LT) must be added.

   b. In DD statement INA, DSN in the third concatenation must be USER1.F228.

   c. In DD statement OUTA, UNIT must be CART.

   d. An entire DD statement,
   //STEPLIB DD DSN=DEV.LOADLIB,DISP=SHR
   must be added.

3. In step S3:

   a. EVEN must be added to the COND parameter.

   b. In DD statement OUT3, RLSE must be removed from the SPACE parameter and the VOL parameter must be nullified.

   c. In OUTPUT statement OT3, DEST must be R5.

Before beginning to do the example, the rules for overriding must be stated:

Common rules for EXEC and DD statement overriding

- Only the contents of the parameter field of an EXEC, DD or OUTPUT statement can be overridden.
- A parameter can be replaced, added, or nullified by means of overriding.
- When replacing an existing parameter, the overriding parameter must be specified in its complete format. DCB is an exception, as will be explained later.
- An overriding parameter replaces the same parameter, if it exists, in the statement inside the procedure. It is added to the statement if it does not exist.
- A syntactical JCL error inside a procedure cannot be corrected by overriding the erroneous parameter. The system checks the overriding as well as the overridden parameter for correct syntax.

Rules for EXEC statement overriding

- To override an EXEC parameter, "parameter.stepname=value" must be coded when adding or replacing a parameter, and "parameter.stepname='" must be coded when nullifying a parameter.
- The PGM parameter cannot be overridden.
- All overriding EXEC parameters must be coded in the EXEC statement that invokes the procedure.
- All overrides to EXEC parameters for a step must be completed before overriding parameters in a subsequent step. Within a par-

ticular step the sequence of overriding parameters is not important.

- An EXEC statement can be neither added nor removed by means
of overriding.
- An overriding EXEC parameter can be coded without the trailing
".stepname." For different parameters, however, the results can be
different. Examples follow:

REGION=800K — All steps in the procedure will be assigned
this parameter.

TIME=(4,30) — All steps in the procedure will be collectively
allowed 4 minutes and 30 seconds of CPU time. This is different
from what happens with the REGION.

PARM=(X,Y) — This PARM parameter will be assigned to the
first step of the procedure, and the PARM parameters of all other
steps will be nullified. This is different from both of the previous
parameters.

COND=(4,LT) — All steps in the procedure will be assigned this
parameter.

PERFORM=17 — All steps in the procedure will be assigned
this parameter.

ACCT=JJ43 — All steps in the procedure will be assigned this
parameter.

Considering that several parameters cause quite different reac-
tions when the ".stepname" is omitted, great caution must be exercised when coding them. Better yet, this practice should be avoided
as too dangerous. The qualifying ".stepname' should always be
coded after an overriding EXEC parameter.

If coded, overriding EXEC parameters that do not contain
".stepname" must precede those that do.

Rules for DD statement overriding

- To override any parameters in a DD statement an independent DD
statement must be supplied in the following format:

```
//stepname.ddname  DD  overriding parameters
```

To replace an existing DD parameter, or to provide an additional
one, the overriding parameter must appear in the parameter field
in its complete format (DCB is an exception). To nullify an existing
parameter, "parameter=" must be coded.

To override any parameters in a concatenation other than the
first one, the following must be coded:

```
//stepname.ddname  DD
//                 DD
   .               .
   .               .
//                 DD  overriding parameters
```

To add an entire DD statement,

```
//stepname.ddname  DD  complete parameter field
```

must be coded.

- The sequence of overriding DD statements must be the same as the sequence of the corresponding overridden statements. The sequence of overriding parameters is not important, except for those which are positional.
- An additional DD statement must the last one in a step's overriding statements. When several additional DD statements are supplied, their relative sequence is not important, unless referbacks are used.
- A DD statement cannot be removed by means of overriding.
- The parameters of an OUTPUT statement can be overridden in the same fashion as parameters in a DD statement
- A DD statement which resides in a step with no stepname cannot be overridden unless the step is the first one in the procedure.
- The stepname which precedes the ddname in an overriding DD statement can be omitted.

```
//ddname  DD  overriding parameters
```

If it is, the default stepname will be:
— The stepname of the last previous overriding DD statement which used the format "stepname.ddname."
— The first step, if no previous overriding DD statement using the format "stepname.ddname" exists.

It is recommended that the stepname be always coded before the ddname to avoid accidental errors.

Now that the rules are in place, the example can be analyzed:

To assist the reader, each requirement will be repeated and every statement to be overridden will be shown.

Since all EXEC parameter overrides will be coded in the EXEC statement invoking the procedure, requirements 1a, 2a, and 3a should be done at the beginning.

Requirement 1a: In S1 the value of the PARM parameter must be (A,B,C,D) and the TIME parameter must be nullified.
Statement in procedure to be overridden:

```
//S1          EXEC  PGM=ED,PARM=(A,B,C,E),REGION=900K,TIME=(5,30)
```

Overriding statement:

```
//ZP          EXEC  LAM,PARM.S1=(A,B,C,D),TIME.S1=
```

This takes care of requirement 1a. Note that if TIME were the last parameter, the "=" would be followed by blanks. For S1, PARM=(A,B,C,D) is now in effect and TIME has been eliminated. Notice that the existing PARM=(A,B,C,E) in the procedure contains most of the needed information, A,B,C. There is no way to take advantage of this similarity. An overriding parameter that replaces an existing one in the procedure must be specified in its complete format.
Proceed with the next requirement.
Requirement 2a: In S2, COND=(0,LT) must be added.
Statement in procedure to be overridden:

```
//S2          EXEC  PGM=FORM,REGION=900K
```

Continued overriding statement:

```
//ZP          EXEC  LAM,PARM.S1=(A,B,C,D),TIME.S1=,COND.S2=(0,LT)
```

COND=(0,LT) is now added to S2 (there is no COND in S2 inside the procedure).
Requirement 3a: In S3, EVEN must be added to the COND parameter.
Statement in procedure to be overridden:

```
//S3          EXEC  PGM=REPO,REGION=400K,COND=(0,LT)
```

Continued overriding statement:

```
//ZP          EXEC  LAM,PARM.S1=(A,B,C,D),TIME.S1=,COND.S2=(0,LT),
//                  COND.S3=((0,LT),EVEN)
```

All the EXEC overrides are done. Care was exercised to finish overriding one step before going to the next one. Had this rule been

violated, a JCL error would have ensued. Consider the EXEC statement above containing a sequence error:

```
//ZP          EXEC  LAM,PARM.S1=(A,B,C,D),COND.S2=(0,LT),TIME.S1=,
//            COND.S3=((0,LT),EVEN)
```

The system will override properly PARM in S1 and COND in S2.
But once the system has gone to S2, it cannot go back to S1 (it is like
a one-way street) and fails to even recognize stepname S1. The result
will be a JCL error:

```
IEF611I OVERRIDDEN STEP NOT FOUND IN PROCEDURE
```

PARM.S1 and COND.S1 can be coded in any sequence relative to
each other, since both belong to the same step.

Next, DD statement parameters will be overridden. According to
the rules stated earlier, for every DD statement in the procedure
where one or more parameters must be overridden, a separate DD
statement must be supplied in the input stream. This mechanism is
completely different from the one for overriding EXEC statement parameters. Also notice that while the stepname follows the parameter
when overriding EXEC parameters, it precedes the ddname when
overriding DD statements — a hard-to-remember detail.

Requirement 1b: In DD statement IN1, DSN must be
USER1.FILE3.

Statement in procedure to be overridden:

```
//IN1       DD    DSN=USER1.FILE2,DISP=OLD
```

Continued overriding JCL:

```
//ZP          EXEC  LAM,PARM.S1=(A,B,C,D),TIME.S1=,COND.S2=(0,LT),
//            COND.S3=((0,LT),EVEN)
//S1.IN1    DD  DSN=USER1.FILE3
```

DSN=USER1.FILE2 is replaced by USER1.FILE3.

Requirement 1c: DD statement IN2 must retrieve data set,
USER1.FILEX as a cataloged data set.

Statement in procedure to be overridden:

```
//IN2       DD    DSN=EXTER.FILEX,DISP=OLD,UNIT=TAPE,
//                VOL=SER=000101
```

There is no need to override DSN or DISP (both are fine as they appear in the procedure). However, the VOL parameter must be nullified (VOL= and VOL=SER= work equally well) in order to permit the use of the catalog (see Section 6.3 in Chapter 6). UNIT need not be overridden, although overriding it is also acceptable.

Continued overriding JCL:

```
//ZP          EXEC  LAM,PARM.S1=(A,B,C,D),TIME.S1=,COND.S2=(0,LT),
//            COND.S3=((0,LT),EVEN)
//S1.IN1      DD   DSN=USER1.FILE3
//S1.IN2    · DD   VOL=         ALTERNATIVE: VOL=SER=
```

Requirement 1d: In DD statement REP, FCB=FCB8 must be added.

Statement in procedure to be overridden:

```
//REP         DD   SYSOUT=*,DEST=R4
```

Continued overriding JCL:

```
//ZP          EXEC  LAM,PARM.S1=(A,B,C,D),TIME.S1=,COND.S2=(0,LT),
//            COND.S3=((0,LT),EVEN)
//S1.IN1      DD   DSN=USER1.FILE3
//S1.IN2      DD   VOL=         ALTERNATIVE: VOL=SER=
//S1.REP      DD   FCB=FCB8
```

Requirement 1e: In DD statement OUT, BLKSIZE must be 23440.

Statement in procedure to be overridden:

```
//OUT         DD   DSN=USER1.PLA,DISP=(,CATLG,DELETE),UNIT=SYSDA,
//            VOL=SER=DEV003,SPACE=(CYL,(20,5),RLSE),
//            DCB=(BLKSIZE=4000,LRECL=80,RECFM=FB)
```

The DCB parameter constitutes the only exception to the rule, which requires that replacement overriding parameters be coded in their complete format. The BLKSIZE subparameter can be overridden without repeating LRECL and RECFM.

Continued overriding JCL:

```
//ZP          EXEC  LAM,PARM.S1=(A,B,C,D),TIME.S1=,COND.S2=(0,LT),
//            COND.S3=((0,LT),EVEN)
//S1.IN1      DD   DSN=USER1.FILE3
```

```
//S1.IN2      DD   VOL=            ALTERNATIVE: VOL=SER=
//S1.REP      DD   FCB=FCB8
//S1.OUT      DD   DCB=BLKSIZE=23440
```

Requirement 2b: In DD statement INA, DSN in the third concatenation must be USER1.F228.

Statement in procedure to be overridden:

```
//INA        DD   DSN=USER1.PLA,DISP=SHR
//           DD   DSN=USER1.F226,DISP=SHR
//           DD   DSN=USER1.F232,DISP=SHR
//           DD   DSN=USER1.F118,DISP=SHR
```

The DD statement to be overridden is a concatenation and has no
ddname. All previous concatenations must be supplied with a blank
parameter field, when no overrides in their parameter fields are
needed. Concatenations following the one to be overridden need not
be supplied, unless they require some overrides also.

Continued overriding JCL:

```
//ZP          EXEC  LAM,PARM.S1=(A,B,C,D),TIME.S1=,COND.S2=(0,LT),
//            COND.S3=((0,LT),EVEN)
//S1.IN1      DD   DSN=USER1.FILE3
//S1.IN2      DD   VOL=            ALTERNATIVE: VOL=SER=
//S1.REP      DD   FCB=FCB8
//S1.OUT      DD   DCB=BLKSIZE=23440
//S2.INA      DD
//            DD
//            DD   DSN=USER1.F228
```

The fourth concatenation can be included (with a blank parameter
field)

```
//            DD
```

but it is not necessary.

Requirement 2c: In DD statement OUTA, UNIT must be CART.

Statement in procedure to be overridden:

```
//OUTA       DD   DSN=USER1.VAT(+1),DISP=(,CATLG,DELETE),UNIT=TAPE,
//           VOL=(,RETAIN),
//           DCB=(TEST.MODEL,BLKSIZE=32700,LRECL=100,RECFM=FB)
```

Continued overriding JCL:

```
//ZP          EXEC  LAM,PARM.S1=(A,B,C,D),TIME.S1=,COND.S2=(0,LT),
//            COND.S3=((0,LT),EVEN)
//S1.IN1      DD   DSN=USER1.FILE3
//S1.IN2      DD   VOL=         ALTERNATIVE: VOL=SER=
//S1.REP      DD   FCB=FCB8
//S1.OUT      DD   DCB=BLKSIZE=23440
//S2.INA      DD
//            DD
//            DD   DSN=USER1.F228
//S2.OUTA     DD   UNIT=CART
```

Requirement 2d: DD statement
//STEPLIB DD DSN=DEV.LOADLIB,DISP=SHR must be added.

Statement in procedure to be overridden: None. This will be an additional DD statement.

As a corollary of the DD statement sequence rule, the additional STEPLIB DD statement must be the last overriding statement in step S2.

Continued overriding JCL:

```
//ZP          EXEC  LAM,PARM.S1=(A,B,C,D),TIME.S1=,COND.S2=(0,LT),
//            COND.S3=((0,LT),EVEN)
//S1.IN1      DD   DSN=USER1.FILE3
//S1.IN2      DD   VOL=         ALTERNATIVE: VOL=SER=
//S1.REP      DD   FCB=FCB8
//S1.OUT      DD   DCB=BLKSIZE=23440
//S2.INA      DD
//            DD
//            DD   DSN=USER1.F228
//S2.OUTA     DD   UNIT=CART
//S2.STEPLIB  DD   DSN=DEV.LOADLIB,DISP=SHR
```

Requirement 3b: In DD statement OUT3, RLSE must be removed from the SPACE parameter and the VOL parameter must be nullified.

Statement in procedure to be overridden:

```
//OUT3       DD    DSN=USER1.TRAIL,DISP=(,CATLG,DELETE),UNIT=SYSDA,
//                 VOL=SER=DEV012,SPACE=(CYL,(50,15),RLSE),
//                 DCB=(BLKSIZE=23440,LRECL=80,RECFM=FB)
```

To eliminate RLSE, the SPACE parameter must be replaced with one that contains identical information but without RLSE.

Continued overriding JCL:

```
//ZP          EXEC  LAM,PARM.S1=(A,B,C,D),TIME.S1=,COND.S2=(0,LT),
//            COND.S3=((0,LT),EVEN)
//S1.IN1      DD  DSN=USER1.FILE3
//S1.IN2      DD  VOL=          ALTERNATIVE: VOL=SER=
//S1.REP      DD  FCB=FCB8
//S1.OUT      DD  DCB=BLKSIZE=23440
//S2.INA      DD
//            DD
//            DD  DSN=USER1.F228
//S2.OUTA     DD  UNIT=CART
//S2.STEPLIB  DD  DSN=DEV.LOADLIB,DISP=SHR
//S3.OUT3     DD  SPACE=(CYL,(50,15)),VOL=
```

Requirement 3c: In OUTPUT statement OT3, DEST must be R5. Statement in procedure to be overridden:

```
//OT3     OUTPUT  DEST=R7,LINECT=50,COPIES=3
```

Parameters in an OUTPUT statement can be overridden the same way as parameters in a DD statement.

Continued overriding JCL:

```
//ZP          EXEC  LAM,PARM.S1=(A,B,C,D),TIME.S1=,COND.S2=(0,LT),
//            COND.S3=((0,LT),EVEN)
//S1.IN1      DD  DSN=USER1.FILE3
//S1.IN2      DD  VOL=          ALTERNATIVE: VOL=SER=
//S1.REP      DD  FCB=FCB8
//S1.OUT      DD  DCB=BLKSIZE=23440
//S2.INA      DD
//            DD
//            DD  DSN=USER1.F228
//S2.OUTA     DD  UNIT=CART
//S2.STEPLIB  DD  DSN=DEV.LOADLIB,DISP=SHR
//S3.OUT3     DD  SPACE=(CYL,(50,15)),VOL=
//S3.OT3   OUTPUT DEST=R5
```

All the overrides are complete. Care was taken to supply the overriding DD statements in the same sequence as those being overridden. The override for the OUTPUT statement also had to be coded in the right sequence in relation to DD statements.

An example of what happens when the sequence rule is violated follows. Consider the same procedure, LAM, used in the previous example but with only requirements 1b and 1c.

```
//ZP         EXEC  LAM,PARM.S1=(A,B,C,D),TIME.S1=,COND.S2=(0,LT),
//           COND.S3=((0,LT),EVEN)
//S1.IN2     DD    VOL=
//S1.IN1     DD    DSN=USER1.FILE3
```

The two overriding DD statements shown above have been coded in the wrong sequence. After the procedure has been invoked, the system reads the overriding DD statements and attempts to match them against those in the procedure. But, as with the EXEC overrides, it is again a one-way street and once a DD statement from the procedure has been passed, the system will never go back to it. When an overriding DD statement cannot be matched, it will be treated as an additional statement.

The system always reads the overriding DD statements first and tries to match them with those in the procedure. In the example, the first overriding DD statement is:

```
//S1.IN2     DD    VOL=
```

The system tries to match it against IN1, the first DD statement found in the procedure. No match! The next DD statement, IN2, is read in from the procedure. A match is found and IN2 is overridden properly. The system now reads again from the input stream, the second overriding DD statement:

```
//S1.IN1     DD    DSN=USER1.FILE3
```

Since the system cannot go backward, no match will be found and IN1 will be treated as an additional DD statement. Luckily, IN1 contains insufficient parameters to be a complete DD statement and the result will be a JCL error (UNIT is needed because DISP defaults to NEW).

Depending on overriding requirements, an error in the sequence can have much more harmful results than a mere JCL error.

To demonstrate, change requirement 1b so that DISP=OLD must be overridden with DISP=SHR in DD statement IN1. The new overriding JCL is:

```
//ZP          EXEC  LAM,PARM.S1=FAIL,TIME.S1=,COND.S2=(0,LT),
//            COND.S3=((0,LT),EVEN)
//S1.IN2      DD  VOL=
//S1.IN1      DD  DSN=USER1.FILE3,DISP=SHR
```

Note that IN1 now contains a complete parameter field and no JCL error will result. Instead there are two DD statements by the same ddname. The first one retrieves data set USER1.FILE2 and the second one data set USER1.FILE3. This duplicate ddname does not generate an error condition. Rather, both are allocated but when the program opens for IN1, only the first of the two will be used. Unfortunately, this DD statement retrieves the data set that was meant to be overridden and, clearly, the wrong one. Most likely, execution will appear to be successful. No manifestation of any failure is apparent, unless one notices the sequence error (a tough error to detect). It may be a long time before the problem is discovered. This is the kind of problem that can give nightmares.

Because of this possible danger, it is strongly recommended that a procedure be always in view when coding JCL to override it, even if it contains only one DD statement. In this case, a sequence error cannot be made but misspelling the ddname of the overriding DD statement will produce the same potentially disastrous result.

12.6 THE OUTPUT OF A PROCEDURE

When invoking and overriding a procedure, it would be nice to be presented with the resulting JCL in the output.

For example, if a DD statement in a procedure

```
//IN          DD    DSN=USER1.FILEX,DISP=OLD,UNIT=CART,
//            VOL=SER=002523
```

were overridden by

```
//S2.IN   DD   VOL=,UNIT=
```

the resulting DD statement is

```
//IN      DD   DSN=USER1.FILEX,DISP=OLD
```

Unfortunately, this resulting DD statement will not be shown. Instead, all JCL that came from the procedure and all JCL that was supplied in the input stream will be shown mixed together, producing a messy and confusing output.

```
//S2.IN    DD    VOL=,UNIT=
X/IN       DD    DSN=USER1.FILEX,DISP=OLD,UNIT=CART,
XX               VOL=SER=002523
```

EXEC statements do not fare any better when it comes to clarity and friendliness of output.

The JCL discussed earlier in this section which executed and overrode procedure LAM (see Figure 12.2),

```
//ZP           EXEC  LAM,PARM.S1=(A,B,C,D),TIME.S1=,COND.S2=(0,LT),
//             COND.S3=((0,LT),EVEN)
//S1.IN1    DD    DSN=USER1.FILE3
//S1.IN2    DD    VOL=         ALTERNATIVE: VOL=SER=
//S1.REP    DD    FCB=FCB8
//S1.OUT    DD    DCB=BLKSIZE=23440
//S2.INA    DD
//          DD
//          DD    DSN=USER1.F228
//S2.OUTA   DD    UNIT=CART
//S2.STEPLIB DD   DSN=DEV.LOADLIB,DISP=SHR
//S3.OUT3   DD    SPACE=(CYL,(50,15)),VOL=
//S3.OT3  OUTPUT DEST=R5
```

would appear as follows in the output:

```
//USER1X    JOB   FB12,MC,CLASS=K
//ZP           EXEC  LAM,PARM.S1=FAIL,TIME.S1=,COND.S2=(0,LT),
//             COND.S3=((0,LT),EVEN)
XXS1        EXEC  PGM=ED,PARM=(A,B,C,E),REGION=900K,TIME=(5,30)
XXSTEPLIB DD DSN=DEV.LOADLIB,DISP=SHR
//S1.IN1    DD    DSN=USER1.FILE3
X/IN1      DD    DSN=USER1.FILE2,DISP=OLD
//S1.IN2    DD    VOL=         ALTERNATIVE: VOL=SER=
X/IN2      DD    DSN=EXTER.FILEX,DISP=OLD,UNIT=TAPE,
XX               VOL=SER=000101
//S1.REP    DD    FCB=FCB8
X/REP      DD    SYSOUT=*,DEST=R4
//S1.OUT    DD    DCB=BLKSIZE=23440
X/OUT      DD    DSN=USER1.PLA,DISP=(,CATLG,DELETE),UNIT=SYSDA,
```

```
XX              VOL=SER=DEV003,SPACE=(CYL,(20,5),RLSE),
XX              DCB=(BLKSIZE=4000,LRECL=80,RECFM=FB)
XXS2        EXEC  PGM=FORM,REGION=900K
//S2.INA    DD
//          DD
//          DD  DSN=USER1.F228
X/INA       DD  DSN=USER1.PLA,DISP=SHR
XX          DD  DSN=USER1.F226,DISP=SHR
XX          DD  DSN=USER1.F232,DISP=SHR
XX          DD  DSN=USER1.F118,DISP=SHR
//S2.OUTA   DD  UNIT=CART
X/OUTA      DD  DSN=USER1.VAT(+1),DISP=(,CATLG,DELETE),UNIT=TAPE,
//              VOL=(,RETAIN),
//              DCB=(TEST.MODEL,BLKSIZE=32700,LRECL=100,RECFM=FB)
XXPRNT      DD  SYSOUT=*,COPIES=2
//S2.STEPLIB DD  DSN=DEV.LOADLIB,DISP=SHR
XXS3        EXEC  PGM=REPO,REGION=400K,COND=(0,LT)
XXIN3       DD  DSN=USER1.VAT(+1),DISP=OLD
//S3.OUT3   DD  SPACE=(CYL,(50,15)),VOL=
X/OUT3      DD  DSN=USER1.TRAIL,DISP=(,CATLG,DELETE),UNIT=SYSDA,
XX              VOL=SER=DEV012,SPACE=(CYL,(50,15),RLSE),
XX              DCB=(BLKSIZE=23440,LRECL=80,RECFM=FB)
//S3.OT3    OUTPUT DEST=R5
X/OT3       OUTPUT DEST=R7,LINECT=50,COPIES=3
XXOT4       OUTPUT DEST=N4,CLASS=C
XXPRNT      DD  SYSOUT=(,),OUTPUT=(*.OT3,*.OT4)
```

A very confusing output, to say the least. This may well be the reason why many people are intimidated by procedures.

The notations "//," "X/," and "XX" have a meaning. They are intended to provide the user with certain information related to overriding and where the statement comes from.

// means that the statement came from the input stream (user supplied). It could be an EXEC, DD, or OUTPUT statement.

XX has two meanings:

- When found in front of an EXEC statement, it means that the EXEC statement came from the procedure. It may or may not have been overridden.
- When found in front of a DD or OUTPUT statement, it means that the statement came from the procedure and it has *not* been overridden.

X/ means that it is a DD or OUTPUT statement that came from the procedure and *has* been overridden. The corresponding overriding statement will be found immediately preceding it. Note, however, that in the case of continuation or concatenation, X/ appears only in the first line. The rest of the lines will show XX.

Overriding and overridden DD or OUTPUT statements are always paired back to back: first the overriding, then the overridden statement.

12.7 OVERCOMING SOME RESTRICTIONS

According to the rules of overriding, as stated in Section 12.5 earlier in the chapter, an EXEC statement can be neither added nor removed by means of overriding. Actually, it would not be particularly useful to be able to add or remove an EXEC statement unless its DD statements were also added or removed, in essence adding or eliminating an entire step. This can be done in many cases through other means.

An independent step, which is not part of the procedure, can be placed before or after the procedure or both, as in the example that follows. EXEC statements which execute programs and others that invoke procedures can be mixed together in any fashion as long as the total number of steps for the job does not exceed 255.

```
//STEP1   EXEC   PGM=P1
--- needed DD statements ---
//PSTEP   EXEC   LAM
--- needed overrides ---
//STEP2   EXEC   PGM=P2
--- needed DD statements ---
```

What cannot be done by means of overriding is insert a step between steps S1 and S2 of procedure LAM (see Figure 12.2). If such a step is needed, the procedure must be modified.

Eliminating a step from a procedure can always be accomplished by overriding the COND parameter of the step to be eliminated. Using procedure LAM again, the second step, S2, can be eliminated as follows:

```
//PSTEP   EXEC   LAM,COND.S2=(0,LE)
```

If step S1, or any previous step (there may other EXEC statements before PSTEP), executes without ABENDing, it will issue a return code. It makes no difference what the return code is. Test (0,LE) will always be satisfied and, therefore, step S2 will not be executed (see Section 4.3.2 in Chapter 4). Not executed and eliminated have the same meaning. If step S1, or any previous step, ABENDs, step S2 will not be executed again, since neither EVEN nor ONLY is included in its COND parameter. The only time this technique will fail is when no previous steps have executed. In this unlikely event, the (0,LE) test will be ignored and step S2 will be executed.

If it is necessary to eliminate the first step, S1, a different technique must be used:

```
//PSTEP   EXEC   LAM,COND.S1=(ONLY,(0,LE))
```

If PSREP is the first EXEC statement in the job, the (0,LE) test will be ignored, but ONLY will cause step S1 not to be executed since no previous step has ABENDed (no previous steps exist). If there are previous steps, if at least one of them has executed without ABENDing, (0,LE) will cause step S1 not to be executed. The only time this technique will fail is when all previous steps have ABENDed. In that case (0,LE) will be ignored, and, since ONLY requests execution in the event of a previous ABEND, step S1 will be executed.

If PSTEP is the first EXEC statement in a job, the first step can be bypassed by coding RESTART=PSTEP.S2 in the JOB statement.

12.8 COMPILE-LINKEDIT-GO PROCEDURES

Compile-Linkedit-Go procedures are frequently used by programmers to test source programs.

Figure 12.3 shows a typical such procedure. It also shows Linkedit-Go and Linkedit procedures.

Here is an example of executing procedure COBUCLG with the following override requirements:

1. In step COB
    a. PARM must be nullified.
    b. A //SYSIN DD * statement must be added (to supply source statements to the compiler).
    c. In DD statement SYSLIN the primary allocation of the SPACE parameter must be five cylinders.

Procedure COBUCLG

```
//COB       EXEC PGM=IKFCBL00,PARM=(LOA,NODEC,SEQ,CLI,
//          SXR,OPT,LIB,SUP)
//SYSPRINT  DD  SYSOUT=*
//SYSUT1    DD  UNIT=SYSDA,SPACE=(CYL,(3,1))
//SYSUT2    DD  UNIT=SYSDA,SPACE=(CYL,(3,1))
//SYSUT3    DD  UNIT=SYSDA,SPACE=(CYL,(3,1))
//SYSUT4    DD  UNIT=SYSDA,SPACE=(CYL,(3,1))
//SYSLIN    DD  DSN=&&LOADSET,DISP=(MOD,PASS),UNIT=SYSDA,
//          SPACE=(CYL,(2,1)),DCB=BLKSIZE=6000
//LKED      EXEC PGM=IEWL,PARM=(LIST,LET,XREF),
//          COND=(5,LE,COB)
//SYSLIN    DD  DSN=&&LOADSET,DISP=(OLD,DELETE)
//          DD  DDNAME=SYSIN
//SYSLIB    DD  DSN=SYS1.COBLIB,DISP=SHR
//          DD  DSN=SYS2.LINKLIBX,DISP=SHR
//          DD  DSN=SYS2.LINKLIB2,DISP=SHR
//SYSLMOD   DD  DSN=&&GODATA(RUN),DISP=(NEW,PASS),UNIT=SYSDA,
//          SPACE=(CYL,(1,1,1))
//SYSUT1    DD  UNIT=SYSDA,SPACE=(CYL,2)
//SYSPRINT  DD  SYSOUT=*
//GO        EXEC PGM=*.LKED.SYSLMOD,COND=((5,LE,COB),
//          (9,LE,LKED))
```

Procedure LKEDG

```
//LKED      EXEC PGM=IEWL,PARM=(LIST,LET,XREF)
//SYSLIN    DD  DDNAME=SYSIN
//SYSLMOD   DD  DSN=&&GODATA(RUN),DISP=(NEW,PASS),UNIT=SYSDA,
//          SPACE=(CYL,(1,1,1))
//SYSUT1    DD  UNIT=SYSDA,SPACE=(CYL,2)
//SYSPRINT  DD  SYSOUT=*
//GO        EXEC PGM=*.LKED.SYSLMOD,COND=(9,LE,LKED))
```

Procedure LKED

```
//LKED      EXEC PGM=IEWL,PARM=(LIST,LET,XREF)
//SYSLIN    DD  DDNAME=SYSIN
//SYSLMOD   DD  DSN=&&GODATA(RUN),DISP=(NEW,PASS),UNIT=SYSDA,
//          SPACE=(CYL,(1,1,1))
//SYSUT1    DD  UNIT=SYSDA,SPACE=(CYL,2)
//SYSPRINT  DD  SYSOUT=*
```

Figure 12.3 Some typical Compile-Linkedit-Go procedures.

2. In step LKED
   a. The LET option must be removed from the PARM parameter.
   b. A concatenation for library TEST.COBLIB (cataloged) must be added to DD statement SYSLIB.
   c. DD statement SYSLMOD must retrieve cataloged data set USER1.LOADLIB and create member FRUN.
   d. A //SYSIN DD * statement must be added (to supply Linkage Editor control statements).

3. In step GO
   a. The COND parameter must be ((5,LE,COB),(5,LE,LKED))
   b. Two DD statements must be added:

```
//IN  DD  DSN=USER1.FIL1,DISP=SHR
//OUT DD  SYSOUT=*,OUTLIM=500
```

The JCL below will satisfy the overriding requirements:

```
//USER1A       JOB   XE55,SMITH,CLASS=D
//CLG          EXEC  COBUCLG,PARM.COB=,PARM.LKED=(LIST,XREF),
//                   COND.GO=((5,LE,COB),(5,LE,LKED))
//COB.SYSLIN   DD    SPACE=(CYL,(5,1))
//COB.SYSLIN   DD
--source program--
/*
//LKED.SYSLIB  DD
//             DD
//             DD
//             DD    DSN=TEST.COBLIB,DISP=SHR
//LKED.SYSLMOD DD    DSN=USER1.LOADLIB(FRUN),DISP=OLD,UNIT=,SPACE=
//LKED.SYSIN   DD    *
--Linkage Editor statements--
/*
//GO.IN        DD    DSN=USER1.FIL1,DISP=SHR
//GO.OUT       DD    SYSOUT=*,OUTLIM=500
```

Most of the overrides are straightforward. Two of them require some discussion:

Requirement 2b. Even though the DD statement at the end of the concatenation is an additional one, it need not be at the end of the step's overrides. It belongs to DD statement SYSLIB and will not be treated as an independent DD statement added to the step.

Requirement 2c. Overriding DSN and DISP are self-explanatory. UNIT was overridden (and nullified) because SYSDA will be used if it is a subset of the the device type in the catalog entry. While SYSDA is appropriate for a temporary data set, it may not be consistent with the device where the volume that contains data set USER1.LOADLIB is mounted, resulting in a JCL error (see Section 7.3.1 in Chapter 7):

```
IEF702I  USER1A CLG LKED SYSLMOD - UNABLE TO ALLOCATE
```

The SPACE parameter was overridden (and nullified) because if data set USER1.LOADLIB exhausted all its available space while member FRUN was being added, the system would have supplied the secondary allocation coded in the SPACE parameter (one cylinder) as opposed to the secondary allocation specified when the data set was created (see Section 7.9 in Chapter 7). This may be undesirable.

12.9 REFERRING TO A PROCEDURE FROM OUTSIDE

Continuing on the same example of the preceding section, let one more requirement be added: that the program in step GO be executed a second time inputting data set USER1.FIL2.

```
//CLG          EXEC  COBUCLG,PARM.COB=,PARM.LKED=(LIST,XREF),
 .    .    .      .    .    .    .    .
 .    .    .      .    .    .    .    .
 .    .    .      .    .    .    .    .
 .    .    .      .    .    .    .    .
//GO.IN        DD    DSN=USER1.FIL1,DISP=SHR
//GO.OUT       DD    SYSOUT=*,OUTLIM=500
//SECGO        EXEC  PGM=*.CLG.LKED.SYSLMOD
//IN           DD    DSN=USER1.FIL2,DISP=SHR
//OUT          DD    SYSOUT=*,OUTLIM=500
```

Note that the referback in the PGM parameter of step SECGO contains three, rather than the usual two names. In this example, reference is made to a step that is inside the procedure, but the statement that contains the referback is outside the procedure. If the EXEC statement that invoked the procedure has a name (the name is optional), this name must be used in the referback:

PGM=*.name-of-EXEC-invoking-procedure.stepname-inside-proce dure.ddname or PGM=*.CLG.LKED.SYSLMOD

If the name of the EXEC statement invoking the procedure were omitted,

```
//                    EXEC COBUCLG,PARM.COB=,PARM.LKED=(LIST,XREF),
//                    COND.GO=((5,LE,COB),(5,LE,LKED)
```

then the referback would contain only two names:

```
PGM=*.LKED.SYSLMOD
```

Omitting the name of the EXEC statement invoking the procedure may be valid syntactically, but it is a poor practice and is discouraged. If the procedure COBUCLG were to be invoked twice, this referback could only refer to the first execution of step LKED.

What was discussed in this section for the PGM parameter, can be generalized to include all referbacks:

When reference is made to an EXEC statement inside a procedure, but the statement that contains this reference is *not* inside this procedure:

• If the EXEC statement that invokes the procedure has a name, then two names must be used in the reference.
— First, the name of the EXEC statement invoking the procedure.
— Then, the stepname inside the procedure.

```
procexecname.stepname
```

Examples:

```
VOL=REF=*.CLG.LKED.SYSLMOD
COND=(0,LT,CLG.COB)
RESTART=CLG.LKED
```

• If the EXEC statement that invokes the procedure has no name, then only the step name inside the procedure must be used in the reference.
Examples:

```
VOL=REF=*.LKED.SYSLMOD
COND=(0,LT,COB)
RESTART=LKED
```

This rule applies to all JCL parameters whose syntax allows them to reference a previous step (in the case of the RESTART JOB statement parameter, a later step):

- The RESTART parameter in the JOB statement.
- The COND, and PGM parameters in the EXEC statement.
- The DSN, VOL, DCB, and OUTPUT parameters in the DD statement.

12.10 SPECIAL OVERRIDES

Most of the overrides discussed in this chapter are ordinary, meaning they are apt to be found often in an everyday environment. This section will discuss certain overrides that are to a small, or high, degree out of the ordinary. Procedure SPEC shown in Figure 12.4 will be used to demonstrate these overrides.

Procedure SPEC is to be executed and overridden as follows:

1. In step S1
   a. DD statement OUT1 must be dummied.
   b. DD statement OUT2, rather than being DUMMY, must output a report.
   c. The second concatenation of DD statement IN1 must be dummied.
   d. DD statement OUT3, rather than being tape, must output a report.
   e. DD statement OUT3, rather than being SYSOUT, must be a 30 track SYSDA temporary data set.
2. In step S2
   a. The third concatenation of DD statement LIBX must be eliminated.
   b. DD statement CNTL must be //CNTL DD *.
   c. In DD statement OUT4, the DCB parameter must be eliminated.
   d. In DD statement OUT5, DSCB model TEST.MODEL must be added to the DCB parameter.
   e. In DD statement OUT6, DSCB model TEST.MODEL must be eliminated from the DCB parameter. All other subparameters must remain intact.
   f. In DD statement OUT7, the BUFNO subparameter must be eliminated from the DCB parameter. All other subparameters must remain intact.

Procedure SPEC

```
//S1      EXEC  PGM=ONE
//OUT1    DD    DSN=USER1.SELL1,DISP=(,CATLG,DELETE),UNIT=TAPE,
//              DCB=(BLKSIZE=32700,LRECL=100,RECFM=FB)
//OUT2    DD    DUMMY,DCB=BLKSIZE=6000
//IN1     DD    DSN=USER1.BRY1,DISP=SHR
//        DD    DSN=USER1.BRY2,DISP=SHR
//        DD    DSN=USER1.BRY3,DISP=SHR
//OUT3    DD    DSN=USER1.SELL3,DISP=(,CATLG,DELETE),UNIT=TAPE,
//              DCB=(BLKSIZE=9040,LRECL=80,RECFM=FB)
//REP1    DD    SYSOUT=*
//S2      EXEC  PGM=TWO,COND=(4,LT)
//LIBX    DD    DSN=USER1.LIBA,DISP=SHR    USER1.LIBA IS A PDS
//        DD    DSN=USER1.LIBB,DISP=SHR    USER1.LIBB IS A PDS
//        DD    DSN=USER1.LIBC,DISP=SHR    USER1.LIBC IS A PDS
//CNTL    DD    DSN=USER1.CTLIB(SRT1),DISP=SHR
//OUT4    DD    DSN=USER1.DBAK4,DISP=(,CATLG,DELETE),UNIT=SYSDA,
//              SPACE=(TRK,(200,50),RLSE),VOL=SER=TEST26,
//              DCB=(BLKSIZE=23400,LRECL=100,RECFM=FB)
//OUT5    DD    DSN=USER1.DRK(+1),DISP=(,CATLG,DELETE),UNIT=SYSDA,
//              SPACE=(23440,(800,300),RLSE),VOL=SER=TEST99,
//              DCB=(BLKSIZE=23440,LRECL=80,RECFM=FB)
//OUT6    DD    DSN=USER1.DBAK6,DISP=(,CATLG,DELETE),UNIT=SYSDA,
//              SPACE=(CYL,(50,15)),
//              DCB=(TEST.MODEL,BLKSIZE=23400,LRECL=100,RECFM=FB)
//OUT7    DD    DSN=USER1.DRL(+1),DISP=(,CATLG,DELETE),UNIT=SYSDA,
//              SPACE=(CYL,(30,10),RLSE),VOL=SER=TEST04,
//              DCB=(TEST.MODEL,BLKSIZE=23400,LRECL=100,RECFM=FB,
//              BUFNO=30)
```

Figure 12.4 Procedure SPEC.

Each override will be individually shown and discussed.
Procedure SPEC is executed below:

```
//USER1B        JOB   XE55,JONES,CLASS=R
//SOD           EXEC  SPEC
```

Requirement 1a: DD statement OUT1 must be dummied.
DD statement to be overridden:

```
//OUT1    DD     DSN=USER1.SELL1,DISP=(,CATLG,DELETE),UNIT=TAPE,
//               DCB=(BLKSIZE=32700,LRECL=100,RECFM=FB)
```

Overriding DD statement:

```
//S1.OUT1  DD    DUMMY
```

Comments: Regardless of the contents of the overridden parameter field, no other parameters are needed (with the only possible exception of DCB). The same would hold true if the DD statement to be dummied were SYSOUT.

Requirement 1b: DD statement OUT2, rather than being DUMMY, must output a report.

DD statement to be overridden:

```
//OUT2    DD     DUMMY,DCB=BLKSIZE=6000
```

Overriding DD statement:

```
//S1.OUT2   DD    SYSOUT=*
```

Comments: Any valid parameter, except DCB, in the overriding statement will have the effect of negating DUMMY.

Requirement 1c: The second concatenation of DD statement IN1 must be dummied.

DD statement to be overridden:

```
//IN1    DD     DSN=USER1.BRY1,DISP=SHR
//       DD     DSN=USER1.BRY2,DISP=SHR
//       DD     DSN=USER1.BRY3,DISP=SHR
```

Proposed overriding DD statement:

```
//S1.IN1    DD
//          DD   DUMMY
```

Comments: This will not work. Overriding and dummying the second concatenation will cause the third concatenation to also act as a dummy. The desired result can be accomplished by some rearranging:

```
//S1.IN1    DD
//          DD   DSN=USER1.BRY3
//          DD   DUMMY
```

The data set of the second concatenation is now effectively dummied, since the two remaining concatenations are for data sets USER1.BRY1 and USER1.BRY3.

Requirement 1d: DD statement OUT3, rather than being tape, must output a report.

DD statement to be overridden:

```
//OUT3    DD     DSN=USER1.SELL3,DISP=(,CATLG,DELETE),UNIT=TAPE,
//               DCB=(BLKSIZE=9040,LRECL=80,RECFM=FB)
```

Overriding DD statement:

```
//S1.OUT3   DD    SYSOUT=*
```

Comments: All parameters in the overridden DD statement which are incompatible with SYSOUT (such as DSN and DISP) are effectively eliminated. Individually nullifying such parameters can result in JCL errors (i.e., //S1.OUT3 DD SYSOUT=*,DSN=,DISP= must be avoided).

Requirement 1e: DD statement OUT3, rather than being SYSOUT, must be a 30 track SYSDA temporary data set.

DD statement to be overridden:

```
//REP1    DD    SYSOUT=*
```

Proposed overriding DD statement:

```
//S1.REP1    DD    UNIT=SYSDA,SPACE=(TRK,(30,5))
```

Comments: This override will accomplish nothing. Neither UNIT nor SPACE is incompatible with SYSOUT (both are ignored when found with SYSOUT), and, as a result, SYSOUT is still in effect. A parameter incompatible with SYSOUT must be present.

```
//S1.REP1    DD    UNIT=SYSDA,SPACE=(TRK,(10,5)),DISP=(,DELETE)
```

Even though DISP=(,DELETE) is the default, DISP is needed to nullify SYSOUT. Another observation can be made here. BLKSIZE need not be coded with SYSOUT as long as LRECL is available. This is not the case with an ordinary disk data set. Therefore, DCB=BLKSIZE should be added to avoid a possible S013-34 ABEND failure.

```
//S1.REP1   DD   UNIT=SYSDA,SPACE=(TRK,(10,5)),DISP=(,DELETE),
//               DCB=BLKSIZE=9040
```

Requirement 2a: The third concatenation of DD statement LIBX must be eliminated.

DD statement to be overridden:

```
//LIBX    DD    DSN=USER1.LIBA,DISP=SHR    USER1.LIBA IS A PDS
//        DD    DSN=USER1.LIBB,DISP=SHR    USER1.LIBB IS A PDS
//        DD    DSN=USER1.LIBC,DISP=SHR    USER1.LIBC IS A PDS
```

Proposed overriding DD statement:

```
//S2.LIBX   DD
//          DD
//          DD  DUMMY
```

Comments: This appears similar to requirement 1c and, since the concatenation to be overridden is the last one, the override above should do.

It will not do. The concatenated data sets are partitioned and dummying a PDS will cause an S013-64 ABEND failure. To find a solution, one must understand how concatenations which specify DSN=pds — but not DSN=pds(member — are normally used. The program, using access method BPAM, searches the PDS directory of the first concatenation for one or more members. If found, the search stops. If not, the search continues to the next concatenation, and so on.

Consider the override:

```
//S2.LIBX   DD
//          DD
//          DD  DSN=USER1.LIBB
```

This causes the third concatenation to be the same as the second. Assume that the concatenations are searched for member KER. If member KER is found in the directory of the first concatenation, the other two will not be searched. If not found, the second concatenation will be searched and, if found there, the third concatenation will not be used. If not found, the third concatenation, which is the same as the second, will be searched again to no avail. Aside from the fact that the directory of PDS USER1.LIBB will be searched twice (a rather benign event), the override above has effectively eliminated the third concatenation.

This technique will run into a problem only if the program lists the directory contents, in which case the directory of USER1.LIBB will be listed twice.

There is a another way to successfully override this concatenation:

```
//S2.LIBX   DD
//          DD
//          DD   UNIT=SYSDA,SPACE=(TRK,(1,,1)),DCB=USER1.LIBC
```

This method overrides the third concatenation with a new temporary PDS with the same DCB characteristics as the overridden PDS. This PDS has an empty directory, which is virtually equivalent to having no PDS at all. This temporary PDS will be deleted when the job terminates.

Requirement 2b: DD statement CNTL must be //CNTL DD *.

DD statement to be overridden:

```
//CNTL    DD    DSN=USER1.CTLIB(SRT1),DISP=SHR
```

Overriding DD statement:

```
//S2.CNTL   DD    *
```

Comments: Regardless of the contents of the parameter field of the overridden statement, none of its parameters will be used. DD * overrides them all.

Requirement 2c: In DD statement OUT4, the DCB parameter must be eliminated.

DD statement to be overridden:

```
//OUT4    DD    DSN=USER1.DBAK4,DISP=(,CATLG,DELETE),UNIT=SYSDA,
//              SPACE=(TRK,(200,50),RLSE),VOL=SER=TEST26,
//              DCB=(BLKSIZE=23400,LRECL=100,RECFM=FB)
```

Proposed overriding DD statement:

```
//S2.OUT4   DD    DCB=
```

This override will accomplish nothing. All other parameters can be nullified in this fashion, but not DCB. Each subparameter must be overridden individually.

```
//S2.OUT4    DD    DCB=(BLKSIZE=,LRECL=,RECFM=)
```

This peculiarity of the DCB is due to the fact that DCB is an exception to the rule (stated earlier) that a replacement overriding parameter must appear in its complete format. With DCB, supplying only those subparameters that need to be overridden without repeating all others that appear in the overridden statement, is acceptable.

Requirement 2d: In DD statement OUT5, DSCB model TEST.MODEL1 must be added to the DCB parameter.

DD statement to be overridden:

```
//OUT5    DD    DSN=USER1.DRK(+1),DISP=(,CATLG,DELETE),UNIT=SYSDA,
//              SPACE=(23440,(800,300),RLSE),VOL=SER=TEST99,
//              DCB=(BLKSIZE=23440,LRECL=80,RECFM=FB)
```

Overriding DD statement:

```
//S2.OUT5    DD    DCB=TEST.MODEL
```

Comments: This override will add the model DSCB to the DCB parameter. There is no need to repeat any of the other subparameters.

Requirement 2e: In DD statement OUT6, DSCB model TEST.MODEL must be eliminated from the DCB parameter. All other subparameters must remain intact.

DD statement to be overridden:

```
//OUT6    DD    DSN=USER1.DBAK6,DISP=(,CATLG,DELETE),UNIT=SYSDA,
//              SPACE=(CYL,(50,15)),
//              DCB=(TEST.MODEL,BLKSIZE=23400,LRECL=100,RECFM=FB)
```

Overriding DD statement:

```
//S2.OUT6    DD    DCB=
```

Comments: This override will remove the model DSCB to the DCB parameter. When overriding a DCB parameter that contains a model DSCB, unless the model is coded in the overriding DCB parameter, it will be lost. The remaining subparameters are unaffected.

Requirement 2f: In DD statement OUT7, the BUFNO subparameter must be eliminated from the DCB parameter. All other subparameters must remain intact.

DD statement to be overridden:

```
//OUT7    DD    DSN=USER1.DRL(+1),DISP=(,CATLG,DELETE),UNIT=SYSDA,
//              SPACE=(CYL,(30,10),RLSE),VOL=SER=TEST04,
//              DCB=(TEST.MODEL,BLKSIZE=23400,LRECL=100,RECFM=FB,
//              BUFNO=30)
```

Overriding DD statement:

```
//S2.OUT7   DD    DCB=(TEST.MODEL,BUFNO=)
```

Comments: This override will remove the BUFNO subparameter from the DCB. As explained earlier, the model DSCB must be repeated or it will be lost. The remaining subparameters are unaffected.

Requirement 2g: Dummy DD statement OUT8.

DD statement to be overridden:

```
//OUT8   DD   DSN=USER1.LIB3,DISP=SHR   USER1.LIB3 IS A PDS
```

Overriding DD statement:

```
//S2.OUT8   DD   UNIT=SYSDA,SPACE=(TRK,(1,,1),DCB=USER1.LIB3
```

Comments: A PDS cannot be dummied, as mentioned earlier. The same method as the last one used for requirement 2a will work here also. The PDS of this DD statement is overriden with a new temporary PDS with the same DCB characteristics as the overridden PDS. This PDS has an empty directory and that is virtually equivalent to DUMMY. This temporary PDS will be deleted when the job terminates.

12.11 EXECUTING A PROCEDURE MORE THAN ONCE

Procedures intended for single execution often cannot be executed more than once without causing problems. Consider a few examples of such procedures:

Example 1: Procedure SE1

```
//S1     EXEC  PGM=P1
//OUT    DD    DSN=USER1.DABAS,DISP=(,CATLG,DELETE),UNIT=SYSDA,
//             SPACE=(TRK,(200,50),RLSE),VOL=SER=TEST26,
//             DCB=(BLKSIZE=23400,LRECL=100,RECFM=FB)
//IN     DD    DSN=USER1.FERE,DISP=SHR
```

Clearly, this procedure cannot be executed twice. The second execution will encounter a "DUPLICATE NAME" JCL error, unless DSN in DD statement OUT is overridden with a different name or a step is added between the two executions to delete data set USER1.DABAS.

Example 2: Procedure SE2

```
//S1      EXEC   PGM=P2
//OUT     DD     SYSOUT=*
//IN      DD     DSN=USER1.FERX,DISP=(OLD,DELETE)
```

This procedure also cannot be executed twice. The second execution will encounter a "DATA SET NOT FOUND" JCL error, unless DSN in DD statement IN is overridden with a different name.

Some procedures can be executed more than once, even though they may have been initially intended for a single execution. Here is an example:

Example 3: Procedure SE3

```
//S1      EXEC   PGM=COPY
//OUT     DD     DSN=&&TEMP,DISP=(,PASS),UNIT=SYSDA,SPACE=(TRK,(50,10)),
//               DCB=(BLKSIZE=23440,LRECL=80,RECFM=FB)
//S2      EXEC   PGM=PRINT,COND=(0,LT)
//INP     DD     DSN=&&TEMP,DISP=(OLD,DELETE)
//PRINT   DD     SYSOUT=*
```

Let this procedure be executed twice:

```
//PS1     EXEC   SE3
//S1.IN   DD     *
---- data ---

/*
//PS2     EXEC   SE3
//S1.IN   DD     *
---- data ---
/*
```

When a procedure is executed twice, the COND parameter should be carefully examined. There may be too much or too little control in the second execution.

Suppose that the two executions are independent of one another and a bad return code from the first execution should not affect the

12.12 SYMBOLIC PARAMETERS AND SYMBOLIC OVERRIDES

The techniques for overriding discussed thus far are unquestionably clumsy and produce even clumsier-looking output. An alternate way of overriding, known as *"symbolic,"* is also available. Symbolic overrides are relatively neater and easier.

Symbolic overrides can be used only when symbolic parameters have been coded inside the procedure. Syntactically, a symbolic parameter is a name preceded by an ampersand (&). It can be coded in place of any parameter, part of a parameter or several parameters in the parameter field of an EXEC, DD or OUTPUT statement. The user can substitute any desired expression or value in place of the symbolic parameter by using a symbolic override in the EXEC statement which invokes the procedure. Normally, symbolic parameters are coded in place of values which are likely to vary from one execution of the procedure to the next. Names which are valid EXEC parameters (i.e., REGION, TIME, COND, etc.) cannot be used as symbolic parameters.

A simple example can best demonstrate the use of a symbolic parameter. Figure 12.5 shows a simple procedure consisting of one step. It is expected that for different executions of the procedure the value of the PARM parameter will change. Rather than coding some value for PARM and later overriding it by coding PARM.S1=value, a symbolic parameter can be used to simplify overriding. PARM=&PEL is coded. When symbolic override PEL=FLD is coded in the EXEC statement which invokes the procedure, a substitution takes place. Figure 12.5 shows pictorially what happens. Whatever follows the "=" sign in the symbolic override (in Example 1, FLD) replaces the symbolic parameter &PEL. Result: PARM=FLD. It is a simple substitution performed at the user's request. The system performs the substitution without questioning if the result is correct. That is the user's responsibility. The resulting JCL appears in the job's output. For Example 1, the following message will appear:

```
IEF653I   SUBSTITUTION JCL - PGM=P1,PARM=FLD
```

In Example 2 of Figure 12.5, the symbolic override is coded as PEL='FLD,TIME=(5,10).' What follows the "=" sign, but without the apostrophes, replaces &PEL.

```
IEF653I   SUBSTITUTION JCL - PGM=P1,PARM=FLD,TIME=(5,10)
```

When coding symbolic overrides, a unique syntactical rule must be followed: If the value that follows the "=" sign contains anything other than alphabetic, numeric or national characters, the entire value must be enclosed in apostrophes. For this reason the apostrophes appear in the symbolic override of Example 2 in Figure 12.5. As mentioned before, the apostrophes are not included in the substitution. When coding symbolic overrides, the use of apostrophes is always acceptable, even if not needed.

There are a great number of ways to code a symbolic parameter that will result in the desired JCL after substitution takes place. For example, procedure SSP could be coded as:

```
//S1   EXEC   PGM=P1,&PR
```

The same result as in Example 1 of Figure 12.5 can be achieved by coding a symbolic override for &PR as follows:

```
//A   EXEC   SSP,PR='PARM=FLD'
```

Procedure SSP could even be coded as:

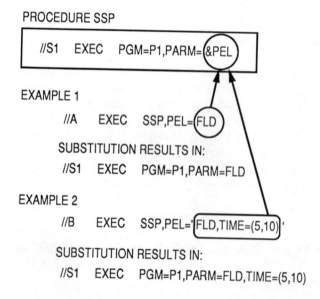

PROCEDURE SSP

```
//S1   EXEC   PGM=P1,PARM=&PEL
```

EXAMPLE 1

```
//A   EXEC   SSP,PEL=FLD
```

SUBSTITUTION RESULTS IN:
```
//S1   EXEC   PGM=P1,PARM=FLD
```

EXAMPLE 2

```
//B   EXEC   SSP,PEL='FLD,TIME=(5,10)'
```

SUBSTITUTION RESULTS IN:
```
//S1   EXEC   PGM=P1,PARM=FLD,TIME=(5,10)
```

Figure 12.5 Symbolic parameters and symbolic overrides.

```
//S1   EXEC   &PF
```

Yes, the entire operand field can be a symbolic parameter, but that is never a good idea. The same result can still be achieved by coding:

```
//A   EXEC   SSP,PF='PGM=P1,PARM=FLD'
```

Clearly, the last two methods are questionable at best. Since only the value of the PARM parameter is subject to variations, it and it alone should be a symbolic parameter. This is basically the philosophy regarding what should be and what should not be a symbolic parameter.

A symbolic parameter may require a delimiter. Consider procedure SSP:

```
//S1   EXEC   PGM=P1,PARM=&PEL
```

Assume the possible values that the PARM parameter can assume are ALD, BLD, CLD, etc. In other words, the last two characters (LD) remain the same while the first varies between A and Z. It would be desirable to code a symbolic parameter for the variable part of the value and code the rest inside the procedure as a constant. Coding procedure SSP as

```
//S1   EXEC   PGM=P1,PARM=&PELLD
```

will not work. Rather than adding the two characters LD at the end of the symbolic parameter as a constant, the spelling of the symbolic parameter is altered instead. To avoid this, a delimiter must be used. The period (.) represents such a delimiter which must be used when an alphabetic, numeric, or national character immediately follows a symbolic parameter. Every other character provides a natural delimiter for a symbolic parameter, making the use of the period unnecessary (but harmless).

Procedure SSP coded as

```
//S1   EXEC   PGM=P1,PARM=&PEL.LD
```

will work. Now the procedure can be invoked as follows:

```
//A   EXEC   SSP,PEL=F
```

In this case "F" replaces "&PEL." resulting in PARM=FLD. Note that the period is treated as part of the symbolic parameter: it will be included in the substitution and, as a result, disappear.

There are two facts that, if kept in mind, can make the use of the period easy:

Fact 1: When a period is found in a procedure at the end of a symbolic parameter, it will *always* be treated as a delimiter and it will disappear during substitution.

Fact 2: When coding a procedure, there is no need to agonize whether or not to code a period. It is always acceptable at the end of a symbolic parameter whether or not it is needed.

There are no exceptions to these two facts.

The use of a period as a symbolic parameter delimiter is often found in the DSN parameter. Consider procedure BLTX below:

```
//S1   EXEC  PGM=BL
//IN   DD    DSN=&HQ..INFILE,DISP=SHR
//OUT  DD    DSN=&HQ..OUTFILE,DISP=(,CATLG,DELETE),UNIT=TAPE,
//           DCB=(BLKSIZE=32700,LRECL=100,RECFM=FB)
```

The first period is a delimiter. The second is the period that separates the levels of a qualified data set name. When procedure BLTX is executed,

```
//PSK  EXEC  BLTX,HQ=PROD
```

the DSN for the IN and OUT DD statements become PROD.INFILE and PROD.OUTFILE respectively.

There is an interesting question, however. Why is the first period necessary as a delimiter? What follows the symbolic parameter &HQ is neither an alphabetic nor a numeric nor a national character. It is another period. Therefore, the delimiter period is not required. True! But note that if the first period were not coded, the one that is intended to separate the levels of the data set name would be assumed to be a delimiter and disappear during substitution, causing the names to become PRODINFILE and PRODOUTFILE.

Let procedure BLTX be coded with only one period in the DSN,

```
//S1   EXEC  PGM=BL
//IN   DD    DSN=&HQ.INFILE,DISP=SHR
```

```
//OUT DD    DSN=&HQ.OUTFILE,DISP=(,CATLG,DELETE),UNIT=TAPE,
//          DCB=(BLKSIZE=32700,LRECL=100,RECFM=FB)
```

and execute it as follows:

```
//PSK   EXEC  BLTX,HQ='PROD.'
```

Clearly, the resulting data set names for IN and OUT will be correct, PROD.INFILE and PROD.OUTFILE. Does it make any difference, then, which of the two versions of the procedure is used? The answer is yes! In the first approach, the symbolic override must be coded as HQ=PROD, and that's fairly simple. In the second approach, HQ='PROD.' must be coded, and that is far more difficult. One must keep in mind that a procedure is normally written only once, but it can be used thousands of times by many people. Therefore, ease of use is of the greatest importance. A minor inconvenience while writing the procedure is well worth it if it simplifies its use.

12.13 THE PROC STATEMENT

Thus far, symbolic overrides have been shown to be part of the EXEC statement invoking the procedure. It would be a serious problem if all symbolic overrides had to be coded every time the procedure was executed. The PROC statement eliminates this problem.

The purpose of the PROC statement is to contain symbolic override defaults. It is an optional statement but highly recommended if the procedure contains symbolic parameters. If coded, it must be the first statement in a procedure. When a procedure is executed, the system will substitute symbolic parameters using the symbolic overrides coded in the EXEC statement. For those symbolic overrides not found in the EXEC statement, the default symbolic overrides in the PROC statement will be used. If a symbolic override is not coded in either EXEC or PROC statement, the symbolic parameter receives no substitution. With the exception of DSN=&name (and possibly the PARM parameter), the "&" will always result in a syntactical JCL error. Figure 12.6 shows pictorially the use of symbolic overrides from both EXEC and PROC statements. The name in a PROC statement is optional.

The PROC statement is mandatory for in-stream procedures. This will be discussed later in Section 12.16 of this chapter.

PROCEDURE SWP

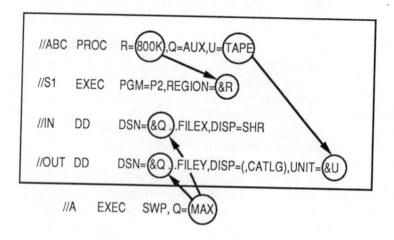

SUBSTITUTION RESULTS IN:

```
//S1    EXEC   PGM=P2,REGION=800K
//IN     DD     DSN=MAX.FILEX,DISP=SHR
//OUT   DD     DSN=MAX.FILEY,DISP=(,CATLG),UNIT=TAPE
```

Figure 12.6 The PROC statement.

12.14 RULES FOR SYMBOLIC OVERRIDING

In this section the rules governing symbolic parameters and symbolic overrides will be stated. Some of these rules have already been mentioned in previous sections.

1. A symbolic parameter is normally found inside a procedure. However, it is possible for a symbolic parameter to be coded in an overriding DD statement, as will be shown later in this section.
2. An EXEC statement keyword (such as TIME, REGION, etc.) cannot be used as a symbolic parameter.
3. A symbolic parameter which is immediately followed by an alphabetic, numeric, or national character ($, @, or #) must have a period at its end.
4. A symbolic override can be coded only once in an EXEC or only once in a PROC statement.

5. A symbolic parameter can be coded many times in a procedure. When substitution occurs, all of the occurrences will receive the same value.
6. When executing a procedure, the symbolic overrides coded in the EXEC statement (invoking the procedure) will be used.
7. If any needed symbolic overrides are not coded in the EXEC statement, those found in the PROC statement will be used.
8. If a symbolic parameter still remains unresolved, no substitution takes place.
9. When nothing must be substituted for a symbolic parameter, "symbolic-override=" must be coded in the EXEC or PROC statement. No blanks will appear in place of the symbolic parameter.
10. The sequence of symbolic overrides in either the EXEC or the PROC statement is not important.
11. A symbolic override in either the EXEC or PROC statement that has no corresponding symbolic parameter inside the procedure will result in a "SYMBOL NOT DEFINED" JCL error. In much older releases of MVS this message failed to identify which symbol was not defined, making the resolution of this problem very difficult. Later releases identify the symbol. It is doubtful that such an old release of MVS would be in use today.
12. When a symbolic override cannot produce the desired result, then a regular override must be used.
13. Symbolic overrides can be mixed with regular EXEC statement overrides in any way. However, the sequence rule for regular overrides is always in effect. If the symbolic overrides were to be removed, the remaining regular EXEC overrides must be in the proper sequence.
14. If a symbolic and a regular override conflict, the regular override always prevails. This holds for both EXEC and DD statement parameters.

Some of these rules require further explanation.
Procedure XYZ can be used for this purpose:

```
//P1    PROC   DATE='''12/31/1999''',XI=APP3,
//             SET=50,BLK=9040,SOUT='*'
//S1    EXEC   PGM=PROM,PARM=&DATE
//DD1   DD     DSN=&XI..SETA,DISP=SHR
//DD2   DD     DSN=&XI..SETB,DISP=(,CATLG,DELETE),UNIT=SYSDA,
//             SPACE=(TRK,(&PRIM,100),RLSE),
```

```
//          DCB=(BLKSIZE=&BLK,LRECL=80,RECFM=FB)
//PRT   DD  SYSOUT=&SOUT
//S2    EXEC PGM=PROX
```

Let the procedure be executed:

```
//USER1C  JOB   SR44,JONES,CLASS=R
//EMA     EXEC  XYZ,DATE='''5/12/1990''',TIME.S1=(1,30),
//              REG=800K,XI=DEV,PARM.S2=FORTA
//S1.DD2  DD    DSN=APP7.SETB
```

Regarding rules 11, 9, and 1

Default symbolic override SET=50 appears in the PROC statement, but there is no symbolic parameter &SET in the procedure. This is a "SYMBOL NOT DEFINED" JCL error (rule 11). Removing SET=50 from the PROC statement or adding &SET in the procedure would eliminate the error. In either case the procedure must be modified, which may be inconvenient or, based on security considerations, impossible.

The error can be corrected without modifying the procedure, by introducing the &SET symbolic parameter via an overriding DD statement:

```
//USER1C  JOB   SR44,JONES,CLASS=R
//EMA     EXEC  XYZ,DATE='''5/12/1990''',TIME.S1=(1,30),
//              REG=800K,XI=DEV,PARM.S2=FORTA,SET=
//S1.DD1  DD    DISP=SHR&SET
//S1.DD2  DD    DSN=APP7.SETB
```

The DISP parameter in DD1 is selected to contain the symbolic parameter &SET. Any parameter could have served the purpose. The overriding DD statement for DD1 causes DISP=SHR to be replaced with DISP=SHR&SET (see rule 1), thus eliminating the "SYMBOL NOT DEFINED" error.

"SET=" is added to the EXEC statement. This causes &SET to be replaced by nothing (see rule 9), resulting in DISP=SHR. Had "SET=" not been coded in the EXEC statement, the result would be DISP=SHR50 and a JCL error (SET=50 is the default in the PROC statement).

One of the most common causes of the "SYMBOL NOT DEFINED" error is removing or "commenting out" DD statements. Consider procedure XYZ again and assume that DD statement RPT is no longer needed. By updating the procedure this DD statement can be removed or, possibly, "commented out." This means that the DD statement is not really removed but made into a comment instead, by placing an asterisk (*) before the ddname:

```
//        PROC   DATE='''12/31/1999''',XI=APP3,
//               SET=50,BLK=9040,SOUT='*'
//S1       EXEC   PGM=PROM,PARM=&DATE
//DD1      DD     DSN=&XI..SETA,DISP=SHR
//DD2      DD     DSN=&XI..SETB,DISP=(,CATLG,DELETE),UNIT=SYSDA,
//               SPACE=(TRK,(&PRIM,100),RLSE),
//               DCB=(BLKSIZE=&BLK,LRECL=80,RECFM=FB)
//*PRT     DD     SYSOUT=&SOUT
//S2       EXEC   PGM=PROX
```

Since the system ignores comment statements, &SOUT is no longer present in the procedure.Unless the SOUT='*' symbolic override is also removed from the PROC statement, a "SYMBOL NOT DEFINED" JCL error will result. With a "commented out" statement, this error becomes more difficult to detect because &SOUT is still visible to the user. It is, of course, invisible to the system.

Regarding rules 12 and 14

Assume that in DD statements DD1 and DD2, DSN=DEV.SETA and DSN=APP7.SETB are needed, respectively. Symbolic override XI=DEV will generate a substitution for &XI, resulting in DSN=DEV.SETA for DD1 and DEV.SETB for DD2. A regular override is needed to provide the desired DSN for DD2 (see rule 12).

This, however, creates a conflict in the DSN parameter. The symbolic substitution will provide DSN=DEV.SETB, and the regular override DSN=APP7.SET8. The substitution will take place, but ultimately the regular override will prevail. The result: DSN=APP7.SETB (see rule 14). If it were not for this rule, sometimes it would impossible to override correctly. Note that the system fails to inform the user which of the two overrides prevails.

Regarding rule 10

Note that the sequence of symbolic overrides in the PROC as well as the EXEC statement have been given no particular sequence.

Regarding rule 8

Symbolic parameter &PRIM appears in the procedure (SPACE parameter of DD statement DD2). There is no symbolic override in either the PROC or the EXEC statement. No substitution will take place, resulting in SPACE=(TRK,(&PRIM,100),RLSE) and a syntactical JCL error.

Regarding rule 13

Note that the EXEC statement invoking the procedure contains symbolic as well as regular overrides. Their relative sequence is not important as long as the TIME.S1 override comes before the PARM.S2 override.

12.15 CHOOSING SYMBOLIC PARAMETERS

Many individuals coding procedures have the tendency to introduce an excessive number of symbolic parameters. This is counterproductive. When a procedure is being developed, the user should examine each parameter (EXEC and DD) and determine if the value of the parameter is likely to vary from one execution to the next. If so, then the value (or the part of the value which varies) should be a symbolic parameter. If not, the parameter should be coded without symbolic parameters. If this parameter must be overridden at some point, a regular override can always be used.

Here is an example of using a symbolic parameter appropriately: The amount of records being sorted in a step varies. The work files in the procedure should be coded as:

```
//SORTWK01   DD   UNIT=SYSDA,SPACE=(CYL,&SP)
//SORTWK02   DD   UNIT=SYSDA,SPACE=(CYL,&SP)
//SORTWK03   DD   UNIT=SYSDA,SPACE=(CYL,&SP)
```

The procedure below abuses symbolic parameters:

Procedure BET

```
//PS     PROC   REG=500K,PG=LET,NOUT='USER1.DSETB',NIN='USER1.DSETA'
//              DF1=',',DF2=CATLG,DF3=DELETE,UN=SYSDA,
//              D='(BLKSIZE=9040,LRECL=80,RECFM=FB)',V=PACK33,
//              TYP=CYL,PR=20,SEC=5,OPT=RLSE,DF4=SHR
```

```
//S1     EXEC   PGM=&PG,REGION=&REG
//OUT    DD     DSN=&NOUT,DISP=(&DF1,&DF2,&DF3),UNIT=&UN,
//              VOL=SER=&V,DCB=&D,SPACE=(&TYP,(&PR,&SEC),&OPT)
//IN     DD     DSN=&NIN,DISP=&DF4
```

This procedure contains an excessive number of symbolic parameters, many of which are not justifiable. This has two negative effects:

• Every time the procedure is executed, all symbolic parameters must be substituted for. This is overhead.
• The procedure is very difficult to work with, especially when it is viewed in proclib without the benefit of substitution JCL messages. Even though the symbolic override defaults are shown (PROC statement), too many symbolic parameters are detrimental to clarity and ease of use.

An analysis of which parameters in the procedure above are good candidates for symbolic parameter use (under ordinary circumstances) follows:

PGM — not a good candidate, programs seldom vary from one execution to the next: PGM=LET

REGION — not a good candidate, it seldom varies: REGION=500K

DSN — possibly a good candidate. Data set names sometimes vary. Normally, however, not all the levels of the name vary. DSN=USER1.&NOUT (if the high qualifier is always the same).

DISP — not a good candidate, DISP seldom changes. DISP=(,CATLG,DELETE)

UNIT — not a good candidate, UNIT seldom changes. UNIT=SYSDA

VOL — possibly a fair candidate. The volume may have to be changed to circumvent space problems.

DCB — possibly a good candidate, but probably not for all the DCB subparameters. BLKSIZE is the true variable in the DCB parameter, the others are usually not. Also, one of the reasons for using symbolic overrides is to get away from the clumsy nature of the other overrides. The symbolic override

D="(BLKSIZE=23440,LRECL=80,RECFM=FB)" is pretty clumsy.

DCB=(BLKSIZE=&BLK,LRECL=80,RECFM=FB) is much better.

SPACE — possibly a good candidate. If the data set has different space needs for different executions, the primary allocation will have to vary. Secondary allocation can vary to a lesser degree. The other symbolic parameters in SPACE are undesirable. SPACE=(CYL,(&PR,&SEC),RLSE)

DSN and DISP in DD statement IN — the same can be said about these parameters as for the same parameters in DD statement OUT. DSN=USER1.&NIN, DISP=SHR

The rewritten procedure BET makes a lot more sense:

```
//PS     PROC    NOUT=SETB,NIN=SETA,V=PACK33,
//               PR=20,SEC=5,BLK=9040
//S1     EXEC    PGM=LET,REGION=500K
//OUT    DD      DSN=USER1.&NOUT,DISP=(,CATLG,DELETE),UNIT=SYSDA,
//               VOL=SER=&V,DCB=(BLKSIZE=&BLK,LRECL=100,RECFM=FB),
//               SPACE=(CYL,(&PR,&SEC),RLSE)
//IN     DD      DSN=USER1.&NIN,DISP=SHR
```

12.16 IN-STREAM PROCEDURES

An in-stream procedure is a procedure which is part of the input stream. It is not a member of proclib. Consider the JCL below:

```
//USER1D JOB    1122,TAYLOR,CLASS=F
//PS     PROC   QQ=DEV1,V=PACK33,PR=20,SEC=5,BLK=9040
//S1     EXEC   PGM=LET,REGION=500K
//OUT    DD     DSN=&QQ..FILE2,DISP=(,CATLG,DELETE),UNIT=SYSDA,
//              VOL=SER=&V,DCB=(BLKSIZE=&BLK,LRECL=100,RECFM=FB),
//              SPACE=(CYL,(&PR,&SEC),RLSE)
//IN     DD     DSN=&QQ..FILE1,DISP=SHR
//S2     EXEC   PGM=GET,REGION=500K,COND=(0,LT)
//IN     DD     DSN=&QQ..FILE2,DISP=SHR
//PRNT   DD     SYSOUT=*
//              PEND
```

A new statement appears in this JCL: the PEND statement. It has a blank parameter field and no name (a name can be coded but has no useful function and is seldom used). Its only purpose is to delimit an in-stream procedure. A PROC statement also appears.

When the system finds a PROC statement while reading in a job, it saves it and goes to a special routine which reads and saves all following statements up to the PEND statement. All the saved statements are placed as a group in the job's region and given a name. This saved JCL is now an in-stream procedure and its name is the name of the PROC statement (PS, in this example). The contents of the saved statements are not checked for syntax. It is as if a temporary mini-proclib is created in memory and the in-stream procedure becomes a member. This in-stream procedure can now be executed later in the same job, the same way as a cataloged procedure.

```
//AA   EXEC   PS
```

The system recognizes the syntax of this statement and knows that a procedure PS is to be executed. But before it goes to search any of the procedure libraries, it checks for an in-stream procedure by that name saved in memory. If found, it will execute it and not go to the procedure libraries. If not found, the procedure libraries will be searched. The execution will be the same regardless where the procedure came from.

In-stream and cataloged procedures work 100% identically. All the rules discussed for cataloged procedures apply to in-stream procedures as well and will not be repeated. There are some trivial differences between the two:

- A cataloged procedure is a member of a proclib and remains there until it is deleted. An in-stream procedure is part of a job's input stream and exists only for the duration of the job. When the job terminates, it disappears, along with the job's memory.
- The PROC statement in a cataloged procedure is optional and its name is also optional. Its only function is to contain default symbolic overrides. The PROC statement in an in-stream procedure is mandatory and serves two functions: (a) it signals the beginning of the in-stream procedure and (b) it contains default symbolic overrides. Its name is also mandatory.
- The PEND statement cannot be coded in a cataloged procedure. The PEND statement must be coded in an in-stream procedure to provide a delimiter.
- The X/ and XX notations found in the output when executing and overriding cataloged procedures become +/ and ++ for in-stream procedures.

The differences stated above do not affect executing and overriding. Both are the same for cataloged and in-stream procedures.

12.17 RULES FOR IN-STREAM PROCEDURES

As mentioned before, any rules that exist for cataloged procedures apply to in-stream procedures with no differences. Some rules apply only to in-stream procedures:

382 Expert MVS/XA JCL

- The EXEC statement that executes an in-stream procedure must be coded after the procedure has been defined.
- A maximum of 15 in-stream procedures can be coded in a job. All must begin with a PROC statement and end with a PEND statement.
- An in-stream procedure can be executed once or many times and it can be combined with the execution of cataloged procedures and independent steps in any way desired, as long as the total number of steps in the job does not exceed 255. Or it may not be executed at all.
- An in-stream procedure cannot be placed before the JOB statement (neither can any other JCL statement). Few other restrictions exist regarding placement:
  - An in-stream procedure cannot be placed in the middle of a continuation of any statement. For example,

```
//S1     EXEC  PGM=U7
//IN     DD    DSN=USER1.TESTFL,
//DAE    PROC  - - - -
//      - - - - - - - - - - - -
//      - - - - - - - - - - - -
//      - - - - - - - - - - - -
//       PEND
//              DISP=SHR
```

is an invalid placement for in-stream procedure DAE. One may ask, of course, why anyone in his right mind would want to place an in-stream procedure in such a strange place.
  - An in-stream procedure cannot be placed in the middle of sysin data. This placement is even stranger than the previous one.

Anywhere else, placement of an in-stream procedure is valid. It is, however, advisable to place in-stream procedures in easy-to-find places, such as right after the JOB statement, to avoid possible confusion.

Consider the placement of the in-stream procedure below:

```
//S1     EXEC  PGM=U7
//IN1    DD    DSN=USER1.TESTFL,DISP=SHR
//DAE    PROC  - - - -
//      - - - - - - - - - - - -
//      - - - - - - - - - - - -
//      - - - - - - - - - - - -
//       PEND
//IN2    DD    DSN=USER1.TRANFIL,DISP=SHR
```

This is a valid placement, but it will tend to confuse everyone except the one who coded it. Causing unnecessary confusion must be discouraged.

12.18 USING IN-STREAM PROCEDURES

One of the main purposes of in-stream procedures is to use them as testing tools. It is easier to test JCL, which will ultimately go into production, using in-stream as opposed to cataloged procedures. Take some JCL in testing, using an in-stream procedure:

```
//DEVA     JOB   1122,TEST,CLASS=T
//PPERS    PROC  MSG='*',Q=PROD,BLK=20000,DATE='''XX/XX/XXXX'''
//S1       EXEC  PGM=PER1,PARM=&DATE
//IN1      DD    DSN=&Q..DAILY(0),DISP=OLD
//OUT1     DD    DSN=&Q..DAILY(+1),DISP=(,CATLG,DELETE),
//               UNIT=CART,VOL=(RETAIN),
//               DCB=(MODELGDG,BLKSIZE=&BLK,LRECL=80,RECFM=FB)
//TRAN     DD    DSN=&Q..DTRANFIL,DISP=SHR
//STEPLIB  DD    DSN=&Q..LOADLIB,DISP=SHR
//S2       EXEC  PGM=PER2,COND=(4,LT)
//IN       DD    DSN=&Q..DAILY(+1),DISP=OLD
//PERORT   DD    SYSOUT=&MSG
//         PEND
//STEPLIB  DD    DSN=&Q..LOADLIB,DISP=SHR
//EX1      EXEC  PPERS,DATE='''09/30/89''',Q=DEVA
//S2.CD    DD    *
```

Assume that testing is complete and the JCL will become production. The migration process is simple:

1. Take the in-stream procedure away from the input stream, remove the PEND statement and make it a member of the appropriate production proclib, giving it the same name as the PROC statement, PPERS.
2. Take the remaining JCL, change any parameters required for production (i.e., remove Q=DEVA from the EXEC statement, thus defaulting to Q=PROD), and make it a member of the production JCL library.

The job is now ready to run under production.

In-stream procedures can also be convenient when a set of JCL must be executed many times in only one job. Consider the following scenario:

The IEBGENER utility must be used to copy 10 cataloged disk data sets named OPS.FILE1, OPS.FILE2, OPS.FILE3, etc., to data sets on tape, named OPS.FILEA, OPS.FILEB, OPS.FILEC, etc., each tape data set residing on a different volume.

```
//COPYJOB   JOB    FJ55,OPS,CLASS=O
//COPY      PROC   DN=1,TN=A
//GEN       EXEC   PGM=IEBGENER,COND=(4,LT)
//SYSPRINT  DD     SYSOUT=*
//SYSIN     DD     DUMMY
//SYSUT1    DD     DSN=OPS.FILE&DN,DISP=SHR
//SYSUT2    DD     DSN=OPS.FILE&TN,DISP=(,CATLG,DELETE),UNIT=TAPE
//          PEND
//S1        EXEC   COPY              DN=1,TN=A ARE DEFAULTS
//S2        EXEC   COPY,DN=2,TN=B
//S3        EXEC   COPY,DN=3,TN=C   .     .     .     .     .
     .          .     .     .     .
     .          .     .     .     .     .
//S10       EXEC   COPY,DN=10,TN=J
```

In-stream procedures can be very valuable in an emergency. Suppose that a job in production,

```
//PROD1E   JOB    PP34,'DAILY REPORT',CLASS=P
//E113     EXEC   PS113
```

executes procedure PS113, which contains a syntactical JCL error,

```
//PS113    PROC   QQ=PROD,V=PROD14,PR=20,SEC=5,BLK=23440
//S1       EXEC   PGM=LET,REGION=500K
//OUT      DD     DSN=&QQ..FILE2,DISP=(,CATLG,DELETE),UNIT=SYSDA,
//                VOL=SER=&V,DCB=(BLKSIZE=&BLK,LRECL=100,RECFM=FB),
//                SPACE=(CYL,(&PR,&SEC),RLSE)
//IN       DD     DSN=&QQ..FILE1,DISP=SHR
//S2       EXEC   PGM=GET,REGION=500K,COND=(0,LT)
//IN       DD     DSN=&QQ..FILE2,DISP=SHR
//PRNT     DD     SYSOU=*
```

SYSOU=* is a misspelled version of SYSOUT=*. Syntactical JCL errors cannot be corrected by overriding. The procedure must be

modified, but suppose the person with authority to modify the protected production proclib is unavailable. Using in-stream procedures,
the problem can be resolved:

1. Copy the JCL from the production JCL library to a member of
   a nonprotected library.
2. Copy the contents of procedure PS113, inserting them between
   the JOB and EXEC statements of the member created in 1. A
   proclib is never protected against reading, only writing.
3. Insert a "// PEND" statement after the last statement of the
   copied procedure.
4. Correct the syntactical error. The member resides in a nonprotected library.
5. Submit this member for execution.

13

Utilities and IDCAMS

MVS/XA comes with a number of programs which are intended to perform some very common non-VSAM functions. These programs are known as utilities, and they are part of Data Facility Product (DFP).

Most of the utilities were developed at the same time as the original version of the operating system in the mid-1960s and, through the years, many of them have become obsolete or semi-obsolete.

This chapter does not profess to cover all the functions of all utilities (the IBM utilities manual is over 400 pages). It intends to show mostly examples of those utilities still in use and, from these utilities, the functions that are likely to be used in a real environment. As with the rest of the book, functions with little or no practical use will not be discussed.

The following utilities are still in use and can be constructively used in today's environment:

- IEBGENER
- IEHPROGM
- IEBCOPY
- IEBPTPCH
- IEHLIST

IDCAMS, or Access Method Services, is a program developed by IBM to provide for VSAM the kind of services provided by JCL and utilities for non-VSAM and much more. IDCAMS, however, can also perform some very important non-VSAM functions that supplement and often parallel those of JCL and utilities. This chapter will focus on the non-VSAM capabilities of IDCAMS.

A few examples of IDCAMS in a VSAM environment will also be discussed.

13.1 JCL FOR UTILITIES

Utilities are divided into two broad categories: IEB and IEH utilities. IEB utilities normally deal with ordinary data sets. IEH utilities normally deal with system data sets (i.e., the VTOC, the catalog and PDS directories).

The typical JCL for an IEB-type utility is:

```
//IEBUT     EXEC  PGM=utility
//SYSPRINT  DD    message data set, usually sysout
//SYSIN     DD    control information for the utility
//SYSUT1    DD    input data set
//SYSUT2    DD    output data set
```

Note: The above does not apply to the IEBCOPY utility.
The typical JCL for an IEH-type utility is:

```
//IEHUT     EXEC  PGM=utility
//SYSPRINT  DD    message data set, usually sysout
//SYSIN     DD    control information for the utility
//ddname    DD    UNIT=device,VOL=SER=volser,DISP=OLD
//ddname    DD    UNIT=device,VOL=SER=volser,DISP=OLD
```

The last two DD statements are unusual and can only be used by utilities or comparable vendor-written software packages. Rather than defining a data set, as an ordinary DD statement does, they define a volume, permitting the utility to perform many operations to different data sets on the volume without requiring a separate DD statement for every data set. The spelling of the ddname in such statements is arbitrary.

```
//D1    DD    UNIT=SYSDA,VOL=SER=PACK42,DISP=OLD
```

All utilities reside in SYS1.LINKLIB, a fact which makes the use of JOBLIB or STEPLIB unnecessary.

All utilities issue return codes with the following meanings:

0 — successful completion

4 — warning, usually benign

8, 12 and 16 — all bad return codes

13.2 UTILITY CONTROL STATEMENT SYNTAX

All utilities during execution open and read the data set described in DD statement SYSIN. Its purpose is to contain control statements which tell the utility what action to take. The SYSIN DD statement will normally appear in one of two formats:

```
//SYSIN DD *
-- control statements --
/*
```

```
//SYSIN DD DSN=TEST.CTLLIB(UT5),DISP=SHR
```

The first of the two is typically used in a testing environment, the other in a production environment. UT5 is a member containing utility control statements.

A utility control statement has the following format:

[label] operation parameter field

The syntactical rules are:

- A label is available but has no practical value and is virtually never used. Without a label, the operation must begin with position 2 or beyond. A label, if used, must begin in position 1 and it must be followed by at least one blank. A label has the same syntax as a "name" in JCL.
- The operation must be followed by at least one blank.
- The operation field consists of parameters which must be separated by commas. Imbedded blanks are not permitted unless found within apostrophes.
- To continue a utility control statement, the last valid character of the line must be a comma and a nonblank character must be coded in position 72 (some utilities do not require this). Coding on the continuation line must begin at position 16. There is no limit to the number of continuations.

• The parameters of a utility control statement are never positional.

This syntax is clearly an imitation of JCL syntax with some differences. It may be of historical interest to note that the same rules applied to the original version of JCL. These rules were later simplified for JCL. Utilities did not follow suit. Example:

```
                                                          <-- pos 72
CATLG DSNAME=USER1.FILD,                                  X
              VOL=3380=PACK44
     pos 16-->
```

13.3 THE IEBGENER UTILITY

Despite the fact that the IEBGENER utility can perform many functions, it is practically always used to perform a straight sequential copy operation. When the utility is given no control statements (//SYSIN DD DUMMY), it copies the data set from DD statement SYSUT1 to the data set in SYSUT2.

BLKSIZE, LRECL, and RECFM are not hard-coded in either of the DCBs corresponding to SYSUT1 or SYSUT2.

Example 1:

```
//GEN1       EXEC   PGM=IEBGENER
//SYSPRINT   DD     SYSOUT=*
//SYSIN      DD     DUMMY
//SYSUT1     DD     DSN=XSITE.NLSET,DISP=OLD,UNIT=TAPE,LABEL=(,NL)
//                  VOL=SER=000367,DCB=(BLKSIZE=4000,LRECL=100,RECFM=FB)
//SYSUT2     DD     DSN=USER1.DFILE,DISP=(,CATLG,DELETE),
//                  SPACE=(CYL,(20,5),RLSE),UNIT=SYSDA,
//                  DCB=(BLKSIZE=23400,LRECL=100,RECFM=FB)
```

In this example, a nonlabeled tape data set is copied to a new disk data set and reblocked in the process. When DUMMY is used in the SYSIN DD statement, the LRECL and RECFM of SYSUT2 must be the same as SYSUT1. The BLKSIZE can be different.

The IEBGENER utility can be called upon to perform a valuable service for the user: If the SYSUT2 DD statement contains no DCB parameter, it will be assigned the same DCB attributes as SYSUT1. A warning message will appear in SYSPRINT to indicate this. If the SYSUT2 DD statement, however, contains a DCB parameter not containing all three subparameters, LRECL, RECFM and BLKSIZE, strange results can occur. For example, assume that SYSUT2 contains DCB=BLKSIZE=23400. The copying operation will be performed but the output data set will have the following attributes: BLKSIZE=23400, LRECL=0, RECFM=U. Rather than copying the LRECL and RECFM from SYSUT1 the utility assumes the default RECFM=U. LRECL=0 is a natural consequence of RECFM=U.

Interestingly, the utility will issue a return code of 0, denoting successful execution. The user may have problems using the output data set with RECFM=U, and a return code of 0 seems inappropriate.

Figure 13.1 shows what IEBGENER will do with various combinations of the DCB parameter in SYSUT2. All but one of the partial combinations of the three DCB subparameters in SYSUT2 give bad or questionable results.

IF SYSUT2 CONTAINS			SYSUT2 WILL USE THE FOLLOWING DCB ATTRIBUTES	WILL IEBGENER WORK?
BLKSIZE	LRECL	RECFM**		
NO	NO	NO	All attributes copied from SYSUT1	YES
YES	YES	YES	As specified in the DCB parameter	YES
YES	NO	NO	Specified BLKSIZE. LRECL=0, RECFM=U	NO*
NO	YES	NO	BLKSIZE=10, LRECL=5, RECFM=U	NO - RC = 12
NO	NO	YES	Specified RECFM. BLKSIZE=10, LRECL=5	NO - RC = 12
YES	YES	NO	Specified BLKSIZE & LRECL. RECFM=U	NO*
YES	NO	YES	Specified BLKSIZE & RECFM. LRECL copied from SYSUT1	YES
NO	YES	YES	Specified RECFM. BLKSIZE=10, LRECL=5	NO - RC = 12

* IEBGENER will copy with RC=0, but output data set will have RECFM of U.
** The RECFM of the input data set (SYSUT1) is assumed to be FB.

Figure 13.1 The DCB of SYSUT2 in IEBGENER. Note: It is assumed that LRECL for SYSUT1 and SYSUT2 is the same when IEBGENER works. //SYSIN DD DUMMY is assumed.

It is, therefore, strongly recommended that, when using the
IEBGENER utility, all or none of the three DCB subparameters be
coded.

Example 2:

```
//GEN2      EXEC  PGM=IEBGENER
//SYSPRINT  DD    SYSOUT=*
//SYSIN     DD    DUMMY
//SYSUT1    DD    *
- data -
/*
//SYSUT2    DD    DSN=USER1.TFILE,DISP=(,CATLG,DELETE),UNIT=TAPE,
//                DCB=(BLKSIZE=32720,LRECL=80,RECFM=FB)
```

In this example, all three of the DCB subparameters are coded. If
none were, the output BLKSIZE would be 80. Sysin data appears to
be using a blocksize of 80, when in reality it is much higher. In view
of the detrimental effect of a small blocksize, the DCB parameter
should be coded with all three of the subparameters when SYSUT1
describes sysin data.

Example 3:

```
//GEN3      EXEC  PGM=IEBGENER
//SYSPRINT  DD    SYSOUT=*
//SYSIN     DD    DUMMY
//SYSUT1    DD    DSN=USER1.AFILE,DISP=OLD
//SYSUT2    DD    SYSOUT=*
```

In this example, no DCB parameter is coded in either SYSUT1 or
SYSUT2. This is perfectly normal and desirable. In SYSUT1 all
needed DCB attributes will come from the data set's standard label.
In SYSUT2, DCB attributes from SYSUT1 will be assigned, and they
are likely to be correct, especially in reference to RECFM=FB as opposed to RECFM=FBA, which can have a serious effect on printing.

Example 4:

```
//GEN4      EXEC  PGM=IEBGENER
//SYSPRINT  DD    SYSOUT=*
//SYSUT1    DD    DSN=USER1.F22,DISP=SHR
//*        SYSUT1 DCB: BLKSIZE=15000, LRECL=120, RECFM=FB
//SYSUT2    DD    DSN=USER1.REFMT,DISP=(,CATLG,DELETE),
//                SPACE=(CYL,(40,10),RLSE),UNIT=SYSDA,
//                DCB=(BLKSIZE=23440,LRECL=80,RECFM=FB)
```

```
//SYSIN     DD    *
     GENERATE  MAXFLDS=2
     RECORD  FIELD=(30,1,,51),FIELD=(50,51,,1)
/*
```

This example demonstrates some of the rarely used features of IEBGENER. The records of the input data set are reduced in size with some of the fields rearranged.

Control statements are used in this case. The GENERATE statement must contain the MAXFLDS parameter to identify that the FIELD parameter will be used twice.

The first FIELD parameter of the RECORD statement requests that 30 bytes beginning in position 1 of the input record be placed, without any conversion (that's the extra comma), in position 51 of the output record.

The second FIELD parameter of the RECORD statement requests that 50 bytes beginning in position 51 of the input record be placed, without any conversion, in position 1 of the output record.

Figure 13.2 shows the results pictorially. The DCB parameter must be coded in SYSUT2 since it is different from that of SYSUT1.

13.4 THE IEHPROGM UTILITY

The IEHPROGM utility is a semi-obsolete utility. With the exception of the BLGD/DLTX control statements, all of its other functions can be performed (in most cases better) by some other facility.

Although using this utility will not be recommended in the majority of cases, several of its functions will be mentioned in this section. The utility is still in use, and it is likely to be found in older production jobs.

The main functions of the utility are to catalog, uncatalog, delete, and rename data sets, delete and rename members of a PDS and

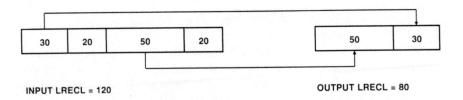

INPUT LRECL = 120   OUTPUT LRECL = 80

Figure 13.2 IEBGENER example.

build a GDG base (index) the last function only if CVOL catalogs are in use.

Example 1:

```
//CATU      EXEC   PGM=IEHPROGM
//SYSPRINT  DD     SYSOUT=*
//SYSIN     DD     *
  CATLG    DSNAME=USER1.FSET,VOL=SYSDA=PACK32
  CATLG    DSNAME=USER1.TAP1,VOL=TAPE=(002365,1,000153,1)
  UNCATLG  DSNAME=USER1.KSET
/*
```

The first two control statements catalog data sets USER1.FSET and USER1.TAP1. Usually data sets are cataloged via JCL by using DISP=(,CATLG). The IEHPROGM utility can be used to catalog a data set which exists but, for some reason, is not cataloged.

Several other available facilities can accomplish the same goal: JCL, IDCAMS, TSO, and ISPF, as discussed in Section 6.6 of Chapter 6. IEHPROGM is simply one of several ways to provide a catalog entry for an existing noncataloged data set, and, as will be seen, not the best one.

When using IEHPROGM to catalog a data set, a number of considerations should be kept in mind:

- If the wrong name is supplied in DSNAME, the utility will catalog it. It simply does not verify that the data set resides on the specified volume.
- If the wrong volume serial is supplied in the VOL parameter, again the data set will be cataloged whether or not the wrong volume exists.
- If the wrong device type is supplied in the VOL parameter, again the data set will be cataloged provided that the device specified is a valid one. The validity of the device is the only item the utility checks (but it does not check if it is the appropriate device for the volume).
- The use of a generated unit name (i.e., SYSDA or TAPE) in the VOL parameter can cause a problem. When cataloging via JCL, a parameter like UNIT=SYSDA or UNIT=TAPE will never cause a problem. The allocation routines (see Figure 1.7) for disk and the open routines for tape determine what type of device the allocated volume resides on and the catalog entry will eventually contain not SYSDA, but the exact device type, such as 3380 or 3480. The

IEHPROGM utility, however, has nothing comparable to the Allocation or open routines, and places a notation indicative of "SYSDA" or "TAPE" in the catalog entry. Upon reconfiguration, such entries can become invalid. If, therefore, IEHPROGM is used to provide an entry in the catalog, it is recommended that a generic name (i.e., 3380) be used in the VOL parameter as opposed to a generated name (i.e., SYSDA).

```
CATLG     DSNAME=USER1.FSET,VOL=3380=PACK32
CATLG     DSNAME=USER1.TAP1,VOL=3480=(002365,1,000153,1)
```

Clearly, this is a dangerous facility for cataloging, and great care must be exercised when using it. Note that no tape device will be allocated in order to catalog a tape data set. This fact may make IEHPROGM relatively attractive when existing tape data sets must be cataloged. Cataloging through JCL will always result in allocating a tape drive, and that, under certain conditions, may be undesirable.

Note that the danger in using a generated unit name exists only for the CATLG function. VOL=SYSDA=volser can be safely used with all other functions of IEHPROGM.

The second control statement catalogs a multivolume tape data set. The VOL parameter, VOL=3480=(002365,1,000153,1), identifies the two volume serials, each followed by the sequence number of the data set on the volume. Both sequence numbers are 1. Interestingly, VOL=3480=(002365,1,000153,2) will also work. If the tape data set to be cataloged resides on one volume, the sequence number need not be coded, unless the sequence of the data set is higher than one:

```
CATLG     DSNAME=USER1.TAP2,VOL=3400-5=000294        if it is data set #1
CATLG     DSNAME=USER1.TAP2,VOL=3480-5=(001961,2)    if it is data set #2
```

When cataloging a generation of a GDG, the absolute name must be used:

```
CATLG     DSNAME=PROD.TRANSF.G0125V00,VOL=3380=PROD42
```

Coding a relative name, such as DSNAME=PROD.TRANSF(-1), will result in a syntactical error.

The third control statement uncatalogs a data set. This function works fine without any peculiarities or dangers. If the data set is not cataloged, the operation will fail and benign return code of four will be issued.

IEHPROGM can add or remove catalog entries in CVOL, VSAM, or ICF catalogs.

Example 2:

```
//DELR       EXEC  PGM=IEHPROGM
//SYSPRINT   DD    SYSOUT=*
//D1         DD    UNIT=SYSDA,VOL=SER=PACK00,DISP=OLD
//D2         DD    UNIT=SYSDA,VOL=SER=PACK04,DISP=OLD
//D3         DD    UNIT=SYSDA,VOL=SER=PACK17,DISP=OLD
//SYSIN      DD    *
   SCRATCH   DSNAME=USER1.BSET,VOL=SYSDA=PACK00
   SCRATCH   DSNAME=USER1.CSET,VOL=SYSDA=PACK17,PURGE
   SCRATCH   DSNAME=USER1.PDS1,VOL=SYSDA=PACK00,MEMBER=X12
   RENAME    DSNAME=USER1.YSET,VOL=SYSDA=PACK04,NEWNAME=USER1.FABE
   RENAME    DSNAME=USER1.PDS2,VOL=SYSDA=PACK17,NEWNAME=CAT,       C
             MEMBER=DOG
/*
```

The first control statement deletes a data set. Several handicaps can be noted in this operation:

- The VOL parameter, identifying the volume and unit, is required. The catalog cannot be used to locate the data set to be scratched.
- A DD statement describing the volume where the data set resides must be included in the step:

```
//D1         DD    UNIT=SYSDA,VOL=SER=PACK00,DISP=OLD
```

If it is not, the operation fails.
- The SCRATCH operation only deletes the data set. It does not uncatalog it. If both are required, as is practically always the case, two control statements must be supplied:

```
SCRATCH   DSNAME=USER1.BSET,VOL=SYSDA=PACK00
UNCATLG   DSNAME=USER1.BSET
```

The second control statement deletes an unexpired disk data set by including the parameter PURGE. If PURGE is not coded, an unexpired data set will not be deleted. Expiration dates are seldom used with disk data sets. A DD statement describing the volume containing the data set to be deleted must be included in the step.

Such a DD statement is necessary fo all SCRATCH, and RENAME operations, but not for CATLG, UNCATLG, BLDG, and DLTX.

The third control statement deletes a member of a PDS (something that cannot be done through the DISP parameter in JCL). Note that if the MEMBER parameter is accidentally omitted, the entire data set will be deleted.

The fourth control statement renames a data set. The data set will be renamed in the VTOC but not in the catalog. To accomplish both, three control statements must be supplied:

```
RENAME    DSNAME=USER1.YSET,VOL=SYSDA=PACK04,NEWNAME=USER1.FABE
UNCATLG   DSNAME=USER1.YSET
CATLG     DSNAME=USER1.FABE,VOL=3380=PACK04
```

The fifth control statement renames a member of a PDS (in this case from DOG to CAT). Note that if the MEMBER parameter is accidentally omitted, the entire data set will be renamed.

Example 3:

```
//DIB       EXEC  PGM=IEHPROGM
//SYSPRINT  DD    SYSOUT=*
//SYSIN     DD    *
  BLDG      INDEX=PROD.DAILY,ENTRIES=8,DELETE
  DLTX      INDEX=PROD.WEEKLY
/*
```

The first control statement builds a GDG base in a CVOL catalog. This is prerequisite to using a DD statement with DSN=PROD.DAILY(+1) and DISP=(,CATLG).

ENTRIES=8 indicates that when the total number of generations exceeds eight, the oldest generation will be uncataloged. DELETE indicates that when the oldest generation is uncataloged, it will also be deleted. If not coded, the uncataloged generations will not be deleted. DELETE is meaningful only for disk generations.

The second control statement deletes a GDG base in a CVOL catalog. Before this operation can be performed, all generations of this GDG must be uncataloged.

Neither BLDG nor DLTX will work in VSAM or ICF catalogs. For those catalogs, IDCAMS must be used (see Section 13.8.4 later in this chapter).

Neither the CATLG nor the UNCATLG nor the SCRATCH control statements can identify a GDG generation by a relative name. Absolute names must be used:

```
SCRATCH   DSNAME=PROD.WEEKLY.G0014V00,VOL=SYSDA=PROD32
```

Coding a relative name, such as DSNAME=PROD.WEEKLY(0), will result in a syntactical error.

13.5 THE IEBCOPY UTILITY

IEBCOPY is not a typical IEB-type utility. It was rewritten in the early 1970s, acquiring a format which is unique among ordinary utilities but imitated by more sophisticated software, such as IDCAMS and DFDSS. Its control statements, rather than referring to data set names, refer to ddnames. Also, rather than performing a single function during one execution (IEBGENER, for example, can copy only one data set in one execution), IEBCOPY can perform multiple functions dealing with many data sets.

The IEBCOPY utility deals almost exclusively with partitioned data sets. It is intended to perform complete or partial copy operations from one or more PDSs to another PDS. The utility can also unload a PDS to tape and, using the unloaded tape data set as input, load the PDS back to disk. IEBCOPY can also *compress* a PDS.

Example:

```
//COPY        EXEC  PGM=IEBCOPY
//SYSPRINT    DD    SYSOUT=*
//SYSUT3      DD    UNIT=SYSDA,SPACE=(TRK,(2,1))
//SYSUT4      DD    UNIT=SYSDA,SPACE=(TRK,(2,1))
//LIB1        DD    DSN=USER1.LIBA,DISP=SHR
//LIB2        DD    DSN=USER1.LIBB,DISP=(,CATLG,DELETE),
//                  UNIT=SYSDA,SPACE=(CYL,(25,10,40)),VOL=SER=TEST14,
//                  DCB=(BLKSIZE=23440,LRECL=80,RECFM=FB)
//LIB3        DD    DSN=USER1.LIBC,DISP=OLD
//LIB4        DD    DSN=USER1.LIBD,DISP=OLD
//TAP1        DD    DSN=USER1.TDSX,DISP=(,CATLG,DELETE),UNIT=TAPE
//LIB5        DD    DSN=USER1.LIBE,DISP=(,CATLG,DELETE),
//                  UNIT=SYSDA,SPACE=(CYL,(10,5,20))
//SYSIN       DD    *
  COPY     INDD=LIB1,OUTDD=LIB3        ABBR:  C  I=LIB1,O=LIB3
  SELECT   MEMBER=(CAT,DOG,SPELL)      ABBR:  S  M=(CAT,DOG,SPELL)
  COPY     INDD=LIB1,O=LIB4
  EXCLUDE  MEMBER=(FELT,TIK,BOLT)      ABBR:  E  M=(FELT,TIK,BOLT)
  COPY     INDD=LIB1,OUTDD=LIB2
  COPY     INDD=LIB4,OUTDD=LIB4
  COPY     INDD=LIB3,OUTDD=TAP1
  COPY     INDD=TAP1,OUTDD=LIB5
```

```
EXCLUDE MEMBER=(DEMO)
COPY    OUTDDD=LIB2,INDD=(LIB3,LIB4)
COPY    OUTDDD=LIB4,INDD=((LIB3,R))
COPY    INDD=LIB1,OUTDD=LIB4
SELECT  MEMBER=(RX1,(RX2,RX3),(RX4,RX5,R),(RX6,,R))
/*
```

DD statements SYSUT3 and SYSUT4 are called "spill" data sets. They will be needed only if the virtual storage provided by the RE-GION parameter is not large enough to satisfy directory-related operations. They are rarely needed, but it is a good idea to always code them, just in case. They require a very small amount of disk space (a couple of tracks will do).

DD statements LIB1 through LIB5 and TAP1 describe data sets that will be used by the utility. The spelling of the ddnames is arbitrary. However, the spelling must be matched later in the control statements.

The first two control statements will be used together. This happens when the COPY statement is followed by a SELECT or EX-CLUDE statement.

```
COPY    INDD=LIB1,OUTDD=LIB3
SELECT  MEMBER=(CAT,DOG,SPELL)
```

Members CAT, DOG, and SPELL from the library described in DD statement LIB1, USER1.LIBA, will be copied to the library described in DD statement LIB3, USER1.LIBC. If any of the members to be copied already exist in the the receiving library, it will not be copied.

The next two control statements will also be used together because the COPY statement is followed by an EXCLUDE statement.

```
COPY    INDD=LIB1,O=LIB4
EXCLUDE MEMBER=(FELT,TIK,BOLT)
```

All members, except FELT, TIK, and BOLT, from the library described in DD statement LIB1, USER1.LIBA will be copied to the library described in DD statement LIB4, USER1.LIBD. If any of the members to be copied already exist in the the receiving library, it will not be copied.

The next control statement will be used alone because it is followed by neither a SELECT nor an EXCLUDE statement.

```
COPY    INDD=LIB1,OUTDD=LIB2
```

All members from the library described in DD statement LIB1, USER1.LIBA will be copied to the library described in DD statement LIB2, USER1.LIBB. Duplicate members will not be copied.

The next control statement compresses the library described in DD statement LIB4, USER1.LIBD:

```
COPY    INDD=LIB4,OUTDD=LIB4
```

All unusable space within the library, resulting from deleting or replacing members, will be reclaimed. A COPY control statement performing a compress operation cannot be followed by a SELECT or an EXCLUDE control statement. If the system fails or the job is cancelled during a compress operation, the library being compressed can become unusable. It is advisable to ensure that a backup exists before compressing an important library, which does not have a recent backup.

The next control statement unloads a library to tape:

```
COPY    INDD=LIB3,OUTDD=TAP1
```

All members from the library described in DD statement LIB3, USER1.LIBC will be unloaded to the tape data set described in DD statement TAP1. No DCB parameter is required for DD statement TAP1.

The next two control statements load a tape data set containing an unloaded libray, to a new library.

```
COPY    INDD=TAP1,OUTDD=LIB5
EXCLUDE MEMBER=(DEMO)
```

All members from the unloaded tape data set described in DD statement TAP1, USER1.TDSX, will be loaded to a newly created library described in DD statement LIB5, USER1.LIBE. No DCB parameter is required for LIB5. The DCB attributes of the original library will be assigned.

The next control statement concatenates two input libraries.

```
COPY    OUTDD=LIB2,INDD=(LIB3,LIB4)
```

All members from the library described in DD statements LIB3 and LIB4 USER1.LIBC and USER1.LIBD will be copied to the library described in DD statement LIB2, USER1.LIBB. If any of the members to be copied already exist in the receiving library, it will not be copied.

The next control statement allows the replacement of identically named members.

```
COPY    OUTDD=LIB4,INDD=((LIB3,R))
```

All members from the library described in DD statement LIB3, USER1.LIBC will be copied to the library described in DD statement LIB4, USER1.LIBD. Identically named members will be replaced in the receiving library.

The last two control statements show how members can be renamed while being copied, and how replacement can be controlled at the member level.

```
COPY    INDD=LIB1,OUTDD=LIB4
SELECT  MEMBER=(RX1,(RX2,RX3),(RX4,RX5,R),(RX6,,R))
```

Selected members from the library described in DD statement LIB1, USER1.LIBA will be copied to the library described in DD statement LIB4, USER1.LIBD as follows:

- Member RX1 will be copied to the output library. If a member RX1 already exists there, it will not be replaced.
- Member RX2 will be copied to the output library and renamed to RX3. If a member RX3 already exists there, it will not be replaced.
- Member RX4 will be copied to the output library and renamed to RX5. If a member RX5 already exists there, it will be replaced.
- Member RX6 will be copied to the output library. If a member RX6 already exists there, it will be replaced.

When coding a SELECT control statement to select and rename one member, it is easy to make a mistake:

```
SELECT  MEMBER=(OLDMEM,NEWMEM)
```

This control statement will attempt to copy two members, OLDMEM and NEWMEM, rather than copying OLDMEM and renaming it to OLDMEM. A double set of parentheses must be used in order to convey the correct meaning:

```
SELECT  MEMBER=((OLDMEM,NEWMEM))
```

A double set of parentheses is never needed in JCL. This, of course, is not JCL. It is a utility control statement, and its syntax is not exactly the same as JCL.

13.6 THE IEBPTPCH UTILITY

The IEBPTPCH utility can print sequential data sets, entire partitioned data sets, or specific members. It can also punch (punching is largely obsolete and will not be discussed).

Example 1:

```
//PPDS        EXEC   PGM=IEBPTPCH
//SYSPRINT    DD     SYSOUT=*
//SYSUT1      DD     DSN=USER1.LIB1,DISP=SHR
//SYSUT2      DD     SYSOUT=*
//SYSIN       DD     *
  PRINT    TYPORG=PO,MAXFLDS=1,STOPAFT=100
  RECORD   FIELD=(80)
/*
```

SYSUT1 describes a PDS that will be used as input. SYSUT2 is the output DD statement, and it normally describes sysout. If the DCB parameter is not coded IN SYSUT2, the default is DCB=(LRECL=121,BLKSIZE=121,RECFM=FBA). If a different LRECL or BLKSIZE is needed, the DCB parameter should be coded. RECFM cannot be changed.

In this example, all the members of the PDS will be printed. The TYPORG=PO parameter is needed in the PRINT statement to identify the input data set as partitioned — if omitted, the default is PS, which stands for physical sequential. MAXFLDS=1 identifies the number of FIELD parameters that will be used subsequently, in this case one. STOPAFT=100 requests that only the first 100 records of every member be printed.

The FIELD=(80) parameter is needed in the RECORD statement because of a peculiarity. If not coded, the utility inserts two blank characters every 8 characters in the output record (similar to an ABEND dump). The FIELD parameter requests that 80 characters be grouped together, thus eliminating the blanks.

Even though the directory is alphabetically organized, IEBPTPCH may print the member in non-alphabetical sequence. This will not happen if the library is compressed before IEBPTPCH is executed.

Example 2:

```
//PMEM      EXEC  PGM=IEBPTPCH
//SYSPRINT  DD    SYSOUT=*
//SYSUT1    DD    DSN=USER1.LIB1,DISP=SHR
//SYSUT2    DD    SYSOUT=*
//SYSIN     DD    *
  PRINT   TYPORG=PO,MAXFLDS=1,MAXNAME=1,SKIP=5
  MEMBER  NAME=MAY
  RECORD  FIELD=(40,41,,41)
/*
```

In this example member MAY of the input library will be printed.
MAXNAME identifies the number of NAME parameters that will be
used later. SKIP=5 will cause every 5th record to print. The FIELD
parameter requests that 40 bytes beginning in position 41 of the
input record be placed in position 41 of the output record with no
hex conversion. If LRECL=80 is assumed, the last 40 bytes of the
output record will be the same as those of the input record. The first
40 bytes will be blanks.

Example 3:

```
//PSEQ1     EXEC  PGM=IEBPTPCH
//SYSPRINT  DD    SYSOUT=*
//SYSUT1    DD    DSN=USER1.FILZ,DISP=SHR
//SYSUT2    DD    SYSOUT=*
//SYSIN     DD    *
  PRINT   TYPORG=PS,MAXFLDS=4
  TITLE   ITEM=('EXPANDED PERSONNEL REPORT',30)
  TITLE   ITEM=('FOR 1770 BROADWAY SITE',32)
  RECORD  FIELD=(20,1,,1),FIELD=(20,21,,26),           C
          FIELD=(20,41,,51),FIELD=(20,61,,76)
/*
```

In this example a sequential data set will be printed. The purpose
of the four FIELD parameters will be to insert five blanks every 20
characters in the output record (see Figure 13.3, Part I). The input
record has a length of 80.
   The two TITLE statements will place a title, EXPANDED PER-
SONNEL REPORT and a subtitle, FOR 1770 BROADWAY SITE, at
the top of each page, offset 30 and 32 positions, respectively, from
the left of the page. No more than two TITLE statements can be
used.

Example 4:

```
//PSEQ2      EXEC   PGM=IEBPTPCH
//SYSPRINT   DD     SYSOUT=*
//SYSUT1     DD     DSN=USER1.TPE3,DISP=OLD
//SYSUT2     DD     SYSOUT=*
//SYSIN      DD     *
  PRINT    TYPORG=PS,MAXFLDS=2,STRTAFT=12
  RECORD   FIELD=(10,'**********',,1),FIELD=(10,71,XE,41)
/*
```

In this example a sequential data set will be printed.
STRTAFT=12 causes the first 12 records to be omitted. The first
FIELD parameter requests that 10 asterisks be placed in position 1
of the output record. The second FIELD parameter requests that 10
bytes from position 71 of the input record be converted to hexadecimal and be placed in position 41 of the output record. Bytes 21
through 40 of the output record will remain blank (see Figure 13.3,
Part II).

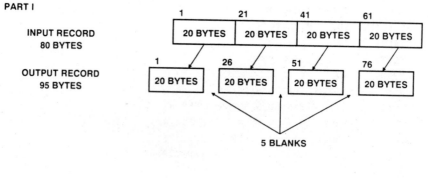

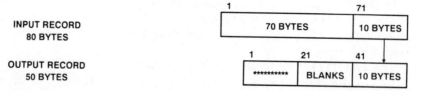

Figure 13.3 IEBPTPCH examples.

13.7 THE IEHLIST UTILITY

The IEHLIST utility can print the VTOC, the directory of a PDS and a CVOL catalog.

```
//LIST       EXEC   PGM=IEHLIST
//SYSPRINT   DD     SYSOUT=*
//D1         DD     UNIT=SYSDA,VOL=SER=PACK11,DISP=OLD
//D2         DD     UNIT=SYSDA,VOL=SER=PACK12,DISP=OLD
//D3         DD     UNIT=SYSDA,VOL=SER=PACK17,DISP=OLD
//SYSIN      DD     *
  LISTVTOC   VOL=SYSDA=PACK11
  LISTVTOC   VOL=SYSDA=PACK12,FORMAT,DSNAME=(USER1.F1,USER1.F3)
  LISTVTOC   VOL=SYSDA=PACK17,DUMP
  LISTPDS    DSNAME=USER1.LIB3,VOL=SYSDA=PACK11
  LISTPDS    DSNAME=USER1.LOAD,VOL=SYSDA=PACK12,FORMAT
  LISTCTLG   VOL=SYSDA=PACK17
  LISTCTLG   VOL=SYSDA=PACK11,NODE=USER1
/*
```

DD statements D1, D2, and D3 are needed to describe the volumes PACK11, PACK12, and PACK17 that will be used later in the control statements.

The first control statement lists all the entries in the VTOC of volume PACK11.

```
  LISTVTOC   VOL=SYSDA=PACK11
```

An abbreviated, edited format is used in which much of the important information (such as, BLKSIZE, LRECL, RECFM space allocated, space used, etc.) is not shown.

The second control statement lists the entries of data sets USER1.F1 and USER1.F3 in the VTOC of volume PACK12.

```
  LISTVTOC   VOL=SYSDA=PACK12,FORMAT,DSNAME=(USER1.F1,USER1.F3)
```

A comprehensive, edited format is shown which displays all of the important information.

The third control statement lists all the entries in the VTOC of volume PACK17.

```
  LISTVTOC   VOL=SYSDA=PACK17,DUMP
```

A nonedited format in hexadecimal is used. This is not particularly useful because the meaning of the various hexadecimal fields is not explained.

The fourth control statement lists the contents of the PDS directory for data set USER1.LIB3.

```
LISTPDS    DSNAME=USER1.LIB3,VOL=SYSDA=PACK11
```

A nonedited format in hexadecimal is used. This may not be very useful because the meaning of the various hexadecimal fields is not explained.

The fifth control statement lists the contents of the PDS directory for data set USER1.LOAD.

```
LISTPDS    DSNAME=USER1.LOAD,VOL=SYSDA=PACK12,FORMAT
```

A comprehensive, edited format is shown, which displays all of the important information, if the members of the PDS are load modules. FORMAT will provide meaningless information if the members of the PDS are not load modules.

The sixth control statement lists the contents of a CVOL catalog residing on volume PACK17.

```
LISTCTLG   VOL=SYSDA=PACK17
```

The output of the control statement is an edited format which shows all of the important information of each catalog entry. However, GDG base information is not shown and the device type of each entry appears as an eight-digit hexadecimal number, which is meaningless to the average user (see Section 6.1 in Chapter 6 for explanations).

The last control statement lists only the entries of data sets whose high qualifier is USER1 in a CVOL catalog residing on volume PACK11.

```
LISTCTLG   VOL=SYSDA=PACK11,NODE=USER1
```

The same format as in the previous control statement is used.

The LISTCTLG control statement can list only a CVOL catalog. To list VSAM or ICF catalogs, IDCAMS *must* be used.

13.8 IDCAMS

IDCAMS is a program product that became available with the virtual operating systems. Its primary intent was to define and handle VSAM objects (clusters, alternate indexes, paths, VSAM and ICF catalogs, etc.).

IDCAMS, however, has several non-VSAM functions, some of which parallel and some of which supplement those provided by JCL and the utilities. This section will concentrate on these functions.

Some examples of IDCAMS defining and handling VSAM objects will also be shown. There will be no attempt to cover VSAM to any extensive degree. Only a few examples will be shown. VSAM is an entire subject in itself, and several good books are dedicated to it.

IDCAMS is part of Data Facility Product (DFP).

13.8.1 Required JCL for IDCAMS

IDCAMS requires only two DD statements: SYSPRINT and SYSIN.

```
//AMS        EXEC  PGM=IDCAMS
//SYSPRINT  DD     message data set, usually sysout
//SYSIN     DD     control information (commands) for IDCAMS
```

Optional additional DD statements may sometimes be needed, as examples will demonstrate later.

IDCAMS resides in SYS1.LINKLIB, a fact which makes the use of JOBLIB or STEPLIB unnecessary.

IDCAMS is a multifunction program. Many operations can be performed in a single execution of IDCAMS.

During execution, IDCAMS opens and reads the data set described in DD statement SYSIN. This data set contains commands which tell IDCAMS what action to take. Note that what was called a "control statement" for utilities is called a "command" for IDCAMS. Both have the same meaning: information supplied to the executing program telling it what to do. The SYSIN DD statement will normally appear in one of two formats:

```
//SYSIN DD *
  -- commands --
/*
```

```
//SYSIN DD DSN=TEST.CTLLIB(ID3),DISP=SHR
```

The first of the two is typically used in a testing environment, the other, in a production environment. ID3 is a member containing IDCAMS commands.

With the exception of certain commands (such as, IF, THEN, ELSE, DO, SET), IDCAMS commands can be used interactively under TSO the same way as TSO commands. However, this may not be advisable for commands that are very time-consuming. The performance group assigned to TSO may cause such commands to take more time than the same commands in batch.

13.8.2 IDCAMS Command Syntax

The syntax of IDCAMS commands is drastically different from that of JCL and the utilities. It is basically identical to TSO command syntax.

```
command parameter-list
```

A command can begin anywhere, except position 1. The parameter list can go up to (and including) position 72. The command and the parameter list must be separated by one or more blanks. Parameters are separated by commas, blanks, comments (any string of characters surrounded by /* and */) or any combination of the three. In a real environment, blanks are by far the most commonly used separators.

The vast majority of parameters have no particular sequence (keyword parameters). A few must be placed at the beginning of the parameter list (positional parameters). In the examples discussed in this chapter, the type of parameter will be mentioned only if it is positional. If no mention is made, the parameter is keyword.

To continue a command to another line, a hyphen (-), preceded by at least one blank, must be placed at the end of the line to be continued. Coding on the continuation line can begin anywhere, except position 1. Note that the hyphen is an extraneous character used only for continuation purposes. Blanks are ignored as long as they are not found in the middle of keywords, values, or names. For example,

```
REPRO   INFILE(IN1) OUTFILE(OUT1) SKIP(1000)
```

can also be coded as:

```
REPRO   INFILE  (  IN1  ) OUTFILE  (  OUT1  )  SKIP  (  1000  )
```

Commands and keywords cannot be broken in a continuation. Values and names can, if a plus (+) is used (not preceded by a blank) at the end of the line to be continued.

Examples of continuation:

```
REPRO   INFILE(IN1) OUTFILE(OUT1) -
SKIP(1000)

REPRO   INFILE(                    -
IN1) OUTFILE(OUT1                  -
)                                  -
SKIP(1000)
```

The second example contains perfectly valid continuations, but one would be hard-pressed to explain why lines are broken in such strange places. This is not recommended.

Many commands can be executed during each execution of IDCAMS. Each command issues a return (condition) code with the following meaning:

0 — successful completion

4 — warning, usually benign

8 — command execution questionable. IDCAMS continues with other commands

12 — command execution unsuccessful. IDCAMS continues with other commands

16 — terminal error has occurred. IDCAMS execution terminates, and no more commands can be executed.

The highest return code issued by any of the commands becomes the return code of the step.

13.8.3 Examples of IDCAMS Used with VSAM Objects

In this section several examples will be shown for some common IDCAMS commands to perform the following functions for VSAM objects *in an ICF catalog environment*:

- Define a KSDS cluster
- Define an alternate index for a cluster
- Build an alternate index
- Define a path for an alternate index
- Delete a cluster or alternate index
- Alter the characteristics of a cluster or alternate index
- Load, update, or copy a cluster
- Print a cluster
- List the entries of a VSAM or ICF catalog

Each example will be followed by a brief discussion. To make the parameters easier to understand, no abbreviations will be used in the examples. Abbreviations, however, are very common in a real environment.

13.8.3.1 Define a KSDS Cluster

```
//AMS       EXEC  PGM=IDCAMS
//SYSPRINT DD    SYSOUT=*
//SYSIN     DD    *
    DEFINE    CLUSTER   (NAME(USER1.BASE)                 -
                        CYLINDERS(100 30)                 -
                        VOLUMES(PROD22 PROD04)            -
                        RECORDSIZE(100 120)               -
                        FREESPACE(10 15)                  -
                        KEYS(20 4)                        -
                        SHAREOTIONS(2 3)                  -
                        SPEED)                            -
              DATA      (NAME(USER1.BASED)                -
                        CONTROLINTERVALSIZE(8192))        -
              INDEX     (NAME(USER1.BASEI))
/*
```

A KSDS cluster consists of two components: the data component and the index component. In a define command it is a good practice to include most parameters under the cluster portion of the command and let IDCAMS apply the parameters to the two components appropriately.

NAME(USER1.BASE) identifies the name of the cluster. This is the name that will be used in the DSN parameter of a DD statement to retrieve the cluster.

CYLINDERS(100 30) specifies primary and secondary allocation for the data component of the cluster. The index components will be assigned an adequate amount of space by IDCAMS. This parameter works the same way as the SPACE parameter in JCL, with the following two exceptions:

- The cluster can have as many as 123 extents on a volume as compared to 16 for a non-VSAM data set.
- If the cluster extends to the second volume, the primary allocation will be repeated and followed by the secondary allocations. For a non-VSAM data set, only secondary allocations are used on volumes other than the first.

VOLUMES(PROD22 PROD04) specifies the volumes where the data set will be defined. The second volume will not be used unless no more secondary allocations can be supplied on the first volume. The sequence of the volumes may be changed by IDCAMS, if necessary.

RECORDSIZE(100 120) identifies the average (100) and maximum (120) record size. VSAM records are always assumed to be variable (except for RRDS clusters).

FREESPACE(10 15) indicates that VSAM will not use 10% of each control interval and 15% of each control area when the cluster is loaded with data. This free space can be used later to accommodate inserted or enlarged records.

KEYS(20 4) specifies that the size of the key is 20 bytes and it begins in position 5 (offset 4) of each record.

SHAREOTIONS(2 3) indicates that, once this cluster is opened, another user in the same system can read the cluster but cannot write on it. Another user executing in a different system has full access to the cluster.

SPEED requests that no checkpoints be taken when the cluster is loaded with data.

NAME(USER1.BASED) identifies the name of the cluster's data component. This name cannot be used in JCL. It may be used in the ALTER and LISTCAT commands.

CONTROLINTERVALSIZE(8192) defines the control interval size to be 8192 bytes. This parameter, if included in the cluster portion but not in the index portion of the command, would cause the same size to be assigned to the data and index control intervals, which may not be desirable. In this command, the control interval size of the index component will be determined by IDCAMS.

NAME(USER1.BASEI) identifies the name of the cluster's index component. This name cannot be used in JCL. It may be used in the ALTER and LISTCAT commands.

There are many more parameters available in the DEFINE CLUS-TER command. For these parameters, defaults are assumed.

13.8.3.2 Define an Alternate Index for a Cluster

```
//AMS      EXEC  PGM=IDCAMS
//SYSPRINT DD    SYSOUT=*
//SYSIN    DD    *
  DEFINE  ALTERNATEINDEX (NAME(USER1.BASEA)          -
                         RELATE(USER1.BASE)          -
                         UPGRADE                     -
                         CYLINDERS(30 10)            -
                         VOLUMES(PROD22)             -
                         FREESPACE(5 5)              -
                         KEYS(9 33)                  -
                         SHAREOTIONS(2 3)            -
                         SPEED)                      -
          DATA          (NAME(USER1.BASEAD)          -
                         CONTROLINTERVALSIZE(4096))  -
          INDEX         (NAME(USER1.BASEAI))
/*
```

An alternate index is a structure virtually identical to that of a KSDS cluster. As a result the command to define it is very similar. Explanations will be given only where the meaning of parameters is different.

NAME(USER1.BASEA) identifies the name of the alternate index. This is not the name that will be used in JCL when the base cluster is to be accessed using the alternate key. Rather, the name of the path must be used (see DEFINE PATH, later).

RELATE(USER1.BASE) identifies the base cluster.

UPGRADE requests that the alternate index be automatically up-dated to reflect changes to the base cluster.

KEYS(9 33) identifies the size, 9, and the position, 34, (offset 33) of the key of the alternate index.

There are many more parameters available in the DEFINE AL-TERNATEINDEX command. For these parameters, defaults are as-sumed. Note that the RECORDSIZE parameter, which is required for the DEFINE CLUSTER command, is omitted. A default for this parameter exists for the DEFINE ALTERNATEINDEX command and it is a common practice to assume this default.

13.8.3.3 Build an Alternate Index

```
//AMS       EXEC   PGM=IDCAMS
//SYSPRINT  DD     SYSOUT=*
//IN        DD     DSN=USER1.BASE,DISP=SHR
//OUT       DD     DSN=USER1.BASEA,DISP=SHR
//IDCUT1    DD     UNIT=SYSDA,VOL=SER=PACK32,DISP=OLD,AMP=AMORG
//IDCUT2    DD     UNIT=SYSDA,VOL=SER=PACK18,DISP=OLD,AMP=AMORG
//SYSIN     DD     *
     BLDINDEX    INFILE(IN)   -
                 OUTFILE(OUT)
/*
```

Before this command can be used, the base cluster must be loaded with its data (a REPRO example shown later).

This command loads the alternate index with its appropriate records. The BLDINDEX command always involves a sorting operation. The records of the alternate index will be placed in alternate key sequence.

The spelling of the IN and OUT ddnames is arbitrary. This spelling, however, must be matched in the INFILE and OUTFILE parameters.

IDCUT1 and IDCUT2 constitute work areas for sorting. In this example, a parameter INTERNALSORT is implied. If the REGION of the step is large enough, the sorting operation can be performed in memory. If not, IDCAMS will define two clusters on the volumes identified in DD statements IDCUT1 and IDCUT2, use them for sorting and then delete them.

INFILE(IN) identifies the DD statement describing the input data set, the base cluster.

OUTFILE(OUT) identifies the DD statement describing the output data set, the alternate index.

The command can also be coded as:

```
     BLDINDEX    INDATASET(USER1.BASE)   -
                 OUTDATASET(USER1.BASEA)
```

This command does not require DD statements IN and OUT. The data sets will be dynamically allocated by IDCAMS.

13.8.3.4 Define a Path for an Alternate Index

```
//AMS       EXEC  PGM=IDCAMS
//SYSPRINT DD     SYSOUT=*
//SYSIN    DD     *
  DEFINE  PATH   (NAME(USER1.ALTKEY)
                  PATHENTRY(USER1.BASEA))
/*
```

NAME(USER1.ALTKEY) defines the name of the path. When alternate index USER1.BASEA must be used to access cluster USER1.BASE, it is the pathname that will be used in the DSN parameter, not the alternate index name.

PATHENTRY(USER1.BASEA) identifies the alternate index that is associated with the path.

13.8.3.5 Delete a VSAM Object

```
//AMS       EXEC  PGM=IDCAMS
//SYSPRINT DD     SYSOUT=*
//SYSIN    DD     *
  DELETE   USER1.BASE
/*
```

USER1.BASE is a positional parameter which identifies the object to be deleted, in this case a cluster. When a cluster is deleted, any associated alternate indexes and paths are also deleted. When an alternate index is deleted, its associated path is also deleted, but the cluster remains unaffected.

```
  DELETE   USER1.BASEA
```

When a path is deleted, its associated alternate index and cluster remain unaffected.

```
  DELETE   USER1.ALTKEY
```

13.8.3.6 Alter Characteristics of a VSAM Object

```
//AMS       EXEC  PGM=IDCAMS
//SYSPRINT DD     SYSOUT=*
```

```
//SYSIN     DD      *
   ALTER    USER1.BASED    ADDVOLUMES(PROD35)
   ALTER    USER1.BASE     NEWNAME(USER1.BASEX)
   ALTER    USER1.BASEA    NOUPGRADE
/*
```

The first parameter is positional and identifies the object to be altered.

ADDVOLUMES(PROD35) requests that one more volume, PROD35, be added to the existing ones. The cluster can extend into this volume if it becomes necessary. Note that the data component name is coded. The cluster name cannot be used. It is important to check the appropriate IBM manual to determine what type of name must be used with the various parameters of the ALTER command.

NEWNAME(USER1.BASEX) identifies the new name of the cluster. The name of the cluster is changed from USER1.BASE to USER1.BASEX. The names of the data and index components will not change.

Renaming a cluster can present a certain danger. Consider the following command,

```
ALTER    USER1.BASE    NEWNAME(USER5.LOPUB)
```

If the high qualifiers USER1 and USER5 are alias names of different user catalogs, the catalog entry for the cluster will change but the entry remains in the original user catalog, which is now the wrong one. A DD statement

```
//DD1      DD   DSN=USER5.LOPUB,DISP=SHR
```

will result in a "DATA SET NOT FOUND" JCL error. A JOBCAT or STEPCAT DD statement must be used to point to the correct catalog.

```
//DD1    DD    DSN=USER5.LOPUB,DISP=SHR
//STEPCAT    DD   DSN=usercatlog,DISP=SHR
```

NOUPGRADE requests that the alternate index USER1.BASEA attribute of UPGRADE be changed to NOUPGRADE. The alternate index now will not reflect any changes made to the base cluster.

13.8.3.7 LOAD, UPDATE and COPY a VSAM Cluster

```
//AMS        .EXEC  PGM=IDCAMS
//SYSPRINT DD       SYSOUT=*
//OUT1      DD       DSN=USER1.BASE,DISP=SHR
//OUT2      DD       DSN=USER1.TPBK,DISP=(,CATLG),UNIT=TAPE,
//                   DCB=(BLKSIZE=32760,LRECL=32756,RECFM=VB)
//IN1       DD       DSN=USER1.FILE1,DISP=SHR
//IN2       DD       DSN=USER1.TRANS,DISP=SHR
//SYSIN     DD       *
      REPRO          INFILE(IN1)    -
                     OUTFILE(OUT1)
      REPRO          INFILE(IN2)    -
                     OUTFILE(OUT1)  -
                     REPLACE        -
                     COUNT(1500)    -
                     SKIP(50)
      REPRO          INFILE(OUT1) -
                     OUTFILE(OUT2)
/*
```

The spelling of the IN1 IN2, OUT1 and OUT2 ddnames is arbitrary. This spelling, however, must be matched in the appropriate INFILE and OUTFILE parameters.

INFILE(IN1) identifies the DD statement describing the input data set.

OUTFILE(OUT1) identifies the DD statement describing the output data set.

The first REPRO command uses as input a sequential data set which has been sorted in prime key sequence. The output data set is an *empty* KSDS cluster. This command will load the cluster with the data of the sequential data set.

The second REPRO command uses as input a sequential data set which has been sorted in prime key sequence. The output data set is a *loaded* cluster. The first 50 records of the input data set will not be used — SKIP(50). The next 1500 records will be used — COUNT(1500). No other records will be copied. Records in the cluster which contain keys identical to those of incoming records will be replaced (REPLACE). Records with new keys will be added.

The third REPRO command uses a cluster as input. The output data set is a new data set on tape. The DCB parameter on the output DD statement must be coded. Since VSAM assumes variable format, it is a good practice to code RECFM=VB. BLKSIZE=32760 and LRECL=32756 are maximum values and will always work.

If dynamic allocation is used, the REPRO command can also be coded as:

```
REPRO INDATASET(USER1.FILE1) -
      OUTDATASET(USER1.BASE)
```

If the output data set is to be created, dynamic allocation cannot be used. JCL must be used to create the data set.

13.8.3.8 Print a VSAM Cluster

```
//AMS       EXEC  PGM=IDCAMS
//SYSPRINT  DD    SYSOUT=*
//IN1       DD    DSN=USER1.BASE,DISP=SHR
//SYSIN     DD    *
      PRINT       INFILE(IN1)   -
                  FROMKEY(BAKER) -
                  TOKEY(JONES)   -
                  CHARACTER
/*
```

The spelling of the IN1 ddname is arbitrary. This spelling, however, must be matched in the INFILE parameter.

INFILE(ddname) identifies the DD statement describing the input data set.

OUTFILE(ddname) could be included to identify the DD statement describing the output data set, but it is optional. If omitted, SYSPRINT will be used.

The PRINT command uses as input a VSAM KSDS cluster. Printing will begin with the record whose key is "BAKER." It will stop with the record whose key is "JONES." The records will be printed in character format.

If dynamic allocation is used, the PRINT command can also be coded as:

```
PRINT INDATASET(USER1.BASE) -
FROMKEY(BAKER) -
TOKEY(JONES) -
CHARACTER
 /*
```

13.8.3.9 List the Entries of an ICF Catalog

```
//AMS       EXEC  PGM=IDCAMS
//SYSPRINT DD    SYSOUT=*
//SYSIN    DD    *
    LISTCAT    ENTRIES(USER1.BASE   USER1.BASEA)   -
               ALL
    LISTCAT    LEVEL(USER1) CLUSTER               -
               ALL
/*
```

The first LISTCAT command will list only the specified entries. All information for each entry will be displayed.

The second LISTCAT command will list all entries which are VSAM clusters and whose names begin with a high qualifier of USER1. All information for each entry will be displayed.

If a command contains neither the ENTRIES nor the LEVEL parameters, a user catalog must be identified in one of two ways:

• Using JOBCAT or STEPCAT:

```
//AMS       EXEC  PGM=IDCAMS
//STEPCAT  DD    DSN=ICF.CATALOG3,DISP=SHR
//SYSPRINT DD    SYSOUT=*
//SYSIN    DD    *
    LISTCAT    CLUSTER   ALL
/*
```

• Using the CATALOG parameter

```
//AMS       EXEC  PGM=IDCAMS
//SYSPRINT DD    SYSOUT=*
//SYSIN    DD    *
    LISTCAT    CLUSTER   ALL      -
               CATALOG(ICF.CATALOG3)
/*
```

Note: A VSAM catalog can be listed the same way as an ICF catalog.

13.8.4 Examples of IDCAMS Used with Non-VSAM Data Sets

IDCAMS possesses some important non-VSAM data set facilities. In this section several examples will be shown for some common

IDCAMS commands to perform the following functions for non-VSAM data sets.

- Catalog and uncatalog a data set
- Delete (and uncatalog) a data set
- Delete a member of PDS
- Rename a data set and a member of a PDS
- Define a GDG base and delete a GDG base
- Change the limit of a GDG
- Copy a sequential data set or a member of a PDS
- Print a sequential data set or a member of a PDS
- List the entries of a VSAM or ICF catalog

Each example will be followed by a brief discussion. To make the parameters easier to understand, no abbreviations will be used in the examples.

Non-VSAM data sets are not always cataloged. IDCAMS commands, other than the DEFINE command, cannot handle non-cataloged data sets.

13.8.4.1 Catalog and Uncatalog a Data Set

```
//AMS        EXEC  PGM=IDCAMS
//SYSPRINT DD    SYSOUT=*
//SYSIN    DD    *
      DEFINE    NONVSAM   (NAME(USER1.FSET)              -
                          VOLUMES(PACK23)               -
                          DEVICETYPES(SYSDA))
      DEFINE    NONVSAM   (NAME(USER1.TAP1)             -
                          VOLUMES(002365 000153)        -
                          DEVICETYPES(TAPE)             -
                          FILESEQUENCENUMBERS(1 1))
      DELETE    USER.KSET NOSCRATCH
/*
```

The first two commands add entries in the catalog. Usually data sets are cataloged as they are created — DISP=(,CATLG). This facility can be used if a data set exists but it is not cataloged. There are other facilities — JCL using DISP=(OLD,CATLG), IEHPROGM, TSO, and ISPF (for disk only) — that can accomplish the same goal.

When using IDCAMS to catalog a data set, a number of considerations should be kept in mind:

- If the wrong name is supplied in the NAME parameter, IDCAMS will catalog it. It simply does not verify that the data set resides on the volume.
- If the wrong volume serial is supplied in the VOLUMES parameter, again the data set will be cataloged whether or not the wrong volume exists.
- If the wrong device type is supplied in the DEVICETYPES parameter, again the data set will be cataloged but only if the device is a valid one. The validity of the device is the only thing IDCAMS checks (but it does not check if it is the appropriate device for the volume)
- The use of a generated name (i.e., SYSDA or TAPE) in the DEVICETYPES parameter can cause a problem. When cataloging via JCL, a parameter like UNIT=SYSDA or UNIT=TAPE will never cause a problem. The allocation routines (see Figure 1.7) for disk and the open routines for tape determine what type of device the allocated volume resides on and the catalog entry will eventually contain not SYSDA, but the exact device type, such as 3380 or 3480. IDCAMS, however, has nothing comparable to the allocation or open routines and places a notation indicative of SYSDA or TAPE in the catalog entry. Upon reconfiguration, such entries can become invalid. It is, therefore, recommended that if IDCAMS is used to provide an entry in the catalog, a generic name (such as 3380 or 3480) be used in the DEVICETYPES parameter as opposed to a generated (also known as esoteric or group) name.

```
DEFINE    NONVSAM    (NAME(USER1.FSET)              -
                      VOLUMES(PACK23)               -
                      DEVICETYPES(3380))
DEFINE    NONVSAM    (NAME(USER1.TAP1)              -
                      VOLUMES(002365 000153)        -
                      DEVICETYPES(3480)             -
                      FILESEQUENCENUMBERS(1 1))
```

Clearly, this is a dangerous facility for cataloging, and great care must be exercised when using it. Note that no tape device need be allocated in order to catalog a tape data set. This fact may make IDCAMS relatively attractive when existing tape data sets must be cataloged. Cataloging through JCL will always result in allocating a tape device and that, under certain conditions, may be undesirable.

The second command catalogs a multivolume tape data set. The VOLUMES parameter identifies the two volume serials. The FILESEQUENCENUMBERS parameter identifies the sequence number of the data set on the volume. Both sequence numbers are 1. Interestingly, FILESEQUENCENUMBERS(1 2) will also work. If the tape data set to be cataloged resides on one volume, the FILESEQUENCENUMBERS parameter need not be coded, unless the sequence of the data set is higher than one.

The third control statement uncatalogs a data set. The DELETE applies to the catalog entry. The NOSCRATCH applies to the VTOC entry

IDCAMS can add catalog entries in ICF (as well as VSAM) catalogs, but not CVOL catalogs. It can remove an entry from any type of catalog.

13.8.4.2 Delete a Data Set or a Member of a PDS

```
//AMS        EXEC   PGM=IDCAMS
//SYSPRINT DD      SYSOUT=*
//SYSIN     DD     *
      DELETE     USER1.FERY
/*
```

This will cause the data set to be deleted and uncataloged. IDCAMS can never delete without uncataloging. This is a highly desirable feature. Unfortunately, there is a weakness. If the data set has already been deleted and uncataloged, the DELETE command will issue a return code of 8, which may become the return code of the step. This return code is normally treated as a questionable one and will cause a subsequent step using COND=(4,LT) or COND=(0,LT) not to be executed, while there is really nothing wrong. This problem can be eliminated by using IDCAMS execution control commands, IF/THEN and SET:

```
//AMS        EXEC   PGM=IDCAMS
//SYSPRINT DD      SYSOUT=*
//SYSIN     DD     *
      DELETE     USER1.FERY
      IF LASTCC=8 THEN -
      SET MAXCC=4 (or SET MAXCC=0)
/*
```

Instead of 8, the return code is now 4 (or 0) and the problem no longer exists.

The member of a PDS can be deleted as follows:

```
//AMS       EXEC  PGM=IDCAMS
//SYSPRINT DD    SYSOUT=*
//SYSIN    DD    *
    DELETE     USER1.LIB1(FDA)
/*
```

This DELETE command will delete member FDA only.

To delete a generation of a GDG, the absolute name must be used.

```
DELETE     USER1.DAY.G0038V00
```

Relative names, such as USER1.DAY(0), cannot be used.

13.8.4.3 Rename a Data Set or a Member of a PDS

```
//AMS       EXEC  PGM=IDCAMS
//SYSPRINT DD    SYSOUT=*
//SYSIN    DD    *
    ALTER      USER1.FILEA   NEWNAME(USER1.FILEK)
    ALTER      USER1.LIBA(SEVB)    NEWNAME(USER1.LIBA(SEVA))
/*
```

The first command will rename the data set from USER1.FILEA
to USER1.FILEK. The catalog will be automatically updated to reflect the renaming operation.

Renaming a data set can present a certain danger. Consider the
following command:

```
ALTER    USER1.FILE1   NEWNAME(USER3.FILEA)
```

If the high qualifiers USER1 and USER3 are alias names of different catalogs, the catalog entry for the data set will change but the
entry remains in the original catalog which is now the wrong one. A
DD statement

```
//DD1      DD  DSN=USER3.FILEA,DISP=SHR
```

will result in a "DATA SET NOT FOUND" JCL error. A JOBCAT or
STEPCAT DD statement must be used to point to the correct catalog.

```
//DD1    DD   DSN=USER5.LOPUB,DISP=SHR
//STEPCAT  DD   DSN=ICF.CATALOG2,DISP=SHR
```

In such a situation, it would be best to uncatalog the data set using STEPCAT and then catalog it again. The entry will now be automatically routed to the appropriate user catalog, thus eliminating any need for further using the dangerous STEPCAT or JOBCAT.

The second command will rename member SEVB of PDS USER1.LIBA to SEVA.

13.8.4.4 Define and Delete a GDG Base in an ICF Catalog

Before a DD statement containing DSN=gdgbase(+1) with a DISP of NEW can be used, the GDG base must be defined to the catalog. For an ICF catalog, IDCAMS must be used to perform this function (the same holds true for a VSAM catalog).

```
//AMS       EXEC  PGM=IDCAMS
//SYSPRINT DD    SYSOUT=*
//SYSIN    DD    *
      DEFINE  GDG  (NAME(PROD.DAY) LIMIT(5) SCRATCH)
/*
```

PROD.DAY is the GDG base.

LIMIT(5) identifies the maximum number of generations that can be concurrently available (5). The maximum LIMIT is 255.

SCRATCH requests that when the oldest disk generation is uncataloged, when the LIMIT is exceeded, it should also be deleted (see Section 11.2 in Chapter 11). The GDG base can be deleted from the catalog as follows:

```
//AMS       EXEC  PGM=IDCAMS
//SYSPRINT DD    SYSOUT=*
//SYSIN    DD    *
      DELETE    PROD.DAY
/*
```

This command will fail unless all generations belonging to this GDG are uncataloged.

13.8.4.5 Change the Limit of a GDG

Sometimes it becomes necessary to change the LIMIT of a GDG after several generations already exist. Changing the LIMIT is a messy operation. It cannot be accomplished by using the ALTER command.

A detailed description of how to accomplish this appears in Section 11.3 of Chapter 11.

13.8.4.6 Copy a Sequential Data Set

```
//AMS      EXEC  PGM=IDCAMS
//SYSPRINT DD    SYSOUT=*
//OUT1     DD    DSN=USER1.TPBK,DISP=(,CATLG),UNIT=TAPE,
//               DCB=(BLKSIZE=32720,LRECL=80,RECFM=FB)
//IN1      DD    DSN=USER1.FILE1,DISP=SHR
//SYSIN    DD    *
    REPRO        INFILE(IN1)    -
                 OUTFILE(OUT1)  -
                 COUNT(2000)
/*
```

The spelling of the IN1 and OUT1 ddnames is arbitrary. This spelling, however, must be matched in the INFILE and OUTFILE parameters.

INFILE(ddname) identifies the DD statement describing the input data set.

OUTFILE(ddname) identifies the DD statement describing the output data set.

The REPRO command uses as input a sequential data set. The output data set is also a sequential data set, newly created. Only the first 2000 records will be copied — COUNT(2000).

Note that the DCB parameter is required in the output DD statement. It will not be copied from the input data set as in IEBGENER.

Dynamic allocation can be used but in this case only for the input data set (the output data set is new). DD statement IN1 is now unnecessary.

```
REPRO    INDATASET(USER1.FILE1) -
         OUTFILE(OUT1)
```

13.8.4.7 Print a Sequential Data Set

```
//AMS        EXEC  PGM=IDCAMS
//SYSPRINT DD     SYSOUT=*
//IN1        DD    DSN=USER1.FILEX,DISP=SHR
//SYSIN      DD    *
      PRINT       INFILE(IN1)    -
                  SKIP(10)       -
                  COUNT(100)     -
                  CHARACTER
/*
```

The spelling of the IN1 ddname is arbitrary. This spelling, however, must be matched in the INFILE parameter.

INFILE(IN1) identifies the DD statement describing the input
data set, USER1.FILEX.

OUTFILE(ddname) could be specified to identify the DD statement
describing the output data set, but it is optional. When omitted, SYS-
PRINT will be used.

The first 10 records will not be printed — SKIP(10). Printing will
stop after 100 records have been printed — COUNT(100). The records will have character format. Other format options available are
HEX (hexadecimal) or DUMP (combination of hex and character format). If none are coded, DUMP is the default.

If dynamic allocation is used, the PRINT command can also be
coded as:

```
PRINT       INDATASET(USER1.FILEX)   -
            SKIP(10)         -
            COUNT(100)       -
            CHARACTER
/*
```

DD statement IN1 is now unnecessary.

In the example below, member SOR1 of PDS USER1.CTLIB will
be printed in character format:

```
//AMS        EXEC  PGM=IDCAMS
//SYSPRINT DD     SYSOUT=*
//INM        DD    DSN=USER1.CTLIB(SOR1),DISP=SHR
//SYSIN      DD    *
      PRINT       INFILE(INM)    -
                  CHARACTER
/*
```

13.8.4.8 List the Entries of an ICF Catalog

Non-VSAM data set entries residing in an ICF catalog can be listed in a very similar fashion as VSAM objects.

```
//AMS       EXEC   PGM=IDCAMS
//SYSPRINT DD     SYSOUT=*
//SYSIN    DD     *
     LISTCAT    ENTRIES(USER1.FILEA   USER1.FILEC)   -
                ALL
     LISTCAT    LEVEL(USER1) NONVSAM
     LISTCAT    ENTRIES(USER1.DAY)                   -
                ALL           /* USER1.DAY IS A GDG BASE */
/*
```

The first LISTCAT command will list only the specified entries, USER1.FILEA and USER1.FILEC. All information for each entry will be displayed.

The second LISTCAT command will list all entries which are non-VSAM data sets and whose names begin with a high qualifier of USER1. Only the name for each entry will be displayed.

The third LISTCAT command will list all information about the GDG base USER1.DAY. It will not show individual generations, only the characteristics of the GDG base (LIMIT, SCRATCH, etc.).

To list individual generations, the absolute names must be used.

```
LISTCAT    ENTRIES(USER1.DAY.G0033V00)    -
           ALL
```

Relative names, such as USER1.DAY(0), cannot be used.

If a command contains neither the ENTRIES nor the LEVEL parameters, user catalog must be identified in one of two ways:

• Using JOBCAT or STEPCAT:

```
//AMS       EXEC   PGM=IDCAMS
//STEPCAT  DD     DSN=ICF.CATALOG1,DISP=SHR
//SYSPRINT DD     SYSOUT=*
//SYSIN    DD     *
     LISTCAT    NONVSAM  ALL
/*
```

• Using the CATALOG parameter

```
//AMS        EXEC   PGM=IDCAMS
//SYSPRINT DD     SYSOUT=*
//SYSIN     DD     *
     LISTCAT    NONVSAM  ALL      -
                CATALOG(ICF.CATALOG1)
/*
```

Note: A VSAM catalog can be listed the same way as an ICF catalog.

14

MVS/ESA JCL Considerations

In the first quarter of 1988, IBM announced MVS/System Product Version 3 (MVS/SP 3), commonly known as MVS/ESA (Enterprise System Architecture). It was initially scheduled for release in the third quarter of 1988. As of the writing of this book (late 1988), MVS/ESA had not yet been released.

MVS/ESA is designed to enhance an installation's choice of facilities and remove certain constraints, especially those of virtual storage.

Under MVS/SP Version 1 (commonly referred to as MVS/SP), each batch user gets a 16-megabyte address space from which usually less than 8 megabytes are available to the user (the rest is used by MVS Nucleus and Common Areas).

Under MVS/SP Version 2 (commonly referred to as MVS/XA), each batch user gets a 2-gigabyte address space. The storage lost to MVS use is negligible when compared to the overall address space size. An ordinary user is limited to virtual storage below the 16 megabyte line, which is usually in the range of 9 megabytes.

Under MVS/ESA, each batch user has the same 2-gigabyte address space as under MVS/XA. In addition, a maximum of 7999 data spaces can also be made available (see Figure 14.1). Each data space is the same size as an address space, and it is intended to contain data only. The address space can contain code as well as data.

An incredible 8000 x 2 = 16000 gigabytes (or 16 terabytes) are available to the user in MVS/ESA. A database of any conceivable size can be loaded into virtual storage, providing the user with enhanced I/O performance.

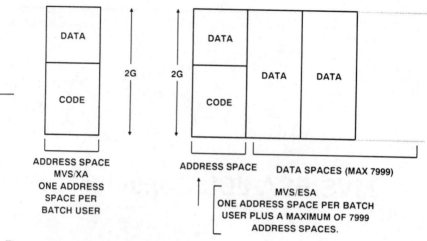

Figure 14.1 MVS/XA and MVS/ESA Address Spaces and Data Spaces.

MVS/ESA introduces a new product, the Storage Management Subsystem, or SMS. This product provides new functions for storage and data management. An installation using MVS/ESA may or may not install SMS. Many of the new JCL features provided by MVS/ESA will only be available if SMS is installed and active.

14.1 JCL CHANGES FOR MVS/ESA

MVS/ESA provides significant enhancements to JCL, mostly in the form of new facilities:

* New JCL parameters are available (if SMS is used).
* Some existing parameters are changed (if SMS is used).
* Alternate syntax is available for certain subparameters
* Some new default options are provided.

The two most notable changes that are likely to have an immediate effect on the user are: •

* When creating a data set, DCB BLKSIZE information need not be provided. While this would result in an S013-34 ABEND failure in all previous versions, under MVS/ESA an optimum blocksize will be supplied by default.
* While previous versions could neither create nor delete a VSAM cluster via JCL, MVS/ESA can (but only with SMS).

14.2 NEW JCL PARAMETERS

Eight new DD statement parameters are available in MVS/ESA, but only if SMS is in use. When SMS is not installed, or installed but not active, all the new parameters will be syntactically checked and ignored.

- AVGREC — average record
- DATACLASS — data class
- KEYOFF — key offset
- LIKE — data set model
- MGMTCLAS — management class
- RECORG — record organization
- REFDD — DD statement referback
- STORCLAS — storage class

There is a ninth new parameter, SECMODEL, intended for use with RACF. RACF is an optional facility and not discussed in this book.

Most of the new parameters apparently attempt to simplify JCL by providing the user with "modeling" capabilities. This relieves the user of the responsibility of being familiar with all details and minimizes the complexity of coding all attributes when creating a data set. An installation will establish the needed data classes, management classes, storage classes, etc., and a data set can be modeled after their attributes when appropriate. The user must be familiar with the names of the available classes and what attributes each class provides.

14.2.1 The AVGREC Parameter

This parameter is meaningful only if SMS is active. Otherwise, it will be syntactically checked and ignored.

When creating a data set, the purpose of the AVGREC parameter is to:

- Identify that the SPACE parameter supplied explicitly or implicitly defines logical record length as opposed to blocksize.
- Allow the primary and secondary quantities of the SPACE parameter to represent units, multiples of 1024 (K), or multiples of 1048576 (M).

General Syntax

```
AVGREC=U|K|M|                                    keyword parameter
```

U — Identifies that the primary and secondary quantities of the SPACE parameter represent the number of logical records

K — Identifies that the primary and secondary quantities of the SPACE parameter represent the number of logical records multiplied by 1024

M — Identifies that the primary and secondary quantities of the SPACE parameter represent the number of logical records multiplied by 1048576

The AVGREC parameter is ignored if the DD statement describes a new data set which is not supported by SMS, such as a tape data set.

The AVGREC parameter overrides the AVGREC provided by the DATACLAS parameter.

Example 1:

```
//D1 DD DSN=USER1.EDAT,DISP=(,CATLG,DELETE),UNIT=SYSDA,
//      VOL=SER=PACK14,SPACE=(80,(100,20)),AVGREC=K,
//      DCB=(LRECL=80,BLKSIZE=23440,RECFM=FB)
```

Example 2:

```
//D2 DD DSN=USER1.XDAT,DISP=(,CATLG,DELETE),UNIT=SYSDA,
//      DATACLAS=PCLASS,AVGREC=M
```

In Example 1, the primary quantity will be calculated on the basis of 100x1024 or 102400 80-byte logical records. The secondary quantity will be based on 20x1024 or 20480 80-byte logical records.

In Example 2, the primary and secondary (if available) quantity will represent millions (actually 1048576) of logical records. Parameters such as SPACE, VOL, UNIT, and DCB will be supplied by the DATACLAS parameter.

The AVGREC parameter should not be coded if the SPACE parameter denotes TRK or CYL.

When the AVGREC parameter is not provided, the primary and secondary in the SPACE parameter will be computed on the basis of blocks.

14.2.2 The DATACLAS Parameter

This parameter is meaningful only if SMS is active. Otherwise, it will be syntactically checked and ignored.

When creating a data set, the purpose of the DATACLAS parameter is to provide predefined data set allocation attributes:

- RECORG
- RECFM
- LRECL
- KEYLEN (VSAM only)
- KEYOFF (VSAM only)
- AVGREC
- SPACE
- RETPD or EXPDT
- VOL count
- For VSAM clusters, IMBED, REPLICATE CISIZE, FREESPACE and SHAREOPTIONS

General Syntax

```
DATACLAS=class-name                         keyword parameter
```

class-name — Name, 1 to 8 characters, defined by the installation storage administrator to be used for allocating new data sets. These data sets can be sequential (PS), partitioned (PO), or VSAM.

The DATACLAS parameter will be ignored if:

- The DD statement describes an existing data set.
- The DD statement describes a new data set not supported by SMS, such as a tape data set.

The following parameters when coded in the DD statement will override what is provided by the DATACLAS parameter: RECORG, RECFM (in DCB or standalone), LRECL (in DCB or standalone), KEYLEN, KEYOFF, AVGREC, SPACE, RETPD or EXPDT (in LABEL or standalone), VOL (volcount only).

When the DATACLAS parameter is omitted, and some or all of the attributes that are supplied by the DATACLAS parameter are not supplied by other JCL parameters:

- An installation-written automatic class selection (ACS) routine will select a data class for the data set.

or

- The result will be a JCL error.

An ACS routine can be coded in such a way as to override the DATACLAS parameter and any related attributes coded in the DD statement.

Example 1:

```
//D1 DD DSN=USER1.SETA,DISP=(,CATLG,DELETE),UNIT=SYSDA,
//        VOL=SER=PACK14,DATACLAS=U1CLASS
```

Example 2:

```
//D2 DD DSN=USER1.SETB,DISP=(,CATLG,DELETE),UNIT=SYSDA
//        DATACLAS=PCLASS,LRECL=120
```

In Example 1, SMS will handle the data set based on the attributes of data class U1CLASS.

In Example 2, SMS will handle the data set based on the attributes of data class PCLASS. LRECL will override the corresponding value supplied by the data class.

14.2.3 The KEYOFF Parameter

This parameter is meaningful only if SMS is active. Otherwise, it will be syntactically checked and ignored.

When creating a KSDS VSAM cluster, the purpose of the KEYOFF parameter is to identify the key offset, the position of the first byte of the key, relative to the first byte of the logical record. The first byte of the record has an offset of 0.

General Syntax

```
KEYOFF=offset                                      keyword parameter
```

offset — Identifies beginning position of the key relative to the beginning of the record (which begins at 0). The maximum value is 32760 minus the length of the key (KEYLEN).

The KEYOFF parameter will be ignored if:

- The DD statement describes an existing data set.
- The DD statement describes a new data set with an organization other than VSAM KSDS.

The KEYOFF parameter must be coded only for RECORG=KS — a KSDS cluster.

The KEYOFF parameter will override the corresponding value provided by the DATACLAS parameter.

Example:

```
//D1 DD DSN=USER1.SETF,DISP=(,CATLG,DELETE),
//       STORCLAS=VDA,DATACLASS=VCALSS,KEYOFF=3
```

In the example, the KEYOFF parameter will override the corresponding parameter in DATACLAS. It identifies the fourth byte of each record as the beginning of the key. VOL and UNIT are supplied by STORCLAS.

14.2.4 The LIKE Parameter

This parameter is meaningful only if SMS is active. Otherwise it will be syntactically checked and ignored.

When creating a data set, the purpose of the LIKE parameter is to provide a model data set from which the following attributes can be copied:

- RECORG
- RECFM
- LRECL
- KEYLEN (VSAM only)
- KEYOFF (VSAM only)
- AVGREC
- SPACE

General Syntax

```
LIKE=model                                   keyword parameter
```

model — Specifies the name of a cataloged disk data set. The volume where this data set resides must be online. The attributes (listed above) of this data set will be used (if possible) for a data set being created.

The following notations are invalid in the LIKE parameter:

- LIKE=USER2.PDS1(MEM3) PDS and membername
- LIKE=USER2.ANNUAL(0) relative GDG name
- LIKE=&&TEMP temporary data set name
- LIKE=*.STEP4.DD2 referback

The LIKE parameter will be ignored if:

- The DD statement describes an existing data set.
- The DD statement describes a new data set which is not supported by SMS, such as a tape data set.

The following parameters when coded in the DD statement will override what is provided by the LIKE parameter: RECORG, RECFM (in DCB or standalone), LRECL (in DCB or standalone), KEYLEN, KEYOFF, AVGREC, and SPACE.
    Example:

```
//D1 DD DSN=PROD.BAS1,DISP=(,CATLG,DELETE),
//        LIKE=SITE.MOD3,STORCLAS=NVC
```

In the example, the appropriate attributes of cataloged disk data set SITE.MOD3 will be supplied to data set PROD.BAS1. VOL and UNIT will be supplied by STORCLAS.

14.2.5 The MGMTCLAS Parameter

This parameter is meaningful only if SMS is active. Otherwise, it will be syntactically checked and ignored.
    When creating a data set, the purpose of the MGMTCLAS parameter is to provide a management class for the data set. Once the data set is created, the management class will control:

- The migration of the data set using hierarchical storage manager facilities.
- The frequency of backup, the number of backup versions and their retention criteria.

General Syntax

```
MGMTCLAS=management-class-name                    keyword parameter
```

management-class-name — Name, 1 to 8 characters, defined by the installation storage administrator to be used for managing the data set after it is created.

The DATACLAS parameter will be ignored if:

• The DD statement describes an existing data set.
• The DD statement describes a new data set which is not supported by SMS, such as a tape data set.

The MGMTCLAS parameter cannot be overridden by any JCL parameters.

When the MGMTCLAS parameter is omitted, an installation-written automatic class selection (ACS) routine may select a management class for the data set.

An ACS routine can be coded in such a way as to override the MGMTCLAS parameter.

Example:

```
//D1 DD DSN=USER1.PERF,DISP=(,CATLG,DELETE),UNIT=SYSDA,
//       VOL=SER=PACK14,DATACLAS=U2CLASS,MGMTCLAS=MAG2
```

In the example, SMS will use the attributes of management class MAG2 to handle migration and backup for data set USER1.PERF

14.2.6 The RECORG Parameter

This parameter is meaningful only if SMS is active. Otherwise, it will be syntactically checked and ignored.

When creating a VSAM cluster, the REORG parameter must be coded. It identifies the organization of the records in the cluster.

General Syntax

```
RECORG={KS|ES|RR|LS}                          keyword parameter
```

KS — Identifies a VSAM key-sequenced (indexed) data set.

ES — Identifies a VSAM entry-sequenced (nonindexed) data set.

RR — Identifies a VSAM relative record (numbered) data set.

LS — Identifies a VSAM linear space data set.

The RECORG parameter will be ignored if the DD statement describes an existing data set or a non-VSAM data set.

If the RECORG parameter is omitted, the data set will not be VSAM. It will be a sequential (PS), partitioned (PO), or direct (DA) data set.

The RECORG parameter will override the corresponding value provided by the DATACLAS parameter.

Example:

```
//D1 DD DSN=USER1.DART,DISP=(,CATLG,DELETE),
//        STORCLAS=VDA,DATACLASS=VCLASS,RECORG=KS
```

In the example, the RECORG parameter will override the corresponding parameter in DATACLAS. It identifies the data set being created as a KSDS cluster.

14.2.7 The REFDD Parameter

This parameter is meaningful only if SMS is active. Otherwise, it will be syntactically checked and ignored.

When creating a data set, the purpose of the REFDD parameter is to refer to a previous DD statement in the same job from which the following attributes can be copied:

- RECORG
- RECFM
- LRECL
- KEYLEN (VSAM only)
- KEYOFF (VSAM only)
- AVGREC
- SPACE

General Syntax

```
             ⎡ *.stepname.ddname            ⎤
REFDD =      ⎢ *.ddname                     ⎥      keyword parameter
             ⎣ *.procexec.stepname.ddname   ⎦
```

*.stepname.ddname — Requests that the attributes be copied from DD statement "ddname" found in a previous step "stepname."

```
REFDD=*.STEP2.OUT
```

*.ddname — Requests that the attributes be copied from a previous DD statement "ddname" found in the same step.

```
REFDD=*.DD1
```

*.procexec.stepname.ddname — Requests that the attributes be copied from DD statement "ddname" found in a previous step "stepname' found within a procedure "procexec" (name of EXEC statement invoking the procedure).

```
REFDD=*.PR4.STEP9.OUT4
```

The REFDD parameter will be ignored if:

• The DD statement describes an existing data set.
• The DD statement describes a new data set which is not supported by SMS, such as a tape data set.
   The following parameters when coded in the DD statement will override what is provided by the REFDD parameter: RECORG, RECFM (in DCB or standalone), LRECL (in DCB or standalone), KEYLEN, KEYOFF, AVGREC, and SPACE.
   Example:

```
//D1 DD DSN=PROD.BAS2,DISP=(,CATLG,DELETE),
//      REFDD=*.STEP2.DD3,STORCLAS=SDT11
```

In the example, the appropriate attributes of DD statement DD3 found in previous step STEP2 will be applied to data set PROD.BAS2. VOL and UNIT will be supplied by STORCLAS.
   The REFDD parameter serves a function very similar to the LIKE parameter. The two are mutually exclusive.

14.2.8 The STORCLAS Parameter

This parameter is meaningful only if SMS is active. Otherwise, it will be syntactically checked and ignored.

When creating a data set, the purpose of the STORCLAS parameter is to provide UNIT and VOL information. A data set created using the STORCLAS parameter is referred to as an "SMS-managed" data set.

General Syntax

```
STORCLAS=storage-class                          keyword parameter
```

storage-class — Name, 1 to 8 characters, defined by the installation storage administrator. It determines the device and volume characteristics of data set when it is created.

The STORCLAS parameter will be ignored if:

* The DD statement describes an existing data set.
* The DD statement describes a new data set which is not supported by SMS, such as a tape data set.

The STORCLAS parameter cannot be overridden by coding the UNIT and VOL parameters in the DD statement unless the storage administrator has specified GUARANTEED SPACE=YES for the storage class. If so, the UNIT and VOL parameters coded in the DD statement will override those supplied by the STORCLAS parameter.

When the STORCLAS parameter is omitted, an installation-written automatic class selection (ACS) routine may select a storage class for the data set.

An ACS routine can be coded in such a way as to override the STORCLAS parameter.

For SMS-managed data sets JOBCAT and STEPCAT are ignored.
Example 1:

```
//D1 DD DSN=USER1.SMSDS,DISP=(,CATLG,DELETE),
//        DATACLAS=NCLASS,STORCLASS=U9CLASS
```

Example 2:

```
//D2 DD DSN=USER1.NSSET,DISP=(,CATLG,DELETE),
//        DATACLAS=FCLASS,STORCLASS=SPCLASS,
//        VOL=SER=PACK22
```

In Example 1, data set USER1.SMSDS will be created on a volume designated by storage class U9CLASS. The remaining attributes will be supplied by the DATACLAS parameter. This data set will be SMS-managed.

In Example 2, data set USER1.NSSET will be created on volume PACK22 because the storage administrator specified GUARANTEED SPACE=YES for storage class FCLASS. The remaining attributes will be supplied by the DATACLAS parameter. This data set will be SMS-managed.

14.3 MODIFIED JCL PARAMETERS

The SPACE parameter can be coded in a new format, but only if SMS is installed and active. None of the other parameters is affected.

    SPACE=(,(,,,directory))

Example:

```
//POUT DD DSN=USER1.LIBC,DISP=(,CATLG,DELETE),
//         DATACLAS=NCLASS,STORCLASS=U9CLASS,
//            SPACE=(,(,,12))
```

In the example, the SPACE parameter specifies 12 directory blocks. This value will override the one supplied by the DATACLAS parameter.

When the AVGREC parameter is coded, the SPACE parameter can also have a different meaning. Consider two DD statements:

```
//OUT1  DD   DSN=USER1.SETA,DISP=(,CATLG,DELETE),UNIT=SYSDA,
//            VOL=SER=PACK01,SPACE=(4000,(200,50))
```

```
//OUT2  DD   DSN=USER1.SETB,DISP=(,CATLG,DELETE),UNIT=SYSDA,
//            VOL=SER=PACK01,SPACE=(4000,(200,50)),AVGREC=K
```

In the first DD statement, the system will allocate (for the primary allocation) the number of tracks needed to contain 200 blocks, 4000 bytes each.

In the second DD statement, if SMS is active, the system will allocate, for the primary allocation, the number of tracks needed to contain 200 x 1024 = 204800 logical records, 4000 bytes each. This is much greater. If AVGREC=U were coded, the two allocations would be equal. If SMS is not active, the AVGREC parameter will be ignored and the two DD statements will allocate the same way.

14.4 ALTERNATIVE PARAMETERS

Under MVS/ESA, with or without SMS, all DCB subparameters can also be coded as parameters omitting the keyword DCB.

Example:

```
//DD3   DD   DSN=USER1.SET3,DISP=(,CATLG,DELETE),UNIT=SYSDA,
//           VOL=SER=PACK03,SPACE=(23440,(500,80)),
//           DCB=(LRECL=80,RECFM=FB,BLKSIZE=23440)
```

can also be coded as:

```
//DD3   DD   DSN=USER1.SET3,DISP=(,CATLG,DELETE),UNIT=SYSDA,
//           VOL=SER=PACK03,SPACE=(23440,(500,80)),
//           LRECL=80,RECFM=FB,BLKSIZE=23440
```

Also, with or without SMS, the EXPDT and RETPD subparameters of the LABEL parameter can be coded as parameters omitting the keyword LABEL.

Example:

```
//DDT   DD   DSN=USER1.TAP2,DISP=(,CATLG,DELETE),UNIT=CART,
//           LABEL=EXPDT=1992/155,
//           DCB=(LRECL=100,RECFM=FB,BLKSIZE=32700)
```

can also be coded as:

```
//DDT   DD   DSN=USER1.TAP2,DISP=(,CATLG,DELETE),UNIT=CART,
//           EXPDT=1992/155,
//           DCB=(LRECL=100,RECFM=FB,BLKSIZE=32700)
```

The EXPDT and RETPD parameters have the same syntax and meaning as do the subparameters (see Section 5.7 in Chapter 5). The EXPDT format shown in the examples above, which allows dates beyond 99365 to be specified, is inherent in Data Facility Product (DFP) Version 3, which is part of MVS/ESA.

14.5 MISCELLANEOUS CHANGES

For SMS-managed and non–SMS-managed data sets:

- If BLKSIZE is not specified through any means when creating a data set, the system determines an optimum blocksize for the data set. In other versions of MVS this always results in an S013-34 ABEND failure (except for sysout data sets.)

For SMS-managed non-VSAM data sets:

- A nonspecific request for a new SMS-managed data set will fail if an SMS-managed data set by the same name already exists on any volume.

```
//NSPEC  DD   DSN=USER1.NDSET,DISP=(,CATLG,DELETE),
//                STORCLAS=NSCLASS,DATACLAS=BIGCL
```

A similar request for a non–SMS-managed data set works differently.

```
//TDD    DD   DSN=USER1.STSET,DISP=(,CATLG,DELETE),
//                UNIT=SYSDA,SPACE=(CYL,(20,5),RLSE),
//                DCB=(LRECL=80,RECFM=FB,BLKSIZE=23440)
```

If the volume selected by the system to allocate this data set already contains one by the same name, the system will try a different volume, if possible.

- DISP=(NEW,KEEP) will default to DISP=(NEW,CATLG). If DISP=(MOD,KEEP) is coded and MOD defaults to NEW, then KEEP will default to CATLG.
- DISP=(OLD,UNCATLG) and DISP=(SHR,UNCATLG) will default to DISP=(OLD,KEEP) and DISP=(SHR,KEEP), respectively.
- DISP=(OLD,CATLG) and DISP=(SHR,CATLG) will default to DISP=(OLD,KEEP) and DISP=(SHR,KEEP), respectively.

For VSAM data sets:

- DISP=(NEW,KEEP) will default to DISP=(NEW,CATLG).
- DISP=(NEW,PASS) will default to (NEW,CATLG).
- DISP=(OLD,PASS) and DISP=(SHR,PASS) will default to DISP=(OLD,KEEP) and DISP=(SHR,KEEP), respectively.
- DISP=(OLD,UNCATLG) and DISP=(SHR,UNCATLG) will default to DISP=(OLD,KEEP) and DISP=(SHR,KEEP), respectively.
- DISP=(OLD,CATLG) and DISP=(SHR,CATLG) will default to DISP=(OLD,KEEP) and DISP=(SHR,KEEP), respectively.

14.6 EFFECT OF ESA ON EXISTING JCL

Without SMS, all JCL used under MVS/XA or MVS/SP should work under MVS/ESA without any problems.

With SMS, when dealing with VSAM data sets, some caution may be required. Consider a DD statement which retrieves a VSAM data set as follows:

```
//VDD   DD   DSN=PROD.KMAST,DISP=(OLD,DELETE)
```

DELETE was probably coded accidentally as there is no intent to delete the data set. Under all previous versions of MVS or MVS/ESA without SMS, DISP=(OLD,DELETE) defaults to DISP=(OLD,KEEP) and, therefore, the data set is kept.

With SMS, the data set will be deleted.

For SMS-managed data sets, some of the defaults for the DISP parameter are different, and that can cause certain difficulties:

- A DD statement contains DISP=(OLD,UNCATLG). While in previous versions of MVS this parameter would cause the data set to be uncataloged, it will default to (OLD,KEEP) for an SMS-managed data set. This may result in future problems.
- A job may be using a nonspecific nontemporary request for a new data set such as the one below more than once:

```
//DD1    DD   DSN=USER1.TRANS,DISP=(,CATLG,DELETE),
//             UNIT=SYSDA,SPACE=(CYL,(10,2),RLSE),
//             DCB=(LRECL=80,RECFM=FB,BLKSIZE=23440)
```

This is clearly a poor practice. All data sets after the first one will be created but not cataloged (NOT CATLGD 2) and no failure occurs. If, however, the data sets are SMS-managed, a failure will occur during the second attempt to create the data set. This may cause a job that ran without a failure to fail with SMS.
- A DD statement contains DISP=(NEW,KEEP). In previous versions of MVS this parameter would cause the data set to be created and kept even if a data set by the same name already exists on a different volume. For an SMS-managed data set, DISP=(NEW,KEEP) will default to DISP=(NEW,CATLG). and if such a data set exists, a failure will ensue.
- For a non-SMS-managed data set, the JCL below would cause the data set DEV1.MAPP to be cataloged in user catalog ICF.CAT3.

```
//S2       EXEC  PGM=PERT
//OUT      DD    DSN=DEV1.MAPP,DISP=(,CATLG,DELETE),UNIT=SYSDA,
//               VOL=SER=DEV009,DCB=(BLKSIZE=23400,LRECL=100,
//               RECFM=FB),SPACE=(CYL,(40,10),RLSE)
//STEPCAT DD     DSN=ICF.CAT3,DISP=SHR
```

If we assume that DEV1 is not an alias name for a user catalog (admittedly an unlikely event), and data set DEV1.MAPP becomes SMS-managed, as shown in the JCL below, the data set will not be cataloged, or it will be cataloged in the master catalog. For SMS-managed data sets, STEPCAT and JOBCAT are ignored.

```
//S2       EXEC  PGM=PERT
//OUT      DD    DSN=DEV1.MAPP,DISP=(,CATLG,DELETE)
//               STRORCLAS=DEV05,DCB=(BLKSIZE=23400,LRECL=100,
//               RECFM=FB),SPACE=(CYL,(40,10),RLSE)
//STEPCAT DD     DSN=ICF.CAT3,DISP=SHR
```

Even if DEV1 were an alias name for a user catalog, the data set would be cataloged but possibly in a user catalog other than the one identified in the STEPCAT statement. This can potentially become a problem.

Disk Characteristics

3330, 3350, 3375, and 3380 Disk Characteristics

DISK	TRACK CAPACITY	TRK/CYL	CYL PER VOL	VOL MAX CAPACITY
3330 MOD I	13,030	19	404	100 M
3330 MOD II	13,030	19	808	200 M
3350*	19,069	30	555	317 M
3375*	35,616	12	959	409 M
3380* SINGLE DENSITY	47,476	15	885	630 M
3380* DOUBLE DENSITY	47,476	15	1770	1260 M
3380* TRIPLE DENSITY	47,476	15	2655	1890 M

* Physically nonremovable

B

3380 Disk Capacity Table

EQUAL LENGTH BLOCKS (WITHOUT KEYS)

MAXIMUM BLKSIZE	BLOCKS PER TRACK	BLOCKS PER CYLINDER	% UTILIZATION
47,476*	1	15	100.0
23,476	2	30	98.8
15,476	3	45	97.9
11,476	4	60	96.7
9,076	5	75	95.6
7,476	6	90	94.5
6,356	7	105	93.7
5,492	8	120	92.5
4,820	9	135	91.4
4,276	10	150	90.1
3,860	11	165	89.4
3,476	12	180	87.9
3,188	13	195	87.3
2,932	14	210	86.5
2,676	15	225	84.5
2,484	16	240	83.7
2,324	17	255	83.2
2,164	18	270	82.0
2,004	19	285	80.2

1,876	20	300	79.0
1,780	21	315	78.7
1,684	22	330	78.0
1,588	23	345	76.9
1,492	24	360	75.4
1,396	25	375	73.5
1,332	26	390	72.9
1,268	27	405	72.1
1,204	28	420	71.0
1,140	29	435	69.6
1,076	30	450	68.0
1,044	31	465	68.2
980	32	480	66.1
948	33	495	65.9
916	34	510	65.6
852	35	525	62.8
820	36	540	62.2
788	37	555	61.4
756	38	570	60.5
724	39	585	59.5
692	40	600	58.3
660	41	615	58.1
628	42	630	55.6
596	44	660	55.2
564	45	675	53.4
532	46	690	51.0
500	48	720	50.6
468	49	735	48.3
436	51	765	46.8
404	53	795	45.1
372	55	825	43.1
340	57	855	40.8
308	59	885	38.3
276	62	930	36.0
244	65	975	33.4
212	68	1020	30.4
180	71	1065	26.9
148	74	1110	23.1
116	78	1170	19.1
84	83	1245	14.7
52	88	1320	9.6
20	83	1395	3.9

* This blocksize is not available with ordinary access methods.

Appendix

C

3375 Capacity Table

EQUAL LENGTH BLOCKS (WITHOUT KEYS)

MAXIMUM BLKSIZE	BLOCKS PER TRACK	CYLINDER	% UTILIZATION
35,616*	1	12	100.0
17,600	2	24	98.8
11,616	3	36	97.8
8,608	4	48	96.7
6,816	5	60	95.7
5,600	6	72	94.3
4,736	7	84	93.1
4,096	8	96	92.0
3,616	9	108	91.4
3,200	10	120	89.8
2,880	11	132	88.9
2,592	12	144	87.3
2,368	13	156	86.4
2,176	14	168	85.8
2,016	15	180	84.9
1,856	16	192	83.4
1,728	17	204	82.5
1,600	18	216	80.9
1,504	19	228	80.2

1,408	20	240	79.1
1,312	21	252	77.4
1,248	22	264	77.1
1,152	23	276	74.4
1,088	24	288	73.3
1,056	25	300	74.1
992	26	312	72.4
928	27	324	70.4
896	28	336	70.4
832	29	348	67.7
800	30	360	67.4
768	31	372	66.8
736	32	384	66.1
704	33	396	65.2
672	34	408	64.2
640	35	420	62.9
608	36	432	61.5
576	37	444	59.8
544	38	456	58.3
512	40	480	57.5
480	41	492	55.3
448	43	516	54.1
416	45	540	52.6
384	46	552	49.6
352	48	576	47.4
320	51	612	45.8
288	53	636	42.3
256	56	672	40.3
224	59	708	37.1
192	62	744	33.4
160	66	792	29.6
128	70	840	25.2
96	75	900	20.2
64	80	960	14.4
32	86	1032	7.7

* This blocksize is not available with ordinary access methods.

D

3350 Capacity Table

EQUAL LENGTH BLOCKS (WITHOUT KEYS)

MAXIMUM BLKSIZE	BLOCKS PER TRACK	BLOCKS PER CYLINDER	% UTILIZATION
19,069	1	30	100.0
9,442	2	60	99.0
6,233	3	90	98.1
4,628	4	120	97.1
3,665	5	150	96.1
3,024	6	180	95.1
2,565	7	210	94.2
2,221	8	240	93.2
1,954	9	270	92.2
1,740	10	300	91.2
1,565	11	330	90.3
1,419	12	360	89.3
1,296	13	390	88.4
1,190	14	420	87.4
1,098	15	450	86.4
1,018	16	480	85.4
947	17	510	84.4
884	18	540	83.4
828	19	570	82.5

777	20	600	81.5
731	21	630	80.5
690	22	660	79.6
652	23	690	78.6
617	24	720	77.7
585	25	750	76.7
555	26	780	75.7
528	27	810	74.8
502	28	840	73.7
478	29	870	72.7
456	30	900	71.7
436	31	930	70.9
416	32	960	69.8
398	33	990	68.9
381	34	1020	67.9
365	35	1050	67.0
349	36	1080	65.9
335	37	1110	65.0
321	38	1140	64.0
308	39	1170	63.0
296	40	1200	62.1
284	41	1230	61.1
273	42	1260	60.1
262	43	1290	59.1
252	44	1320	58.1
242	45	1350	57.1
233	46	1380	56.2
224	47	1410	55.2
216	48	1440	54.4
207	49	1470	53.2
200	50	1500	52.4
192	51	1530	51.4
185	52	1560	50.4
178	53	1590	49.5
171	54	1620	48.4
165	55	1650	47.6
158	56	1680	46.4
152	57	1710	45.4
146	58	1740	44.4
141	59	1770	43.6
135	60	1800	42.5
130	61	1830	41.6
125	62	1860	40.6

120	63	1890	39.6
115	64	1920	38.6
111	65	1950	37.8
106	66	1980	36.7
102	67	2010	35.8
98	68	2040	34.9
94	69	2070	34.0
90	70	2100	33.4
86	71	2130	32.2
82	72	2160	31.0
78	73	2190	29.9
75	74	2220	29.1
71	75	2250	27.9
68	76	2280	27.1
65	77	2310	26.2
61	78	2340	25.0
58	79	2370	24.0
55	80	2400	23.1
52	81	2430	22.1
49	82	2460	21.1
46	83	2490	20.0
44	84	2520	19.4
41	85	2550	18.3
38	86	2580	17.1
36	87	2610	16.4
33	88	2640	15.2
31	89	2670	14.5
28	90	2700	13.2
26	91	2730	12.4
24	92	2760	11.6
22	93	2790	10.7

3330 (MOD 1 or MOD 11) Capacity Table

EQUAL LENGTH BLOCKS (WITHOUT KEYS)

```
------------------------------------------
|         |    BLOCKS PER     |            |
|MAXIMUM  |-----------------|      %      |
|BLKSIZE  | TRACK |CYLINDER|UTILIZATION|
------------------------------------------
```

MAXIMUM BLKSIZE	TRACK	CYLINDER	% UTILIZATION
13,030	1	19	100.0
6,447	2	38	99.0
4,263	3	57	98.2
3,156	4	76	96.9
2,498	5	95	95.9
2,059	6	114	94.8
1,745	7	133	93.7
1,510	8	152	92.7
1,327	9	171	91.7
1,181	10	190	90.6
1,061	11	209	89.6
962	12	228	88.6
877	13	247	87.5
805	14	266	86.5
742	15	285	85.4
687	16	304	84.3
639	17	323	83.4

	596		18		342		82.3	
	557		19		361		81.2	
	523		20		380		80.3	
	491		21		399		79.1	
	463		22		418		78.2	
	437		23		437		77.1	
	413		24		456		76.1	
	391		25		475		75.0	
	371		26		494		74.0	
	352		27		513		72.9	
	335		28		532		72.0	
	318		29		551		70.8	
	303		30		570		69.8	
	289		31		589		68.8	
	276		32		608		67.8	
	263		33		627		66.6	
	252		34		646		65.8	
	241		35		665		64.7	
	230		36		684		63.5	
	220		37		703		62.5	
	211		38		722		61.5	
	202		39		741		60.5	
	194		40		760		59.6	
	186		41		779		58.5	
	178		42		798		57.4	
	171		43		817		56.4	
	164		44		836		55.4	
	157		45		855		54.2	
	151		46		874		53.3	
	145		47		893		52.3	
	139		48		912		51.2	
	133		49		931		50.0	
	128		50		950		49.1	
	123		51		969		48.1	
	118		52		988		47.1	
	113		53		1007		46.0	
	108		54		1026		44.8	
	104		55		1045		43.9	
	100		56		1064		43.0	
	95		57		1083		41.6	
	91		58		1102		40.5	
	88		59		1121		39.8	
	84		60		1140		38.7	

80	61	1159	37.5
77	62	1178	36.6
73	63	1197	35.3
70	64	1216	34.4
67	65	1235	33.4
64	66	1254	32.4
61	67	1273	31.4
58	68	1292	30.3
55	69	1311	20.1
53	70	1330	28.8
50	71	1349	27.2
47	72	1368	26.0
45	73	1387	25.2
42	74	1406	23.9
40	75	1425	23.0
38	76	1444	22.2
35	77	1463	20.7
33	78	1482	19.8
31	79	1501	18.8
29	80	1520	17.8
27	81	1539	16.8
25	82	1558	15.7
23	83	1577	14.7
21	84	1596	13.5

Bibliography

In the author's opinion, the following IBM publications should be available to the reader of this book for reference purposes.

MVS/XA Publications

MVS/Extended Architecture JCL Reference, GC28-1352

MVS/Extended Architecture JCL User's Guide, GC28-1351

MVS/Extended Architecture Integrated Catalog Administration: Access Method Services Reference, GC26-4135

MVS/Extended Architecture VSAM Catalog Administration: Access Method Services, GC26-4075

MVS/Extended Architecture Data Administration: Utilities, GC26-4018

MVS/Extended Architecture Magnetic Tape Labels and File Structure Administration, GC26-4003

MVS/Extended Architecture Data Facility Product Version 2, GC26-4147

MVS/ESA Publications

MVS/ESA JCL Reference, GC28-1829

MVS/ESA JCL User's Guide, GC28-1830

MVS/ESA General Information for System Product Version 3, GC28-1359

Glossary

ABEND — A failing condition normally encountered during the execution of a program. The system interrupts the program, removes it from execution, and associates the ABEND failure with a completion code, also known as an ABEND code (such as S0C7).

ABEND code — See completion code

absolute name — The actual name of a generation of a GDG. The format of the name is gdgbase.GnnnnVmm, where nnnn is a number between 0001 (and rarely 0000) and 9999. mm is a number between 00 and 99 (almost always 00).

Access Method Services — An IBM-developed program product with a comprehensive set of facilities for creating and manipulating VSAM objects. It also has certain facilities for non-VSAM data sets. It is commonly called IDCAMS.

address space — Virtual storage made available to each batch and TSO user. In MVS/SP an address space is 16 megabytes. In MVS/XA an address space is 2 gigabytes.

alias of catalog — Another name for a user catalog. This is normally a simple (nonqualified) name, and if it is used as the high qualifier of a data set name, it determines the user catalog with which the data set is associated.

application program — A user-written program.

backup — A copy of a data set or a volume. It can be used to reconstruct the data set or volume, if necessary.

Basic Direct Access Method — An access method which reads and writes blocks directly, without having to read previous blocks.

Basic Partitioned Access Method — An access method which reads and writes blocks of members within a partitioned data set sequentially but can access or create members randomly.

Basic Sequential Access Method — An access method which reads and writes blocks sequentially.

block — The unit of data transfer for non-VSAM data sets. No I/O operation can be performed for less than an entire block. Maximum size is 32,760 bytes. Also known as physical record.

BPAM — See Basic Partitioned Access Method

BSAM — See Basic Sequential Access Method

catalog — See user catalog and master catalog

Central Processing Unit — The "brain" of a computer where all arithmetic calculations and memory manipulations are performed. It is also known as a processor or by its acronym, CPU. Mainframe, system, box, and host can also be used as synonyms as long as they contain one CPU (as many as six are possible).

channel — A high-speed (millions of bytes per second) medium connecting the CPU and a control unit. It is a powerful minicomputer in itself. A maximum of 255 channels can be available within one mainframe (16 maximum under MVS/SP).

completion code — A code identifying an ABEND failure. System completion codes consist of three hex characters preceded by the letter S. User completion codes consist of four hex characters preceded by the letter U. The last two digits of most system completion codes identify the SVC (supervisor call) where the failure occurred. Also known as ABEND code.

condition code — A number between 0 and 4095 issued by an executing program to denote the conditions encountered during its execution. A condition code of zero is normally treated as indicative of successful execution. Also known as return code.

CPU — See Central Processing Unit

cluster — See data set

compress — A copying operation which eliminates any unusable disk space within a PDS resulting from deleting and replacing members.

CVOL catalog — A catalog structure intended for non-VSAM data set entries in a non-ICF environment. Also known as OS catalog.

cylinder — All the tracks on a disk volume which have the same diameter. Each of the tracks of a cylinder resides on a different recording surface. After the read/write head of a disk device is positioned on a cylinder, all the tracks of that cylinder can be accessed without moving the access arm of the device.

data set — An organized collection of information that can be read from, written to, or both. Also known as file or (for VSAM only) cluster.

data set control block — A VTOC entry. There are six different types, Format 1 to Format 6. Often referred to by its acronym DSCB. A Format 1 DSCB is effectively the standard label of a disk data set.

data set label — Two 80-byte records which precede a tape data set label and two 80-byte records which follow it. The leading records are called HDR1 and HDR2 and the trailing ones EOF1 and EOF2. On disk, a DSCB is considered a data set label.

device — Equipment which has the ability to read or write (or both) information using a medium normally other than memory. Examples: a tape device can read from or write to tape volumes; a printer device can only write on paper; an optical scanner device can only read from paper. For disk or tape, it is also referred to as drive or unit. A solid state disk device uses memory as its medium.

direct access storage device (DASD) — A magnetic medium of data storage where any data can be accessed directly, without need to access preceding data. Currently, all direct access devices are disk. A fixed-head disk is also known as a drum. There are no up-to-date drum devices available.

dynamic allocation — Allocation of a data set or a volume without the use of a DD statement in JCL. It is performed via application program instructions.

drive — See device

DSCB — See data set control block

Entry Sequenced Data Set — A nonindexed VSAM data set. Records can be read or written only in sequence.

ESDS — See Entry Sequenced Data Set

expanded storage — Real storage optionally available in many 3090 mainframe models which is used as auxiliary storage instead of disk for paging and swapping purposes.

extent — A contiguous area of disk storage allocated to a data set (at one time).

file — See data set

forward reference — A notation in JCL enabling a DD statement to access information from a subsequent DD statement.

generated unit name — A device name, such as SYSDA, whose meaning is determined by the installation during system generation. Any valid installation-chosen names can be used. Also known as esoteric name or group name.

generic unit name — A device name, such as 3380, whose meaning is determined by MVS/XA. Generic names are not installation dependent.

host — See Central Processing Unit

IBG — See interblock gap

IBM 3350 disk — A disk device which contains a nonremovable volume with a maximum capacity of 317 megabytes. It contains 555 cylinders, each cylinder consists of 30 tracks, and each track has a maximum capacity of 19,069 bytes.

IBM 3380 disk — A disk device which contains a nonremovable volume with a maximum capacity of 630 megabytes. It contains 885 cylinders, each cylinder consists of 15 tracks, and each track has a maximum capacity of 47,476 bytes.

IBM 3380 disk (double density) — A disk device which contains a nonremovable volume with a maximum capacity of 1260 megabytes. It contains 1770 cylinders, each cylinder consists of 15 tracks, and each track has a maximum capacity of 47,476 bytes.

IBM 3380 disk (triple density) — A disk device which contains a nonremovable volume with a maximum capacity of 1,890 megabytes. It contains 2655 cylinders, each cylinder consists of 15 tracks, and each track has a maximum capacity of 47,476 bytes.

ICF — See Integrated Catalog Facility

IDCAMS — See Access Method Services

Indexed Sequential Access Method — An access method which can read update or insert logical records or blocks, without having to read all previous ones, by using indexes. ISAM is obsolete.

Integrated Catalog Facility — A catalog structure replacing VSAM and CVOL catalogs. It is part of the original DF/EF program product.

interblock gap — A physical separation between blocks, often referred to by its acronym, IBG. Also known as interrecord gap or IRG.

IRG — See interblock gap

ISAM — See Indexed Sequential Access Method

Key Sequenced Data Set — An indexed VSAM data set. Records can be read updated or inserted with the aid of keys and indexes.

KSDS — See Key Sequenced Data Set

library — See partitioned data set

logical record — A data record of fixed or variable size which resides inside a block or (rarely) spans across more than one block (variable- spanned only).

magnetic tape storage device — A magnetic medium of data storage where data can be accessed only sequentially.

mainframe — See Central Processing Unit

master catalog — A VSAM or ICF catalog whose main contents are entries of user catalogs (along with their alias names) and system data sets. There is only one master catalog per MVS/XA system and it is write-protected against unauthorized users.

model DSCB — A cataloged disk data set whose DCB attributes are copied by another data set by means of the DCB parameter.

multiprogramming — The concurrent use of one CPU by several executing programs.

multiprocessing — Two or more tightly coupled CPUs working together in a single operating system environment.

multitasking — Two or more programs executing concurrently within the same address space.

partitioned data set — A data set which consists of members, each containing sequentially organized data and a directory at its beginning describing the members. Also known as PDS or library.

PDS — See partitioned data set

physical record — See block

processor — See Central Processing Unit

qualified data set name — A data set name that contains at least one period.

qualifier — A name that precedes a period in a qualified data set name. For an example, if the data set name is A.B.C.D, A is the high qualifier, B is the second qualifier and C is the third qualifier. D is not a qualifier. Also known as qualification level or index.

Queued Sequential Access Method — An access method which reads and writes logical records sequentially.

QSAM — See Queued Sequential Access Method

reason code — A two-digit hex number which often follows a completion code. In ABEND failure S013-14, 14 is the reason code.

referback — A notation enabling a JCL (EXEC or DD) statement to access information from a previous JCL (EXEC, DD, or OUTPUT) statement. Also known as back reference or backward reference.

relative name — The name often coded in the DSN parameter, such as DSN=gdgbase(n). n is a number between -254 and +255.

Relative Record Data Set — A numbered VSAM data set. Records can be located directly based on their relative position within the data set.

return code — See condition code

rotational delay — The time it takes for data on a disk track to be positioned under the read/write head via the rotation of the volume.

RRDS — See Relative Record Data Set

seek time — The time it takes for the access arm of a disk device to move so that its read/write head is positioned over the track (or cylinder) where the desired I/O operation will take place. Sometimes referred to as arm movement.

shared DASD — A disk device which is accessible from two or more MVS/XA systems.

simple data set name — A data set name, 1 to 8 characters, that contains no periods. Also known as nonqualified name or unqualified name.

track — A circular electromagnetic groove on a recording surface of a disk volume where information can be stored (written) and retrieved (read). All tracks on a recording surface are concentric.

transfer time — The time it takes for the data to be transferred form a device to virtual storage (read) or vice versa (write) during an I/O operation.

UCB — See Unit Control Block

unit — See device

Unit Control Block — An area of virtual storage in the nucleus of MVS/XA describing a device.

user catalog — A VSAM, ICF or CVOL catalog whose main contents are entries of the user's data sets. The high qualifiers of these data sets are normally alias names for the user catalog.

virtual storage — A mapping technique which combines real and auxiliary storage enabling the user to use the two together as if they were real storage.

Virtual Storage Access Method — An access method which can read and write logical records sequentially, directly, or by using indexes. Normally referred to as VSAM.

volume — An electromagnetic medium where information can be written to and read from. A volume either permanently mounted on a device or mounted upon request For disk, it is also referred to as pack. For tape, it is also referred to as reel, cassette, or cartridge (the last two for 3480 tape only)

volume label — A label which contains a volume's characteristics such as volume serial. On standard labeled tape it is the first 80-byte record on the volume. On disk it resides on track 0 of the volume.

Volume Table Of Contents — A data set whose entries (known as DSCBs) describe each individual data set (except non-ICF suballocated VSAM clusters) on the volume as well as the entire volume. Often referred to by its acronym, VTOC. Every disk volume must have one VTOC.

VSAM — See Virtual Storage Access Method

VSAM catalog — A catalog structure intended for VSAM data set entries in a non-ICF environment.

VSAM object — An entity created by VSAM such as a cluster, an alternate index, a path, a user or master catalog, a page space, an alias, etc.

VTOC — See Volume Table of Contents

Index

ABE, 137, 239
ABEND, 67-70
  S001-1, 70, 137
  S001-4, 192, 310
  S013-10, 297
  S013-14, 125, 206
  S013-18, 181
  S013-20, 192, 238
  S013-34, 238, 361, 430
  S013-64, 297, 362
  S122, 70, 82, 92, 269
  S23708, 195
  S213-04, 103, 152, 172, 173,
    177, 196, 263, 264
  S222, 70, 82, 92, 269
  S322, 43, 58, 69, 82, 92
  S413-04, 113, 194, 235, 312
  S522, 43, 58, 69, 225
  S637-0C, 312
  S813-04, 174, 175, 195, 227, 332
  S804, 40, 56
  S806-04, 52, 300, 301, 303
  S80A, 40, 56
  S822, 40, 56
  S837-04, 118, 229
  S878, 40, 56
  SA13-18, 231
  SB14, 181, 188
  SB37-04, 69, 124, 126, 208,
    211, 212, 214, 216, 218, 219,
    220
  SD37-04, 124, 190, 208
  SE37-04, 118, 124, 208, 229
  SE37-08, 220

absolute name (GDG), 316
ABSTR, 128, 207
ACC, 137, 239
Access Method Services
  See IDCAMS
access methods
  See organizations
account number, 33, 60
accounting information, 33, 60
ACCT, 60
ACS, 434, 437, 440
address space, 38, 55
ADDRSPC
  in JOB statement, 37
  in EXEC statement, 54
AFF, 110, 112, 113, 193, 194, 196,
  197, 235
AL, 131
allocation, step, 18-20
ALTER IDCAMS command, 320,
  414, 415, 422
ALX, 123, 127
AMORG, 413
AMP, 198, 413
ANYLOCAL, 284
apostrophe, 27
ASP, 2
asterisk (*)
  See DD *
AUL, 131
automatic class selection
  See ACS
AVGREC, 431, 432

BLDG, 319, 397
BLDINDEX IDCAMS command, 413
BLKSIZE, 135, 237, 238, 240-246
blocking factor, 215, 246
blocksize allocation in SPACE, 123, 214, 215
blocksize, selecting proper, 240-246
BLP, 130, 183-185, 330
BPAM, 9, 97, 180
BSAM, 8, 9
buffers, 241, 242
BUFND, 197, 198
BUFNI, 197, 198
BUFNO, 137, 192, 237, 239, 242
BURST, 284
bypassing step execution, 70

catalog
    CVOL, 141, 142
    VSAM, 141, 142,
    ICF, 142
    contents of entry, 143, 144
    adding an entry, 150, 151, 394-396, 419-421
    removing an entry, 160-163, 394, 395, 419, 421
    failing to catalog, 151-155
cataloged procedures
    restrictions, 336
    executing, 335
    overriding, 336-352
    special overrides, 358-365
    symbolic parameters, 369-373
    symbolic overrides, 369-373
CATALOG IDCAMS parameter, 418, 426, 427
CATLG, 101, 105, 106
CHARS, 284, 285
CLASS,
    in JOB statement, 41, 42
    in OUTPUT statement, 289
CLOSE, 139, 140, 193-195, 235, 236
closing data sets, 20, 224, 225
cluster, 407, 410
command statement, 21, 22
comment statement, 21

concatenation, 195-197, 309-313, 326, 327
COND
    in JOB statement, 41, 76-80
    in EXEC statement, 57, 58, 80-86
condition code
    See return code
CONTIG, 123, 126
CONTROL, 190, 191
COPIES, 278, 279
CPU, 4-6
creating data sets
    disk
        temporary, 203-205
        nontemporary, 201-203
        sequential, 201-205
        partitioned, 205, 206
        direct, 206, 207
        multivolume, 218-221
    tape
        multivolume, 229, 230
        on multifile volumes, 230, 235
CYL, 123
cylinder vs track allocation, 209, 210

DATA parameter, 272, 273
data set control block
    See DSCB
data control block
    See DCB
Data Facility Product
    See DFP
data space, 429, 430
data class
    See DATACLAS
DATACLAS, 433, 434
DCB
    description, 133, 241
    when creating, 236-240
    when retrieving, 191, 192
    with DUMMY, 297
    with GDGs, 321-323
    with sysout, 277
DD statement: description, 21

DD *, 271-274
DDNAME parameter, 298-300
DEFAULT, 287, 291, 292
DEFER, 110, 112
DEFINE ALTERNATEINDEX
    IDCAMS
    command, 412, 413
DEFINE CLUSTER IDCAMS command, 410-412
DEFINE GDG IDCAMS command, 318, 319, 423
DEFINE NONVSAM IDCAMS command, 419-421
DEFINE PATH IDCAMS command, 414
deleting data sets, 176-180, 396, 421, 422
deleting members of a PDS, 396, 397, 422
DELETE
    in DISP, 101, 104
    IDCAMS command, 321, 414, 421, 422
delimiter statement (/*), 121, 272, 273
DEN, 136, 137, 237, 239
DEST, 281-284
DFP, 96, 131, 132, 301, 302, 310, 311, 442
device count, 110, 111, 185, 218, 219, 229, 230
directory quantity, 123, 125, 206, 441
DISP, 101
DLM, 273
DSCB, 12
DSN, 96
DSORG, 125, 240
DUMMY, 100, 296, 297
dynamic allocation, 21

end of file, 309, 242
EROPT, 137, 138, 192, 237, 239, 240
ES, 437, 438

ESA
    See MVS/ESA
ESDS, 9, 438
EVEN, 57, 70, 81, 82, 91
EXEC statement: description, 50
EXPDT, 129, 131, 442
external writer, 275, 289

failures under MVS/XA, 63
FB, 10, 136
FCB, 279, 280
FLASH, 285
FORMS, 290
forms, 275, 276
FREE, 139, 140, 193-195, 235, 236

GDGs
    defining the GDG base, 318, 319, 397, 423
    changing characteristics, 320, 321
    using a GDG model, 321-323
    peculiarities, 323-326
    concatenating generations, 326, 327
    recovery, 328, 329
generated unit name, 110, 111, 158, 349, 420
generation data groups
    See GDGs
generic unit name, 110, 111, 158, 394, 420
GROUPID, 293, 294

HASP, 2
HOLD, 281
holding jobs, 49

IDCAMS
    JCL, 407, 408
    command syntax, 408, 409
IEBCOPY398-402
IEBGENER, 390, 393
IEBPTPCH, 402-404
IEHLIST, 405, 406
IEHPROGM, 393-398

IF IDCAMS command, 163, 180, 421

in-stream procedures, 333, 334, 380-385

initiation
    job, 18, 20
    step, 19, 20
initiator, 17, 18
input stream, 16
internal reader
    See INTRDR
INTRDR, 275, 276

JCL
    statements, 20- 22
    syntax, 22-30
    errors, 63-66
JCLHOLD, 49
JESDS, 292, 293
JES2, 2, 17, 274, 275
JES2 accounting information, 33-35
JES2 log
    See log
JES3, 2, 17, 274, 275
JES3 log
    See log
JOB statement: description, 31, 32
job, 15-17
job control language
    See JCL
JOBCAT, 147-150, 304
JOBLIB, 301, 302
jobname, 32

KEEP, 101, 105, 172
KEYOFF, 434, 435
keyword parameter, 23
KS, 437
KSDS, 9, 437

LABEL, 129-133
library
    See PDS
LIKE, 435, 436
LIMIT, 318, 423
LINECT, 293

LISTCAT IDCAMS command, 418, 426
LOCAL, 282, 283
log, 292
LRECL, 135, 137, 138
LS, 437, 438
LTM, 130, 184

management class
    See MGMTCLAS
member, 12-14, 180, 181, 205, 206
messages, 36, 66, 292
MFT, 1, 2
MGMTCLASS, 436, 437
MOD, 101, 102, 161, 179, 186-189, 246, 247
model DSCB, 134, 135, 321-323
MSGCLASS, 46, 47
MSGLEVEL, 36, 37
multiprogramming, 4-6
MVS/ESA, 3, 429, 430
    new JCL parameters, 431
    modified parameters, 441
    alternative parameters, 442
    miscellaneous changes, 442,443
MVS/SP, 3
MVS/XA, 3
MVT, 1, 2
MXIG, 123, 127

NEW, 101
NL, 130, 183, 184, 228
NOTIFY, 44, 45
NSL, 131
null statement, 121
NULLFILE, 96, 100, 297

OLD, 101, 182
ONLY, 57, 70, 80, 81
opening a data set, 241
OPTCD, 193, 237, 239
organizations, 8-10
OS, 1, 2
OUTLIM, 279
OUTPUT
    parameter, 286, 287
    statement, 287-296

output data set
    See sysout data set
output group — GROUP
overriding procedures
        EXEC parameters, 339, 340,
            342, 343
        DD parameters, 340, 341, 343-
            349, 358-365
        OUTPUT parameters, 341
        symbolic, 369-373

P
    See paralell mount
paging, 7, 8
parallel mount, 110, 11, 112, 185,
    186, 218
PARM, 52-54
paritioned data set
    See PDS
PASS, 101, 106, 107
passing data sets, 249-270
PDS, 12, 97, 180, 181, 205, 206
PEND statement, 336, 380-382
PERFORM
        in JOB statement, 45, 46
        in EXEC statement, 59, 60
permanently resident volume, 224
PGM, 51, 52, 300
positional parameter, 23
primary allocation, 103, 208
PRINT IDCAMS command, 417,
    425
PRIVATE, 116
private volumes, 221-223
PROC statement, 373, 380-382
procedure libraries, 333-335
procedures
    See cataloged procedures
proclibs
    See procedure libraries
PROC in //*MAIN, 335
PROCLIB in /*JOBPARM, 335
programmer's name, 35, 36
PRTY, 42, 43
public volumes, 221-223

QSAM, 8, 9
qualified data set name, 97

REAL, 37, 38, 54, 55
receiving passed data sets, 249-270
RECFM, 135, 137, 238
RECORG, 437, 438
record formats, 10, 11
REF, 116, 120, 121
REFDD, 438, 439
REGION
        in JOB statement, 38-40
        in EXEC statement, 55-57
relative name (GDG), 316
REPRO IDCAMS command, 416,
    417, 424
reserved volume, 223, 224
RESTART, 47-49
RETAIN, 116, 117
return code, 41, 57, 73, 76
RETPD, 132, 142
retrieving data sets
        disk, 171-174
        tape, 174-176
        VSAM, 197, 198
        multivolume, 185, 186
RJE, 282, 283
RLSE, 123, 126, 190, 191
Rn, RMn or RMTn, 282
ROUND, 123, 127, 128
RR, 437, 438
RRDS, 9, 438

secondary allocation, 123, 124, 125
SER, 116, 120
SET IDCAMS command, 163, 180,
    421
SHR, 101, 182
simple data set name, 96
SKP, 137, 192, 239
SL, 130
SMS, 430, 431
SMS-managed data set, 440
SUL
SP
    See MVS/SP

SPACE, 122, 123
SPOOL pack, 117, 274
standard labels
  See SL
step, 16
STEPCAT, 147-150
STEPLIB, 302-304
stepname, 50
storage, virtual, 7, 8
storage class
  See STORCLAS
storage management subsystem
  See SMS
storage volumes, 221-223
STORCLAS, 439-441
SUL, 130
SVS
syntax
  See JCL
SYSABEND, 305, 306
SYSMDUMP, 305
SYSOUT, 275
sysout data sets, 275
SYSUDUMP, 305, 306

temporary data sets, 96-99
termination
  step, 19, 20
  job, 20
  abnormal
    See ABEND
THEN, 163, 180, 421
TIME
  in JOB statement, 43, 44
  in EXEC statement, 58, 59
tracks, 209, 210
TRK, 123
TYPRUN, 49, 50

U — undefined, 136, 391
UCB, 144
UCS, 280, 281
uncataloging data sets, 160-163,
  394, 395, 419, 421
UNCATLG, 101, 106
UNIT, 110

unit affinity
  See AFF
unit control block
  See UCB
utilities
  JCL, 388
  control statement syntax, 389,
    390

VB, 10, 136
VBS, 10, 136
VIO, 307, 309
VIRT, 37, 38, 54, 55
virtual I/O
  See VIO
VOL, 115
volume count, 116, 117-120
volume sequence, 116, 117
volume table of contents
  See VTOC
VSAM, 9, 10, 197, 198, 407, 430
VS1, 2
VS2, 2
VTOC, 12, 13

writer, external, 275, 289
WRITER, 289

XA
  See MVS/XA